CW00763226

Eyes Wide Open
True Tales Of A Wishbone Ash Warrior
Andy Powell with Colin Harper

To Richard, Aynsley, and Lawrence—Big Love.

A Jawbone Book
First edition 2015
Published in the UK and the USA by
Jawbone Press
3.1D Union Court
20–22 Union Road
London SW4 6JP
England
www.jawbonepress.com

ISBN 978-1-908279-81-1

EDITOR Tom Seabrook
JACKET DESIGN Mark Case

Volume copyright © 2015 Outline Press Ltd. Text copyright © Andy
Powell and Colin Harper. All rights reserved. No part of this book
covered by these copyrights may be reproduced or copied in any
manner at all without written permission, except in the case of brief
quotations within articles or reviews, where the source should be
made clear. For more information contact the publishers.

Printed in the Czech Republic by PB Print UK

1 2 3 4 5 19 18 17 16 15

CONTENTS

sounds
ANDY
POWELL
OF
WISHBONE
ASH

FOREWORD

BY IAN RANKIN

There was a little shack next to a railway bridge near my primary school, and that's where I bought my weekly copy of *Sounds*. There were other music papers out there, but *Sounds* was the only one that included a free colour poster. I was twelve years old in 1972, and growing up in a small town on the east coast of Scotland made it tough to be a music fan. I relied on the radio, my regular fix of *Sounds*, and the record collection of a friend's big brother. That record collection had introduced me to Frank Zappa, Jethro Tull, and Led Zeppelin, while *Sounds* filled my head with dreams of loon pants, peace badges, and denim waistcoats, along with bands I would probably never get to see, since the nearest venues were miles away. One day I pinned the latest poster to my bedroom wall. The guitarist was playing a Gibson Flying V. I'd never seen a guitar like that before. Its owner's name was Andy Powell and he played in a band called Wishbone Ash. Almost a year later, I did a swap in the playground of my new high school—a Genesis album I'd grown tired of in exchange for a Wishbone Ash album with a magnificent gatefold sleeve, showing a sentinel and a UFO. What I found inside was even better: a band with chops, mixing the old and the new, capable of spine-tingling solos and soaring guitar interplay. That was *Argus*, and Wishbone Ash had a new fan. Who became, as it turns out, a lifelong fan.

So it's a great pleasure to be able to say that the man behind the Flying V can write a bit, too. Here's the story of the band in his distinctive voice. There are tales of tour antics with The Who, of sessions with Ringo Starr, of hair-raising trips to India and beyond. The highs and lows of band life are laid bare, and, yes, there's even room for some courtroom drama, too. Above all, Andy never forgets that the music is what it's all about—making great albums and then sharing those songs with fans worldwide. Wishbone Ash is still very much a band hard at work, and as Andy himself says the line-up you'll see at a gig these days is as tight and scintillating as any in the history of the group.

From the austere landscape of 1950s Britain, through the swinging 60s and rocking 70s, right up to the very different world of the present day, this is a book written by someone who's seen it all and lived to tell the tale. From early influences such as Django Reinhardt and Chuck Berry, to the small ad in *Melody Maker* that would change his life, and from there to the rollercoaster ride of five decades of Wishbone Ash, here is Andy Powell's story, told for the first time.

Enjoy the ride …

Ian Rankin,
July 2015

INTRODUCTION

If there is one song in our large back catalogue that sums it all up for me then it has to be the one called 'Warrior', visualised on the sleeve of our best-known album, *Argus*. It's a collectively written piece with lyrics by our original bassist, Martin Turner; it speaks about fighting for what you believe in and has a prophetic vision that belies our youth.

To me, the song is a metaphor for life itself—or, at the very least, life in a band on a musical quest. The lyrics could be applied to any worthwhile endeavour in any walk of life where you have to fight the good fight. I've had soldiers, actual warriors of our own time, come to me and tell me how that song gave them comfort in battle.

I am never happier than when I have a clear musical mission and, yes, a clear mission in life. I think it's the same for most of us. We need to know where we stand; what our purpose is. We've all been there, one way or another. This book is the story of my struggles, my insecurities, challenges, successes, and achievements. It's my life as I see it: an acknowledgement of who I am.

It took a long time for me to really grow into the role of a professional musician, to feel that I was not only comfortable in those shoes but running in them. It even took me some years as a professional musician before I'd state it under 'occupation' in my passport. It was always a work in progress. In the lyrics of this song one hears a wistfulness, but one also hears a strong resolve at the same time. I like that. There's an understanding that at some point you'll be needing to go down to that valley, to gather there, gird up your loins, and put your world to rights. And often it'll be just when you are feeling the most content with your lot—you'll have no option but to face change, don the armour, and wade into battle once more. There's also that quest to be a slave of no man, throwing off the shackles or the ties that bind, while fighting the good fight once more.

> *I'll have to be a warrior,*
> *A slave I couldn't be,*
> *A soldier and a conqueror,*
> *Fighting to be free.*

The best songs—and this one is one of them—have a kind of yearning to them: a yearning for a better life, a quest for the truth and often, above all else, a quest for true love. It's the same with the singer. An audience can tell in an instant if the song is coming from the heart, regardless of whether or not the singer was the writer.

Guitar playing is like this too. The best soloists have a yearning within their style. Certainly Jimi Hendrix had that—he was on a mission. Clapton at his best could move you like this; Peter Green, most definitely. And I've always known this in my own approach—known when I was transcending or was merely paying lip service to the song. That, for me, is music.

Victor Hugo said, 'Music expresses that which cannot be put into words and that which cannot remain silent.' And, of course, in addition to songs with words, Wishbone Ash are known for producing a large body of music propelled forward by those intertwining guitars. When these ingredients, the music and the words, are blended in the right way, when the harmony and synergy is present in the song, you have one hell of a great band.

That, to me, is Wishbone Ash. It's a band for which I'm proud to have fought for in excess of four decades. I was proud to be in it in the 70s, and I'm just as proud to be in it today. I've been buffeted and bruised by the cold winds of ill fortune along the way, but one always gains from experience. I'm a better person today than I was yesterday, and I've got there by accentuating the positives in a business where, as others might say, if you're not up, you're down. I've found the middle way, and whatever may happen tomorrow, that sun keeps on shining. In the words of 'Eyes Wide Open', a Wishbone Ash song from the twenty-first century, I've made it thus far in a business that knows no mercy by 'taking hold of my life'. This book is my story.

CHAPTER 1

GROWING UP

The 1950s in Britain are often described as bleak, stuffy, austere, and monochrome. And trust me, they were. The 60s, on the other hand, are always paraphrased as vibrant, loose, colourful, exciting, and optimistic. The tint becomes rosier as time goes on, but even at the time it felt as if something had changed for the better.

It was about time, too. In 1965 Roger Miller was able to tell people around the world that 'England Swings (Like A Pendulum Do)', and Roger's take, rather more so than his grammar, felt pretty accurate to me. The 60s really *were* 'Swinging', or at least they were if you went out and looked. And I did. I was born in the East End of London in 1950 but grew up in Hemel Hempstead, just north of the city, exactly the right age to drink deep from this well of hope. I was outside London, the magic cauldron momentarily at the heart of global culture, but I was close enough to get there, to see and hear what was about to have a major impact on the world. It was a golden time and place for pop music—and it seems to have defined the era in a way that it never had before and never really would again.

There would be an awful lot of kids like me enthralled by music and swept along by the dream of being a part of what Andrew Loog Oldham, the game-changing manager of The Rolling Stones, called the 'industry of human happiness'. You might think 'beats working for a living' would have been a thought at the centre of that equation but actually, no, it wasn't. My generation, it seems to me, were grafters. You had to be—growing up, there just wasn't a lot of money around. There was a desperation to *build* something new and exciting, something colourful and loud, and building required effort. We had the energy and the will to do that.

Prime Minister Harold Macmillan told the nation in 1957 that we'd 'never had it so good'. He was the very antithesis of the sort of person who would come to represent the good times coming: starchy, old-school, upper class and with a bumbling voice. But move that remark on a few years, and I'd have to agree: we never did have it so good. And, if I put on my best pair of rose-tinted spectacles, I'd probably have to say we never quite managed it again.

My band, Wishbone Ash, was a '70s band'. I can't deny we did our best to give those halcyon 60s a run for their money, and if the past is another country, it's always worth a visit.

My mother, though, might have thought differently. Ruby Alfreda Powell, born in 1921, had a past much tougher than mine. Her father died, aged twenty-one, on Christmas Day 1930, and she basically brought up her two younger stepbrothers herself. She always learned her lessons well. She did everything correctly because corrected she was, spending a good portion of her time in the workhouse, after her mother couldn't manage. As a child she would have done quite menial work to earn her keep. No easy road, to coin a phrase.

My nan was quite a character. She would actually go out into the street and sing for their supper. Somewhere or other the 20s were supposed to be 'Roaring', but I imagine in Britain it was just like the 50s would be— the decade after a ruinously expensive war, another grinding procession of penury and gloom and wishing to be somewhere else (preferably America). When the Wall Street crash came along in 1929, even America was no good.

Nan was quite industrious, though. She was in service—a live-in servant to the relatively wealthy, just exactly the same as her mother, Great Grandma Pudney, had been. Various liaisons ensued and the family history becomes a little bit vague, I must admit. I daresay it would fuel a few plotlines in *Downton Abbey*, but then my nan's experiences were hardly unusual. The tough times made life hard for young Ruby. The workhouse system of dealing with the poor in society was abolished in 1930, although many of the places were still functional up to 1948. It's a sobering thought. Maybe Macmillan's line wasn't so ridiculous after all.

Amazingly, however awful it was, the whole experience didn't give my mum a ball and chain of bitterness to haul around. What it did give her was a fantastic survival instinct and work ethic, which she passed on to us, me and my brother Len, who came along four years after me.

* * *

'What did you do during the war, dad?'

I might have asked this at some point. To which my dad, also called Len, would surely have replied, 'Run for cover.' My mum and dad married in 1944 and lived at 43 High Street North, East Ham, in the East End of London, inconveniently central to the thinking of German Bomber Command. Dad was deemed to be more useful to the war effort working in the armaments industry than gallivanting off somewhere with a rifle and a tin hat. He was lucky in that respect. That was the sad lot of his older brother Eddie, the star of the family, who perished on Omaha Beach, Normandy, on D-Day. My mum packed parachutes. She was eventually evacuated off to Northampton, and my dad would cycle up there to visit—on his bike at first, and later on a motorcycle. After the war, he was an engineer for Vauxhall Motors in Dunstable, Bedfordshire, an English outpost of the General Motors empire. The company spent most of the war making Churchill Tanks and then moved on to the Bedford Van. Like most of the British rock fraternity, I'd spend a fair proportion of my music apprenticeship trundling uncomfortably along minor roads for interminable distances in Bedford vans. Funny, you often thought you'd made it when your band finally got a van.

My dad was the only one of his brothers who moved out of the East End. The youngest of four brothers and two sisters, he was the only one who took the plunge and probably went above his station in taking a gamble, getting a job in the provinces. People didn't move much in those days. It was a big deal. Dad was a hard-working guy so we were one of the first in our street to get a television and a car. My mum was a housewife—in the rather patronising terminology of the time—but she actually did all sorts of things: she kept books for a local garage, she worked in the school canteen preparing school dinners, she did whatever she needed to do to supplement the income.

Hemel Hempstead was apparently founded in the eighth century, receiving an honourable mention in William the Conqueror's *Domesday*

Book, and it was granted a town charter from Henry VIII a few centuries later. As far as everyone was concerned, however, the place was a 'New Town', designated as such by the government in 1946, along with various other places like Stevenage and Crawley, and open for business—or at least for an in-rush of immigrants from the Blitzed-out East End—in 1949.

We would often go back and visit my relatives in East Ham, and you'd see the war damage lingering on well into the 50s. But we were growing up in a squeaky clean, wonderful Utopia of new housing estates with new schools, playing fields and the countryside where we could climb trees, ride our bikes, and play hide-and-seek. Everything was fresh and brand new. It was, to use an Americanism, *awesome*. The kitchen cupboards were still pretty uninspiring places, though. Food rationing didn't stop in Britain till 1954 but everything was homemade and made with love.

Growing up in the 50s had an effect, I think, on a whole generation of Britons. If you look at The Beatles, the Stones—any pop groups of the 50s and 60s who were British—everyone was tiny. We were no different. I can still remember going to the local health centre and getting our ration of orange juice and cod liver oil. Mum made life more pleasant by being able to stretch the food budget with wonderful wholesome meals like oxtail soup, lamb stew, and of course homemade cakes, which were a magnet for local kids.

Travelling was always a bit of an ordeal. There were no motorways, no service stations, and during the Suez crisis of 1956 there wasn't much petrol either. Nevertheless, my family liked to go to Polzeath, Cornwall, for holidays, and it would take us at least ten hours to drive there. You can do it in half that time now. It would seem like an unattainable quest to find this remote corner of Britain—windswept moors and winding roads, Arthurian castles and clotted cream scones. It all felt very exotic at the time. I remember my mum would pack sandwiches and a flask of tea for the trip, and then we'd get down there, bundle into a caravan or a guest house, and freeze for the two weeks!

All the photographs of me in the 50s are by the seaside—I've got swimming trunks on, but I've got a home-knitted sweater on as well. And it was the same for every kid in Britain. It was misery! Everybody in the family looks so undernourished. But we absolutely loved it.

Looking back on it, going to Cornwall for holidays was quite middle-class and probably a bit eccentric at the time. The era tends to be characterised by Butlin's and Pontin's holiday camps—these rather grim, whitewashed Gulags erected around the unforgiving British coastline and purportedly offering affordable holidays in week-long increments for inner-city families … as long as your idea of a good time was bingo, ballroom dancing, and a kind of militaristic approach to communal fun with people you didn't know. It sounds pretty ghastly to me, and clearly my dad had a similar view. Holiday camps played a big role in the careers of The Beatles and others in the very early 60s—well-paid summer residencies for weeks on end in front of captive audiences, at a time when the infrastructure of rock music in Britain was yet to be created—but fortunately I escaped.

My dad, I suspect, thought he was above this sort of thing. He wanted something a bit more rugged, and pottering about old tin mines and smugglers' coves in Cornwall was certainly that. He had a great romantic streak in his own way. He'd sing Italian opera round the house and, not speaking a word of Italian, he'd make up his own language. But he *could* sing it. He really could hold a tune. I suppose, in a way, he was rebelling against his lot. He was a virtuoso whistler. I used to listen to my dad working in the back garden from my bedroom. He'd be whistling away, and I really believe this had an impact on the way I would use vibrato and develop my melodic guitar style later on.

* * *

It's very convenient to talk in decades, but for me, being born in 1950, my life has seemed to evolve in sync with the turn of each decade. One of my earliest memories of music on TV is *Sunday Night At The London Palladium*—I'd always sit and watch it with mum and dad. It was presented at first by Tommy Trinder, a cheeky chappie from the Music Hall era, and then later by Bruce Forsyth—a man who, however implausibly, was until recently still playing to millions on weekend light-entertainment vehicles in Britain. When people ask me, 'Are Wishbone Ash still going, then?' I really ought to point out the towering totem of Brucie.

The *Palladium* show was a kind of entertainment revolution in its day—a rambunctious hour of cheer from the still-new ITV. Not only a second television channel but one that seemed prepared to have some fun. You didn't get much fun from the BBC in those days. Everything that wasn't clipped or deemed culturally educational was designated 'light entertainment'—Light Entertainment was just that: a sort of aural blancmange, prescribed and regimented to the general population like a laxative.

The only chink in the armour of this scrupulous regime, it seemed, was 'Uncle Mac' on the radio—on the BBC Light Programme, as it was. A man known to his adult friends as Derek McCulloch, Uncle Mac had been involved in broadcasting for children on the BBC since the 30s. His *Children's Favourites* show ran from 1954 to '64, and that was when it got really free—we'd hear stuff from America, we'd hear Burl Ives, folk songs, Pete Seeger, things like that. His stated aim was to fire children's imaginations, broaden their horizons, and he met the brief. Some people say they heard Elvis Presley, old bluesmen, all sorts of oddities on his show. Certainly, it was about the only slot on BBC radio at that time that broke away from the constant diet of dance bands and *The Billy Cotton Band Show*.

Leaving aside Uncle Mac and *Sunday Night At The London Palladium*—which even had Bill Haley & His Comets on the bill on one occasion—there wasn't much exposure to music at home. We never had a record player when I was growing up. My aunt Rene had a radiogram, though, and I would hear songs like 'Mack The Knife' and 'Fever' by Peggy Lee or the odd Sinatra song. Other delights on the radiogram included Acker Bilk, a strange man from the West Country with a clarinet and a bowler hat; Edmundo Ros, maestro of Latin-American supper club music; and The Mike Sammes Singers, a soothing harmony act that later managed several discreet appearances on Beatles records. But for me, the first thing that really captured my ear was Django Reinhardt and his Hot Club de Paris.

I had no idea what this was. I think my dad turned me on to it, but it really resonated with me. I would have been about nine or ten. I heard that music, and it was streets ahead of anything else—and yet this was a pre-war act. Django himself had died in 1953. But this sort of information wouldn't have been particularly known and certainly not pertinent at the time. (The curious, accelerating obsession with 'newness' is perhaps one of pop music's least loveable gifts to the world.)

For me, hearing it as a kid, Django's music rocked—the rhythm guitars were just pumping away—and over the top of this rhythm, with these incredible, emotional outbursts of fire, was this man playing lead guitar with, apparently, only two fingers. As I said, in those days, certainly in my neighbourhood, lots of people whistled: the milkman, the rag-and-bone man, the postman; all these guys whistled. And some of them were really bloody good! When you heard Django play guitar it was just another version of that: trilling away there, his strings like a human voice; a lot of passion, a lot of emotion. You didn't hear that normally in the 50s. There was no place for naked emotion in post-war Britain. But the French, or the gypsies, seemed to know something we didn't, and it was intoxicating stuff.

Toward the end of the 50s we were moving from light music on the BBC to the first inklings of rock'n'roll. I was hearing stuff that was loosely rock'n'roll, like Tommy Steele—the first in a series of rather ersatz British rock'n'rollers, usually with descriptive surnames, like Vince Eager and Johnny Gentle, and usually managed by the same man, Larry Parnes. It was all a bit camp and peculiar, in retrospect, but it was relatively exciting at the time.

Lonnie Donegan was, in a way, a magical one-off, though he seemed to be the start of this loosening-up of popular music in Britain. Skiffle was a British phenomenon: folk song with a jazz beat, they called it; three chords, a tea-chest bass, a washboard, and some thimbles. Everyone could do it— and, for a couple of years, everyone did.

Lonnie had kicked it all off with 'Rock Island Line' in 1956. This was seriously fun music, a breath of fresh air. He was the father of 'letting it all go'. I was quite young then but anyone of any age could relate to the excitement—the energy of Lonnie's performances in the 50s still comes across from old clips on YouTube. His hits dried up at precisely the time The Beatles arrived, but he was still holding festival crowds in the palm of his hands right up to his death in 2002. There has to be a lesson there: you can work hard at musicianship but you can't buy charisma.

At some point before the decade's end I became aware of Chuck Berry, a man who had both musicianship and charisma, counterbalanced by the sort of personality flaws you only hear about later in life. I'd hear Chuck's guitar playing and think, *Wow!* This was something incredible. It's remarkable that what Chuck did in the 50s is still the bedrock, the basic template of rock'n'roll in almost all its forms to this day. That chugging rhythm, the lead guitar that sounds like car horns, the riffs, the poetry in the lyrics—it started for me a lifelong love of all things American.

This seemed to be typical in my peer group. We maybe didn't quite rationalize it all as 'America' but everything we cared about was coming from there. My aunt Doris and my uncle Tosh had a newsagents and sweet shop in Dagenham, about an hour away from where we lived. That was the first place I drank a Coca-Cola, and it was the first place I ever read a *Superman* comic. Anything from America had a huge impact. Everything in post-war Britain was just grim and drab and grey, and so you craved the colour and the fun of America: Coca-Cola, comics, burgers, films. When we got the TV I remember a series called *77 Sunset Strip* and I became a fan of Chevrolet Impala cars, these vehicles that seemed to glide in and out of parking lots on cushions of air. I was definitely a devotee of the lead character, Kookie, played by the ultra-cool Edd Byrnes, who presented my first glimpse of what was to become, in the UK, the sharp mod style. The mind boggled. We just loved it, we craved it.

Many years later, on one of the first Wishbone Ash tours, I can remember sitting on my own on Miami Beach thinking, *My God, I'm in a Technicolor movie! I am actually living the dream, right here, right now!* I was there on the beach thinking, *This is actually Technicolor!* When you're nineteen or twenty, that sort of thing is very impactful. I guess I was, and still am, a sensualist. I crave sensual experiences, and of course music is one of the best.

* * *

Most people of my age who gravitated into making music for a living owe some kind of a debt to Cliff Richard & The Shadows. Some of them even admit to it! Brian May, Al Stewart, Peter Frampton, Jeff Beck, Ritchie Blackmore, Pete Townshend, Dave Gilmour, Tony Iommi; even Neil Young and Frank Zappa are among the great and the good who have happily acknowledged the primal influence of Hank Marvin, Shadow-in-chief, a cheery looking man with Buddy Holly spectacles and a red guitar in a monochrome age. Was I any different? No! Joining the boy scouts and hearing pop music—specifically the instrumental music of The Shadows—on a transistor radio was the sunlit path. The road to rock was signposted by Hank's twang. Baden-Powell's orienteering skills, cowboy hat, and old-school camaraderie would help you find the way.

By the end of the 50s, Cliff and the boys were all over the airwaves, all over the TV variety shows. But I wasn't particularly interested in Cliff and the singers at the time—not in Tommy Steele or Billy Fury or any of those other Larry Parnes 'stable' guys, whose names all seemed to be abstract nouns. Truth be told, I didn't really care much for Elvis Presley either. I was never into the rebellious aspect of rock'n'roll; I just didn't understand it. I wasn't drawn to that side of rock until much later, when I became a mod and a fan of bands like The Action and The High Numbers. That's when I felt rebellion—but that was a few years down the road. As a ten year old, sticking it to the man—even if I'd known how to do so or, for that matter, quite who 'the man' was—just didn't grab me.

What *did* grab me, though, was the ear candy of The Shadows sound, and Hank Marvin in particular. I liked what was going on in the band—in the boiler room, so to speak. How did the actual players create the sound of the band? For a period of time, it seemed as if that was all that was played on British radio. You might occasionally hear The Ventures—instrumental West Coast Americans—but you mostly heard our British version of it, which was The Shadows. Hank just did it better than anyone else. It was totally cool, it was smooth; he had the finesse, the touch and the tone. It stands up even today.

At the time of writing, Hank has a new album out, his first in a while, and if it all sounds pretty similar to what he was doing fifty-five years ago, who could possibly knock him for it? He found something unbreakable very early on in his career and he hasn't needed to fix it yet—and nobody has realistically wanted him to. Sometimes *not* changing what you do is exactly the right thing, though you always have to keep the longer term, bigger picture in mind. Having the confidence not to blow with the wind or attempt to move with the times can often be the path of wisdom, though it might seem costly in the short term. I'll admit that Wishbone Ash came close a couple of times to getting mired in emulating others. These days we simply adhere to our 'sound' and play to our strengths. Very few fans would wish for us to return to 80s-type production values.

But getting back to Hank, what was it about him that was so compelling back in the day? Well, partly at least it was the instrument he played. It just looked so cool. Toward the end of 1959 he acquired a red Fender Stratocaster with gold-plated hardware and a tremolo arm. It's probably impossible to fully appreciate the novelty of this today, but between 1951 and '59 American instruments were banned from import into Britain. It was actually Cliff who acquired the instrument, through the back door, direct from Fender's factory in America, for Hank to use. Apparently it's now in Bruce Welch's loft—Bruce being the Shadows' rhythm guitarist—and Cliff has quipped that, after a lifetime on permanent loan, he'll leave it to Hank in his will. I think that guitar has repaid Cliff's investment a thousand fold by now.

The funny thing was, the decision to buy a Stratocaster was an accident: Hank was aspiring to the guitar sound he was hearing on Ricky Nelson's records at the time, which was down to James Burton and a tremolo-free Telecaster. I suppose all those guys I mentioned above would now agree that this was a fortuitous mistake to make. It's probably less well known that Hank was also directly responsible for Vox Amplifiers creating the A.C.30 amp, a bit of gear that really defined the live sound of virtually all British bands in the 60s, from The Beatles downward.

* * *

While all this was fuelling my musical fantasies, I still had to contend with the business of education. At five years of age I started at Hobbs Hill Primary School and then moved up to the Junior School. I enjoyed school but it was always the art classes that captured my interest. I even won an art contest once. However, like all youngsters, I had to participate in sports as well, and it was during an away game with the school cricket team that an event came to light that was to turn into a big scandal for the school and the whole town.

One of our team had been seriously distraught all afternoon and, after we questioned him, admitted that he had been assaulted in the school stock room by the headmaster. I went home and told my parents. My mother later went round to my friend's house and told his father, but he was in total denial. Eventually the police were informed and the whole situation was taken very seriously.

As it turned out, Reginald Swell—yes that really was his name—had been abusing a lot of boys in the school, but luckily not me. He was a local councillor, too, which somehow made it a bigger deal. Other teachers were aware of it and were obviously fearful for their own jobs. We were taken out of school for weeks as the scandal exploded. For those who like to think the past was a kinder, simpler place, that might be the case in some respects. In other respects—like having layers of safeguards, accountability, and retribution against bastards like Reginald Swell—it would be chilling to regress from the modern era.

There were two options in those days in Britain when you reached the end of junior school: it was all down to an exam called the 11-plus. If you passed, you went to a grammar school; if you failed, you went to a secondary modern. To a great extent it impacted the rest of your life and the options and expectations you might have. In 1961 I ended up at Apsley Grammar School. Meanwhile, several of my friends—and in due course my brother—ended up at the local secondary modern.

I had a lot of friends from the same social background and suddenly there was this line in the sand between us. It was a terrible, divisive line. But I still kept in touch with friends from both sides of that line because music was the thing that cemented our friendships. Most of my friends in bands were from schools in different neighbourhoods. Friendships require effort from all involved, but I can't think of an instance where that tiny bit of effort every so often—the time to make a phone call or send an email to catch up and keep a connection going—has not been worthwhile. Later, after I had joined Wishbone Ash and moved to London, I was to invite an old drummer friend of mine, Terry Finn, to help out with some of our crewing needs.

Back in the early 60s, the effort involved was less apparent: there were shared goals, shared interests, and the sun always seemed to be shining. If you were musically inclined you could exploit those musical talents in the summer. Summer holidays were long and we kids were bored, so we'd all hang out at community centres, youth clubs, and so on, and that's when I started playing music.

It seemed that kids from my social strata were not encouraged to play music at school. If you didn't have music lessons and you weren't from a middle-class family—and I wasn't—you weren't deemed to be musical. Consequently I got little encouragement in music at school other than communal lessons on the recorder. So thank goodness for those summer holidays: that's when the chance to participate in music really happened. The closest I came to learning any musical theory was when I bought a book by Bert Weedon called *Play In A Day*. As simple as that book was, along with the promise it made, I never learned more than three chord patterns in different keys. I simply trusted my ear more. Years later, it amazed me how much musical experience my own boys would be given in their new American schools. Everyone was encouraged to join the school band or orchestra, and lessons in multiple instruments were made available to all the students.

I can recall at some point in the early 60s, presumably after that import ban had been lifted, word spreading around my neighbourhood that a real live Stratocaster had been seen in our local music shop in town—a salmon-pink one, no less. Kids from my housing estate would make pilgrimages down there to gawp in the window.

Around the same time we'd also make similar pilgrimages to London on the train or even the bus, which was a two-hour journey, to visit the music stores around Charing Cross Road, like Macari's and Selmer's, just to simply see a Stratocaster. We were young and easily intimidated, so we wouldn't even dare go in the store, we'd just stare in awe at these artefacts from another world, glowing in the window.

There were two or three of us involved in these field trips to the edge of the dream world. My friend Bob Moreton in particular led the way. We couldn't even begin to aspire to own one of these instruments but what we could do was try to make our own approximations. We didn't dare get close to them to make accurate measurements so we had to guess it all, do it from memory. The first guitar I ever made, with my dad, was a copy of a Stratocaster. He made some of the metal hardware parts and one of the other fathers helped with the electronics. We didn't have a hope in hell of buying an amplifier, so someone took the guts out of a TV and I used the speaker from that. I've got photographs of myself with that guitar, and actually it was rather good! I played it onstage—and finding those stages was the next step.

Everyone has to start somewhere, and in my case it was the Ovaltine factory in Kings Langley. (I note that a blue plaque from English Heritage marking this prestigious event has yet to be erected.) The occasion was one of their annual social events. There's a photograph of myself there: I think I was thirteen, and actually it was my future father-in-law Jack Langston who had finagled it so we could play. This was huge for us, and it was enough to give us the impetus to carry on as a band.

The next stage was playing at a Saturday-morning cinema before a screening of a Disney movie at the local Luxor Movie House in Hemel Hempstead. Once again, this nerve-wracking experience of public performance in a proper theatre was invaluable to me.

At this point we would have played the odd song like 'House Of The Rising Sun' or 'Rockin' Robin'—a 1958 hit for one Bobby Day—but our repertoire was mostly instrumentals by The Shadows, plus a particular favourite, 'Cruel Sea' by The Dakotas. Everything was learned by ear. It was a typical four-piece Shadows line-up. I became known in later life as a lead guitar player, but for me rhythm guitar was a huge part of rock and would remain so. Bruce Welch was my first hero. He was such a smooth player. I never did the moves, though.

* * *

There's a very clear dividing line in British popular music, and it's simply this: before and after the arrival of The Beatles. You could feel it at the time. The Shadows continued to have hit singles throughout the 60s, and you could still see Billy Fury or Johnny Kidd popping up now and again on *Ready Steady Go!*, but virtually everyone else who had made some kind of mark during that first flowering of British rock in the late 50s quickly faded away into cabaret or obscurity (or both).

I know where and when I first heard The Beatles: I was at school, and I remember hearing 'Please Please Me' on a transistor radio during the mid-morning break. The metaphorical clouds parted and the sun burst forth.

It was the first time that what we call 'production' hit me. In those days, the norm for a recording artist was to be either a featured vocalist or an instrumental act. The Beatles broke the mould: it was all singing, all playing. They had this vocal sound, a homogenous texture of three voices, the chiming guitars, the arrangement—everything was so clear. I wasn't able to articulate it as 'production' at the time but I knew it was something new and distinct. *How did they create that sound?* It was so different and so powerful.

From that point on, all of the talk was about The Beatles. *Who is this band? Where are they from? Liverpool, where's Liverpool? How do they talk up there?* We were intrigued with these distinctly Liverpudlian sayings, which soon became common currency, like randomly adding 'whack' to perfectly adequate questions. 'How ya doing, whack?' became the catch phrase in the school corridors. And thus we all walked around for a week or two, trying to talk Liverpudlian. Everything before that had been London, London, London, and now, all of a sudden, it was all about Liverpool. Then we got to see them on TV, and the whole journey—for a whole nation and then a whole world—began. After that, every single, every album became an event.

* * *

The Beatles were an entity apart; that was obvious to us. There was something that was obviously groomed about them, but it wasn't 'London'. They had this German thing going on with their suits and haircuts, which was kind of mod but not really mod, so they stood apart from the London scene somehow which made it very interesting. Somebody once asked them in a press conference if they were mods or rockers. Ringo immediately replied, 'Neither: we're mockers,' which spoke volumes. They were above labels, and they were sharp of wit. I, however, was becoming a mod—or at least I was for a while. If you'd have told me that later on I'd actually work briefly with a couple of The Beatles in recording studios, I would not have believed it possible. But this did indeed come to pass.

The mod movement in Britain all started in London in the late 50s with Italian suits, French shoes, smoky basement scenes, and a soundtrack of modern jazz—all a subtle but definite differentiation away from the drab homogeneity of clothing and lifestyle available to men in the buttoned-up Britain of those days. By the middle 60s, the idea of 'mod' had devolved into something slightly different: the clothing aspect was still there, but by the time it was spreading out to the regions, the soundtrack had distilled to a kind of punchy R&B, especially with danceable records from black American artists with horn sections, while amphetamines, an aid for all-night dancing, were all the rage. British bands with horn sections would start to multiply voraciously a year or two down the line—one or two of them featuring me on rhythm guitar—but in 1964, thirty miles north of London, the bands we considered mod were four-piece guitar/vocal units typified by The Small Faces and The High Numbers (soon to become The Who).

I was fourteen when my band, The Dekois, opened for The High Numbers at the Trade Hall in Watford. Given the advanced levels of published Who archaeology these days, I can fairly certainly pin it down to August 1 or 22 1964. For me it was an epiphany. I'd never seen anything like it. Pete Townshend was playing a Marshall stack and he had his Rickenbacker guitar, a curly guitar lead—all intriguing stuff, let alone their stage act, their music, their energy. We went backstage, to their dressing room, and I can remember thinking, *My God, these people are so professional—they've got stage clothing!* It was all hanging up on hangers. They travelled in a Ford Transit and I'm thinking, *That's so pro…*

I can't say they were particularly welcoming on that occasion, but I sensed there needed to be a kind of arrogance to get anywhere—which is a lesson in itself. I saw Steampacket with Rod Stewart and the ultimate female mod icon, Julie Driscoll, at the same venue, the following year. These were older guys, three or four years older, so I was watching them for signs to see how they carried themselves—and, once again, it was all about attitude. So I definitely decided that to be a rock musician with any kind of success you had to have attitude. Up to that point I was an attitude-free zone; seeing The High Numbers was when the penny started dropping.

Then I saw The Who, as they now were, at the Dacorum College in Hemel Hempstead. I'd stood in the crowd in front of Townshend watching him play and, to use the vernacular of that time, I was mind-blown. The band by now was into the whole auto destruct thing. I literally ran all the way home. My dad was on the nightshift. I woke my mum up at around one in the morning and said, 'You've no idea—I've just seen the most amazing thing!'

I'm not sure my epiphany was entirely appreciated. Nevertheless, even in the cold light of retrospection, The Who had a huge impact on me. A few years later, in, I suppose, a bit of a fairy-tale sort of denouement, we ended up opening for them in the States. I can't honestly say they were much more welcoming on that occasion, but by then, of course, I had acquired some attitude of my own.

I wasn't a big pill-popping mod, although some of my friends were. For me, it was all about getting an edge over the norm. We were growing up on very regimented 50s housing estates; everybody did things the same. Sooner or later you craved the opportunity to be different. And funnily enough—it seems absurd, in a way, looking back—that usually meant finding someone or something to copy. Individuality by uniform … as long as the uniform wasn't what your dad was wearing.

One of the key guys to emulate in those days, when I was fifteen or sixteen, was Steve McQueen. He was the kind of movie star who dressed in a modernistic way—the lapels were a certain cut, the raincoats were shortened, the shoes were French or Italian. Everything was trimmed down, like the *Mad Men* thing you see on TV these days.

Our aspirations, though, weren't limited to style. Free market economics was a big part of life: we were all hustling. Remarkably, given the penury of a time soon to come, I was never without money in my teens. I wasn't specifically encouraged by my parents to take on lots of part-time jobs as a teenager but I always felt that I should. And, right from the beginning, I equated playing music to making money.

It wasn't that I wanted lots of money, but I was very keenly aware that you had to pay your own way and take responsibility for yourself. It was there in my family background, from my mother's and my grandmother's experiences. More to the point, we didn't get pocket money. All the local kids had jobs and if there were any jobs going you hustled to get them. I delivered newspapers every day of the week: before school I'd get up, come rain or shine, and do a newspaper round. Friday nights I worked in a fish-and-chip shop; Saturdays I worked in an electrical shop. There were milk rounds, and I even had my own ice-cream round for a while—in fact, around 1966 or '67, I had my own ice-cream truck! My future colleagues in Wishbone Ash would never let me forget it, but actually that was how I learned to drive, before I even had a driving licence.

Putting in the hours like this meant I could save enough money, for example, to be able to go up to London and have a bespoke mohair suit made. My shoe place of choice then was called Raoul, with French shoes a speciality. All dressed up, we would then go into London or into Watford. We aspired to the Flamingo Club scene down in Soho, which Georgie Fame had started—jazzy R&B, ska rhythms, Hammond organ, and a classy horn section, all grinding out in a smoke-filled cellar with hipsters, gangsters, and black US servicemen on weekend leave.

It all seemed so sophisticated—and it was. In Watford, where the vibe was somewhat less rarefied, we could go to the Free Trade Hall or Kingdom Hall and see all the London bands that were doing the circuit at the time. By that time my whole musical world was expanding into Stax, Motown, and blues. 'Our' bands were The Action, The Creation, The Who, Zoot Money & His Big Roll Band, Spencer Davis, The Birds, Steampacket, Gary Farr & The T-Bones, Cliff Bennett & The Rebel-Rousers, Georgie Fame & The Blue Flames … it was a good time to be alive.

Around this time my good mate Bob Moreton—who was in a way my artistic guru, turning me on to Salvador Dali among others—played me a song by one Albert King. It was called 'Personal Manager'. I was instantly hooked, and he's still probably my favourite bluesman of all the Kings. I was really intrigued when I saw the photo of him on the record sleeve playing this odd-shaped V guitar by Gibson.

* * *

I left school at eighteen, after completing seven or eight O-levels and two A-levels. I could probably have gone to university if I'd pushed myself. I knew that I was fortunate in having passed the 11-plus and had the advantages of a grammar-school education. However, I never really understood why I was at grammar school, because I never had the direction at home to make full use of it.

I wonder now if perceptions of 'class' in Britain created more of a ball and chain around your ankle in those days than it would today. There are still class differences, of course, but back then society felt more rigidly delineated. Ideas above your station weren't encouraged, though I think my dad gave it a fair go in his own way, despite being a staunch socialist. Maybe I felt university was beyond me, or maybe I just felt the muse too strongly. Either way, that's what I did.

By then I was playing in bands with horn sections—seven or eight-piece ensembles. I was with two bands in my later teens: one was called The Sugarband and one was called The Ashley Ward Delegation. While I was still at school it was pretty much a weekend situation, but there were certainly times when I would stagger into school having done a gig on a Wednesday or Thursday and just about be able to make it through the day.

We were getting gigs in our own little world around St Albans, Watford, Hemel Hempstead—all these little satellite towns of London. Occasionally we'd make forays into London. We always had a Hammond organ, which was pretty unusual, even in those days. Four of us would have to lift this thing in and out of the van, and we were only skinny little kids. And, yes: we actually *had* vans. There were always older guys in the band, and someone would have a driving licence and the wherewithal to sort out a hire-purchase agreement. The van would, of course, be painted with our band name on it—we had a very 'pro' attitude. Yet somehow I felt the need to do two things which, I have to admit, do seem polar opposites. One was to go on the newly invented hippie trail to Marrakesh; the other was to have a go at something like a 'proper job'. In retrospect, I needed to get both of these daft ideas out of my system.

CHAPTER 2

OUTWARD BOUND

(1969–70)

Even at the time, the 60s seemed to move very fast. Every few months there was something new. One minute I was a mod—sharply dressed, sharp music, sharp attitude—and the next minute I was on the hippie trail to Marrakesh. That isn't a euphemism: I actually did go to Marrakesh.

I must have been nineteen, because I'd already spent some time at the John Lewis Partnership on their management-training scheme. Also, as far as I can recall, I'd only just got together with Steve Upton and Martin Turner—the beginnings of Wishbone Ash, the band that I would spend the rest of my life in. We'd had something of a rehearsal, at least, when I broke the news. My mind was made up. I had decided to go overland to Morocco in a Land Rover with a collection of other like-minded hippie wannabes—all complete strangers.

I suppose it was a kind of compressed equivalent to the gap year of today; a bit of fun and experience in between school, and what was to become my university of the road. I'd played in bands since the age of twelve and had always equated earning my keep with playing music, so it was a bit of a shock to find out at age eighteen that I needed to find a career. In my mind I already had a career: I was a musician, but in what I saw as my need to conform, the best thing the school career's officer could come up with was the retail industry. I was conflicted, to say the least.

The curious thing is, none of this was down to parental pressure. I don't think my father ever visited the school while I was there. I don't think I got any real guidance from my parents. My dad certainly wasn't encouraging me to be an engineer on the night shift at Vauxhall Motors. I don't criticise them for that. They were just so busy making a living. It was a different world back then. There were management-training schemes in all kinds of industry at that time in Britain. Retailing was something I'd actually done. I was good at selling. Hell, to be a musician—selling your talents to an audience is one of the basic requirements, after all.

And so it was that I started off in Trewins at an affiliated store in Watford, and from there moved to the flagship branch of John Lewis in London's Oxford Street. I spent my first summer there, sweltering in the oppressive heat, without air conditioning, trussed up in a suit and tie, a far cry from hippiedom. It was pure hell. I could see that there was possibly a real career there, though. In twenty years I might become a department manager. I liked the merchandise that I was selling, and the company had a good ethos. The idea was that we sales people were partners, rather than employees, sharing in the profits.

One happy by-product of the Oxford Street job was that it put me right in the centre of London, albeit as a commuter still living at home. I'd been playing in bands that occasionally made forays into the city, and that was appealing. Life in London promised a whole new level of excitement, but I simply wasn't invested in this new career. I felt like an imposter—an actor playing a role. I give credit to a wonderful personnel officer, Silvia Lieberman, who basically encouraged me to go with my feelings, and that eventually led to me leaving the partnership.

I started growing my hair again; I ditched the suits and put vents in my Levi's. Whilst on holiday in Wales, I answered an ad in *Melody Maker*—one of the foremost music papers in Britain at the time. The wording struck a chord with me:

Wanted—Lead guitarist: Positive thinking, creative and adaptable, for strongly backed group with great future.

I'm hazy about the exact chronology, but probably just before the initial rehearsal with Steve and Martin, I went up to Macari's, a well-known music shop on London's Charing Cross Road, to sell my guitar to fund the Marrakesh trip, which was already scheduled. This was my precious Burns guitar, which I'd saved for with money that I'd made from my newspaper round some years before. I remember my mother had actually pinned the £40 that I'd saved into the inside pocket of my jacket when I'd made the train journey to Surrey to buy the instrument. (The previous owner had actually won it in a competition on the back of a cornflake box.) As a side note, a few years ago I found an identical model and purchased it, with the idea of renovating it for sentimental reasons. That short-scale Burns Jazz guitar really was a great instrument, with an innovative floating vibrato system that surely helped form my lead-guitar style back in those days.

I was determined to experience travel on my own. I needed an adventure, and the trip to Morocco was to be the first time I'd ever left the country. I'm told that when my parents took me to Victoria station to meet my new travelling companions, I never even turned round and waved to them. I was more than ready to get out and experience life. Even as a young kid living on our housing estate, I'd always roamed far afield. When I got a set of roller skates I wasn't content rolling up and down the driveway—I went to the next neighbourhood. Similarly, as soon as I got a bike I rode for miles, visiting different towns.

So there I was, sometime in the summer of 1969, a passenger in a bone-shaking old Land Rover, driving across Europe on the way to somewhere I barely had any idea about. Perfect. I stayed for six weeks, and as one might imagine soon hooked up with a couple of furry freaks from Leeds who had the same idea. There was indeed something in the air, and it smelled rather exotic. Yes, it was the first time I smoked hashish, procured from a man in a tent on the beach who sat crossed-legged on a woven carpet and deftly used a machete to casually chop off a lump from a large hash cake the size of a dinner plate.

The first stop was Tangiers. I saw belly dancers, I heard Moroccan musicians, I travelled on to Fez and Marrakesh, staying just off the Medina, where we saw Bedouins and the strange blue men from the desert. Then we travelled up into the Atlas Mountains, where the Land Rover promptly broke down. We ended up staying with a tribal family and being entertained by one one of their daughters, who danced for us after we had all shared the same family food bowl—my first taste of the wider world. I marvelled at how this little family survived, the women washing clothes in a mountain stream and so on. It was an eye-opener.

And then I came home. My senses had been overloaded and my immediate wanderlust had been satiated.

* * *

The audition that I attended before the trip had been interesting, if somewhat of a long-winded process. I made the call to London from a public callbox in Wales.

> 'Hi, my name is Andy—about that ad in *Melody Maker* …'
> 'Well, you need to come to St John's Wood where we're rehearsing in the basement of our manager's parents' house, 21 Marlborough Place …'

So up I went to leafy North London on the train with my homemade guitar to meet with these two chaps, Steve Upton and Martin Turner. I have a vague recollection that maybe I came back a second time and Ted Turner—'no relation', as we would be forever obliged to keep saying—was there, while Martin and Steve tried to come to a decision about which one of us they would eventually decide on. At one point they told me that they'd been unsure about Ted due to his lack of experience but that his mother had really pleaded with them to give him another try out. Ted had also been for an audition with Jon Hiseman's Colosseum, where they reached the same conclusion as Steve and Mart.

In my mind, when I was auditioning, *I* was also auditioning *them*. I felt that I'd already paid my dues. I had the qualifications to go to university, I'd invested some serious time with John Lewis on the management course, and I'd played with bands for years. It was really a big deal to turn professional, and I wasn't about to jump wildly into the unknown with any old bunch of dreamers or time-wasters. My parents were also very nervous about me taking this step. It had to feel right.

I remembered buying a book featuring The Hollies back in 1965 called *How To Form A Beat Group* (a bit of twenty-first-century Googling reveals that it was written by Anne Nightingale). I'd always had this fantasy in the back of my mind: I'd been in enough 'beat groups', I knew the routine—

buy a van, get some gear on credit, play the local town hall—I'd already done all that. It was time to find a path to the next level.

After I found my way by tube to St John's Wood, I arrived at some large wooden gates behind which stood a grand house. My arm was shaking from carrying the heavy guitar—the second one that I'd made for myself. I was greeted by the preposterously named Miles Axe Copeland III, an ebullient American wearing hopelessly out-of-date horn-rimmed glasses and dressed in a Brooks Brothers tweed jacket. We'll come to him in due course. He took me down an outside staircase to the basement. Martin Turner and Steve Upton were the two musicians looking to complete a band they were trying to form. Steve, by his rather pompous accent, I could tell, was an ex-private-school boy, three or four years older than me—at a time of life when that mattered. He had already been in a band, The Empty Vessels, with Martin and Martin's brother Glenn, and before that he had travelled to Germany and played in Hamburg with a band called The Devarks. It seemed to me that he was the one deferred to in terms of running a band. Apparently, he and Martin had met when both of them had worked for a lumberyard down in Torquay in the West Country—Steve in the offices and Martin in the yard, making deliveries.

It looked as if this relationship had carried through into their musical endeavours, with Steve being the de facto 'producer' or manager of Martin and Glenn. I learned that Miles had discovered the threesome playing in a club on Haverstock Hill in Hampstead. He was to supersede Steve, whose role then became that of road manager—by which I mean overseeing the logistics of hotels, mapping, and travel arrangements. An old friend of theirs, Mark Emery, was eventually enlisted to help with the actual roadie-ing side of things and was, in time, to gravitate toward mixing our front-of-house sound.

The dynamic of that first meeting was, well, a bit odd. During the spoken part of the audition, Martin was verbose—I couldn't get past him. It struck me at the time that the name of their prior outfit might have been most apt. The irony of the band's name seemed to be lost on them both. We were talking one-on-one and he was dressed in what I thought was a kind of caricature of what a rock person would dress like if they came from the provinces. In my mind, at that time, the London fashion scene was where it was at. I'd gone through the mod thing; I was into fashion and I wouldn't have been seen dead wearing a chiffon scarf or a striped sailor shirt. This guy thought he was a ladies' man—that was plain to see. In terms of a band's visual appeal, he was clearly a good-looking guy, but curious outfit aside, I had my doubts about him at the audition, simply because he didn't stop talking.

In complete contrast, over in the corner, Steve Upton was sitting on a desk with his knees drawn up to his chest. At one point I had to say, 'Hey, Martin, it's nice talking, but what does Steve think about all of this?'

I looked over to Steve and raised an eyebrow. These guys seemed to have some relationship where on the one hand Martin had all the front, all the 'rock star' thing, and then there was this other fellow who, I thought, probably pulled the strings. I was trying to figure it out. I wanted to stop any game-playing to see if there was anything worth moving forward with. The moment I threw the spotlight on Steve I could sense a kind of awkwardness. My arrival, obviously, was going to change the dynamic. Could it work?

The other component in this whole process was Miles Copeland. Alongside these two guys whose personas I could at least identify—one a voluble Lothario with a West Country accent, the other a taciturn fellow with somewhat of a private-school accent—was this loud and brash American.

'What kind of music do you like, Miles?'

'Well, pretty much my favourite band is Creedence Clearwater, but then when The Beatles came along, that was it, y'know.'

OK, I thought, *he knows nothing.*

I'd noticed a book called *The Power of Positive Thinking* on the desk. These then were the components: West Country rock star wannabe, minor private schoolboy, bizarre expatriate American ... and a book about positive thought. And then on the periphery, as I remember it, was Ted Turner—the apprentice, so to speak. I liked Ted. He was easy to get on with, and we both liked Peter Green and Fleetwood Mac. Ted was not there on this first day of posturing and prevarication, though, but he was there the next time we got together.

So yes, whatever we all thought of each other, there *was* a next time. Underneath all the swagger, there really was positivity—the beginnings of a team and people who were committed to making something happen. In the end, both Ted and I got the gig, and there we were: a four-piece with two lead guitarists and a very unusual man with a plan—specifically, to be a millionaire before he reached the age of thirty. We had nothing; he had next to nothing. The only way was up.

In point of fact, to show how tentative and undecided things had been during the long audition process of 1969, I believe that two keyboard players had been slated for the gig with one or the other of us guitarists. One was Matthew Fisher, soon to join Procol Harum, who later played as a guest on our song 'Blind Eye', really contributing to the success of that composition. The other, I believe, was Hugh Banton, later to join the band Van der Graaf Generator. In this way, contrary to erroneous information that has been put out there, Wishbone Ash was formed in London.

* * *

If Brian Epstein had been the fifth Beatle, then Miles was certainly our fifth member. In fact, you could argue—and many people have—that it was Miles who formed Wishbone Ash. It was certainly all to come together under his aegis. Miles was drawn instinctively toward band management, although he had little experience of it, but he had done a business course at the American University in Beirut, where he had spent a good deal of time in his formative years. Also, he'd met with an English pop outfit called Rupert's People, who had been visiting Beirut while he was finishing up college, I believe. Miles managed them for a time, once the family moved to London, after things became somewhat unstable in the Lebanon. This band, featuring John Tout, who went on to be the keyboard player in Renaissance, also had a front man by the name of Rod Lynton. In due course, Rod became our publicist, and, much later on, during the Wishbone Ash reunion of the late 80s, my partner in a pine-furniture-restoration business.

Miles Copeland II (Miles's father) had been a founder member of the CIA. He was a classic loud American, from the South—Birmingham, Alabama, to be exact. His wife, Miles Jr's mother Lorraine, an Oxbridge archaeologist from Scotland, had also been involved in espionage, working for Britain's Special Operations Executive (SOE) during World War II, though we didn't know this at the time. Spies and former spies, after all, tend not to broadcast their activities. The whole family had been neighbours with Kim Philby, the defector to Russia, when they'd lived in Beirut.

It was, you might say, a very interesting family. The house in Marlborough Place was full of nonstop activity. Upstairs there would frequently be a Jesuit priest visiting, or a BBC mobile film crew conducting interviews with Miles senior, and downstairs there would be us, jamming away for all we were worth.

If it seems odd that a blistering right-wing spymaster would tolerate a rock band in his basement, well, it seemed pretty odd to us, too. That was the dichotomy. Miles senior was also a trumpet player—he once played with The Benny Goodman Orchestra—and he'd sometimes come down to the basement with his instrument and jam with us. And then, later in the day, Stewart Copeland, his youngest son, would arrive home from school and jam with us on a spare drum kit …

* * *

Starting a band in London at the end of the swinging 60s probably sounds a lot more glamorous today than it was at the time. An adventure, yes; glamorous, no. It wasn't even safe, if the truth be told. I think few musicians today can relate to the serendipity of the way things were in those days; the way you laid everything on the line—not just us but probably every other great British rock band of that era. It was such a gamble, and yet we did it all on a whim. Being in the music game really was going into a life one notch above criminal activity. It was anti-establishment, there was no financial safety net, and trying to get a bank loan or any kind of support from the social services was, well, remote. The advice from older family members and from society at large was, 'Get a real job!'

I arrived in London with my homemade guitar and a Laney amplifier and moved into a flat with Ted. Or, to be more precise, I moved into one rat-infested, depressing room above a convenience store that should have been condemned. The first visitor we had to this establishment was a wizened little man with a cage in his hand: 'Rat Catcher,' he announced himself. The room was rented to us for the sum of five quid a week by an Irish landlady who was later to become immortalised in the song 'Lady

Whiskey'. Neither of us had a clue how we were going to pay for the place. We had no money, and there were days when we just didn't eat. We became very adept at pilfering the odd Vesta readymade curry from the store shelf as we passed through to the back stairs. I weighed 120lbs; I was, in effect, a starving person.

In April 1970 we had a few gigs in France, and by then I was so malnourished I got pleurisy and was sick for about six weeks. Upon returning to London, an attic room was found for me at Marlborough Place until my father could get up to London and collect me. Being under medical care at home, back in my old childhood room, worked wonders, and after a month's recuperation I was back in business. At one point, Steve Upton came to visit me, for which I was grateful. In my feeble and depressed state I told him that I was having second thoughts about returning to the lifestyle we had created for ourselves. We talked it over, though, and I soon found myself back living above the shop.

So there we were, quite literally all starving to death—not taking care of ourselves, without adequate clothing, trying to build a career out of nothing. Our parents just let us go. I have fond memories of stopping at Ted's parents' house when we'd get gigs in the Birmingham area—and at Martin's folks' place, too, down in Devon—and them trying to fill us up with goodies. I think they could see what we were going through. In our minds we were men by now; we were on our own. There wasn't this transitional period where you leave home with the condition that you can go back to mum and dad if it doesn't work out, except in the case of near-death for myself. It literally felt like do or die. I think that perhaps this is the clearest difference between then and the present day. It was a pioneering time in popular music, and the opportunities were there if you fought for them.

During these very early days of the band, Miles was living at his parents' place while we were all living, poor as church mice, in Gloucester Avenue, Chalk Farm, behind the Roundhouse in Camden Town. We'd walk to St John's Wood every day to rehearse. Occasionally we'd see Paul McCartney out walking his sheep dog. We met Kevin Harrington, through Steve Brendell, who had been the drummer with Rupert's People. Both these guys were working at NEMS Enterprises, who handled The Beatles. Kevin later worked directly with 'the boys' (as they were known) as assistant to Mal Evans, The Beatles' famous roadie. Later, Kevin and Rod were instrumental in securing Ted and I some session work. Ted played on John Lennon's *Imagine*, on the song 'Crippled Inside', while I worked with George Harrison and Ringo on a couple of sessions for people like Cilla Black and an Australian songwriter that Ringo was handling for the Apple label. Even though they'd ceased operating as a live band, The Beatles owned London, and to get the opportunity to play on one of their individual projects was a great honour. Through Kevin we met Terry Doran, George's assistant, and sometimes we'd get ferried around by Kevin in one of the band's cars, a Humber Super Snipe.

The session I did at Apple, with George producing Cilla, was great. He was a pleasure to work with, very accommodating and easy-going, making us players feel at ease immediately. There were a couple of George's large-bodied Harptone acoustic guitars in the studio, and I played a six-string model on the Cilla session alongside Rod. Ringo was on drums and Klaus Voorman was on bass. It was surreal standing in the control room listening to playbacks with George and Ringo being so complimentary—deferential, even. Ringo was quite self-effacing actually. I had to pinch myself. One thing immediately struck me: I was a skinny guy but these chaps were even tinier than me. People often say it's like that when you meet your idols in the flesh. They seem much smaller than you imagine.

The other session was at Tittenhurst Park, the famous country house owned at that time by Ringo but previously owned by Lennon. It was where the iconic photos for the *Imagine* album were shot, where John is with Yoko, sitting at that white Steinway grand piano. This was a bigger live session with more players. Again, Ringo was the epitome of a welcoming host. No big rock-star attitude—extremely down to earth.

* * *

Unsurprisingly, given his rarefied family background, everything Miles did was larger than life. He created a culture around him and you wanted to be on board, for fear of missing out. He had boundless energy. With the end of the Vietnam War and the bourgeoning youth movement, and the popularity of the long-playing vinyl record, the way forward was 'progressive' music. That was deemed to be the future for the next decade, and we were going to part of it, with Miles leading our charge. He was chief among the proselytizers of positivity with his outrageous sense of fun about the business. He didn't care about making mistakes, which was a remarkably useful quality. He was all about making waves, and we got swept up in the idea.

Miles was a unique figure in the music business in London in those days, and later on, when we went to the States, he would occupy a similarly singular position. People did not forget an encounter with him easily. He could outrage and polarise on a regular basis but he would still be taken very seriously. He was a very effective businessman—and, luckily for us, he was on our side.

Of course, none of Miles's moves would have had any traction if he were peddling rubbish. He was a magician, not a miracle worker. Although it was clear to us that there was no great visionary songwriter or front man among us, it was very clear that we had a unique and exciting sound. Miles would come to every show with us, keeping a very sharp eye on our development and how audiences were responding to us. He went headlong into a world where there were some very big sharks and I don't think we realised at the time what he had to contend with in order to have his voice heard. We ribbed him mercilessly about being the 'straight' guy in the outfit—the one wearing the suit. But he stood by us, and I have to say that none of the plans we had in those early years could have been manifested without Miles behind us.

We weren't prolific writers to start with. I think Martin had parts of the songs 'Queen Of Torture', 'Doctor', and 'Handy' from the days of The Empty Vessels, and these would all end up on our first album. I'd started writing and came up with the song 'Errors Of My Way'. Ted had most of the idea for 'Blind Eye,' the lyric and so forth, while I contributed to the guitar lick that became the hook of the song: a huge dynamic sound, with Steve's jazzy drum fills, with which to open our set and later our first album, *Wishbone Ash*.

What I brought, from my soul-band days, was not so much songs but a sense of how to groove. I didn't think Steve or Martin had a really solid 'groove' that was commercial enough to become successful. They could rock with great gusto but we needed to move people—make them want to dance to our music. I remember having to teach Martin what a shuffle was, and the fact that you could alter the picking and hence the movement within a piece of music. He played bass with a pick and didn't get that it was not necessary to play every note on the downstroke, or that a smoother sound could be achieved by picking on the upstroke as well. In addition, apart from complete songs of mine like 'Valediction', I was also more interested in creating arrangements, guitar parts, openings, melodies; finding colour in the music with which to pull in the listener. Our long rehearsal sessions were so much fun in those days. We were intensely driven, unlike anything I've known since.

The aforementioned gigs in France during March and April of 1970 turned out to be a rite of passage for both us and Miles. We arrived in Calais having no idea that a carnet—a kind of equipment manifest—was needed in order to bring musical instruments into the country. Europe was different then: a place of borders and bureaucracy. The only thing to do was for Miles to return to England on the next ferry to get the necessary paperwork while we waited in a café for something like twelve hours until he returned. All credit to him: he did it. He got back on that ferry, went to the carnet office in London, probably lined up for hours, achieved a result, and then turned around and came right back on another ferry.

* * *

In retrospect, the fourteen or fifteen months between starting the band and releasing our first album seems like remarkably swift progress. Time gets compacted in hindsight, and you tend to dismiss those miserable bed-sits, the lack of food and the hard graft, and look instead, with some awe, at the date sheet and the billings with acts like Deep Purple, Free, The Who, ELP. I was part of something special, and sometimes it takes a bit of distance to be able to recognise that.

Around this time I acquired a nickname: 'Snap'. I think it speaks of my general impatience, since I was often disparaging and eager to get going. I know it was the same for the other guys. I just probably voiced my frustration more, making off-hand comments or snappy comebacks to suggestions by Miles or some of the others.

Things did get better, though, thanks to a concerted focus on the job at hand. When you have five guys totally focused on making something happen, you are bound to get results, although there were a few setbacks. Miles used his wiles in a couple of ways, capitalising on each and every little contact or connection along the way. The French dates were helped along by a couple of Miles's old school buddies and their connections in Paris. One friend had the equally preposterous name of Tulliver Brooks, and yet another invited us to his parents' very upmarket apartment on the Left Bank where—over a formal dinner complete with the family's butler waiting on us at the table—I inadvertently tipped a silver tureen full of soup over a beautiful inlaid Louis XV dining table. What can I say? The handle had been loose …

The reality was that we were all staying in a one-room *pensione* near St Germain called L'Hôtel des Balcones, at 3 Rue Casimir Delavigne, which I can still remember to this day. It smelled of coffee, furniture polish, and bad French plumbing. We met up with some *jolie* French girls and one came back to the room with young Ted. I remember us all trying to get some sleep while he was sharing a bed with this sweet young thing—Chantelle, perhaps, was her name. She was saying softly, in broken English, 'I am not ze groupie.' Of course we ribbed him mercilessly about that, while being secretly jealous that he was able to get her into his bed.

We played venues like the Rock & Roll Circus, which seemed quite a decadent place, and later a place called Le Golf-Drouot. The DJ's name was Jaques Chabiron, I remember. It was all very exciting, and we felt like an anomaly in the *trés cool* environs of Paris. I particularly enjoyed tasting the different foods and checking out the clothes shops. Steve did the driving, if I recall, navigating our trusty yellow Transit van around the Arc de Triomphe, being quite shocked at the pace and intensity of Paris traffic.

In May 1970 we supported Deep Purple at The Civic Hall in Dunstable. During the summer we played festivals in Bath and at the Plumpton Racecourse, and in August we secured our first BBC session on Bob Harris's *Sounds Of The Seventies* followed by our first TV slot on BBC2's *Disco 2* that December.

Barring those initial French gigs we were playing exclusively and exhaustively in Britain that year—something like 100 to 200 shows in and around London and up and down the motorways. At one point it felt as if we were the house band at the Speakeasy, the musicians' hangout in London, given the number of times we played or partied there.

One night Keith Moon got up and jammed with us. I remember it clearly because Steve had just taken delivery of a brand new pink Slingerland sparkle-finish drum set. Keith got behind it, pretty drunk by then but intent on playing to his group of hangers-on. I think we played Chuck Berry's 'Johnny B. Goode', Keith giving it the whole bug-eyed ludicrous rock drummer caricature, grinning and posing for all he was worth. It was hilarious. At the end, amid much cheering, Keith got up, and instead of walking around the drum kit he walked right through it, kicking parts of it nonchalantly out of the way and off into the crowd. Steve was mortified. I can still see his look of chagrin. It all worked out and came good a few months later, however, when we were lucky enough to be supporting The Who on a tour of the States. Keith gave Steve a bottle of Courvoisier cognac and took him under his wing. It was a case of 'Who cares' both times!

* * *

The first British Invasion of America involved 1964, The Beatles, Ed Sullivan, and anyone else who managed to grab the coat tails and surf the biggest wave in pop music. The Dave Clark Five and Herman's Hermits, as a result, meant a great deal more in the USA than they did back home. Even Freddie & The Dreamers had a US number 1. Weirdly, rock acts like The Who and Jimi Hendrix would often be opening for acts like these, waiting for the market to catch up with them.

The second British Invasion started in the late 60s, with acts like The Who and Cream of course, but by the time Wishbone Ash arrived to conquer the US, in February 1971, a whole new touring infrastructure had been opened up and defined very largely by British bands over the previous two years. The likes of Led Zeppelin, Ten Years After, Jethro Tull, and Fleetwood Mac criss-crossed America frequently and extensively from the beginning of 1969 onward. A typical tour could begin with two or three nights at the Fillmore East, a crumbling old cinema in New York, and stop off at legendary 'underground' clubs in Boston, Detroit, Anaheim, and Los Angeles, often on bills with domestic acts like The Doobie Brothers or The Allman Brothers, and, in between, meander around huge college gymnasiums and prototypical open-air festivals, state fairs, and hockey arenas, in the Midwest, the South, and everywhere else.

Our second album, *Pilgrimage*, was released in the US during August, a good month before it appeared in Britain—one of the quirks of having a US record label, MCA. This was beneficial for us since we had our second US tour booked—or so we thought. Arriving once again on US soil we discovered there were no gigs. We found ourselves in Wildwood, New Jersey, a coastal resort town, where we hung around for about ten days killing time. I remember going crabbing, sunbathing, and celebrating Ted's twenty-first birthday by jamming outside on the hotel deck. We had our British crew with us, Chris Runciman and Mark 'The Hobbit' Emery. It was fun but not what I'd had in mind.

After we'd spent time kicking our heels, Miles eventually made contact with a guy called Ron Sunshine. I don't know how Miles discovered him, but at this point in time Ron was booking dates for The Who. We had played a show with Steppenwolf; the good word had gone out and suddenly we were being offered five shows supporting The Who. What an opportunity! So we stopped bothering the local crustaceans and started work. We played shows in Cleveland, Dayton, Detroit, and Minneapolis and then, most memorably, the Mississippi River Festival in Edwardsville, Illinois. This was truly an eye- and ear-opener. The crowd was monstrous. I remember going up to the mic—I'd never heard my voice amplified like that before. I think the PA system was set up with delay towers to synchronise the sound coming from the stage and the back of the festival site.

The whole touring experience was an induction into rock'n'roll mayhem. We were staying at the same hotels as The Who and their entourage, and they were all drinking and making merry, buzzing with the sheer joy of being young, successful, and having the time of their lives. The partying would be taking place backstage and then everyone would scramble into a bunch of waiting limos heading to the hotel; Daltrey in most cases would grab a bevy of the best looking women before speeding away. At the hotel one night— one of those two-storey Holiday Inn motel-style places—I can remember Townshend and Moon going into their *Goons* skits and the Americans in the room wondering what was going on. Remy Martin was consumed as if there was no tomorrow, and the odd TV would find itself hurled over the balcony into the swimming pool. John Entwistle was roaming about filming everything. Moon was blowing up toilets with cherry bombs and travelling with a caseload of guns—hopefully replicas. My wife Pauline was on the road with us at that time. At one point he burst into our room and aimed one of his weapons, a Thompson sub-machine gun, at us in the bed, shouting, 'Your money or your wife!' Another time he was heard yelling 'Bring me sunshine.' This was not so much a tribute to Morecambe & Wise, the much-loved comedy act of the day, as a warning for Ron Sunshine, the promoter that The Who had little regard for, to go hide in the nearest cupboard.

We were also opening for bands like Steppenwolf and Three Dog Night—both great bands but not stadium-rock material at that time. They did not have their sound systems together, nor were they able to make the massive gestures that were needed in order to take control of a very large audience. Watching The Who was like being at the feet of the masters. As a Brit, it was easy to feel diminished by the sheer scale of America at first, but seeing this glaring disconnect between what the audiences wanted and what US acts were not delivering was good for our morale. We had a fighting chance.

One of the tricks up our sleeve—one of the things that allowed us to make an impact—was that we always shipped our own equipment over to the States with us. We had powerful, clean-sounding Orange amps, cabinets fitted out with JBL speakers, and the amount of wattage coming off the stage before even being miked up was huge. We also had a gadget called an AMS—a professional studio-grade digital delay unit, which ironically enough was invented by Mark Crabtree, father of Joe Crabtree, the current drummer for Wishbone Ash. Simply put, we were able to do things with this digital technology that the Americans had yet to hear in a live context, such as to create what sounded like double-tracked guitars or double-tracked vocal effects. It enhanced our sound, making it both powerful and clear.

More to the point, the sound was ours. Everywhere we went we astounded the sound companies who would hear us onstage and be intrigued to learn how we approached live sound. Shipping all this equipment came at great expense, of course, but it was money well spent. We had a tour manager, Mel Baister, who carried $100 bills with which to ease the way through the various freight issues we might encounter at airports on a daily basis as we flew from gig to gig, city to city. In this way, we went in a short period of time from being a supporting act to headlining our own shows.

Toward the end of that second US Tour we played at the Satsop River Festival in Washington State to a massive number of people. Festivals back then were not the efficient events that they have become today. A large part of what went on was building a vibe by word of mouth and watching the event take on a life of its own. Consequently, organisers of such things were often adapting everything to accommodate more and more audience numbers as things went forward. This festival was no different. Eventually it became so unwieldy that the only way for the artists to get in or out of the stage area was by helicopter. We made a particularly strong impact on that show, which had a line-up featuring War, Steve Miller, Delaney & Bonnie, Billy Preston, and others. The estimated size of the audience was between 100,000 and 150,000!

On reflection, this was the start of a three- or four-year period of intense touring, with us sometimes being away from home for eight or nine weeks at a time. It would prove to be the solid foundation on which the rest of my life as a touring musician was built.

Some of my favourite places to play at that time were Pirates' World in Miami, the Warehouse in New Orleans, the Agora Ballroom in Ohio, Cain's Ballroom in Tulsa, Oklahoma, and the Academy of Music in New York City. We played prestigious places like Carnegie Hall and also the Schaefer Music Festival in Central Park, which was an early free event. The pace at which we travelled was intense. It was a crash course in American geography and regional culture. One minute you would be in the hustle and bustle of New York City and the next arriving into the crazy laid-back party atmosphere of the French Quarter in New Orleans, staying in a gentle old Southern hotel like the Marie Antoinette, its rooms filled with genuine French antiques. Texas was a whole other world, of course, and we had some of the best hospitality shown us, not least by our MCA promotions manager Henry Withers, whose family barbecued for us on their ranch. Our promoter Leon

Tsilis's family also showed us their Greek-American-style home cooking on one of our few precious off days in Washington, DC. It seemed in those days that if you were a British person in America, you could do no wrong. No wonder we fell in love with the place.

At the end of the US tour we were to meet with one Allen Grubman, a New York lawyer who Miles had discovered. He was later to team up with partners Artie Indursky and Paul Schindler. Allen, soon to become the biggest music-business lawyer in America, was representing us and the rest of Miles's stable of acts; later on he would represent Madonna, Billy Joel, and Bruce Springsteen, to name but three. Between all of the groups Miles was managing, there was a lot of business to be done. After all, we were off to an amazing start with the MCA deal, which we'd signed for a cool quarter of a million dollars—probably several million dollars in today's money. Of course, that label would own our music in perpetuity both on this planet and throughout the known universe. At that time we were still paying ourselves a monthly wage, which I believe had gone up to around £100 each.

All the elements were now in place with which to do what every other act from the UK craved, and that was to crack the US market. We had a killer record deal, a direct signing with a US label, not with one of their European subsidiaries, so we had a global reach with our releases. We had a crack promotions team with people like Leon working all the regional outlets in connection with the live promoters, exposure on the expanding national network of FM radio stations, a great music lawyer fighting with us from our corner, a great road crew, a fresh new sound, a state of the art live presentation, and of course an expert booking agency to make it all happen on the road. Our dedicated booker at the Jerry Heller Agency was Richard Halem, and his diminutive co-booker, soon to become a giant in the music business, was Irving Azoff. These guys were our Jewish Mafia, and then we had the real Mafia in LA working the record. It was colourful to say the least, and a total eye-opener as to how things needed to be in order to crack the giant US market.

PAULINE

'Rock Wife' is a term my wife Pauline would absolutely detest, since it conjures up an image of some American reality show like *Mob Wives* or *Basketball Wives*—in many respects something cheap and tabloid-y. But based on the idea that behind every successful man there is a great woman, Pauline is the supreme Rock Wife. In using the term 'successful', I'm thinking more of being productive and fruitful rather than simple monetary success.

She's seen it all, of course, having travelled with me on the road right from the beginning, in broken-down tour vans as teenagers, when I played in homespun soul outfits and beat groups at village halls, to the huge stadiums where we played with some of the biggest bands of our era. She's been there for me through it all, indulging my passions and artistic tantrums, as well as calmly getting on with being a wife to the supreme boy who refused to grow up, and mother to our three sons. She is the voice of reason and good sense. Coming from a largely female family, she found change and challenge in our all-male nuclear family, but I can happily say we now have a balance in our lives, with two daughters-in-law and two beautiful granddaughters.

Pauline and I were married on January 1 1972 at the Priory Church in Dunstable, Bedfordshire. It was a day when she took on two marriages: one to me and the other to the music business. Even on New Year's Eve, the night before our wedding, with me being flush with our early success, the music intruded. Wishbone Ash had a show at London's famous Marquee Club in Wardour Street. It was some night, with Pauline being dragged onto the stage at the end of the evening and both of us being presented with cake and champagne by Jack Barry, the club's manager. She always says she gatecrashed my stag night, but it is a night we both will never forget. The rag-tag gang of hungover rock'n'rollers that somehow made it to the church and reception the next day only added to the memories and colour of our big day.

It was no easy task, though, to strike out from the clannish *Boy's Own* culture of Wishbone Ash. When I first declared to our manager, Miles Copeland, that she and I were getting married, he for one was horrified, fearing that all the work he and we had put into the band might be destroyed by something so bourgeois as a marriage. Of course, it had happened that way for many bands, not least of all The Beatles, when Yoko incurred the wrath of the fans and John's fellow band members alike. So Miles sat Miss Langston down and gave her a stern talking to. He told her in very specific terms that she was in no way going to be permitted to upset the apple cart by making wifely demands that might focus my attention away from anything other than the band and its upward trajectory. She in turn told him what was what and we all moved on from there. Happily, Pauline and Miles shared a good relationship, and there was never any tension about her interfering with any of the band's plans.

Pauline had been on numerous tours with us but was quite determined to have her own life as well as participating in the fun of a touring rock band. It was somewhat surprising to me when she chose teaching as a profession, given the healthy disdain she had always shown to the teachers in the school where we had met. She was always having to write and rewrite the 'Codes of Conduct' for some misdemeanour or other. I, of course, loved this feistiness of hers right from the beginning. The ability she has to not suffer fools gladly has been a lifelong boon to me because, as most people can imagine, the music business definitely attracts its fair share of fools, charlatans, and naïfs. I'd occasionally suffer them but she never would, and she will not to this day.

She is not remotely materialistic; I'm much more so. Always, the life and colourful journey that the music business has offered our family has been the paramount thing. I've rarely had to compensate for time spent away from the family with expensive gifts and demands. She's been the most pragmatic and patient of people, which is all to the good because the life has been very taxing on her at times, I'm sure, though you would never know it. Again, having the confidence of her own career as a teacher has been extremely rewarding. The long summer holidays always afforded us the time to travel together as a family. Our sons have often teased us that they have been into just about every cathedral and art gallery in Europe, although we did the obligatory Disneyworld trip as well—fun as well as 'culture'. I consider us one of the fortunate few couples to have been able to weather the storms that this crazy business throws at a family.

As a teenager, Pauline was definitely mod in her fashion sense, and we'd both push the boundaries within the restrictions of our school uniform. On weekends, Pauline and her buddies would gravitate to the same dance clubs that we boys would, all pale-pink lipstick, long leather coats and knee-length leather boots. Then, come Monday, it'd be back to the blazers and school ties, modest-length skirts and polka-dot summer frocks.

Pauline invariably dated Mini-Cooper-driving guys, older and cooler than I could possibly hope to be. The best travel option I could offer was a Honda 50 moped. But eventually my persistence won out and she got to witness the beginnings of that whole tedious hurry-up-and-wait thing that goes into producing a gig at some little youth club in a converted wartime Nissen hut. Being crammed into the back of a very shaky and unsafe van was hardly the most romantic of ways to conduct a relationship, especially when on at least two different occasions the van actually caught fire. The fact that I rescued my guitar before her is not one of my prouder moments, and I still wonder if she fully realised what she was taking on.

Early on in our marriage we moved out of London to a sixteenth-century cottage in the village of Edlesborough in Bedfordshire. This move wasn't made without criticism from a certain member of the band who felt moving to the provinces did not gel with a rock'n'roll lifestyle. Nonetheless, Steve for one soon followed suit with his own country cottage. Pauline and I wanted to return to our roots and start a family, and for us, London was not the place to do this. Richard was born in August 1978, Aynsley followed in February 1982, and suddenly life took on a whole new meaning.

Around this time, Penny Gibbons, who had been running the Wishbone Ash fan club, decided to call it quits with that particular aspect of the workload, while getting busy with her own family life, and Pauline offered to take over those responsibilities. Our cottage was suddenly overrun with fan paraphernalia as well as all of the necessities two small children require. I had by this time added a studio to the back of the cottage, so there were days when chaos reigned as Pauline tried to get autographs signed for fans, write a newsletter, take care of the boys, and stay sane, whilst we were making music into all hours of the night.

When we discovered baby number three was on the way, some decisions had to be made. The fan club found a new secretary and the cottage went on the market. By the time Lawrence was born in May 1984, we had moved farther afield, to a farm in Great Brickhill, Buckinghamshire, and Pauline became focused on caring for our boys full time.

There was a point in the early 70s, before children and the need for security took over, when the band moved to America, and we were all thrown together much more than would be deemed healthy. Consequently, for a brief time, the rock wives—all quite different in personality—would be forced into social situations none of them would necessarily have chosen for themselves. While we slaved together in the band's basement studio in Connecticut, wives and girlfriends were left to integrate themselves into the lifestyle we had essentially chosen for them. Pauline, for one, soon realised that shopping excursions to New York and hanging around a pool all day was not going to cut it. She became heavily involved with dance and exercise and then took a job as receptionist for a local hairdresser, Martin Pinto. It was Martin and his wife Jill who introduced us to the friends who we can thank for us living in the US today. We found like-minded souls in Robert and Elyse Shapiro, with whom we shared similar ideas on family life, and they were instrumental in later years in helping us make the transition to our new American home, becoming surrogate aunt and uncle to our lads as we fulfilled the same role for their daughter Anna. We would all join forces at tour manager Russell Sidelsky's house, and were charmed to meet his new wife Woody and welcome into the ever-expanding clan their daughters Layla and Romy. Life was good.

Martin, however, yearned for a return to Blighty. America was not working for him. I think everyone else on the other hand was very happy drinking in everything America had to offer—not least of all the amazing weather offered by the New England seasons—making full use of it by enjoying bike-riding, trips into New York, learning to water ski, snow ski, and generally partying. It was, to use a variation on the Stevie Wonder line,

'America—just like I pictured it', and Pauline and I felt a real affinity for New England. We really did not want to return to England. We were building new relationships and living life to the fullest. We did, in fact, return to England for work, but the US had grabbed our hearts and continued to be a big draw for us. The Powell family kept its feet in both camps, and we have continued to live here for a number of years without one ounce of regret.

Citizenship eventually became something we needed to approach, and I have to say that the moment we took the plunge, everything really began to fall into place, and our commitment to the American way of life consolidated itself. It was a happy discovery that we would never be required to rescind our UK citizenship due to a reciprocal treaty between the two countries. In fact, our family members are all now dual citizens, and that status perfectly demonstrates our lives as we've lived them, with all of us having a very dual concept of our lives and roots.

Over the years people have tried to pry into my marriage to Pauline, some with malevolent intent. There have been petty jealousies, and Pauline has had to weather these more so than myself in a way. I remember her being harassed in Kensington Market for being with me at the time when my face was all over the music press, and there have been a few unpleasant phone calls to deal with. In the world of social media that we have now, cruel and idiotic statements get posted on Facebook that would, if they weren't so ridiculous, test even the strongest of relationships. You have to wonder at the minds of some folk. In true fashion, given her sense of humour, Pauline finds much of the fan/musician thing quite amusing, and she keeps me absolutely grounded with her common sense.

At the time of writing, now that our kids are grown with families of their own, Pauline works with me on managing our complicated touring logistics, and we find ourselves together 24/7. It is a true test of our commitment to one other. It's very timely because it frees us up to enjoy the journey together, spreading out the pressures and alleviating much of the stress involved in the constant travel. We have come full circle, and as with a lot of long-standing marriages, have found that true friendship and commitment arrive only through the tests of adversity that you go through as a couple. The band still charges forward and we both with it, just like always. It's quite something.

CHAPTER 3

ARGUS
(1972–74)

A couple of things happened in 1972 that have defined the rest of my life. Firstly, Pauline and I were married on New Year's Day, and secondly, Wishbone Ash recorded an extraordinary album. We called it *Argus*. In retrospect, nothing else we did would be quite so significant. And the funny thing is, we sort of knew it at the time. We were all in our early twenties, and none of us were Lennon or McCartney, but we had huge self-belief. With the spirit of the times—and all sorts of other factors—we crafted a forty-four-minute, seven-song body of work that immediately resonated widely with people and continues to do so all these years later.

Argus was recorded early in the year at De Lane Lea Studios in London, the same place as our previous two albums (though the premises had by then moved from from Holborn to Wembley), and with the same team: Derek Lawrence producing and Martin Birch engineering. We didn't set out to create a 'concept album'—the phrase itself a hot new concept at the time—but inadvertently I suppose that's what we ended up doing. We had been gaining experience playing to much larger audiences and had come to the realisation that simpler yet more grandiose musical gestures in the construction of our songs were proving to be more impactful in stadiums and arenas. Martin wrote most of the words and all of us, to varying degrees, crafted the music. It turned out to be an album of powerful if loosely connected themes: time passing, aspiration, conflict, good and evil.

More than anything, the unifying theme of *Argus* was yearning, as I said in the introduction to this book—a spiritual yearning, a yearning for justice, a yearning for love, a yearning for nature and freedom. Backing up these universal emotions was a sense of backbone, grit, the determination not to be trodden on or swept aside without a fight; the realisation that everyone can to an extent, at least, make their own future through values, commitment, and resolve. The guitar lines throughout the album were very lyrical and melodic in themselves and meant to be heard in just the same way as the vocal lines.

We welded together the reflective, self-analysing world of the singer-songwriter with the muscular sweep of stadium rock. It was a particular kind of stadium rock: 'English pastoral' mixed with 'West Coast cool'; sun-kissed Californian country-rock with vocal harmonies in damp British denim. Add a few of J.S. Bach's simpler ideas on counterpoint fused with the sheer exuberance of youth and the listener is in the zone.

In these few songs we had defined ourselves both by the lyrics and the ensemble sound of a unique British band. We were able to capture something in the arrangements and input by the four band members that was greater than the sum of the parts and which clicked with a great number of people worldwide.

We were empowered and we were empowering. We weren't jaded by the business at this point, and that, perhaps, was what made *Argus* such a once-in-a-lifetime work: that mixture of enthusiasm with experience before the inevitable tipping point was reached.

Pilgrimage, which we'd released prior to *Argus*, was pretty much our live set performed in the studio. You can hear that it's an album more suited to being replicated live in the clubs, not in stadiums. Yet on the title track, 'The Pilgrim', and also on the song 'Phoenix' from the very first album, we were already experimenting with the musical processes that would be used to even greater effect on the *Argus* album, particularly on the core trilogy of songs: 'The King Will Come', 'Warrior', and 'Throw Down The Sword'. After our experiences travelling around the world we now had a more global vision. It all came together on this album.

'The King Will Come'—a song that has been in Wishbone Ash's live set pretty much constantly since then, spoke of a second coming, with lyrics that had been lifted from the Bible by Martin and from Kahlil Gibran's *The Prophet* by Steve Upton. No matter, the song was selling hope. It was a hopeful time. Hopefulness dates but hope itself never does. Nostalgia and hope make perhaps the most powerful combination in all of art. *Argus* was just an accident of human interactions, but it feels like it might have had intelligent design. Maybe the king did come, after all. It was certainly a blessing on the professional lives of those who were involved with it.

For such a windswept pinnacle of 70s rock, the songs that became *Argus* were mostly created in fairly prosaic circumstances. I remember how we worked the songs out on acoustic guitars at St Quintin Avenue just off Ladbroke Grove, which was where Martin, Steve, and Ted were living. I was living with Pauline on Wallingford Avenue, just 'round the corner. We were all feeling pretty excited about the material so we rewarded ourselves by going to Jubilee Studios, a basement rehearsal place in Covent Garden. I can vividly remember us working on 'The King Will Come' all night and emerging from that basement at four o'clock in the morning, just when all the barrow boys were loading up their barrows with fruit and vegetables. We were coming out into the sunlight and thinking, *I think we've really just created something amazing*. We got such a high from transitioning the songs from this acoustic songwriting process onto the electric instruments. It felt as if we were on the verge of something exciting.

Aside from 'The King Will Come', the most immediate song on *Argus* was 'Blowin' Free'. Quite why we did not release it as a single I really don't know, because it had major elements of commerciality about it: the shuffle rhythm, the harmonised vocals, the upbeat guitar parts. Martin came up with the lyrics, which concerned a girl he'd been chasing in the Empty Vessels days, while the music was a happy accident inspired by the music of Steve Miller, among others. I'd been fooling around on guitar with a friend, Mick Groome, later of Ducks Deluxe, inverting some chord progressions from songs by The Beatles and The Who, and lo and behold this immortal riff in the key of D major emerged. It grew from there, and the finished article, especially the stacked guitar and bass parts at the song's end, rather like a horn section, seem to have been an influence on a slew of other songs and other bands—parts of Steely Dan's 'Reelin' In The Years' (they even borrowed the apostrophe) and Thin Lizzy's 'The Boys Are Back In Town' are the most obvious examples.

It has been said that 'Blowin' Free' has a wonderful exuberance. This is true. It captured, for me, what was best about the 70s—it fits right into the zeitgeist. It encapsulated the feeling of the time. If you can imagine: you're young, you're a Brit travelling America for the first time, there's nothing but the vast expanse of freeways and open road; the sun is shining and life is full of possibilities. If it sounds like a song to play at maximum volume in an open-topped convertible on a Midwest freeway, that's exactly what it is. In fact, I can remember us putting it together during 1971, driving across the cornfields of Iowa. By the time we got to the West Coast it was done—we played it at a soundcheck at the Whisky A Go Go in Los Angeles. And that was the first step toward *Argus*.

Just read here what blogger and LA music insider Bob Lefsetz said about the song in his Lefsetz Letter blog (dated April 5 2010) after he'd discovered a You Tube clip of it from the 70s:

Clive Davis would say Wishbone Ash can't sing, that the song is too long. Jimmy Iovine would say they're not good-looking enough, that there's no way to tie in with the Fortune 500. And a band this good wouldn't make a deal with a major label today anyway, they wouldn't give up 360 degrees of revenue, wouldn't sell their souls, they'd want to be free, on stage, where they belong!

I never even HEARD this song until today! Sitting at the light, waiting to turn from Sunset onto Barrington. When I heard the live rendition done at XM. Which is not the take I'm going to point you to here, that one had better vocals, but this ancient one just WAILS!

Wanna know what it was like in the seventies? WATCH THIS CLIP! Catch the audience clapping, grooving, moving to the music. Others standing in sheer admiration … how do they DO this?

We know how Britney did it. On sheer desire. Flashing her lashes for aged men. But that didn't used to be the recipe we admired. We liked acts that truly cooked. Who assembled the ingredients and every night attempted to make that cake RISE!

Watch this clip. Doesn't it make you want to raise your arms in exultation like the dude in the black shirt at the end? Doesn't it make you want to grab your wallet, put on your jacket and go to the gig?

You can't get this feeling anywhere else. Only music can light such a spark inside, transport you three fifths of a mile in ten seconds.

> Hang in there, through the intro ad, through the first few notes, until the guitars lock in and start to WAIL!
>
> In the old days, music was sealed up, you could visit it in the store, but it was hard to hear. But via the miracle of the Internet, you can hear Wishbone Ash's 'Blowin' Free' right now! TURN IT UP!

While 'Blowin' Free' was the most obviously 'American'-sounding piece on the album, the American touring experience was crucial to the whole album. The birth of FM radio in the States was certainly one of the factors leading into the *Argus* material, with all these young DJs given the license to play songs that were no longer restricted to being three minutes and available as a single. Then you had this wave of British bands going over to the States and showing the Americans how to really do stadium rock—how a band could make big musical and visual statements able to fill that environment.

We knew what we had to do. I don't think we ever consciously said, 'We're going to write this thing and hopefully it'll be big on FM radio,' but we were on these long tours, we were listening to FM radio all day long, we were smoking weed, we were immersed in the stuff of the times. The youth movement was burgeoning—we were golden. It was a moment in time where you're so busy and so thrilled with what you're doing and the opportunities presenting themselves to you that everything is living in the moment. It happens, I've no doubt, to most successful bands and to lucky young people at some point, however briefly. At that point in time we had money, we had travel, we had access to audiences, hungry audiences. We had pot and technology. And most of all, with our manager and record label behind us, we had massive self-belief.

To put it simply, we were doing the best we could—and, in hindsight, we were at our best at that precise point in time. There were simple elements in the songwriting but, as with all the best songwriting, everything culminated and came together to make something magical. When we put that music into a big auditorium it had heft.

* * *

Another aspect of the whole music world at that point of time that can't be emphasised too forcefully is that this was the moment at which the 'art of the rock album' was at its absolute zenith. In those days, labels nurtured their artists, and there was the capacity both in time and finances to do so. The move from physical to download as a retail medium in recent times has various pros and cons but one result—whatever one's opinion of it may be—is that the idea of an artist creating a body of work which represents a strong period of creativity has been diminished. We now live essentially in a world of tracks rather than albums and music seems to have a very short shelf life.

'The album' was the format we all worked toward in those days, and to a large extent Wishbone Ash fans still measure our progress in albums and expect to have a new one every year or two. I guess at the time I also thought it helped to have something to work toward in that sense. Some of the albums I most enjoyed and was most inspired by prior to 1972 included *Hard Road* by The Bluesbreakers, *Disraeli Gears* by Cream, *Song To A Seagull* by Joni Mitchell, and *Harvest* by Neil Young.

Argus was our grand artistic statement, a kind of concept album. Part of that analogy is borne out by the sleeve design. The Beatles had Peter Blake; we had Hipgnosis. Others of our era had Roger Dean, Rodney Matthews, and so forth—masters of the LP sleeve format in this fairly brief window of time. Everyone was creating epics in those days, and that's something *Argus* has got going for it: it was our epic.

There was this wonderful cinematic imagery of 'The Warrior' on the cover, the artwork bringing a visual dimension to the music within. Steve Upton came up with the album's title, *Argus*, taken from Greek mythology's one-eyed watcher. It fitted neatly with this cover design of a solitary sentinel seen from the back, looking out over a mist-covered vale, clothed in the garb of the ancient world. I've got notebooks from when I was a nine-year-old at school, full of nothing but drawings of Greek warriors—I was obsessed with all of that.

The two Hipgnosis partners, Storm Thorgerson and Aubrey Powell, convinced Miles to let them go on a junket to the south of France where the figure, one of their employees, was photographed using clothing from Ken Russell's movie *The Devils*. Amusingly, while *Argus* went on to win 'Best Album' in the *Melody Maker*'s annual poll, it was Jethro Tull's *Thick*

As A Brick that won 'Best Album Cover' for its elaborately created spoof local newspaper, poking gentle fun at the mundane aspects of regional life in 70s Britain. Our epic mythologizing stood no chance, but in retrospect it has had far greater long-term impact. Some even say that the character and image of Darth Vader himself was inspired by our album cover.

* * *

Argus was released at the end of April 1972, a few weeks after a headlining city-hall tour of Britain. We were lucky enough to get a lot of support at the BBC: we featured each of the album's seven songs at least once across three Radio 1 sessions in the middle of the year (including the two that we would hardly play live at all again until the twenty-first century, 'Sometime World' and 'Leaf And Stream') and performed five at a Radio 1 *In Concert* in May.

But life is never entirely simple. Three weeks into a US tour in June, all our equipment was stolen after a show in St Louis. We had no choice but to fly home and assemble new gear—during which time Martin was hospitalised with appendicitis. Keen-eyed archaeologists examining old copies of *Melody Maker* will find that in July, while back in London, we were reported as planning to re-record 'Blowin' Free' for single release as soon as Martin was back on his feet. Apparently we had planned to do this while in America before the gear went south. A month later, the same paper announced the single's release—the A-side being a new song with a Rolling Stones vibe, 'No Easy Road'.

'Blowin' Free' has turned out to be perhaps our most popular song, certainly our most recognisable to the general public. Did we miss a trick by sticking it on the B-side? Possibly. As far as I recall, we were quite happy with the recording but erred toward a far more generic sounding song as the A-side. At my suggestion, we beefed it up later with horns but the whole single idea coincided with ditching our tried-and-tested production team and going into Olympic studios with engineer Keith Harwood. Perhaps this was the Rolling Stones influence taking precedence over our classic song 'Blowin' Free'. I think a genuine producer would have said, 'Guys, WHAT do you think you are doing?'

For better or worse, Wishbone Ash were never much good at singles.

We did keep trying over the years, right up to the end of the 80s, but we never quite cracked it. Still, we had one more go as recently as 2010—as much for the novelty as anything else—with 'Reason To Believe', written and recorded specifically for single release.

We went back to the States and fulfilled our remaining dates in July and August 1972. We even, at the suggestion of our promotions manager, Leon Tsilis, cut a live album in a studio in Memphis called *Live In Memphis.* The idea of this was to hand it out to the FM radio stations as a kind of insider glimpse of a hot new band from England. It was a brilliant idea and it really worked, giving the DJs the sense that they were personally discovering us. I remember the recording was very stressful, as these things often are, particularly in this case, because upon arrival at the airport in town, Ted's vintage Stratocaster fell off the luggage cart when it was removed from the plane's hold. We watched out of the plane's window as it was literally run over by the same cart. Ted frantically tried—and actually succeeded—in rebuilding it prior to the recording, which took place in front of an invited studio audience.

Argus reached number 3 in the UK chart and hung around it for twenty weeks. It was 'Album Of The Year' in both *Sounds* and *Melody Maker*, at a time when these things really mattered, and we were invited to play at a *Melody Maker* poll-winners' concert at the Oval cricket ground, London, in September in front of 18,000 paying customers. We shared the bill with Genesis, Focus, Argent, and ELP, which was great on paper but perhaps a bit of a mistake on the day due to the lateness of our arrival. This caused the headliners, ELP—the overall band of the moment—to go on earlier and for us to finish the show. They had a dynamic show planned with a giant smoking Tarkus model. I think we certainly did ourselves proud in terms of performance, but having not been there to receive our awards along with the other artists was seen as a direct snub.

* * *

A few years ago, if I was asked by a fan or an interviewer what I thought our best album was, I'd probably have given a waffly answer involving whatever our recent releases were. But now, in the fullness of time, I agree with the critics—*Argus* really was our high point, the coming together of everything. And that was 1972! It's the view of the public, too, and they are the most discerning of all.

One band member who seemed to know that an era was coming to an end was Ted Turner. He left the band after the subsequent recording for his own private and some would say self-interested reasons. In so doing, he also broke the spell, the internal dynamic intrinsic to the band's ensemble sound. We all had to adapt to that. Steve Upton's response was to pen the harsh lyric to the song 'Don't Come Back', which appeared on *There's The Rub*. My response had been to go out and find a replacement for Ted. The show had to go on.

This ushered in a twelve-year career with Ted's replacement, Laurie Wisefield, who was relegated to forever chasing the ghost of *Argus* without really understanding what he was chasing. Sometimes providing technically far more complex guitar lines than anything we'd attempted with Ted in the band, Laurie's ideas were always overshadowed by the sheer simplicity of the melodic lines we'd explored on this classic album. For example, the killer opening to the song 'Don't Come Back' was in itself as dynamic an opening as anything we could come up with after *Argus*—but the song itself was just so-so. It was to be the case time and time again as both Martin and Laurie attempted their own versions of what they thought we were actually about, while we embellished these songs with tons of guitar ear candy, the likes of which no other band was doing at the time. Me, I was as confused as the next guy while Martin and Laurie explored their new love affair. To be fair, a new generation of younger fans came on board, receiving some good new music but having missed out on the great 'flowering'.

Post-*Argus*, where were the signature double tracked harmony vocals between Martin and myself? Where were the simple, strong, double-tracked guitar lines? I'd pushed Derek Lawrence to do this on pretty much every song and it had worked. Certainly we came close once more to a concerted band feel on the *New England* album after decimating our audience with *Wishbone Four* and *Locked In*. But in reality it would take two decades to fully reconcile ourselves with *Argus*'s success, during which time everything had changed.

Speaking for myself, I had major input on the arrangements. The guitar lines I came up with on *Argus* demanded the listener's attention. I provided the intros and endings to many of the songs, from 'Throw Down The Sword' to 'Blowin' Free', as well as soloing on pretty much everything that required a solo on the album. It's been said that some of my most inspired soloing was exemplified on songs like 'Sometime World'. I was working with Martin on bass lines and providing the best bass hook of the album all in the same song, just as he was working on guitar lines with Ted and me. The vocal line that flies through the piece, seemingly at odds with that bass line but complementing it immensely, was mine. Keeping score, though, is pointless. We really were a great team at that point. No amount of grandstanding over who wrote what means a damn forty years later. We simply had great synergy as a band, and importantly, Martin and I worked to bring out the best in each of us. It was never to be repeated.

My personal vision was for an album that would really feature English folk-rock with some bluesier American influences thrown in for good measure. Others were doing it with the emphasis more on folk, but we could take a harder-edged stance. An album starts with the drums and, in no small extent, we purloined the drumming style of Fairport Convention's Dave Mattacks, which Steve Upton was to adopt. Just listen to the drum part on the aggressive opening I constructed for the song 'Warrior'. There's no question in my mind that had Martin simply tried to compose a song like 'The King Will Come' as a complete entity—the lyrics and simple chord structures without serious work on the arrangements, intros, outros, and chord embellishments—he would have fallen flat on his face, despite what he now says.

However, it can't be denied that Martin was the instigator of much of the album's material, and he was to feel that he needed more and more recognition in this regard. He took matters into his own hands as much as he could, also in terms of attempting to be the band's producer on the subsequent album, *Wishbone Four*—a move that none of the rest of us was happy with. I'm convinced that this eventually led to his demise. I often wonder why his idea of his much-talked-about 'creative force' and abilities as a writer have not borne more fruit in the years since. There has been nothing but a dearth of creativity in that particular camp. It's a shame; he promised so much.

Ted also rose to the occasion, here and there, with his rhythm and lead parts—the complete intro to the song 'Time Was', for example. Lap steel guitar was heard once more on this album, and Steve rose magnificently to the occasion with his song 'Leaf And Stream', inspired by a chord sequence and guitar arrangement I came up with, embellished by Ted's chord voicings. We were all singing from the same hymn sheet, and it was, at times, as if the album was producing itself, demanding a direct and clear approach from all of us. All the producer and engineer had to do was to make things as sonically clear as possible, which of course they did, aided in no small part by the advent of the new sixteen-track recording format. This in itself was a major catalyst for what we were doing, and of course is now often overlooked. We could indulge in overdubbing.

I understand and accept that when people are buying any of the current music from Wishbone Ash, they're looking for a thread of DNA back to *Argus*—and it does exist. And I think, being the last man standing in the Wishbone Ash story, a lot of that is invested in me. Writing this now, at sixty-five years of age, I feel really proud about it, and I feel really privileged that *Argus* made album of the year in the UK music papers. I still get the shivers, along with the audience, when I'm playing 'Warrior' or 'Throw Down The Sword' live. I never tire of those. To this day, once the wind gets under my sails, I'm there, and I can lift a band of musicians along with me—they all feel it, and I think the fans feel it. I wouldn't be still doing this if there wasn't something important that I was capable of delivering, which on the one hand means something to other people and, on the other, which gives me a shot of adrenalin, too. Obviously the guys that were with me at that time gave up on all that; they were defeated eventually by the enigma of it all. Martin self-consciously even derides and lampoons some of that *Argus* material now, with his new outfit, which is a travesty in my book—and in that of many of the fans, no doubt.

Wishbone Ash have been blessed with incredibly loyal fans, and they're all hooked on that thread of emotion that goes back to *Argus*. They recognise that the band's sound, at its best, is a transcendent experience, and *Argus* was the one studio album that itself transcended the live experience. I've often pondered the fact that we never took a deep breath after the huge achievement of that album. This perhaps is where Miles fell down as manager. Musicians are often the last people to have an objective viewpoint on such things as career strategy. That's the job of management. That's why you pay them. We should have waited and done some analysis of what we'd produced. We should have taken much more time before diving into the studio again and flogging ourselves senseless on the road. If it had been the Pink Floyd, for example, they would have left a five or eight year gap after the release of a milestone like *Argus*. Ted could have been brought back into the fold. Coulda, woulda, shoulda.

One thing's for certain: with vinyl albums only containing forty-five minutes of music but CDs allowing for seventy-five minutes, it's an interesting idea to imagine the songs from *Argus* being augmented by standout tracks that appeared sporadically through subsequent albums, but which most definitely had that DNA thread. I'm thinking of 'Ballad Of The Beacon', 'Sorrel', 'Lady Jay'. Those examples of English pastoral would have sat right at home with the material featured on *Argus*. I'd take that any day over some of the pointless, derivative tributaries we meandered down during the end of the 70s and certainly into the wilderness years of the 80s. It's only recently, in my humble opinion, that things have coalesced in a natural, non-forced manner. Of course, it's a completely different set of players and the times are so different, but that strand of DNA is intact. I never gave up on it.

You can also hear early hints of the *Argus* style in my songs like 'Errors Of My Way' and 'Valediction', and of course the band's epic, 'Phoenix'. When a band is truly flying and connecting with its own true energy, the players and the audience can feel it and that was definitely the case on that particular song. It is, to this day, an extraordinary piece of music. I like to think that I'd be objective enough to know and to accept when the magic has gone. After all that I've gone through, I would knock this band lark all on the head immediately. But I feel really good about the material we've produced during the last twenty years or so, and I'm still chasing that *Argus* sound and feeling as much as I know the fans are. We're still all on the same path.

HOTELS

I literally spend half my life in hotels. 'What?' you say. But no, I actually love hotel living, and I have this fantasy where I can, at some point, see myself living in a penthouse of some luxury hotel, simply calling down for room service or requesting a cab into town whenever my heart desired it. Think about it. Life is pretty easy in a hotel. Laundry, messaging, breakfast—all handled quietly and efficiently behind the scenes while you sip Martinis by the pool at the end of a long day.

It's not all four- and five-star experiences, however. We've seen every kind of on-the-road hostelry, from the homely to the desperate English B&Bs just barely hanging on to existence, like some throwback to theatrical digs for travelling vaudeville stars from two centuries back. Some of the best times have been had in these. Others are swanky yuppie places—all steel and chrome Bauhaus edifices in, say, Berlin or Munich. My favourites, though, are grand old hotels like the Atlantic in Hamburg or the Waldorf Astoria in New York, where you get comfort and old-world charm coupled with real efficiency. These professionals really understand the life of being a traveller and do not discriminate in that regard.

You often meet some interesting folks in hotels. Not so long ago, in Edmonton, Canada, we went down to breakfast and who should be there with his wife and son but Mickey Rooney. This was not long before he passed away. He was definitely in his nineties and posed very kindly for the obligatory photo, turning on the charm just as he might have seventy-plus years ago. It was something to behold. They don't make them like that anymore.

Another time, in Glasgow, Steve Upton and I stayed in the same hotel as Billy Connolly; we hung out with him in the lobby, drinking whisky, naturally. He regaled us with stories all night long, until something like 5:00am the next morning. On another occasion, most of the cast of the hit British comedy drama series *Auf Wiedersehen Pet* were staying at the same hotel as us, and we got to hang out at the hotel they used while filming the series, where we could observe some of their world with them, joining in with their humour.

It does not always work, being stuck in one hotel in one place for a period of weeks. Despite my fantasy of living permanently in a grand hotel, I do prefer being on the move, because if one particular establishment is not working for you or found to be lacking, you know that it'll all change the very next night. The next hotel might not use that horrid plastic incontinence sheet on the bed that you only discover in the morning after you've spent the night wretchedly tossing and turning in your own perspiration. In fact, the essence of change, including the linen, is a key draw to touring. Fresh sheets—don't underestimate them, along with the little *Do Not Disturb* sign that you can affix to the door handle when you shut out the world. Once, at the Revere Hotel on Boston Common, Massachusetts, the hotel had a sign you could use that said *Talent At Rest*. I liked that.

One hotel where we had no choice but to spend an extended period was the Thunderbird Hotel, situated on Collins Avenue by the beach in Miami, Florida. This place was a decaying edifice from the glory days of the 60s, but they gave us a great financial deal for the duration of our stay while we worked on *There's The Rub*. You could have made a movie about the antics of the quirky characters who either worked there or remained as semi-permanent residents. It was here that I discovered the music of Bob Marley & The Wailers for the first time, so that was my musical backdrop as I tried to make myself comfortable in my roach-infested room. The manager was always trying to think of new schemes to drum up business, and one day a truck literally dumped tons of earth in the centre of the lobby, right there on the carpet, and palm trees were planted—to improve the ambience, I guess.

The bar, which we'd visit fairly frequently, was manned by a tough old guy, a former prize fighter. We had some pretty crazy evenings spent there with our producer and engineer. Tanqueray and tonic was our drink of choice, I remember, and one night even saw me swinging from a chandelier above the piano, which was being played by a venerable English gentleman resident who was taking great delight in taunting us scruffy rock'n'rollers about our idea of what 'real music' was. He'd play us an ancient tune and say, 'Yes, your music is okay but can you do this?' This was a real hoot to us, of course. It became such a catchphrase later, during overdubs, especially if Laurie or I made a mistake in our playing.

A hotel breakfast is a true indicator of how the day will pan out; as they say, breakfast is often the most important meal of the day—and often the *only* meal you'll get that day while on tour. The German hotels, hands-down, have breakfast nailed. Freshly squeezed orange juice, smoked salmon, excellent breads, real eggs cooked perfectly, excellent coffee—to say nothing of those delightful little wieners or frankfurters that they squeeze onto a plate wherever possible.

Breakfast in America used to be truly the best and was one of the most memorable things about hotel life there back in the 70s. I'll never forget my first night in a hotel in Washington, DC. In the breakfast room the next morning I was asked what I'd like for breakfast. 'Eggs and bacon, please,' I meekly answered. 'Now, honey, how would you like those eggs—over, over-easy, sunny-side-up, shirred, poached, scrambled…?' My mind was forever blown.

These days, all that service has gone. The rooms are clean and efficient enough but there are no budgets anymore for staff and only rarely for real breakfast. The receptionist will boast to you on check-in about the complimentary breakfast buffet, but there will be some sad reconstituted powdered egg omelette brought in on a truck the night before, along with the nitrogen-infused sausage patty and the disgustingly gooey waffle-making machine that the family of five have just destroyed. It's all pretty bad. We often just skip the whole sad experience and find a Denny's or—our favourite—Cracker Barrel restaurant en route to the next show, where breakfast and lunch will mutate into the all American brunch.

There have been some ridiculous and, then again, truly nightmarish hotel experiences, two of which I'll relate here. Starting with the truly ridiculous. Our long-time friend, promotions manager, webmaster, and mentor, Leon Tsillis, was on tour with us in the USA—Milwaukee, to be precise. We were staying at the Park Hotel after a show at the renowned Shank Hall, named after the hotel in the movie *This Is Spinal Tap*. I know, I know—it should have been a sign that things could go wrong! We'd played a great show, and around 2:00am pandemonium broke out. Fire trucks were called out, guests evacuated, sprinkler systems activated. Amazingly, all four of us band members slept through all this, but what had happened was that a radiator valve had blown in Leon's room, shooting hot water up to the ceiling and down onto his sleeping body. Talk about a rude awakening. That must have really been shocking for him.

Shocking? This one stays in my mind forever. I was nineteen or twenty, and we were playing this funky club, well known at the time in Frankfurt, Germany, called the Zoom Club. I remember seeing Arthur Brown there— it might have been the night before we played. An old bass player friend of mine, Phil Shutt, was with him at the time. Anyway, after our show, we were accommodated in a small, cramped doss-house of a hotel behind the club—it might have been part of the club—and I'm sleeping in a tiny single bed in this shoebox-sized room when I'm awoken by a blood-curdling wail in the corridor, probably not two feet from where my head was lying pressed up against the headboard of the bed.

This was bad. I was young and inexperienced. I just lay quaking in bed, fearing the worst. It was no ordinary wail, that's for sure. I must admit, I did not dare to go out and investigate. The next morning, when I did venture out, it turned out that there had been a stabbing—an actual murder, on the floor where I'd been sleeping, literally just outside my room, and there were the blood stains on the carpet to prove it.

In those days, when Miles would travel with us, there would be all kinds of practical jokes and pranks played between the management and the band. Short-sheeting the bed was a classic. The bed sheets would be folded halfway in the bed, and tucked under the mattress very tightly while the occupant—Miles—was out of the room. After a long day of travelling, a raucous show and the inevitable partying, the poor recipient would be driven to distraction trying to figure why he could not fulfil the act of slipping blissfully into his waiting bed.

One time, Miles got back at Ted Turner and me for the constant harassment by beckoning us down to one of the hotel rooms on the floor we were all staying on. He said there was a surprise waiting there. Being naturally inquisitive we could not hold back and as he held the door open, ushering us into this Holiday Inn room, there on the bed in all her glory was an obviously naked young lady—for our enjoyment, one assumes. What was not immediately apparent as we edged up to the bed was that she had one leg encased in a plaster cast. This was all too much for me. I left, but from memory I believe Ted dallied a little. Miles thought this was a huge hoot and dined out on it all for months.

Once, as a celebration for completing one of the recordings we'd made in Miami, Pauline and I found ourselves on the island of St Thomas. We were staying on the beach in one of those small two-storey vacation-style hotels. We were in a deep, blissful sleep. It was hot and perhaps 3:00am. We'd left the sliding doors from the balcony to our room open for some air. All of a sudden we were woken by a very large person literally right there in our room. It wasn't Keith Moon this time. The guy was stumbling about and chuckling to himself in the dark. I could see he looked to be a native of the island. We're both naked in bed; I'm rendered speechless, Pauline is helpless under the covers. I'm wildly gesticulating for him to leave the way he'd come in. I'm shouting at him but nothing is coming out of my mouth. He's obviously drunk, huge, and disorientated. I'm wondering if he's wielding a machete. He did exit the room eventually, and later I figured out he had obviously decided to spend the night in what he'd thought was an empty hotel room, having spied our open sliding door from the beach. You just never know with hotels.

On another occasion, not so long ago, we'd been travelling out of Nashville and decided to use this hotel not far from the Grand Ole Opry. It was 2:00am and the nice Hispanic lady on reception got us six rooms on the ground floor. We were so tired. There had been a couple of guys cleaning the floors in the reception area, eyeing us suspiciously, it seemed to me. It struck me as strange that my sliding door was slightly open when I got to my room. I closed it and the next morning I found out that everyone's sliding door had been open. It was a set up. When our drummer, Ray Weston, awoke, he was missing his wallet and all his tour proceeds with it. It was a few thousand dollars. Needless to say we called the police but nothing was ever resolved. This kind of thing can be heartbreaking after putting in weeks of work as a musician, with bills at home to pay. One false move and it's all gone. On another occasion, I lost a few thousand dollars myself by foolishly leaving a belt pack containing the proceeds of a show on the hood of our vehicle and driving off, after being distracted by a call on my mobile phone—from Ray, as it happened. I went back an hour later, but of course it was gone.

These lessons constantly show you that touring is a risk business. If it's not money, rip-offs, cancelled shows, groupies, dodgy promoters pulling guns on you (it happened to me in Italy), it could be food poisoning and fires, or traffic accidents and nights in the emergency room of some hospital somewhere, far from home, watching as gunshot victims are wheeled in or worse. But at the very least, like in the song, whatever catastrophe occurs, you can always 'check out any time of day …'. Truly, though, there's no place like home.

CHAPTER 4

NEW ENGLAND AND BACK AGAIN
(1975–79)

We were advised, as a lot of bands were in the mid-70s, to go overseas because of the huge amount of income tax we were paying: 83 percent on our gross earnings, I believe. Although we didn't really feel that we were earning any money, because we weren't actually seeing much of it, somebody was—and they were advising us to go abroad. There was a lot of naivety, although we all got the idea that our time in the sun, financially speaking, might be limited.

A lot of bands had a 'tax year' around that time. Jethro Tull did it in the glare of great disapproving publicity, and it lasted about three weeks, until they decided, *What are we doing? We're British!* The Rolling Stones hung out in the South of France and got *Exile On Main Street* out of the experience. A couple of years later, Rick Parfitt from Status Quo endured twelve months of tedium on Jersey—a notably sedate British Territory located in the English Channel but not part of the UK or its tax regime. He managed to get a hit single out of it, 'Living On An Island'. We didn't do any of that—neither the real monetary benefit nor the smash hits, but we did get something more valuable as I see it now: a true immigrant experience in a country that we initially believed to be much like the UK but, as we later found out, was something entirely different.

I believe that part of the reason I took to America like a duck to water was because my own family had uprooted from London when I was a kid, and I felt fairly disconnected from my close-knit East End relatives. Perhaps the cord was severed then. Even though our family would go back to visit at Christmas and so on, we were living a different, suburban reality. Don't get me wrong, I had a good childhood, but I was living in a new town, and in our neighbourhood there were Irish people, Scottish people, Welsh people, Londoners—the point being that I wasn't terribly connected to my roots. Consequently, for me, it was easy to become an expatriate. It wasn't so easy for one or two of the others, but in general some very positive things came out of the emigration adventure.

It was a huge period for the band—a bit of a sink-or-swim experience. Shortly after we went to the States and began the process of being residents in a new country, we went back to Europe and took part in Miles's latest wheeze, a traveling festival called Star Truckin' '75, which was both fantastic and farcical. So at the same time as we were moving to America we were breaking Europe, headlining this colossal rolling festival—the first of its kind—an evolving and revolving cast of the great and the good. It would occupy the whole of August 1975, starting from an airfield near Southend and taking in France, Germany, Italy, Belgium, Holland, Denmark, Sweden, Austria, plus a whole day of that year's Reading Festival in England. What could possibly go wrong?

Miles had come up with the idea with a Dutch accountant and promoter called Cyril van den Hemel, who I think had previously booked some individual shows with us. Miles was becoming well known as an entrepreneur in the music business by then and his contacts and reputation were now obvious enough to give a veneer of credence to what was really an ambitious scheme. Given the logistics involved, the potential for failure was huge. But, being a 'bigger picture' kind of guy, Miles was thinking that there was a big market for rock festivals, and that this would basically be a one-stop shop on that score for promoters across Europe. He was offering an entire festival full of contracted acts available in a town near you. All the local promoter had to do was to find the location, sort out the local regulations, and plug into the concept. It just needed someone in each city to say, 'You're offering us a day with Caravan, Soft Machine, Mahavishnu Orchestra, Wishbone Ash, and Lou Reed? Yes indeed, we'll sign on for that!'

I'm sure the diary took very little time to fill once the acts had been confirmed. The trouble is, no one had told Lou Reed. He was meant to be headlining, his presence being a big deal in Europe at that point. But apparently he was stuck in New York somewhere, having just fired his manager, and seemed to know nothing about any tour. Thus it was that Wishbone Ash, by default, became the headline act. Climax Blues Band and Caravan, in addition to Wishbone Ash, were in Miles's 'stable' of artists. Another of his acts, Renaissance, had been scheduled in as well, but Annie Haslam was unwell at the time. The Renaissance-shaped hole in the tour wasn't as detrimental as Lou Reed's absence, but it did mean the bill needed to be bulked out even more every night.

I don't really remember much of the background in terms of what Miles was telling us, although the business about Lou professing ignorance of the whole venture was in the British music papers on the eve of the tour. We were in Connecticut, trying to get a handle on a new way of life, and whatever Miles told us when he presented the tour to us, after flying over from London, needed a lot of consideration. He was our manager, first and foremost; that was the way we looked at it, but the poor financial climate and the fact that Miles was personally in financial trouble himself was making us very wary of taking such a chance. In hindsight I'm glad that we did sign on for the tour because it was phenomenal. When I look at the posters now and look at the line-up, it was incredible—it's hard to believe it really happened. It's absolutely why I'm still able to tour Europe to this day.

With Lou opting to stay in New York and Wishbone becoming the de facto headliner, a series of other great artists would fill the breach for a night or two in the glaring absence of the man from The Velvet Underground. In Belgium and Holland we added Steve Harley's Cockney Rebel, simply because he was a name artist with that all-important hit single and had the necessary carnets in place to do it. But possibly the oddest act, given the rest of the Anglo-centric bill, was Ike & Tina Turner. They lasted two or three shows and were a lesson in American professionalism, sensuality, and sheer performance once they hit the stage.

Before we could enjoy all this, though, the flight out of Britain was an interesting experience in itself. We imagined there would be a Boeing 747 involved, but when we arrived at the airfield in Southend, along with all of the other bands, our jaws dropped. There was this dumpy-looking little freight aircraft nicknamed 'The Guppy' because it looked like the fish of the same name. Being primarily a cargo carrier it barely got off the ground with all this gear and twenty or thirty musicians on board. There was real and genuine fear that we weren't going to be able to leave the runway. I'm sure I can't have been the only person thinking, *Hmm, this doesn't portend well*. In fact, later on in the tour alternative arrangements had to be made, because with the extra acts and their extra gear, the transport was simply inadequate.

This set the tone for the transport situation every day. Haphazard would be the word. It wasn't like a modern rolling festival: it was a loosely stitched-together bunch of ad hoc arrangements involving various local taxi firms, buses, airports, hotels, local promoters, and whatever else. All in the days before email and mobile telephony. How on earth did we do it? Everything about the touring machinery was ramshackle, and yet the shows themselves, when everyone got there and the hassles of the day were set aside, worked really, really well. In several of the places that the festival visited, Star Truckin' provided that city—or even that country—its first experience of a major rock festival, and it must have had a tremendous galvanising effect on some of the local music scenes.

It was a big rock'n'roll circus every night. It was an opportunity for us to watch our peers onstage. I'm sure it was the same for them. I made a few friends on that tour, particularly the late Pete Haycock from Climax Blues Band. He was a kindred spirit. He could easily have been a guitarist in Wishbone Ash—he had finesse, a real feeling for the blues, and he was an easy guy to get on with. I remember Ralphe Armstrong—bass player with the Mahavishnu Orchestra and a larger-than-life figure. I liked him a lot; he was very warm, very easy to get on with, as was their drummer, Michael Walden. I can't say I made friends with the guys from Soft Machine but they were certainly very amiable. I remember talking to Steve Harley quite a bit, and I thought he was quite a character. I can remember him ripping the head off Charles Shaar Murray, the *NME* writer, one night—maybe he'd given him a bad review or something, but there was certainly a screaming match going on backstage.

In terms of making it a memorable show for the punters, everyone on the tour very much rose to the occasion, giving, I'm sure, some of the best performances of their careers. Acts like Soft Machine went down well in France, which always had a soft spot for music at the esoteric, arty end of rock. Just ask Pink Floyd. The more Anglo-Saxon-oriented rock audiences—in Germany, for example—would have favoured Wishbone Ash. But festivals then, in general, were always really eclectic in their bills—as they've become now, once again—so in general there was a very open mind to the variety of music on offer. They were interesting times.

I saw a little bit of Ike Turner's reputation at close hand. There were a couple of nights where Ike and Tina didn't come onstage on time; one night in particular, they were an hour and a half late. They had a caravan out back, and there were some nasty sounds coming out of that caravan. We were all standing around, people walking back and forth, furrowing their brows. When the Ikettes did emerge, it was obvious there'd been some physical interaction, shall we say. But it was part of their way of being, I think. They had this old showbiz mentality whereby whatever had happened backstage, everyone went onstage and did their act, Tina shaking her booty and rocking it like nothing else. The backstage abuse and then covering it up with this total frenzied professionalism was probably the sort of thing that had gone on for years—it was clearly part of what 'Ike & Tina Turner' was. They bailed out before Spain because they'd been offered a TV show in Germany—just one example of how loose the tour was and how rock'n'roll the whole business in those days. These days, you'd have lawyer's letters for breach of contract, promoters obliged to offer refunds. In addition, I believe that today there would be a horde of health & safety people with clipboards trying to close you down every night—and very probably succeeding.

The highlight for me was the show at Orange, in the south of France. It's gone down in local lore as 'the French Woodstock', and I can understand why: three days of peace and love, all taking place in the totally European glory of a vast Roman amphitheatre and the kind of sunshine and ambience that the denizens of Yasgur's Farm could only dream about. The Festival D'Orange was an event with an almost totally English line-up of acts. Canvey R&B band Dr Feelgood effectively broke Europe—and simultaneously broke into the British press in a big way—through their one performance at Orange. The Star Truckin' bill made up the bulk of the third day. My brother Len turned up on a motorbike, on his way back from Greece. People who were there at the time still come up and talk to me about it, and I've made some great lasting friendships with fans who first saw us there. For example, to this day, I go skiing with a French friend, Michel Sady, who was there, and he and his family have stayed with us in Connecticut just as we visit him and his family in Normandy.

People often marvel at how the original Woodstock came to be, with so many people in the one place—potential chaos with a fabulous entertainment spectacle just about holding it all together—and yet our little tour was like that on a peripatetic basis. It should probably have fallen apart after two or three days, but the wheels stayed on. Miles didn't always worry himself too much about the details—and I think that's the only way you can be. But he had made some great contacts, people who could handle the details, like Entec, a Surrey-based PA company. They were there at every show and were very much a bunch of mates, which helped.

Still, at Orange everything was running so late I can vividly remember sitting in our hotel drinking endless cups of espresso, waiting to be told, 'You're on next.' Nobody seemed to know when it might be—midnight, 1:00am, 2:00am … finally, at five in the morning, we were on. And how fortuitous that was. It was truly magical to be able to play 'Phoenix' just as the sun was rising. Think about it: the sun's rays shooting over the walls, glancing off 2,000-year-old statues, you're in a Roman ruin, for God's sake, and you're playing your most epic number as the dawn was breaking. It was truly a beautiful moment.

Every night we were headlining, but we were ready for it—we'd paid our dues. But every night we were following John McLaughlin's Mahavishnu Orchestra. It would transpire to be a last hurrah for John's band, which had burned brightly since exploding into the consciousness of every musician with their first album, *The Inner Mounting Flame*, in 1971. This was a later version of the Orchestra—the last, in fact, as John disbanded the unit later that year—but, even so, it was intimidating coming on after any entity known as The Mahavishnu Orchestra. You really did feel, *Wow! We're not worthy*. This was a period when John was revered for pushing rock music into another dimension—and that was not something we were doing, nor could do, at least not at that time. We did what we did very, very well, though, and we could always draw from that. We had a proggy element, we had our shtick where we could get the crowd going, we had a 'sound' that was uniquely ours. We knew how to project well on big stages—I knew how to be a performer and not just a muso. And while John McLaughlin could fire out notes like a machine gun, I could at least draw some comfort from feeling that my tone was better—fewer bullets, a better-oiled barrel!

Our stagecraft had also evolved somewhat by this time, honed by all the big stadium dates we'd already played through the years. Laurie Wisefield had brought a kind of 'rock star' element to the band. Ted always brought intensity to our shows, but he wasn't so into the artifice of being a 'rock star' onstage in the same way as Laurie—the stage wear, the choreographed solos, pulling the moves, throwing shapes, and, yes, appealing to the ladies. We might have been following a musically fearsome quartet, but we were no amateurs at working a big crowd, whatever time of day it might have been. And while Mahavishnu John was channelling cosmic energy in his playing, at least at Orange we had the whole burning edifice at the centre of the solar system on our side: a one-all draw there, I think.

I got on well with John on the tour, though he had wisely opted out of the communal travelling experience after that wobbly first flight. He was never in competition with any other act—he seemed only to be in competition with himself—so there were never any issues about the billing. It was a happy band of travellers all 'round. But as musicians you always know what the hierarchy is—which, in a situation like Orange, added an extra level of adrenalin to one's performance, aside from the several extra levels all those espressos had added already.

One unexpected aspect of the tour was that we seemed to be selling a huge amount of merchandise. At the end of the tour Miles said, 'Guys, you've done really well on this merchandise.'

'We have?'

'Yeah, we sold a few T-shirts. My suggestion would be to take some of this money and buy a house in Spain where you guys can be creative and chill out there with your friends and families …'

It all sounded too good to be true. We'd spent so much time working during our career, we almost couldn't imagine really chilling-out. Consequently, we flew down to Alicante on the Costa del Sol. I remember seeing this dilapidated property with great potential, as a real-estate maestro might say—a typical Spanish hacienda with all the arches and porticos, looking out over olive groves and onward to the Mediterranean. I remember thinking, *OK, this is pretty cool*. There was an estate agent there, there were deeds; I believe we put down a deposit on the property. A figure of £8,000 comes to mind. We dutifully signed our names on the legal document and flew back to London—and that was the very last we ever heard of it.

When we got back to Connecticut, Miles paid us a visit and sheepishly said, 'I've got some good news and some bad news. Good news: the tour was great. Bad news: I've lost all the money.' His Dutch business associate, Cyril, who was responsible for counting the money every night, had apparently absconded with all the proceeds—and, like the place in Spain, he was never to be heard of again.

Miles had been ripped off royally. In fact, the financial impact brought down his first empire entirely. We didn't commiserate when he brought us his news. We were outraged. *What? You drag us out of our nice little cocoon over here, you talk us into doing this thing, and now there's nothing to show for it?*

We were quite ungrateful and unsympathetic—which I regret. This man had lost everything. There was also the issue of the villa in Spain, although I think everyone had forgotten about that. There was this explosion of outrage that he, as our manager, had allowed us to be ripped off in that way. We weren't focused on all the positive elements he'd got right, just those that hadn't worked out—specifically not being paid. He could probably have used a shoulder to cry on at that point. Miles is the only one who can really tell the full story of that tour and the subsequent financial meltdown in his management stable, but it can't have been easy for him.

We were all quite devastated about this huge loss of income for the band, but Steve was the one, as our spokesman and road manager, who fired Miles. Some time later, we were doing a British tour, playing the Hammersmith Odeon, and we got word that Miles was downstairs and wanted to come up and wish us well. Steve wouldn't have him in the dressing room. He took what he perceived as being let down really badly. But they would make up in due course.

The bigger picture, though—leaving aside the anger at doing a month of free work and interrupting our great adventure in trying to be American residents—was that Star Truckin' '75 broke Wishbone Ash across Europe like nothing else. It had been hugely successful in the sense that really mattered: thousands upon thousands of people had come to see it and would remember it. Headlining the Reading Festival, which formed part of the Star Truckin' tour, and which we'd previously played in 1971, was our only show in England that year. It took me a long time, many years, to really appreciate how important that tour had been.

* * *

We had all moved—band, wives, crew—to New England, the area of outstanding natural beauty that includes New Hampshire, Maine, Connecticut, Rhode Island, Massachusetts, and Vermont. And it was a real coming of age. We were living in a new country, we had a relatively new recruit in Laurie Wisefield and a new record label, and we were soon to lose our long-term manager. It was a dynamic time but it was all rather daunting.

There's a real dichotomy to being a member of Wishbone Ash, even in the name itself. The 'Wishbone' is a feel-good thing, a good luck charm; 'Ash' suggests death and destruction. That's the way I feel about it—a yin and a yang thing, built right into the very name. The theme follows through to the band's personnel, with this lack of leadership, this adolescent dream—and I still espouse it—that a band can be a democracy. It's an ethos that always leaves room for shattered dreams. There's always been an ecstatic, euphoric thing about the band, but then there's this other side, where youthful euphoria can be laid low. I think that's part of the mystique of Wishbone Ash: it's all there in the name.

When we moved to America it was initially disconnecting but, using that old 'positive energy' analogy from the original ad in the *Melody Maker*, which I really did take to heart, I dived into making America my home. It's still my home. It's one of my greatest achievements, I think: to go to a foreign country, take the immigrant experience—which as anyone who's ever moved to a foreign country will know is no small thing—and make it work for onself. I'm a living example of the American dream. The Hemel Hempstead dream was my dad's equivalent—to get the hell out of the East

End because much of it had been destroyed. *Let's make a fresh start somewhere else*, he thought. And I was really just doing the same thing in a way.

For Pauline and me, at least, the relocation was nothing to be feared, just another transition. When Ted had left, that was when the initial trauma was felt: *Oh my God, all this success then Ted decides to leave—we're doomed!* But that turned out to be something of an exaggeration. These things are huge when you're in the eye of the storm, but to most people it wasn't that big a deal: man leaves rock band; rock band replaces him. After that there were no real traumas, just transitions. If we were on a high, we were on a high; if we were on a low, it was, *OK, let's deal with it and move on …*

We were growing up, getting more mature each year, getting into our mid-twenties and starting to see the bigger picture. Even now it amazes me that people bring along vinyl records for me to sign that were produced by MCA and released in places like Iran and India. I look at these things and think, *Wow!* We had income because they had such powerful distribution. So a career that we created in four years, up to the point where Ted left, wasn't going to just subside overnight, or in a year. It was a slow, slow decline. What we did in those first four years of our career essentially kept us going for the subsequent six.

Moving to America enabled me to distance myself a little from this career in the band, which was all-consuming, and to look at it from a great height and then come back and help to resurrect it and really start to move it forward. It really did feel like 'Phase Two'. Adapting to new situations: that's what was going on with me internally at the time. Externally, in business and in organisational terms, we were thrashing around a bit without the guidance of Miles. He was, literally, miles away. It was time to build something new.

There were pros and cons to this novel state of being. On the one hand, yes, we were now hanging on to more of our earnings, but then on the other hand it was slipping through our fingers pretty easily. We had rented four or five houses around Westport, Connecticut, and we each bought a car. Admittedly, they were used cars. Even in our greatest rock-star excesses there was a thread of old-fashioned prudence and thrift. Nevertheless, we were blowing huge amounts of money while at the same time playing fewer tours *and* keeping our British road crew on a retainer. Crazy! However, in a way, you could say that the twenty percent management commission we'd been paying all those years was being saved and put to a different use.

I was spending an awful lot of time riding my bike, messing about on boats with our tour manager, Russell Sidelsky, learning to do things in America that I would never have had the chance to do in England. Steve and Laurie hung out together a fair bit but I never found it relaxing to hang out in my free time with my workmates. Space from one another was very much needed. We did need a bit of a rest, it's true, after several years of pretty relentless work, but in retrospect, one really good thing about our leafy New World retreat from Blighty was that we completely got out of town while the punk thing came in. If you dealt in melody and harmony and had the wrong sort of trousers it was a really good time not to be in London.

Just before we left Britain, I would go walking along the Kings Road in Chelsea and I'd have people coming up to me asking for autographs. I thought, *Well, this is nice—for five minutes.* I was in every magazine, every other week—I was reasonably recognisable—I wasn't strolling around town with a Flying V strapped on but I didn't want to be that 'rock' person on an everyday basis.

Moving to America meant we became somewhat more anonymous, and we could actually start living a more regular life—trying different hobbies, having a bit of money in our pockets and the breathing space to just grow a little. Speaking for myself, I was beginning to feel really at home there.

* * *

Toward the end of the 70s, a lot of bands of our ilk started to feel that they were drifting into irrelevance—or, worse, finding themselves castigated as bloated old dinosaurs. We never really experienced that, except perhaps in a detached way. In general, there was so much money floating around in the music business at that time that bands were inclined to get an unrealistic sense of their worth. It was only right that punk came along. Aside from the politics and fashion aspect, it was simply resetting the dial back to the way rock had been in the beginning: simple, direct, exciting, rebellious. Much as I might have a soft spot for the likes of Gentle Giant, Mahavishnu, or even Pink Floyd, not even their greatest fan could make a case for street-level accessibility.

Aside from the personnel changes and the portent of punk, we had also opted not to renew our deal with MCA, signing with Atlantic instead. It looked great on paper. Ahmet Ertegun came to one of our East Coast shows and personally signed us—a huge honour. But, as it turned out, we were really up the creek without a paddle—or, to coin a new phrase, in the middle of the Atlantic without a navigator.

There's The Rub, released in 1974, had been Laurie's first album and our last with MCA. *Locked In*, in 1976, would be our first—and last— with Atlantic. Having barely set up camp in Connecticut, we went down to New York and recorded with Tom Dowd. Tom was already a legend, having had years of producing classic artists like Ray Charles, Otis Redding, Aretha Franklin, Cream, and others. We were overwhelmed and we were intimidated when we finally got to meet him, and once we started recording it was all business. There was none of the easy-going camaraderie that Bill Szymczyk had created in the studio, and definitely none of the alcohol and other chemical additives. Tom was like a college professor. He even wore a stopwatch round his neck to record and compare musical measures or bar times. What we didn't realise while we were recording with Tom, however, was that he was going through a period of personal angst—his marriage was breaking up, his good friend Al Jackson from Booker T. & The M.G.'s had just died, and in the midst of all this he was landed with some scruffy guys from England who had little in common with the R&B and deep soul genre around which he'd built his reputation. It wasn't a particularly pleasant experience.

Tom didn't have any huge feeling for Wishbone Ash, twin lead guitars, stadium rock, or anything like that. Great as he was, for us, he was just the wrong man at the wrong time. I suspect Ahmet Ertegun, Atlantic supremo, had just thrown the dog a bone. Tom was house producer and needed employment. We came along as a new signing and needed to make a record. Atlantic had given us a good deal, but at that exact point in time we had just fired our manager and we no longer had someone saying to us, 'Hey guys, this isn't working out. Here's the plan.' Even our songwriting had gone a bit off the rails. We did have some new songs but they were all a bit twee.

'Moonshine' is a not a number likely to be resurrected in a twenty-first-century set list, and I don't hear too many fans complaining about that. The whole disco thing was coming along, and we were actually trying to funk things up on pseudo-disco grooves—which we weren't really competent in doing. The name Wishbone Ash is not written large in the annals of disco. And rightly so, I fear.

By the end of the sessions for what became *Locked In*—the title of which was no accident—Tom had effectively turned us into a New York combo. Our vocals were found to be sorely lacking, so he sent us to a singing coach—a story in itself—and he was in no mood to pander to us. We lost our big British sound. In fact, we lost the plot: there it was, drifting off on the New York breeze as four lost souls from England looked on hopelessly out of a window, in a room where they were making the most appallingly inconsequential music. I remember listening with dread to the playbacks and at one point, playing the cassette in the car as we were being driven home from the studio, I think I went into a foetal position on the back seat. I was listening in horror to what we had just recorded and thinking, *Oh my God, there goes our career*. I really, truly thought that. Even the album design was cheesy: poorly drawn graphic renditions of us looking out at New York through some kind of porthole or something.

However many bumps in the road there may have been, everything up to that point had seemed to be moving in a generally forward direction for our band. I suspect any band of certain longevity will deliver a dud piece of work at some point, and this was certainly ours. Even so, I wouldn't trade those experiences for anything. But you don't do it twice. Lynyrd Skynyrd went through a similar experience with Tom and they actually shelved their third album produced by him, eventually getting it remixed with fresh overdubs in Muscle Shoals Studios. We should have done something similar. We had gone through that intense period of three or four years where we had incrementally and steadily built up our audience—we had this fabulously loyal audience in England who supported us in all the town halls and colleges. It was a market we understood and loved. And then we were breaking into Europe and doing the same.

Then we came to America. There we were, living in the middle of the countryside—in Steve and Laurie's case literally in a log cabin, deep in the woods—and it was like, *What the hell is going on?* Suddenly we were thrust into New York City with a man who has had an almost unbelievably stellar career—he'd recorded Cream, for God's sake—but our recording was a complete failure. It was the very opposite of 'getting it together in the country', that reliable old fallback position for all 70s acts worthy of the name. And thus, almost inevitably—as if guided by some subliminal adherence to that idea—that's exactly, at my insistence, what we did next: we got it together in the country.

* * *

After the disaster of being *Locked In* we built a studio in the basement of the big main house on Goodhill Road Extension in Weston, Connecticut, known as Laurel Edge. It stood on fourteen acres and was occupied by Martin and his wife Maurn, along with Russell Sidelsky. We had brought a couple of our loyal road crew over to the States with us. Mark Emery would be in charge of the live studio sound. We wanted to create a vibe—a sound we could actually play to.

Around this point we were offered a management deal with Lieber & Krebs, a management team who were involved with Aerosmith, a band we'd been playing quite a lot of shows with. Steve Upton, who had drawn the short straw and wound up in the position of being our de facto manager in Miles's absence, was duly sent down to New York to meet with these guys. They sent a limo for him. When that happens you generally know that ultimately you'll be paying for it—or, if no transactional mechanism is yet in place, somebody will be expecting to make a lot of money out of you. And thus it was. When we heard about the outrageous 50 percent commission they wanted in comparison to the 20 percent we had been paying Miles, we decided against their offer. In retrospect, it might actually have done something for us. You never know, but it just felt wrong. After all, we had only just extricated ourselves from the Atlantic hierarchy, and we weren't about to jump from the frying pan into the fire, where we'd relinquished creative control and were now faced with relinquishing financial control.

With that offer behind us, it was time to get on with creating what became the album *New England*. It was a happy period. In a way, I think it was the last hurrah for the kind of communal spirit we had had in the beginning—four people, living more or less together, creating music together with a common purpose. The music business is exactly that: a business. But the trick is in trying to block that out and create music with a kind of purity of spirit, crafting it as best you can but not crushing it beneath the weight of commercial concerns. Unfortunately, we would blow with the wind a bit come the early 80s, but *New England* was really 'us'. Long-term fans still have a good feeling about that album—and so do I.

The house Martin and Maurn occupied was the setting for the recording of this determinedly homespun affair. We hired in a mobile recording truck, operated by a couple of brothers called Howie and Ronnie Albert, who drove it all the way up from Florida. They parked it in the driveway while we set up a PA, put mattresses on the walls, and created a makeshift studio in the basement. *Locked In* was a claustrophobic failure; this would be a sure-fire cellar.

A dusty basement became a cauldron of sound. And, yes, it probably went to 11. You can almost hear it on the record. Ronnie and Howie had a great track record. Their trick was that, as brothers, they had identical 'ears'—they heard and could respond to the music, recording instruments in exactly the same way as each other. In other words, they could record for twenty-four hours straight, being able to take over from each other seamlessly, after a twelve-hour shift. They'd put this to great use with bands like Crosby Stills Nash & Young—with Stills and Crosby's coke habits they'd needed frequently to pull twenty-four-hour sessions.

Mark Emery ran the live, engineered sound in the room so that we could all play off it. This was in stark contrast to the previous experience of playing in a very confined way in an acoustically dead New York studio with tiny studio amps, Fender Champs. English bands didn't do that: they brought their full stage rig into a studio and they played! So that's what we did. We had delays, reverbs, echoes going on in the room through a PA system, which gave us the feeling of creating a big rock sound—the very thing which had been so sorely lacking on *Locked In*.

'Getting it together in the country', invented by Traffic down in

Berkshire in the 60s, was generally understood to involve a more relaxed concept of recording. We managed to combine this with a strong work ethic and got the record done reasonably quickly. The truck and the engineers were on rent, and we were paying for it. We had half to two thirds of the material we wanted to record more or less ready beforehand, and then the rest we put together on the fly. I can certainly remember one song from that album, 'When You Know Love', which was entirely a studio creation: I had a little rhythm guitar pattern, Martin had some lyrics; a song was born.

Both Laurie and Martin were getting into a writing groove with 'Runaway' and 'Mother Of Pearl'. The big rock sound was back and guitar solos were flying everywhere. One of my favourite tracks even to this day is Martin's fully realised song 'You Rescue Me'. It's one of the album's highlights. 'Lorelei' was largely my song, with some minor help from Pauline on the lyrics. To my mind, some of Laurie's most sublime soloing, on his 1954 Fender Stratocaster, appeared on this piece. For some light relief, I put together 'Candlelight', which I'd originally worked on with Ted before Laurie joined the band. This instrumental saw Laurie now replacing Ted around the dining table at Laurel Edge, the intimate recording actually taking place by candlelight. The whole thing was a true group effort and was all the better for it. We were writing for each other again, instead of for some record label or producer's agenda.

New England ended up as a powerful, positive statement. We've considered playing the album live onstage in recent years. It may yet happen. As it is, the current Wishbone Ash often plays snippets from the album. Songs like 'Runaway', 'Mother Of Pearl', and once in a while 'Candlelight'. There's no guitar player in recent years that can do justice to Laurie's playing on 'Lorelei', so we just skip it.

There was a special atmosphere created during the recording of *New England* that completely brings the songs to life. In fact, the album as a whole captured a certain sense of place. It was the antithesis of its predecessor. An album is, after all, the record of a moment in time, and this was a good moment, what we chose to send out to the world that year. I think it was late August when we were recording, and there's a point, just after 'You Rescue Me', where there is this long stretch of genuine New England ambience in the grooves. We actually went outside with the microphones and recorded this incredible sound that had been distracting us during the recording. Yes, we had chanced upon the right moment in the weird seventeen-year lifecycle of the cicada, and there were now millions of them in the trees around the house creating their own collective rhythm. You can hear dogs barking on the album as well. That was the mood: it was very humid, very hot; there was a very funky feeling in a basement with no air-conditioning. And that's what you're looking for in a rock band: a bit of sweat and toil, and a door that isn't locked, metaphorically or otherwise.

Capturing the mood perfectly was the album sleeve design itself, once again supplied by Hipgnosis. It was an eerily lit black-and-white composition depicting vaguely institutionalized young men, sharpening sticks in readiness for action. The ever-provocative Storm Thorgerson had flown out to capture the mood visually and even had us wading up to our armpits in swamp water, which he captured in photographs for the inner sleeve.

As artists, what we wanted was to transcend the circumstances of the making of the album and reach as many people as possible, but at the same time to capture something of the time and place, something of where we were at, and invite people into that world—like a good film or a book. You had forty-odd minutes of audio to create, however impressionistically, a sense of landscape and ideas, questions and answers. *New England* was created there and then by the four of us playing as a group, combining all our individual idiosyncrasies and reflecting something of where we were as people and where we actually were, on the map. Elements of various songs may have been in place before Howie and Ronnie rolled up the driveway, but it took the four of us in that basement to make it come together sonically. We felt comfortable in our skin again.

* * *

With this album we had the tremendous good fortune to be offered a new deal by MCA—the same people we had left behind for the green pastures of Atlantic barely a year earlier. It was fantastic of them to take us back. The deal was very largely down to John Sherry, our agent at that time in England, who slipped effortlessly thereafter into the role of being our manager—and all power to him for doing that. The new MCA deal, which lasted up to 1981, would provide us with shelter in an increasingly stormy environment. We were very much cosseted and protected from all the changes that were going on in the music business back in Britain. We hadn't completely burned our bridges as potential British residents, though. Our New England experience was emigration with a safety net since we all retained properties in the UK while renting homes in America.

Not long after *New England*, the album, we started to gravitate back to Old England for recordings. Martin, in particular, really didn't settle in America. I don't think he ever felt comfortable there. New York might have suited him more than rural Connecticut. There were domestic tensions at home, too. I know that our good friend, tour manager Russell, couldn't wait to get out of the house. Eventually he moved into a cool house designed by Frank Lloyd Wright, just down the road. Laurie and Steve were very happy, it seemed, building new contacts, making friends and living lives as single guys, albeit with steady girlfriends.

Martin had very much pushed for John Sherry to be our manager, so there was an axis of Martin and John wanting us to record at Surrey Sound, in Leatherhead, near where they both had houses. I was easy-going about it. I had a house in Bedfordshire at the time—as well as what was essentially our new home in New England—so when it came to the recording period I found myself doing this huge commute down to Surrey. It was certainly doable; whether it was wise is a question I'd often ask myself when I'd find myself tooling along country roads in my trusty Morgan sports car, navigating through fog at 2:00am after long drug- and drink-fuelled recording sessions under the auspices of Dr Nigel Gray, our producer.

One evening, during an intense recording session, John took a phone call from a slightly hysterical Pauline, who said that she'd arrived home with our young son, Richard, to discover that we'd been robbed. I was overdubbing a guitar solo at the time and John initially refused to hand the phone over to me, thinking that Pauline was making an excuse to chat. The drive home from Surrey seemed longer than ever that night and I arrived at the cottage to find chaos, with detectives, in-laws, and a toddler putting fingerprints all over the crime scene. It turned out that the hours of our routines had been logged by a couple of builders we'd hired to install a front porch. Pauline thought she had seen movement in the back garden as she came down the driveway, and that was apparently the robbers making a hasty getaway through the back gate. My collection of rare and valuable instruments—including at least six extremely rare and valuable Gibson Flying Vs—was left intact as well as my studio recording gear. The thieves had been mostly focused on TVs, jewellery, and hi-fi gear. We lost some precious mementoes and keepsakes from our travels, and they had obviously trashed the place, too, but it could have been so much worse.

Just Testing, recorded over several months at the end of 1979, would be the second of our new phase of 'British albums' and the first of several we recorded at Surrey Sound. In the meantime, though, there would be one more 'American album', *Front Page News*, in 1977. That particular album saw us returning to Miami, with Ronnie and Howie at the helm once more. We lived communally again, this time in a Spanish-style house with a shaded courtyard, once owned by Howard Hughes and set up as a love nest for him and Ava Gardner. We were reunited with our Scottish cook and sailor, Bob Dunlap, who had previously captained a sailboat cruise that Pauline and I had taken with he and his family, island-hopping around the Virgin Islands.

Front Page News was released on October 7 1977, in the middle of our tour of Europe. There are some good songs on that album: '714', 'Come In From The Rain', 'Right Or Wrong', 'Diamond Jack', and so on. A month later, on November 14, we were back in New York, taping *The Mike Douglas Show*. Also on this show were Georgia Brown, Gary Crosby (son of Bing), and Marvin Hamlisch, the distinguished songwriter known for songs from *A Chorus Line*, *Butch Cassidy*, *The Sting*, and so on. This was a huge show in America at the time. After we'd finished our musical slot, Mike came over and interviewed us. Marvin ran over to where we were standing and made a bit of a fool of himself by trying to mimic his idea of a peace-sign-waving rock audience member, while prostrating himself in front of us. He didn't want to lose the limelight.

We were also very happy to be reunited with Derek Lawrence, the man who had produced *Argus*. Together we recorded the album *No Smoke Without*

Fire back in the very same recording studio that had given birth to *Argus*. It would probably be a lie to deny that at the back of everyone's mind was the hope that we might be able to recapture some of whatever it was that had made the music so great a mere six years earlier. Our record sales were dropping off alarmingly and our audience had in many respects lost faith in the band's ability to be certain of our direction. The musical relationship that Martin and I had together around the *Argus* period was pretty much broken. John Sherry saw this and gave Laurie a lot of inspiration to try and come up with something approaching the musical feeling of *Argus*. Songs like 'You See Red' and 'Ships In The Sky' were the outcome of this inspiration, and pretty good they were too, as was 'The Way Of The World', but the grandeur was missing. I think that John also saw that Laurie and I were not in sync as writers at that time—or as people, for that matter—but we could still deliver the goods together in the guitar department and onstage.

* * *

Argus was always 'there'. It was the elephant in the room when it came to recording any new Wishbone Ash album. Or so we thought. Martin saw himself very much as the spearhead of our sound. He was of the mindset that everything he wrote was great art and therefore 'worthy'. His singular belief in his abilities—including his talents as a solo singer—was off the scale. He also thought he could produce the band. On *No Smoke Without Fire*, however, Derek Lawrence was not having any of it, and he and engineer Rafe McKenna got on with the work, paying Martin little heed.

No Smoke Without Fire would be one of those albums referred to in retrospect as 'solid'. I doubt if Derek would have been leaping up and down at De Lane Lea thinking, *Wow! I've just produced the most amazing record!* It's always a producer's job to bring the thing in on budget and to get the best results out of the band in question at that time and place. On that score, he did a damn fine job. But whatever that extra magic rabbit had been in the early 70s, it wasn't being pulled out of the hat again. It was a different moment in time.

It would be fair enough to ask what Derek thought about the eventual *No Smoke Without Fire* as compared to the first three albums we had made together. But, curiously, I don't think any of us asked him. I believe the feeling was that we'd completed the job as required—that's sometimes the way it is at the end of album sessions, and that was probably true of other bands at that time as well. In Britain there had been a loose brotherhood of British rock bands all playing the same venues, all getting record contracts around the same time, producing classic recordings, all touring America in a second 'British Invasion'—shared bills and friendly rivalry. For Wishbone Ash to have had the great good fortune of working with Derek Lawrence, and Martin Birch, the engineer of those great Fleetwood Mac, Deep Purple, and Pretty Things records, there had definitely been something in the air.

By 1978, though, I don't think the same feeling was present in the air—not for us and nor, I suspect, for any band of our era. I was happy to work with Derek because I liked him; he was a Londoner, and he knew instinctively that our real stock in trade was getting it down as live as possible, and that the guitars were always going to be the ace up our sleeve as far as the audiences were concerned. 'It's all about the guitars, innit?' he'd often say. He'd worked with the best and knew what constituted a great rock record, in just the same way as Bill Szymczyk did years earlier, having also worked with so many great American artists.

Nevertheless, bullish and undeterred, we went the whole hog and got Hipgnosis—yes, the *Argus* people—to create the cover art. The attempt to bring the old team together would be hard to deny, wouldn't it?

On November 5 1978—Guy Fawkes Night—John Sherry staged a party to celebrate the release of the album. He decided to operate the pyrotechnics himself, with the help of a few members of our road crew. These were serious fireworks: mortars and rockets all laid out as if in readiness for battle. I remember John running back and forth with lit taper in hand and all the glee of a schoolboy pyromaniac. It was a good time.

* * *

Around this time, Pauline and I were preoccupied with starting a family. Richard was born in August of 1978. It was a life-changing event for both of us, naturally, and I felt the onset of fatherhood more keenly than I could have ever have imagined. When Richard came into the world he was three weeks overdue and born by caesarean section, and while a rather groggy Pauline was recovering, I actually got to hold him first. It was my immediate impression that this was an old soul that I held in my arms. It seemed almost as if he'd been on this earth before. When Pauline did eventually have him in her arms the maternal bond was immediate and strong. She was destined for motherhood, that's for sure. Elation would be my state of mind for the next week at least while I ran around like a chicken with its head cut off, preparing the home for the arrival of mother and son.

In those days, giving birth was not the rushing in and out of hospital that it is today. Time was allowed for mother and baby to get used to new routines and get over the birth itself. We prepared this tiny closet of a room for Richard right next to our cosy bedroom in the eaves of our old cottage. Our first visitor was the midwife—a rather tall, matronly Irish lady—and I immediately warned her of the thousand-year-old petrified oak beams upstairs and explained that she would have to duck her head in order to avoiding hurting herself. The Grade II-listed property had been constructed of beams salvaged from the British Navy after the fleet had been broken up, having done its work defeating the Spanish Armada in 1588. Sure enough, when she reached the top of the stairs she omitted to duck and promptly banged her head on this giant blackened beam and was knocked out cold. So there I was with mother and baby and a rather large, befuddled Irish lady lying prostrate on the landing upstairs. I think I may have revived her with a tot of whisky, if I think about it. This was the same lady who recommended that Pauline drink a pint of Guinness a day for the iron content, which she promptly did, being very health-minded for her children. That wouldn't happen these days.

On September 6 1978, just a couple of weeks after Richard was born, I somehow received an invitation to a special event in the rock fraternity. The Peppermint Park club in London played host to a party thrown by Paul McCartney to celebrate his acquisition of the entire Buddy Holly song-publishing catalogue. There were quite a few celebrities there, of course. Pauline had planned to accompany me but, with a new baby, she had other concerns.

I made the solitary trip to London and, once at the club, I found myself seated at a table with Keith Moon and his girlfriend, Annette Walter-Lax.

He was rather subdued. I'd actually never seen him like that; he was saying how he'd really turned a corner with the whole crazy rock'n'roll lifestyle, especially with all the pills and booze. It's hard to look back and think of him as only thirty-two years of age at that time because he'd already lived so much life, of course. Anyway, it was to be the last time any of us were to see him, because later that night he passed away while staying in Harry Nilsson's flat, 12 Curzon Place. Ironically, he'd been prescribed some sort of drug to wean him off alcohol. I was so shocked to read the newspaper headlines the next day, since I'd been sitting right there across from him at that party. Another macabre irony was that four years earlier, Mama Cass from The Mamas & The Papas had died in that very same apartment of heart failure, also aged thirty-two.

I was having questions about the whole rock'n'roll lifestyle, and the grounding that parenthood was giving me meant that songwriting was taking a back seat. Having said that, there was one song of mine, 'Master Of Disguise', which was recorded for our next album *Just Testing*, and which we still play in concert. With America still on my mind, the song was my reaction to getting to grips with having been an alien in a foreign country. I was just beginning to learn about it and yet here we were, back spending all this time in the UK again. Musically speaking, I was conflicted and in a state of confusion, that's for sure. I'd certainly lost my clear sense of our band identity. When it came to fatherhood, though, I was as sure as I had ever been about anything in my life. I was still enjoying the recording process and playing shows but something was missing about the band.

I was learning some important lessons about recording from Nigel Gray, a fantastic producer and engineer whose talents we were now employing. I didn't realise how much of a 'producer'—a producer of my fellow band members—I actually was too. We all 'produced' results out of each other, as I mentioned earlier, and it was a process that had served us well in the earlier days. When we were living closer to each other and were more involved socially and creatively, it was almost a natural process. As we became less involved with each other, that way of working and its benefits gradually slipped away. Laurie for one was also not so sure during this phase, and on one occasion where we were trying to complete one of Martin's works of art, he simply said, 'It's shit,' after being cajoled by Martin into coming up with a guitar solo. We weren't a particularly happy band. Mutual respect was required.

Whatever the strength of the material, we could always fall back on the guitar playing, which even now I look back on and think was stellar. There were always some new tricks up our sleeves in that department, which was getting more and more competent and professional. Synth guitars came to the fore; slide guitar, voice boxes, effects processors—we used it all and really started to use the studio itself as a creative tool rather than a place you went to record just your songs.

By 1979, with Dr Gray at the helm of *Just Testing* at his studio, Surrey Sound, the location for all those wonderful recordings by The Police, our recorded sound—our productions—were without fault. Great grooves, great guitars, pretty good songs. But I don't think we were ever able to do another epic production like *Argus* again—certainly not before the end of the decade. We had a lot of creative licence, and we used a lot of it to prevent each other interacting together as a true band. All bands of our vintage were doing the same, taking preposterously long periods of time to produce albums and competing for the latest and best snare drum or guitar sound. It was pretty indulgent. We even brought in the songwriter Claire Hamill, who was being represented by John at the time, and she was actually very inspirational, adding backing vocals as well as co-writing with Laurie one of our best songs of that era, 'Living Proof'. That actually was a great move as it really shook things up and inspired us. The stage and touring were where we became more of a band—I guess in part because we were thrust together again for six weeks a time, and because, onstage, you have to play more as a band.

Onstage and in the studio, I could still pull wild solos out of thin air and hated to pre-think the art of soloing. Laurie (and later Roger Filgate) felt much more secure in this way of working, doing their homework the week before in order to know exactly how a solo would end up sounding. Me? I'd just say, 'Roll it,' and I'd go for it, sometimes falling flat on my face but often coming up with some really good ideas on the spur of the moment. Probably my favourite song of Martin's from that period is 'Surface To Air' from *Just Testing*, but I defy anyone to have a clue what the lyrics were about. For me, the best Wishbone Ash music of that era was when a great song idea was brought to the table, even in a bare-bones sense, and the band then breathed life into it. That was certainly the case with that song, and the twin-lead break in the middle is still one of my favourites.

* * *

By the end of the 70s we were all living quite separate lives. We'd come a long way from living in the same flats or the same street as before. You gain something and you lose something in that progression. But by and large we still conceived of ourselves as a band. It was the only reason we were together. Martin often balked at that, in particular with the songwriting aspect, but I truly believe that excellence in the guitar department made what were often mediocre works shine brightly. The inter-band dynamic had changed out of all recognition with the replacement of Ted by Laurie— and, what's more, the sheer amount of work that we did, both in the studio and on the road, seemed to me in retrospect to be a kind of atonement for the mistakes we had made immediately after *Argus*. In many respects we replaced amazing inspiration with sheer work ethic.

Around that time we released a non-album single, 'Come On'. It was a cover of a Chuck Berry song, and to this day I think of it as a brilliant recording. If there was anything we did that should have been in the charts, that was it—a great recording, a fairly daring rearrangement, an inventive production. But, alas, the casual viewer will look in vain for any old *Top Of The Pops* clips showing Wishbone Ash storming the charts with it. Plenty of 'classic rock' bands did manage hit singles in Britain and/or America in the late 70s—Thin Lizzy, UFO, Boston, Journey, the list goes on—but for whatever reason, we weren't one of them.

Toward the very end of the decade there was a lot of frustration about the lack of success in camp Wishbone. We were doing some sterling work in the recording studio but there was a worryingly apparent correlation between getting a lot better at our craft and the sales of our records declining massively.

There had been this return to British studios to record again, this attempt to recreate the old team—but none of it was working. We were still getting decent recording advances but we weren't moving the product. So there was a great frustration from the business side of things from both label and management. We had gone back to MCA and there was very much a sense of, 'We've got to pull something out of the bag here guys.' There were lots of talks down at John Sherry's place and a lot of pacing the cage about what we were going to do next.

Initially, John had thrown his lot in with Martin, politically speaking, and it had been John and Martin who initiated the return to British recording studios from those in America. Although recording in America hadn't particularly brought up our record sales, we had redeemed ourselves in the fans' eyes. *New England* and before it *There's The Rub* were, in my opinion, minor triumphs in sonic and artistic terms. But when we started recording down at Surrey Sound in England, the sales still weren't near where they needed to be. Frustration piled upon frustration.

The times were a-changing, and whatever it was that we needed to do to keep up, we clearly weren't doing it. In America, we'd peaked, chart-wise, with *Wishbone Four* in 1973: a *Billboard* number 44. It was simply the album that had coincided with the peak of our reputation as a live act in America. A national TV broadcast on *Don Kirshner's Rock Concert* around the same time hadn't done any harm—although Martin possibly wishes he hadn't worn that bathrobe. Things had steadily slipped away after that: *There's The Rub*, *Locked In*, *New England*, and *Front Page News* all charted lower and lower in the Top 200. *No Smoke Without Fire*, our grand return to making a 'British album', didn't chart in America at all. We sneaked back in with *Just Testing* in 1980—at the dizzy heights of number 179—but, as it transpired, that would be it for our US chart career.

In Britain, our first eight studio albums, from *Wishbone Ash* in 1970 to *Front Page News* in 1977, all made the Top 30, with *Argus* a clear peak, having reached number 1 or number 2 of the Top 10, depending on which chart you were looking at. Our three albums released between 1978 and '80—*No Smoke Without Fire*, *Just Testing*, and the concert recording *Live Dates Volume 2*—all hovered just within or without the Top 40. There were to be a couple more UK chart entries in the early 80s, including an Indian Summer or glorious swansong of sorts with *Twin Barrels Burning* in 1982—

riding shamelessly on the back of the 'New Wave of British Heavy Metal'—but there endeth our British chart career.

Still, however mediocre the sales, Surrey Sound worked out pretty well for us in terms of results. It was a lively sounding room situated above a dairy, and we were very lucky to be working with Nigel Gray. I loved working with Nigel—a great producer, very pro and very able. So there was no problem with any of that; it's just that the business had changed, the times had changed, and I think our fans had changed. Once we had let down the fans with *Locked In* and, before that, to a degree at least, *Wishbone Four*, it was very hard to get some of those people back on board again.

We were all living life and we took our foot off the pedal. While we felt on a daily and weekly basis that we were making up for lost time as people, to the music-fan masses we just weren't around as much. Britain had a strong weekly music press, with three big magazines—*Sounds, Melody Maker*, and *NME*—and if it was reported that you'd 'left the country' it was like, *Whoa! They've deserted us!*

It took us a long time to get over the charge of desertion. I can remember a front cover of *Sounds* near the end of 1976: a picture of me getting out of a limo, with what was perceived as a rather apologetic expression, and the headline, 'Who's back in Britain, then?' I was simply a man in a rock band who had been living in Connecticut. Despite the rewarding immigrant experience, I'd personally never felt that I'd 'left' Britain entirely.

How times have changed. These days, if you're a professional musician, nobody gives a second thought to where you live—in fact, they're not even interested. If you're at the level of U2, people might care where you pay tax (the Netherlands) vis-à-vis where you collect your post (Ireland) because it actually affects the gross domestic product of a nation, but for the rest of us it's long since ceased to be an issue. But back in those days we were a kind of 'band of the people', and we lost some of that by going to America. That said, we've still got fans from the very early days who've stuck with us—they're still down the front, loyal as ever, and a big part of the process.

FANS

A large part of the reason for the band's longevity and success comes from the fact that Wishbone Ash always respected its fans and catered to their needs, realising that without them we would be nothing. So, right from the beginning, a culture was nurtured of always signing autographs and having time for our folks, often getting to know individuals—and, later, their families—by their faces in the audience, and at post-show record signing sessions. We've only expanded on all this in recent years. We always had fan clubs in the UK, the States, and Japan and would try to cater especially to these folks whenever and wherever possible.

The UK club was started at our request by a lady who worked in Miles's office by the name of Doreen Boyd. She, and later her daughter Lindsay, handled mail-outs and membership cards, and as a side line Lindsay was instrumental in getting the *College Event* magazine going. This was a brilliant idea of Miles's to educate university social secretaries about the acts they could book for their events (most of whom, naturally, were on his agency's roster at the time). Although Doreen was to go on after that to become The Police's fan club secretary, she cut her teeth with our fans, so to speak, and became a kind of auntie to them. Some years later, when we came under the management of John Sherry, his personal assistant, Penny Gibbons, took over the role of fan club secretary. Much later on, in the early 80s, Pauline did the same.

It was a point of pride for me to always answer fan mail and try to grant the small requests from fans whenever possible. I'd always take note of youngsters following the band and often fathers or mothers would be seen bringing their youngsters along after a show to introduce them proudly to us, thereby inducting them into the wider Wishbone Ash family.

It's not hard to see how music can really help create lasting bonds and memories between parents and their children if you imagine a family enjoying music together on a road trip, or celebrating family birthdays with a band's music as the backdrop to all that. Those songs will be forever *their* songs. Only recently, we played a private event where the managing director of a huge company, a lifelong Wishbone Ash fan, was thrown a surprise retirement party by his colleagues with us making his wish come true by inviting him to play onstage with us. His daughter came to me afterwards with commemorative photos for us to sign. She was ecstatic. It had meant so much to her to be involved in celebrating the memories that she and her father had shared through our music. You simply can't quantify that.

Another lifelong fan, now well on his way to becoming successful in the world of business, is one Simon Atkinson, who had discovered the band's music as a very young lad from his dad's record collection. He would turn up to shows with his mother, who would wait outside patiently for him in the car. Finally, on his eighteenth birthday, Simon's greatest wish was granted when he went to Berlin to see the band perform there. In subsequent years, as we've got to know Simon, he's handled all sorts of requests and tasks for us, not the least of which was compiling the most comprehensive list of Wishbone Ash tour dates (presented as an appendix herein). He has sold merchandise and helped with tour management and crewing, becoming very much part of the inner circle.

Nevertheless, while the vast majority respect your space, there are always fans who abuse one's hospitality and good-natured openness. In some cases, you find out there is a kind of innate desire in others to consume you as the host and supersede you and unravel you—an attitude of, 'I can see through the façade of fame and personality, and could probably be doing it myself.'

One such character was Gary Carter, to whom I'd been introduced as a rather gauche teen by his father, an avid fan of the band. One afternoon, during our soundcheck before some show in England, it was pouring with rain. Often fans would hang around outside the venue hoping to listen to a soundcheck and perhaps hear a new song or two. I'd spied young Gary, on his own this time, standing bedraggled outside this venue, literally soaked to the skin. I couldn't see him suffer like this so I invited him inside. And so began a relationship that I could hardly have guessed would prove to be the absolute bane of my life.

Over time Gary, like Simon, became a great authority on the band's history (mostly the second phase of it). He started a fanzine and also became involved in our merchandising. Some of the diehards and more senior fans had reservations about Gary right from the start—and, in the fullness of time, they were proved right. It gradually became clear that he couldn't accept that Martin was no longer in the band and seemed to be looking for someone to blame, namely me.

It all came to a head when he was selling merchandise in Dublin, Ireland, during the *Illuminations* tour. Gary had decided to feature stacks of Martin's new offering, *Walking The Reeperbahn*, on the sales table, while displaying just one of our CDs. This was the last straw. There was a parting of the ways.

I tried to keep civil later on, when Gary and a chap called Mark Chatterton got a project together to write the history of Wishbone Ash. I was in Germany mixing a thirtieth anniversary DVD recording of Wishbone Ash featuring guests and former band members—very intensive work—and was presented with a completed text which I was told was to be ready for the publishers in one week. Should I wish to contribute, I had better get my copy in fast. Like a fool I stayed up each night for a week, after ten-hour video mixing sessions, working with sheaves of paper and editing the blatantly biased text. I'll add that I was working under a solitary bulb while living in a tiny caravan in a field, which was being guarded by a rather irate goose acting as a watchdog. At this point in time I really was a man out standing in his field. In hindsight, I should have had nothing to do with the book. But you live and learn.

* * *

Something I'm very proud of with regard to Wishbone Ash and the fan community concerns our 1995 album *Illuminations*. I talk about it in detail elsewhere, but the key point was that here, with the band needing to firmly stake its place in a new decade and with a new line-up, the album that would do that was made possible through the direct intervention of our fans. Long before PledgeMusic or Kickstarter, Wishbone Ash delivered a fan-funded album. It was, for that time, a very novel gesture toward the band from people who really cared about what we did and who could spare a few pounds each to share in the adventure. I remain deeply grateful to this day for that level of support and commitment.

The profit motive was never the only criteria Wishbone Ash employed when considering tours. A big part is the legacy and keeping fans involved in the music, both current and back catalogue—which I in particular had gone to great lengths to keep available in the record racks. Certain tours, especially in the USA, were inevitably loss-makers due to the cost of travel and accommodation. No matter: the bigger picture was more important. People respected this and felt catered to, and as a result they would show their loyalty by turning up for dates year after year, often travelling great distances to do so, even traversing countries and continents.

All this built up an incredible international community. Fans' sons and daughters from different cultures have even married as a result of this community. Others regularly spend their vacations nurturing friendships in countries with their newfound friends, as a result of meeting at a show somewhere on the planet. It's something the current band and I are immensely proud of.

Three fans of Wishbone Ash of long-standing are especially worth mentioning in terms of having my back throughout all these years: Leon Tsilis, Guy Roberts, and Andy Yates. Leon is a former MCA employee and Special Promotions project manager. It was he who suggested that Wishbone Ash become one of the first bands anywhere to get its own website. He fully saw the future and the way the record labels would lose their grip. Leon's a huge fan of guitar playing and guitar bands (Lynyrd Skynyrd credit him with breaking them nationally in the US) and has a deep love for our band and its music. He encouraged me to promote Wishbone Ash on the web and did an awful lot to help with keeping the band's back catalogue intact— which, of course, has been a huge benefit to all former band members in terms of keeping royalties and residuals steadily flowing to them.

In the UK, Guy Roberts served the band in a similar fashion, helping to expand our international merchandising operation, giving a real personal service to other fans, forever seeking rare recordings or a special T-shirt from some obscure tour. Guy, an incredible archivist, got involved along with another stalwart, Andy Yates, a former policeman who'd become a fan as a young man, prior to joining the force in the UK. These two guys—along with their team of Dave and Daniel Moore, Sue Roberts, Mike Day, Nick DeJong, Mike and Pauline Holt, and a host of others—have overseen many fan conventions in the UK together, with Guy even running one in the USA. Leon put together two on cruise ships, sourcing for us the contact for one at Club Med in Florida, as well as the aforementioned anniversary concerts. It's been a shining example of how folks who started out as fans have really rolled up their sleeves and got stuck in to help out.

These days, with the business as we've always known it imploding on itself, fans have often taken it upon themselves to promote their own shows. John Ford in Indiana, John Winder in Oregon, and Mark Merriman in Tennessee are three who have done so recently in the States. In fact, at the show in Indiana, Dave Cruickshank, a promoter of the band himself, and his son Ruaridh turned up all the way from Bonnie Scotland to support us. Back in the UK, Simon Mills promoted Wishbone Ash at a fabulous country-house event.

Ironically, Andy Nye, originally a fan of Wishbone Ash from forty years ago, now our UK agent of many years standing, could never have foreseen owning a booking agency, let alone becoming our agent, when, all those years ago, I'd personally berated him with foul epithets for not clapping along with the rest of the crowd at our gig at the Dacorum College—finally being told by me to 'fuck off' when he did not comply. I'm very humbled and pleased that he did not do so since, together, we've weathered some pretty rocky storms in keeping the good ship Wishbone a viable performing entity.

In America, Steve Koontz, a super fan from North Carolina, who regularly takes on 3,000-mile road trips to follow the band, has been an immensely proactive supporter, even if you just take into account the sheer exuberance and infectious enthusiasm he displays. Talking of which, I simply cannot ignore super-fan extraordinaire Derek Thomson, from Newcastle, England, who turns up all over Europe with the self-same fire in his eyes that he had when I first met him at those rollicking shows at Newcastle City Hall back in the day, when you wondered whether the balcony would support the crowds of kids leaping up and down on it. Ian

Routledge, another fan from those times in the Newcastle/Durham area, even lobbied to have us appear on a favourite festival of his in Minnesota, USA, the Moondance Jam, which we duly did, appearing on a bill with Tom Petty & The Heartbreakers. Amazing personal efforts by what we would have called 'amateurs' in a previous era. At the time of writing, I'm less than two weeks away from a return trip to South Africa with the band by virtue of the professional efforts of super-fan David Salter. This is very real fan power.

People in bands talk about their 'street teams': well, we have had all this going on for years. There's not a town or city in a foreign country where, even to this day, I can't find a fan on the phone or, more likely, through social media, and ask for some simple job to be done, whether it's collecting posters from a printer or collecting a band member from an airport. Take Fred Renz, who as a young fan and guitar player himself had the good fortune to witness the recording of some of the *New England* album, forever aligning himself to our cause. Fred has become a firm friend, helping out with all sorts of technical issues and tasks when we're on tour, in the course of which he's become a huge expert on 'real ales' of Britain.

I'm also thinking of Big Harry and Nick in Holland and Detlef Assenmacher in Germany who have helped us in so many ways. In California, Atsuko Wolcott was instrumental in helping me secure some recent dates in her native country, Japan. Other Japanese fans from back in the 70s, Yasuko Seto and tsunami survivor Tamiko Bandai in Japan, have not forgotten a birthday of mine in over forty years! To this day we have friends and fans in France that we go skiing with each year, led by self-appointed 'fanager' Christian Guyonnet. There is another gentleman in Germany, Dr Bodo Kirf, who has personally booked us into some great European corporate shows through his sheer love of the band's music. It had formed the soundtrack to his university days in Paris, where he studied at the Sorbonne. In fact, a lot of former students cite similar stories concerning the import of our music, as do war veterans. Only recently, in Southern California, I met a former sailor who served off the coast of Vietnam and recalled how our music would be played over the ship's sound system during maintenance duties all those years ago.

Taking it a little to extremes, on one other occasion I had a request from the family of a lifelong fan in Lichtenstein, now unfortunately terminally ill, to play a show there. I did not bargain for him being wheeled into the venue on a hospital gurney, complete with drip feed, or for his nurse to place him directly below my microphone stand. No matter what I did, it was very hard to consider the rest of the audience. It seemed to me that I was I was playing an entire show for his eyes only.

In the States, years ago, we met a person who for years we simply knew as Dr John. In starting the USA *Hot Ash* fan magazine he became a vital resource to fans all over the world who wanted more information about our activities. It was not until we finally visited his home in Boise, Idaho, that we got the full sense of what industry a fan could simply put into his vocation. John Brady, as we later found his name to be, had even built an extra wing on his suburban home to house his incredible collection of Wishbone Ash memorabilia collected and traded from all over the world. The good doctor had every release of ours, not just from the States but from places like Iran, India, the Soviet Union—anywhere that the long reach of MCA could get to. John has found the rarest of rare recordings of the band, like the original demo recording for the first album, a one-off acetate disc that he located in an auction not so long ago. He graciously passed this on for release so that the original band members, along with the fans, could benefit from this find, the result being the 2007 release *First Light*.

* * *

Over a thousand shows ago, I met three French fans of Wishbone Ash at a fan club convention that we held in Duisburg, Germany: Michel Sady from Normandy; Christian Guyonnet from Paris, soon to become our videographer, among other things; and one Daniel Vetter from Saint-Etienne. Daniel was destined to become one of my closest friends, as well as to join a long list of really great Wishbone Ash front-of-house sound engineers—a position that he still occupies to this day, years later. All three of these gentlemen promoted shows off their own back in France, proactively taking personal financial risks in order to publicise the band's current musical output.

Daniel unfortunately lost money on his one and only foray into promotion, Saint-Etienne not being a particular stronghold for Ash fans. At any rate, soon after, we had a full French tour scheduled, and I invited Daniel to work the sound for us. He had impeccable credentials, having worked in the music business on several different levels. He'd travelled the world as co-guitarist for Steve Waring, an ex-pat American who had introduced the claw-hammer picking style of acoustic guitar playing all through France and in far-flung French territories such as New Caledonia and La Rèunion, so he was no stranger to the road. He had also received training at Apogee Sound Systems in California, and most importantly he knew, like the back of his hand, every Wishbone Ash song, guitar lick, and arrangement, not to mention our individualistic approach to live sound and production.

Fast forward to today, and Daniel has toured the world with us and even mixed live performances for CDs. You might say he's our fifth band member—and my personal sommelier and gourmand. Through him, together with Christian and Michel, the band and I have developed a lifelong love of French culture, but more importantly we've gained true friendship—in Daniel's case, he literally has my back in the fog-of-war, which every band knows can be how it is when you are on some festival stage with no possibility for a soundcheck and you and your front-of-house man need to conjure up a live mix by virtue of sheer intuitive musicality using those abilities that have taken decades to hone.

Lastly, people like Daniel earn their spurs by knowing when to be prudent with strangers—or, conversely, when to tell them to back off, if they are over-stepping the mark. Erstwhile fans who enter the band's inner circle can choose to abuse or nurture one's trust. Happily, I can say that Daniel has not only nurtured our trust but also upgraded our live sound, furthering our music in ways that other fans continuously remind me of when they rave about the quality of our shows from the perspective of the sound.

There's only one other gentlemen who comes close to Daniel's lengthy tenure with the band, and that is Holger Brandes, our German tour manager, who has been with us on tours too numerous to mention after previously working security at clubs on the Reperbahn in Hamburg. Like

Kevin Harrington years before him, Holger is a gentle giant who could certainly use brawn instead of brains to calm down a negative promoter or neutralise a dodgy fan situation. Like all our crew guys, he always chooses the latter. I'm proud to have all these guys on our side.

* * *

People sometimes forget that the term 'fan' is an abbreviation of 'fanatic'. We were to meet a few of these along the way. Somehow, I seemed to get more than my fair share of nutters on my back than the other band members. This was probably due to the fact that I'd stayed the course, never quitting the band. The Ghoul from Goole comes to mind—a person who'll remain nameless, but who I allowed into our circle, and who has subsequently and massively abused the privilege over a period of many years.

Certain fans are stuck with the idea that the line-up featuring the original four members was the only true line-up, and even if those other members did leave to pursue their own lives, these fans would simply not accept it. I myself know what it is like to revere an artist and even to idolise them. I'm a fan of music and of certain musicians, and I'm guilty of projecting all sorts of my own passions and unrealistic expectations on them. So I 'get it' … to a certain extent.

The image of me with my Flying V was the one most used in the music press, so I became particularly closely identified with the band's image. Even the guitar that I played, folks would say, was inspired by the very wishbone in the band's name. They may have had a point. But some of this high profile did not wash with certain fans. That's fair enough, but it wasn't by my choosing or design that (a) certain band members quit or (b) certain magazines liked to push my image above that of another. With the media, for anyone in the public eye, we are *all* pawns in the game—you can only hope to influence it, never steer it or control it. As with pretty much all bands, certain fans favoured their own choice of member to fete. Jealousies among the fans themselves would ensue as to who did what and who was the most important.

Only recently in Germany I met a fellow who told me we'd met in a former life and that, in all seriousness, I should be the president of the

United States. Even more alarmingly, some years earlier, there was the 'fan' from England who told me, in a voluminous handwritten letter, sent to my home, that he had been personally trained by Mossad, the Israeli secret service, and was going to 'relieve me of my millions'. He was, he told me, heavily armed, and was going to come after me for my ill-gotten gains. This one I took rather more seriously and definitely had to report him to our local constabulary. Shortly thereafter, I had him checked out at this address in the UK where he lived in a little bungalow at the end of a cul-de-sac in a quiet Surrey neighbourhood. It turned out that he'd spent some time in certain institutions. Nevertheless, with all the things being reported on the news around the time—the Unabomber and so on—one had to take his threats very seriously.

* * *

One of the most bizarre fan encounters I've ever had happened in the 90s at a show in America. I'd had warning that this person was coming to our show. The venue had been a school house a couple of hundred years ago, and the good folks that ran the place were a kind of music society—real music fans. After our little show, in front of this group of very enthusiastic fans, a man sidled up to me and in a low voice said, 'We've met before.'

'Oh yeah?' I said, looking at him sideways, while signing my autograph on another fan's CD.

'I've been inside your house …'

That caught my attention, and it immediately creeped me out. It transpired that this was Martin Darvill, a man who had become involved in managing Martin Turner's musical 'comeback'. I'd already crossed swords with him on the phone concerning the nature of Martin's return into the business. Now he'd come to this little show of ours to whisper this creepy reminder in my ear. It was a signal of a world of pain that I would endure for the next seven years or so, while, all that time, it seemed to me, he would be chipping away, as the manager of 'Martin Turner's Wishbone Ash', at the long years of goodwill we had enjoyed among the fan community. Ultimately, this would impact my very ability to continue in the band of which I had long been left sole custodian. We'll look at the gory details later, but my personal view remains that without this man in the picture, the issues between Martin Turner and I could have been resolved to everyone's benefit long before it ended up, in 2013, in a court of law.

* * *

Any band of our longevity will inevitably attract, over the years, a handful of genuinely disturbed individuals or followers with odd agendas you could do without. Likewise, any commercially viable business, bands included, will inevitably attract business operators circling around it—from the occasional essentially criminal promoter who disappears with the takings (it's happened many times, to Wishbone Ash as much as anyone) to legitimate businessmen pursuing marketplace activities at odds with one's own.

The reason Wishbone Ash remains something worth fighting for—even in a courtroom, as it would turn out—is not simply because it's my livelihood or the livelihood of my fellow band members at a given time: it's because it means something to tens of thousands of people around the world—to people who have no negative agendas around the band whatsoever, but who simply remain active participants in this fantastic community of people of which I, too, am privileged to be a part. For every good fan gone bad, there are a thousand and one good fans gone better—and that is, of course, all to the good!

CHAPTER 5
PEOPLE IN MOTION
(1980–86)

The first two months of this new decade saw us touring Britain and Ireland following the release of *Just Testing* on January 18. During this tour we recorded music for the *Live Dates Volume 2* album at Newcastle City Hall and Colston Hall in Bristol and also had our Hammersmith Odeon show on February 2 recorded by the BBC.

The last show of the tour on February 22 was in Belfast, at Whitla Hall. It was during the time of the Troubles, and just getting into Belfast from the south was fraught with danger. The fully armed security forces would change the location of the border checkpoints regularly, and we were questioned at gunpoint, all the time feeling very exposed while the whole scenario was being covered from a ditch by yet more armed soldiers. To say that things were tense would be an understatement.

Our driver on this particular occasion didn't really put our minds at rest either. He had apparently had his Mercedes people-carrier blown up on a previous occasion, although, thankfully, his passengers had all exited the vehicle prior to the explosion. Once we got to Belfast, he let it be known that where we were staying was known as the most bombed hotel in Europe—one had to enter it through security and then yet another checkpoint ringed with barbed wire. Finally we made it to that evening's venue. Predictably, during the soundcheck an alarm sounded and word went out that there was a bomb in the building. We were all pretty quick to exit the building but none so fast as Laurie, who ran hell-for-leather from the venue, guitar in hand.

By the time the 80s arrived we'd had a number of years of relative stability but less and less success. Martin had been applying his 'creative force' a lot of late—he was on a roll, ploughing his personal experiences into songs—but looking back, as a recording entity, there was a lot about us trying to go in directions that were really quite directionless. We had briefly returned to an esprit de corps with the *New England* album, but then later on we'd lose our nerve and go off on these Bryan Ferry/David Bowie tangents—whatever was going on at the time. Martin had met Ziggy, even had him turn up at one of his parties in London with Iggy Pop in tow, and he was royally smitten. Martin's vocals subsequently became even more mannered and theatrical, and I for one could not get behind this obviously repressed side of his vocal ambitions. All the while, sales of the albums were going down at an alarming rate.

The MCA contract gave us a lot of security, no doubt about it, and the album advances were decent, although we were spending a lot of the money on indulgent recording time. It was the modus operandi for bands of our era to spend a lot of time recording, even writing stuff in the studio as you went along. That is now a bygone era. These days, things are a lot more efficient. Spending weeks in Florida with *Front Page News* was a case in point. The problem was that Wishbone Ash no longer *was* front-page news, barring a magazine cover apiece for Laurie, Martin, and myself over the last couple of years of the decade, in the modestly circulated British muso monthlies *Guitar* and *Beat Instrumental*. The photo of me stepping out of that limo on the front page of *Sounds* in 1976 was a last hurrah for that sort of thing. The mainstream of the music world had moved on, and we were doing our best to keep up—even if that meant imitating Bryan Ferry.

We were fishing around for a hit single, which was always, to me, a bit of a red herring. The label, of course, would have loved it. This was the era when singles were what you could hang your hat on. Classic rock bands, as they were becoming known, did have hits occasionally—Boston, Journey, Thin Lizzy, UFO, Ritchie Blackmore's Rainbow, even Black Sabbath, for goodness sake. Everyone except us, it seemed. I wasn't exactly gnashing my teeth day in day out trying to write a hit, but I think Laurie more than any of us was doing his best to try and create something to fill that gap.

Strangely, though, the one song we recorded around this time that I thought should have been massive was a cover: 'Come On', written by Chuck Berry, the godfather of rock guitar. The song had been a breakthrough hit for The Rolling Stones back in 1963; our version was sufficiently different and had a certain spark about the performance, with a terrific production. It could have done something with half a chance and a fair wind behind it. The label released it in Britain as a non-album single in August 1979. By coincidence, the British charts were welcoming with open arms a smattering of similarly quirky revamps of early-60s singles around that time, among them Barrett Strong's 'Money' (The Flying Lizards), Dusty Springfield's 'I Only Want To Be With You' (The Tourists), The Zombies' 'She's Not There' (UK Subs), and The Beatles' 'I Want To Hold Your Hand' (Dollar). This was all totally coincidental to our decision to record a Chuck Berry number that had been a hit for the Stones from that same era. It was also totally coincidental, I'm guessing, that the groove on the subsequent Dollar hit was remarkably similar to the one we used on 'Come On'! Alas, even with the fair wind of a British pop trend, the casual viewer will look in vain for any *Top Of The Pops* clips showing Wishbone Ash storming the UK charts.

Rock DJs like Alan Freeman and Tommy Vance at BBC Radio 1, however, were always good to Wishbone Ash, and both had evening shows on air at the time. But if Wishbone Ash ever had a ship at daytime British radio, it had probably sailed by now. Our next single, released in Britain in January 1980, would be 'Living Proof', the lead track from *Just Testing*. It had been co-written by Laurie Wisefield and singer/songwriter Claire Hamill and was destined to become one of Wishbone Ash's perennial stage favourites. But no, that didn't do anything on the charts either.

* * *

Just Testing was released at the very start of a new decade. Having taken a break from the road for almost the entire year of 1979, we now toured Britain and Europe heavily from January through to April, with further British town hall concerts and European festivals up to September. There was a lot of phoning back and forth between John Sherry and some of us band members during this time: 'Things aren't working ... I'm frustrated ... what can we do?' There was one band member who wasn't having a lot of those conversations, however, and it was Martin. So we decided it was time to have that conversation round at his house, a kind of 'come to Jesus' meeting, so to speak.

Thus, in October, along with John Sherry—the person Martin had pushed to handle our affairs and bring us all into more of a British frame of mind again—we all went to Martin's house. We said, 'Look, we think this isn't working. We think we need to have a change of direction, whether it's bringing in a new singer or an outside songwriter. Whatever we need to do, we need to shake things up.' We had dabbled a bit by having Claire Hamill sing backing vocals on *Just Testing*, and in fact she would later join us as a kind of fifth member on the road in 1981. I don't think anyone felt that having Claire more involved was a total solution in itself, but it indicated that we were keen to try to refresh what we were doing. Save for Martin, everyone else was aware that we were losing direction, losing fans. We weren't gaining any ground.

Having said all that, I don't think anyone at the time had really thought through what it was we needed to do, but it certainly came out at that meeting that one thing we lacked was a truly major vocalist, with gravitas, in the way that, say, Boston or Journey or Free had. And maybe we should get one in. No one was suggesting a return to the harmonized vocal style that so marked the sound of *Argus*, which in retrospect strikes me now as strange. It had been such a strong trademark sound, along with the twin harmony guitars. We had already started working on a new album, so if we were going to do it at all, now was the time to grasp that vocalist nettle.

Another big factor that was brought out in the meeting was that decision-making was becoming difficult—if not impossible. The whole thing was becoming turgid, somehow—we were still moving along but without any decisive goals or strategy to achieve tangible results. John Sherry, our very frustrated manager, certainly had his ideas, but he was really nervous about laying down the law in the way that Miles would have done.

So what was the impediment to change? Well, it seemed that the one intransigent fellow in the band, on most things, because he was having it his way and was quite happy with the way things were going, was Martin. He was enjoying it. He quite liked the albums and the direction and didn't seem that concerned with the slump in sales. It's possible that he thought the

MCA deal would just keep going indefinitely. He had a very comfortable middle-class lifestyle in East Sheen, a London suburb. He had a lovely home, he had a studio at home, and he had started a family. He was living a kind of bourgeois rock-star life.

I, on the other hand, certainly didn't feel that I'd arrived in that way at all. I don't think Laurie felt that way, and I think Steve was looking at the two of us thinking, 'Well, I guess if they don't feel that way I don't feel that way either.' As a manager, John needed some kudos among his peer group, too—some tangible achievements—and he was definitely encouraging us to do something. It was seemingly in everyone's interests, bar one, to start making things happen in some way.

Once the meeting got underway, the red flag for Martin was when the dreaded phrase 'lead singer' came up. He kind of flipped out at that, blew a fuse, and immediately showed us to the door. 'You can all fuck off!' were the words he used. In that instant, in effect, he'd fired himself. I guess he thought that an hour or two later we'd call and say, *'Hey, buddy ...'* But we didn't. His old mate Steve wasn't coming to Laurie and me and saying, 'I think we made a mistake here.' It was just like: 'Right then, what are we going to do now?' It was very bizarre. In hindsight, there had been no useful discussion, no alternative suggestions except for the singer thing or indeed any acknowledgement that we were failing. With one leap, though, we were free. That was evident to one and all. It really did feel like that. Suddenly, a lot of pressure that had been coming from one camp was, with the slamming of a door, no longer there. It was simply a matter of getting another bass player who could do some vocals.

At that point John Sherry became very motivated and suggested we get together with a certain John Wetton. This all happened very quickly. John Sherry and his namesake came from the same town on England's south coast, Bournemouth, and had known each other a long time. I'd seen John Wetton playing in bands in the 70s like Mogul Thrash but I didn't know him personally and hadn't followed his later career. Wasting no time, John Sherry brought him up to my house in Bedfordshire. I had a little studio there that I'd had designed by Eddie Veale of Veale Associates and built in a sixteenth century barn in my back garden that had previously almost burned to the ground. John Wetton came along and we jammed, and I'm thinking, 'Wow, this guy can really play.' It seemed like a great fit.

What we didn't realise was that John Sherry had already presented a scenario to John Wetton: a bill of goods whereby he would come into the band as lead singer, possibly also as a principal writer. Whatever had been said, it soon became clear that John Wetton and Wishbone Ash were in possession of different versions of a script, and there could only be one denouement.

By that time the rest of us had actually already written ninety percent of a new album, *Number The Brave*, and we were quite happy with the songs Laurie and I had arranged and tailored to our individual vocals. There would have been issues with keys but also with style if we'd gone back to square one, to say nothing of meeting our delivery schedule for the album, and bearing in mind the tour plans already under way.

I'd seen John with earlier bands but I hadn't seen him in King Crimson or heard the Crimson records where he's featured as a vocalist; I knew his bass playing style but was totally unaware of his vocal style and latter reputation. This might seem strange, especially nowadays, when music and the basics of music history are available at the click of a mouse, but back then if you were a band doing serious touring—as we had been during John's time with Crimson from 1972 to '74—it was inevitable that vast amounts of popular (let alone 'underground') culture could pass you by. As a side note, aside from the jam session we had, John didn't particularly endear himself to me shortly after our first meeting with his dismissal of my country home, saying that he despised that kind of rock-star cliché. *Aye, aye, we've got arrogant lead-singer syndrome in the making again here*, I thought, and so it was to be proven the case once again that first impressions often don't let you down.

Thus, in blissful ignorance of not being on the same page, we all got on the same plane and, at my suggestion, went again to Criteria Studios, Miami. A lot of great records had been made there—*Layla*, *Hotel California*—and we'd had some good recording experiences there ourselves previously, although it was a difficult studio in a way: very dry sounding, all orange shag-pile carpets with no hospitality areas. There's a legend that Wishbone Ash spent so much money on recording time that they built Studio 4 on the basis of it. Whether it's true I have no idea, but it certainly didn't seem that we were skimping at recording.

In fact, we were living quite extravagantly, as we always did in Miami. We were living, commune style, on Palm Island, a fabulous place on the bay with its own swimming pool, later to be bought by the Maharishi Yogi. We'd stayed there previously with Martin and his wife Maurn during the recording of *Front Page News*. Our immediate neighbours were The Bee Gees, and we'd often see Barry whizzing past in his Bowrider speedboat, flashing those famous teeth. I loved this house and being in Miami. It was the feeling of freedom that totally fed my soul. We were able to de-stress between sessions. We were able to bring our families along, too, so our wives, girlfriends, and children were all part of the process. I'd be teaching my son Richard to swim in the mornings and then recording at the studio during the afternoon and evenings.

Back to the studio … John Wetton was playing up a storm. Like Martin, he had this very upfront, English style of bass playing, but with more drive. In between sessions, however, John would sit at the studio piano, singing these ballads—very pianistic pieces—and it later transpired that what he was trying to do was get us to lend an ear to songs he'd been writing, but without formally presenting them. Despite the lead voice thing being on our agenda, John Sherry had misrepresented the idea of him becoming the 'front man', and I think John was also in the studio wondering, 'When am I going to get to sing a lead vocal?' There was a personality issue—a classic English diffidence—where he wasn't sufficiently upfront enough to say, 'Hey, I've got this song … this idea … this direction …' And the direction in his head was what he later did with Asia. Well, that was never going to work with us: we were a guitar band, not a keyboard band; we were riff-orientated, not power-balladeers. The guitars were still very much the combined voice of Wishbone Ash and always had been.

The unfortunate thing was that if John Sherry had clearly presented it to us that John Wetton would like, say, three or four songs on the album and a share of the vocals, I'm pretty sure we could have found the common ground. We weren't going to become a piano band, but there was no reason that we couldn't have developed some of John's ballads into Wishbone-friendly territory in the manner, of, say, 'You Rescue Me' from *New England*, or 'Leaf And Stream' from *Argus*, if only we'd had more time.

As it was, I only came to know John's vocal style from one song. At the end of this whole studio experience, he came up with 'That's That', which was a pretty blatant yet typically sideways way of telling us, 'Thanks guys, but I'm off.' There could be no advantage in shuffling around awkwardly, speaking in code. I'd become used to the American way: nothing is done by innuendo in America. Subsequently I've read in interviews that John really had it in for me. I became this bête noir—the man who stopped him singing on the album—which is just not the case. It was simply ignorance on our part on the range and style of his vocal abilities, his reticence to be upfront with his songs, and John Sherry's miscommunication to him about the nature of the gig. Maybe John Wetton simply thought we would all be aware of his recorded oeuvre, but we weren't—we were in the bubble of Wishbone Ash. I heard him sing in the studio, but although he would later have chart success with his song 'Heat Of The Moment' in Asia, his voice did not make me, for one, sit up and pay attention.

* * *

Number The Brave was released in April 1981, and we hoped it would make a difference. Despite the misunderstandings with John, for that brief moment in the studio we were a 'band' again, albeit a different kind of band than we had been before. There was certainly a lot of energy on the album. There were new guitar sounds, there was Laurie and me taking over the vocals— and doing so reasonably well, I think. Steve Upton collaborated with us on the ripping title track, inspired by the Stephen King novel *The Stand*. Sonically, the whole album was a great recording, as can be heard to great effect on, for example, my song 'Underground'. A new band dynamic was in place, with Steve contributing a lot more to the material and to lyrical ideas on tracks such as 'Where Is The Love' and 'Open Road'. I particularly loved the cover design by the visual artists Cream, which was taken from an old World War I poster featuring weapons (in this case bayonets) honed and ready for battle once more, in true warrior style. With Dr Nigel Gray in the chair, six weeks of studio time, rented houses, and a big drug bill, as far as I remember, it was also the last of what you might call our 'big budget' recordings, right at the point where the 70s wave crashed for the last time onto the shore of the 80s.

As that wave receded and the new era dawned, what should a minor-crisis-prone English classic-rock band do to try and keep up with the times? Yes, that's right: bring in a man from Uriah Heep. I'm seeing the funny side of it on paper, but in truth Trevor Bolder—who had previously played bass in David Bowie's Spiders From Mars and spent several years subsequent to that fighting demons and wizards with the Heep—was exactly the right man at the right time.

Trevor had wanted a change from Uriah Heep and answered an ad we put in *Melody Maker*. Funnily enough, he had replaced John Wetton in Heep several years earlier and would repeat the trick with Wishbone Ash. He'd be with us for the next couple of years: 1981 into 1983. Trev was a very easy guy to get on with, down to earth, good sense of humour, a fantastic bass player who could really dig in rhythmically while propelling the band forward. I always enjoyed having him onstage—he was a really solid guy, whereas John Wetton, I came to see, was a bit precious. I couldn't imagine hanging out with John the way we could with Trevor, who had a nice levelling effect on all of us. In a social context, just traveling around as a band, Trevor was always good company.

The first touring we did together was in the UK and Europe around the middle of 1981. The *Number The Brave* tour was a full production affair with a giant drum riser with stairs for Laurie and me to mount during solos. There was also a walkway that could be reached by two sets of stairs high above the stage at the rear, which we would nervously climb during key choreographed parts. This very expensive set, which was built out of square section steel, welded together during weeks of construction at John Henry's rehearsal and storage studios in Camden Town, was to feature on only one tour. With its giant bayonets, carved in plywood silhouetted by the lighting rig supplied by Entec, it actually made a big impact in the venues we played, but eventually, and wastefully, it was abandoned in some anonymous warehouse in London. No one ever really knew where.

We later augmented the band with Claire Hamill on backing vocals and the odd shared lead vocal. Two or three years down the line, the British charts would see a number of women having chart success with classic rock—the likes of Pat Benatar, Joan Jett, and Grace Slick with Starship. Also, my own favourite band, Fleetwood Mac, had gone all West Coast with not one female band member but two in the shape of Christine McVie and Stevie Nicks. What we were doing with Claire for that moment in 1981 wasn't a million miles away from that territory, but I don't think we could ever have developed into a female-fronted band.

I don't think Claire was ever enough of a 'band person'—she looked like it, she sang like it, but I'm not sure Claire was a 'road animal'. She could certainly hang with the guys and have fun, but to do it year after year? I don't think so. After the European dates she did come over to the States with her future husband, Nick, who ran the record label Beggars Banquet and was managing her at that time. But she didn't finish the tour. Her heart was truly linked to her folk-singing roots. If you wonder what the five-piece Wishbone Ash sounded like, we did a German TV show during that tour playing 'Get Ready', from *Number The Brave*, which can be found online. If you're a Wishbone fan, it's a bit like discovering a Dead Sea Scrolls variation of something from the Old Testament.

After Claire had taken the night flight home from New York, bound for London Heathrow, I found myself at the Tower Theater in Philadelphia the next night, centre stage, pretty much fronting the band before a packed house. I believe that really was one of those sink or swim moments for me—a portent of things to come.

Trevor's membership of the good ship Wishbone saw us move from the sheltered harbour of MCA into a whole new independent era, out on the open sea. We took part in a filmed concert to celebrate the twenty-fifth anniversary of London's Marquee Club during this period, which was later released on video. The studio album we made at this point was *Twin Barrels Burning*. We used Jimmy Page's studio down in Cookham for that one, with Ashley Howe engineering. Jimmy had bought the Sol Studio from Elton John's producer, Gus Dudgeon, who had coincidentally engaged the services of the same respected studio-design firm I had, Veale Associates, in turning this fabulous old watermill into a full residential recording studio.

When it came time for Trevor to do his bass parts he just couldn't get a bass sound he was happy with. I'd also had a hard time getting a guitar sound. Trevor figured out that there was something wrong with the studio monitors. He dug his heels in and was getting angrier by the day, but no results were forthcoming. Eventually, Jimmy himself came down, having received word of our dissatisfaction. He arrived with a silver-tipped walking cane, dressed in white flannels and blazer, looking for all the world like he was living the life of an eccentric country squire, or perhaps playing some role in a period drama. But he was very pleasant and wanted to make things right for us—after all, we were renting his studio. We explained the problem and he summoned Eddie down. They went through everything and found that, sure enough, the speakers were out of phase, which was duly put right. I don't know how much recording Gus had done with the monitors set like this—or Jimmy himself, for that matter—but at least now we were cooking with gas and could objectively analyse what we were laying down on tape.

As a side note, it was fascinating to see Jimmy's old Vox A.C.30 and Fender Telecaster lying casually in the studio—tools of the trade that had been used to record some of his iconic guitar solos. In addition, while mooching around the living room of the house one day, I remember opening a cupboard and seeing that the only items in there at the time were some professional-looking one-inch recording tapes. I looked on the spines and, sure enough, they seemed to be masters of some, if not all, of the key recordings in the Zeppelin catalogue. Amazing that they were just sitting there in a cupboard of one of Jimmy's several houses, unguarded, and not in some vault somewhere, given the value of the Zeppelin recorded legacy.

We had only a passing acquaintance with Page—I'd jammed with him previously at a charity night in a little village hall in Surrey alongside Simon Kirk and others—but in Trevor we had a solid connection to another rock legend, David Bowie, and we had a lot of fun asking him questions about his time with Ziggy and The Spiders From Mars. We were all hugely interested in that period, and he was always happy enough to talk about it, though none of it was good. *Hunky Dory*, just one example of my favourite Bowie's albums, has Trevor's stamp all over it, so I was sad to hear this. There were lots of tales of not getting paid and he didn't have too many good things to say about Bowie's manager or others advising David. I think the Spiders were too busy being a band, delivering the goods in the engine room instead of taking care of business. It's easily done. We'd been there.

Twin Barrels Burning, released on a small label in Britain in October 1982, actually reached number 22 in the British charts—our best chart placing in years. It would also be our last chart placing ever—at least, up to the time of writing. Never say never! But if we had somehow known then that, in purely commercial terms, we had scaled our last peak would we—would I—have had the will to carry on over the next thirty-plus years? Who can say? But I'm glad I did.

In any case, we toured on the back of this release, playing some interesting places along with the UK, like Zagreb, Belgrade, Sarajevo, Pula, and Split in the former Yugoslavia. The port of Split was full of sailors from the British navy, and the gig saw us entertaining what seemed like some rather young, enlisted guys who all, not surprisingly, seemed very shell-shocked, having stopped there on their way home from service in the Falkland Islands, where they'd been under fire below decks and had seen their comrades torpedoed on HMS Sheffield and HMS Ardent, among others.

* * *

After two years of stability and forward momentum, Trevor left us amicably in April 1983, returning to the fold with Uriah Heep, after some changes had been made to the situation there that had disillusioned him a couple of years before. He would remain with Heep until he passed away in 2013.

At this point you could be forgiven for having the impression that Wishbone Ash had become a revolving door situation—Andy Powell, Laurie Wisefield, Steve Upton, and whoever we bumped into on the way to a gig. True enough, years get compressed into sentences when you're looking back, but if there was a bit of scramble for members it was still a couple of years off.

With Trevor gone we recruited Mervyn Spence on both bass and vocals. Mervyn, like Trevor, was with us for over two years and one album. He had been in Trapeze after Glenn Hughes left and he came in very much as a lead singer—yes, at last we were addressing the question that had caused Martin

Turner to slam the door. Mervyn—or Spam, to use his nickname—was also very involved in the writing. This was still the era of the New Wave Of British Heavy Metal that had begun with the likes of Saxon, Judas Priest, Iron Maiden, and Def Leppard in the late 70s, and Mervyn was the right guy to front a band locking on to that particular passing ship like a grateful barnacle. The sole album we made with this quartet—*Raw To The Bone*, recorded at Surrey Sound again, with Nigel Gray at the desk—reflected that style. Merv brought youth, energy, and a screamingly impressive vocal instrument to the table. The rest of us turned up the volume … except for poor Steve.

Steve had succumbed to the newly fashionable technique of sampling drum sounds and the need, created by producers like Mutt Lange and others, for rock drum tracks to be in perfect time and tempo. Briefly, what this entailed was for all the drum patterns to be programmed by the producer, and for the rest of us to play to those sequenced and quantized tracks. There was a smattering of Steve's persona in there, in as much as each of his drums was to be sampled individually. In this way, the producer and engineer were able to make a composite of his actual drum sounds and tunings, but that was as far as it went.

Drummers from the 60s—Steve's era—never played in perfect time, and in Steve's case, his approach was very idiosyncratic, he being a right-handed drummer who set his kit up as a lefty would, resulting in unusual tom rolls and rhythmic patterns. This had all contributed in the past to giving our band its unique sound. All that was now out of the window. It made for a contemporary production, but certainly if someone had been trying to do that with my guitar playing, I would have been off in a shot or at the very least protested to the max. Not so, Steve: he just accepted it all, taking on board that the drum tracks represented the very heart of any production.

At this moment in time we were again getting down to business as usual. A chap called David Potts and an associate whose name I can no longer recall took over briefly as managers. Steve was acting as road manager and accountant and I was enjoying things more on the creative side with Mervyn and Laurie. It was a real band again.

Was this the last roll of the dice? Well at the time, when you're doing it, immersed in it, it doesn't feel like that. In hindsight, other forces outside compound to make it seem like that. But we did some amazing work around that time. I remember some great shows in London, and we played the Loreley Festival in Germany in 1985, with Metallica and heavy bands of their ilk. In fact, there's a clip of us at that show online doing 'Streets Of Shame', a song we'd written about our experiences in the Indian subcontinent. In that video I appear to be wearing leather pants and a leather German-style biker's cap. What can I say? It was the 80s—although that doesn't explain why Mervyn had no shoes on. Or why there's a scale model of Stonehenge on the stage. OK, I made that last bit up. The truth is, we were often the oldest guys on a bill, but we still didn't feel out of place.

The irony was that I was making this pretty heavy music with Wishbone Ash at the time but at home I'd be listening to Scritti Politti, The Fixx, Nik Kershaw. I wasn't listening to the kind of music I was creating! I know a lot of people say the 80s was a dire period for music but I didn't think so at all. I found it all interesting. Digital recording was coming to the fore; these new acts were exploiting it, and that's the kind of stuff I was enjoying. I was not about to shoot myself in the foot and give up on playing the guitar, though, even though synthesizers were really beginning to take over. The guitar had been good to me, and the trusty Flying V had by now well and truly taken on the role as my talisman—despite the fact that a lot of rock music didn't seem to need guitar solos anymore. That would change again, soon enough, when guitar became cool again and younger audiences had a need to seek out us early-70s purveyors. The popularity of the V was now on the rise, soon becoming the definitive guitar of choice of heavy metal acts everywhere around the world. Finally, the instrument originally designed when Gibson was run by Ted McCarty was selling like hot cakes, and other manufacturers were rushing to come up with their own clones of this iconic electric guitar design.

* * *

In May 1984, Pauline and I made plans to sell our beloved little cottage, Holmleigh, in Edlesborough, Bedfordshire, and move to a bigger place in a village a few miles north called Great Brickhill, in the neighbouring county of Buckinghamshire. The cottage had become too small for the four of us, with its single bathroom off the tiny kitchen, restricted bedroom space, and lack of privacy upstairs. Since we had another baby on the way, we went from the sublime to the ridiculous: Ivy Lane Farm, with its six bedrooms and two living rooms, plus dining room and large farmhouse kitchen.

Our move from the damp, foggy environs of Edlesborough to the healthier higher-ground location of the farmhouse in Brickhill, with its fabulous views across several counties, was also spurred on by some alarming events. A predatory stalker was on the loose and had been breaking into houses locally, terrorising our neighbours as well as us and garnering national attention in the media, which had christened this guy 'The Fox'. Only six doors up from our former country idyll, he'd broken into a house that was being looked after by a teenage son and daughter while their parents were on holiday overseas. He'd committed rape and God knows what else, and it began to transpire that other people became the victims of his perversity when he observed them from carefully built hideouts he'd created in their back yards or adjoining property.

A police crime and crisis centre was set up on the village green and all kinds of investigations were ongoing while petrified locals were arming themselves to the teeth in case of any eventuality. This was all going on while our move to Great Brickhill was in progress. Once there, I started work on *Raw To The Bone* down in Surrey, which was a couple of hours drive away, so I was spending time away from home occasionally, rather than face the long daily commute. This was not the best time to be leaving my family, it's true. News quickly reached me via a BBC report that The Fox had struck yet again, a stone's throw from where we'd moved to, attacking an elderly couple while they lay in their beds, actually shooting the husband in the hand.

Lawrence, our third son, was born in May 1984, right when The Fox was on the rampage. It may seem inconceivable but this predator had seemingly moved with us and was now terrorising our new village. Our house was very exposed and open to fields on the hillside, and the family was trying to adjust to this new feeling of remoteness, exacerbated by the now familiar terror in our neighbourhood. Pauline was sleeping with all the boys in the same room, a hammer and a carving knife stashed under the bed. After calling the police and being told that people should take every precaution they could in their homes, she was doing what she could under the circumstances and her parents were making frequent visits. Police surveillance was ongoing, and we got used to seeing helicopters checking things out from the air before eventually, on September 11 1984, a man was arrested in London on charges of rape, indecent assault, aggravated burglary, and burglary. The Fox was given six life sentences on February 26 1985. It had all been a stressful beginning to a new home life with a new baby, as well as a new album to promote.

* * *

Raw To The Bone, garish cover art aside, was pretty solid. Despite the heavy metal clothing there was still plenty of identifiable Wishbone Ash melody and harmony. There are still songs I'm proud of on that album, like 'Cell Of Fame', for example, a Steve Upton lyric with a great chorus vocal and bass line provided by session player Brad Lang. Tommy Vance gave us a chance to feature four of the album tracks on his *Friday Rock Show* in Britain around its time of release in July 1985. Nevertheless, the majority of our work during the Mervyn Spence era was not in Britain, it was in mainland Europe and even India, of all places, where we were poised to make our third tour. The reality is, if you're in a rock band, you're juggling a slightly different set of careers in all these different places. When things were going downhill in Britain for us we were still touring places like Germany very solidly.

We have this repeating pattern in British cultural life: build 'em up, knock 'em down. It doesn't happen anywhere else—or certainly not with as much gusto. Even today, when I travel around the world, it's a wonderful, prideful, secure feeling to hear people in other countries talk about 'British Rock' and the second 'British Invasion'. The respect that bands like Deep Purple, Cream, Ten Years After, Jethro Tull, Black Sabbath, Wishbone Ash, and so forth are held in is tremendous. And then you come back to Britain and, as far as the media goes, it's the cold shoulder. As the saying goes, you can't get arrested. In fact, I'd be far more likely to get British press coverage these days if I actually *was* arrested for something—'70s Rock Star Drink

Drive Drama: Wishbone Ash Man Blowin' Free Into Breathalyser' or the like—than if I did anything involving music.

You always need to keep such realities in your mind. It's much easier to do that now than it was then, although it was during the mid 80s that my view on being a professional musician in a rock band started to change. It wasn't all about the destination—I was finally coming to see that it was about the journey, the road travelled, and I was really getting a firmer perception of the way our generation's music was being viewed not only by our peers but also from the younger crowd.

Fans would come up to me after a concert in the early-to-mid 80s, thumbs aloft, saying, 'Keep it going!' Bands would be crumbling around you. There was very much a feeling of survival, and it was then that I started to understand the concept that a big part of continuing with Wishbone Ash was just that: survival. I'd read interviews with other people, not always musicians, and would quote them to the band. In particular, I always remember reading a Michael Caine interview where he was asked, 'How do you choose the movies that you do and the ones you don't do?' And he said, 'It's quite simple: I just take everything.'

I remember reading that and thinking, *My God—yes! That's it!* If you're not someone like Sean Connery and your career's just ticking along, there's no mystery to this—you just need to work. I saw another interview with Bob Hoskins, another British actor, where he was asked the same question, and he replied, 'Well, it's really simple. If I know the catering company on the set and it's one that I like, that's the movie I go for.' And again I thought, *Bloody hell, it* can *be that simple*, even though Bob was obviously being a tad flippant. I began to realise that one could take one's foot off the pedal of this constant, intense thinking that, *We've got to make it*. This was a constant in the 70s: *We've got to make it … we've got to crack America … we've got to do this, do that …*

It gradually dawned on me that we haven't *got* to do any of these things. It's not about that; it's about the long run. I started to formulate this concept of just 'being in the music game' as an actual career. Ironic really, since I'd been a serious professional for years, with many albums already under my belt.

Dealing with the rough and tumble of the 'music game', as I began to think of it, all became more like water off a duck's back when I started to think less like a musician and more in business terms. I'm still always in my heart and soul a musician but I needed to realise that there was this other thing I could plug into—not taking negative press cuttings so personally and to really see the big picture and realise that making strategic business moves could also be creative and satisfying. Laurie still had this need to 'make it', and the way he did that was as a great sideman, leaving Wishbone Ash in December 1985 and joining Tina Turner and later Joe Cocker, or was it the other way round? I've always meant 'great sideman' as a huge compliment, although I know Laurie has taken umbrage when I've expressed that view in the past. He has this incredible ability to slot himself into a musical unit and improve it. That's a tremendous quality to have as a musician.

The 80s was a time when Western rock bands started widening their horizons. Places like South America, the Middle East, and Eastern Europe began opening up for regular touring, and it didn't matter if you had become unfashionable back home. In fact, it helped if you had a cachet of longevity, and even more so if your 70s records had been released in these essentially new touring territories. A lot of British 'dinosaurs' became conquering heroes in far-flung places during the 80s and 90s. Jethro Tull, who had been huge in the 70s, had a sabbatical during the mid 80s, but when they re-emerged, tours of unusual territories were a big part of their activity, aggressively opening new markets. Ian Anderson definitely became someone I looked up to in terms of the way he took care of business. And I realised it's not rocket science. Much of the time it's about trusting your instincts and, especially, not being afraid of hard work. I'd come to see that a lot of 70s acts had got things round the wrong way; being so used to being 'handled' by very powerful managers, they'd often see themselves as the employees doing their managers' bidding, rather than hiring managers to do their bidding and handle their career moves.

Along with many of our peers, Wishbone Ash had played in Australia, New Zealand, and a few times in Japan back in the 70s and 80s. In fact, like many artists of that time, we had released a live album exclusive to Japan (*Live In Tokyo*, 1979). Yugoslavia was probably the most esoteric territory we played in those times—the most open of the Eastern Bloc nations to

Western tourism and cultural visits. By the end of the 80s we could add tours of Russia and Lithuania to the list, and I would later visit Brazil with Night of the Guitar. But perhaps the most unusual territory was India, which we toured no less than three times between 1981 and 1985: twice with Trevor Bolder, once with Mervyn Spence.

The first booking there came about in a weird way. A promoter by the name of Vikram Singh had come into the agency we were represented by one day in 1981 and said, 'I need a rock band for India. I want to put a Western rock band on tour in India.' And the agent, John Sherry, said to him, 'Well, who do you want? We have several on the books …'

The promoter didn't really know but he looked at a poster of us on the wall and said, 'Well, they seem pretty good.' And so, based on that poster, we ended up going to India. I think the only pop or rock people who'd been there before were Boney M. and The Police. This all fed into my idea that it can all be about the journey travelled rather than this constant idea of getting to point B. Because we'd been signed to MCA, our music had already been released in all these places, so why not let these audiences enjoy the music first-hand, as European or American audiences had been able to? You could buy a Wishbone Ash album in India, or the Lebanon, or Iran. So exploring these new territories became a whole new facet to being in a band. It was a new experience for us, for me, as much as it was for the audiences.

* * *

We had been keeping busy promoting the new album with John Sherry back on board, but sometime in 1985 it became clear to us that the band's finances were in bad shape. John decided to leave what appeared to be a sinking ship. His parting words to us were, 'I'm leaving, and I advise that you declare bankruptcy.' Steve and I were mortified.

Steve was the operations guy, used to keeping the books on the road. I wasn't too hands-on with any of that. I did have a good handle on what fees we were getting, where money was going, but not the day-to-day details, and our fees had certainly plateaued. As a measure of things, we weren't retaining road crews any more. My brother Len came on board from time to time, eventually staying for a six-year stint as guitar tech and driver. I can remember turning up to a rehearsal room carrying in this heavy amplifier, with Laurie already there, and saying to him, 'This is a new experience ...'

Laurie was sitting in that rehearsal room waiting for someone to carry *his* amp in—because that's the way it had always been. Pretty soon it started to get back to the way it was in the old days: four guys scrabbling around, carrying gear, arranging gigs. We hadn't quite got back down to the level of driving a van ourselves. We were doing bus tours in the USA in those days and would have a driver supplied with the tour bus. Driving the van ourselves would come a little later, in the 90s.

Just after our third trip to India, in December 1985, Laurie decided enough was enough. The following month, after a tour of Germany and Scandinavia with Jamie Crompton stepping in on guitar, Mervyn had moved on too. I'd come to know him as a good friend, and this was certainly proven on one occasion when he and his wife Julie visited Pauline, me, and our boys at the farm. It was winter and very cold but we all decided to go for a walk down to the local wildlife area, where there was a pond that was completely frozen over. I had our youngest son, Lawrence, attached to me in a baby sling. Three-year-old Aynsley, who was dressed in a red down jacket with a hood and also, amusingly, a red cape over the top, began running around playing the part of Super Ted, one of his favourite TV characters. We adults were talking and enjoying the winter scene when suddenly Aynsley charged right out onto the ice shouting 'Super Ted' at the top of his lungs. No sooner had he made it out there than the ice broke under his weight and he plunged into the icy water. With six-month-old Lawrence strapped to me, I couldn't move very quickly, but Mervyn was the man of the moment, and with great reflexes plunged into the pond and grabbed our fast-sinking child by the hood of his jacket, thereby saving him. We'll always be grateful to Mervyn for that. It was a scary moment. We wrapped young AJ in a coat and headed back home where we thawed him out in front of the big old range cooker.

Laurie's departure was at the beginning of the year, and we had a tour booked. We needed to be ready to leave in a week. The legal ramifications of cancelling at that late stage were obviously a secondary issue for dear old Lol. That was a week when, yet again, it all got extremely *real* for me. I was very grateful to Jamie for jumping in at the last moment on the recommendation of our tour manager, Phil Griggs. Jamie had a real can-do mentality: he was currently holding down an unlikely touring gig with Suzi Quatro, which he was prepared to put on hold, and we worked like crazy that week to get prepared. Steve was happy to hand over the reins for this. It was guitar business anyway. He was just grateful, no doubt, not to be held legally liable for a cancelled tour. We had no tour insurance.

It was quite a while before I heard from Laurie again, and I realised that, as with Ted in the 70s, there was little love lost. He wasn't looking out for our welfare, he was looking out for his, so we just had to get on with it. There was a period around that time that I connected with another wonderful guitar player by the name of Phil Palmer. Jamie had a prior commitment with the Suzi Quatro Band but we needed to fulfil a few pre-booked shows. Phil, a real pro, came in and woodshedded the material in a way that I could not quite believe.

Thankfully, Steve and I were able to complete our commitments. We were becoming much more proficient at surviving and much less precious about it all. Phil, the nephew of Ray and Dave Davies, went on to be a sideman in Dire Straits and Pink Floyd, also playing stints in Eric Clapton's band. Of all the many guitarists I've worked with, I'd have loved to work more with him since he was such a musical player. He had an effortless ability, whereas I'd been conditioned by my 70s experience to believe that recording and writing had to be this constipated, hard thing to do. It all made me a looser and more adaptable player and set the stage for me to become more of a bandleader and a more prolific writer, as well as becoming more relaxed about my chosen profession. I'd tended to downplay myself in the past, I came to realise. Meeting players like Jamie and Phil, I could see that this was all changing. These guys were grateful to be working, they respected my abilities and the band itself, being real fans, and they knew what it meant to hustle for gigs. For myself, I saw that I liked being in the cut and thrust of all that instead of being in some pampered cocoon.

We had a one-month line-up of Wishbone Ash. And yes, if you want to point a finger and say 'wilderness years', this is where they start. For the next seventeen months we had, at least on paper, several versions of the band with Andy Pyle (formerly of Blodwyn Pig) stepping in on bass and both Jamie Crompton and Phil Palmer, separately, coming in and out on second guitar. It was a bit of a revolving-door thing. But we were still filling the diary. We had a three-month tour of America in 1986—our first sustained visit for some time.

That US tour, by bus, was pretty intense. People think bus touring is glamorous; it's not. We arrived in New York and met everyone else we'd be touring with. The bus itself had been used by heavy metal bands and was most certainly not some pampered cocoon—the bunks were designed like coffins, the lights were like braziers, the decor was dungeon chic. It was horrendous! The bus driver was a Vietnam vet, and I'm sure he was a psychopath. One night we were cruising along the freeway, driving through the night after a show, as was the usual custom, the miles being so many that it was the only way one could fulfil the bookings. We were all partying in a lounge at the back of the bus, which was flying along at 70mph, and then the bus driver walked in. We all thought, *What the hell? Who's driving the bus?!* It turned out that Steve Upton was now driving the bus. They'd done some kind of manoeuvre where one guy slides off the pedals and the seat and the other guy slides on. Steve, at that point, had never driven a bus in his life before.

That was a wake-up call. I'm thinking, *I've got three young kids and a wife at home, I'm stoned at the back of a bus, partying at 70mph and the bus driver's just walked in—a stoned Steve Upton is now the bus driver of this $150,000 vehicle, and this is total madness.* I think it was around about this time that Randy Rhoads had died in a crazy event involving a light aircraft he was in, with the pilot dive-bombing the band's tour bus. It was time to grow up. Rock'n'roll was getting way out of control.

The psychopath idea really took hold later on the tour. I remember sitting in a café with this same bus driver, talking about music and what he'd been doing with his life, and he casually mentioned how he'd torched his neighbour's house because of some drug deal that had gone wrong. And this was the man to whom we were entrusting our well-being every night. There'd be no hotels on that tour, but there'd be a party every night on the bus, and there were some really dodgy characters mixing with us there—

drug dealers, Hell's Angels, skanky women. This really was the armpit of rock'n'roll, the arse end of it. In my mid-thirties, with a wife and three young children at home, I was in danger of becoming a dead rock'n'roll cliché. It was time to change, get real, face up to my responsibilities, and not run off to join the circus.

Our primary concern for those couple of years in the 'wilderness' was simply getting out of debt. When John Sherry quit we had a £20,000 obligation to Barclays bank. It might not sound like much now, but it was a bigger deal then—it's a big deal *any* time when you don't have it—and the bank was looking for it back. We didn't realise it at first but it turned out that we could actually negotiate the debt. Thankfully someone—our accountant I think—advised us, 'Why don't you make them an offer?' And so we went in there and offered them £12,000, as an alternative to bankruptcy—Wishbone cash instead of a Wishbone crash. We just rolled up our sleeves, went out, got gigs, and started to repay it. Another reality check in the art of debt management. I was learning that the business world was not an entirely scary place, and that it could actually be managed and be fun—something Miles Copeland knew years before. Have fun at all costs but take care of business as you go.

When that word 'bankruptcy' had been uttered, it brought us up sharp. It had the effect of focusing the mind. The fact that we opted to fight it really was like the turning of a corner. It was empowering, realising that you could actually control your own destiny. Previously we'd relied on managers and labels for that. I think it took a couple of years of managing the finances but we did it. Steve and I were very much a partnership in this process, making decisions together on how we would spend money, who we would repay in what order, and so on. I was regularly commuting into Europe, playing shows in order to stave off bankruptcy. It's bizarre, isn't it? But it was a manning-up process. There's nothing worse than being confronted with your own demise. My feeling was, a rolling stone gathers no moss. If you keep moving—or, in our case, play shows and work at all costs—bad luck has less chance of catching up with you.

I look back on the early-to-mid 80s as a great period of growth. The only way you can learn any lessons in life is first of all to see them as lessons, as opportunities. Someone from the outside might say, 'Oh my God, they were failing massively there' or 'They were making some wrong moves there' or suchlike. But with a different hat on, I was trying to get some positivity out of it all. These days, despite being around for decades, I'm still all about learning lessons in life. As soon as I began to look at music as being a journey, not a frenzy to get somewhere, I accepted that we were a band somewhat out of time—but my life started to have more meaning and a greater sense of responsibility started to unfold.

There was still a music business then, which there is less of now, so I would have been remiss if I didn't take on board some lessons, not only in business but also in life. When we arrived in the 80s it was clear that the band was no longer going in a linear direction: our career wasn't lifting off, it was moving in a lateral direction, consolidating, in a way. So the question was, 'How can we glean some lessons from this that will prepare us for the 90s?' And in fact we did learn some lessons, and the band would make it through the 90s with a renewed sense of purpose, but with different players, as it turned out.

By 1987 we were turning the corner (metaphorically, and without a nutcase at the wheel), but it was a shaky period. It's certainly possible that Wishbone Ash might have run out of road if we hadn't received a shot in the arm from an unexpected source, but the question is academic because that's what happened next: a phone call from Miles Copeland. And he had a plan.

INDIA

I'm always being interviewed—largely by rock websites these days—but one of the questions consistently asked is this: 'Name for us some of the highlights or standout events of your career in music.' This is really a futile attempt to encapsulate a forty-five-year career into a one-page interview. It can't be done easily.

There are the obvious awards and the globally acknowledged album successes but, in my memory, it's often the new countries that we've visited that stand out in my mind—places that impact you with their different cultures, climate, and customs. The first time we visited America was one such time. Actually, it was returning to dear old England after that first tour, and the culture shock of seeing your familiar country in a completely different way, that was truly shocking—much like an astronaut who leaves the earth and comes back to see it as a very small and vulnerable place. That's how it used to seem to me. Certainly, coming from the UK and diving into big continents has this effect. Such was the case with India, which was a country, or sub-continent, that we visited three times in all, over a four-year period.

I've already mentioned the serendipity as to how that all came about but nothing could prepare us for the first impression when we landed in Bombay on Friday December 4 1981. It was overwhelming. My immediate feeling was that the light seemed brighter, different there from the diffused, northern English light, much as it does in the States, except that this Indian light seemed flatter, yet no less bright. There was the sensation of there being a very fine dust in the air, possibly pollution, and then the visual mayhem of it all.

In the baggage hall, it seemed as if we were transported back in time, to Britain's colonial past. The airport officials were dressed in khaki uniforms straight out of the 1920s, and they possibly *were* that old. It all seemed quite chaotic, yet there was a whimsical order to it all, with lots of form-filling and rubber-stamping. Outside, we were presented to our road crew, some of whom were wearing lungis—skirt-like affairs as an alternative to trousers—and they were all smiling broadly while hanging off an unusual looking three-wheeled truck whose open flatbed was draped with gaily coloured red-and-white gingham mattresses. This would be where our guitars and suchlike would be carefully laid together with the bits and pieces of scavenged backline equipment that our hosts had found for us to use on our shows.

Our promoter was a tall, very amiable man with a moustache and dark curly hair by the name of Vikram Singh. Vikram was rumoured to be an aristocrat, quite wealthy no doubt, and somehow connected to the film industry. Our tour manager was known simply as Nareesh. He was fabulous, an older gentleman of exquisite taste. Immaculately dressed and groomed, Nareesh had a lighter and quite beautiful complexion, with perfectly cut silver-grey hair. He was completely charming but seemed to maintain an imperious control of everything around him. I'd later observe him closely while travelling with us. Each day, he'd emerge from his hotel room in a different magnificent outfit, but he never seemed to carry any luggage whatsoever. Later on, at train stations or airports, he'd simply walk into an empty space, clap his hands together, and half a dozen skinny, dark-skinned fellows would appear at his side out of nowhere, eager to do his bidding.

The journey from the airport to our hotel was like nothing I'd ever experienced before in my life. Jaw-dropping can be the only description. Every aspect of life was being lived out on the streets as we cowered behind the closed windows of the two little vintage Austin cars provided for the journey. At traffic lights, tiny girls, hardly older than ten years of age, with babies on their hips, would knock on the windows, begging with their large imploring eyes trained intensely on you. Our hosts merely brushed them away. There were entire families literally living on the sidewalk, under lean-tos made of palm fronds, cardboard boxes, corrugated iron—anything that

133

could be scavenged. Yet inside, one would see a TV flickering on and off. Dogs, cats, severely disabled people, policemen, entire families riding on one moped, oxen pulling carts of vegetables or hardware goods—it was a truly chaotic scene. And this was only just the beginning.

We wondered what our hotel would be like, but it turned out to be something else entirely. It was off-the-scale luxury, which made it all the more shocking. We were greeted with much bowing and scraping and festooned by beautiful smiling ladies with garlands of woven jasmine and magnolia flowers. 'Namaste, Namaste'—the traditional Hindu greeting with palms held together in front of the chest—and we were all anointed by our greeters with the universal bindi mark in the centre of the forehead between the two eyebrows. Hindus believe this is a major nerve point, we were to discover, and everywhere we went people would dab one of these marks on you. In talking to our hosts, I was immediately struck by how eloquent they were in our mother tongue—so much more so than us, using an almost quaint, gentrified kind of colonial/Victorian English. All the time their words were accompanied by exquisite manners and the typically Indian way of bobbing the head from side to side, so that you'd never seem to get a direct answer about anything. 'Yes' could be 'no', or it could be 'maybe'. You never quite knew. That's because, as we were to find out, nothing is quite a certainty in India. There is always that feeling that, no matter what we mortals may wish to happen, everything is in the hands of the gods.

If I remember correctly, the hotel was on the beach, behind a high wall over which one could survey this vast mass of humanity that seemed to live out there permanently, by the ocean. We'd see people conducting their ablutions right there in the open, and it was up to you to look away, thereby affording them some sort of modesty. Everywhere around us, entertainers were vying for the coins in our pockets, with the most incredible circus of magic tricks, acrobatics, and musical performances. There were monkey trainers and snake charmers, and one chap was putting rocks between his teeth and super-heating them with what seemed like it was just his breath until they glowed bright red and sparks were flying off them.

A German came up to us on the patio and offered us a toke on a large hash spliff. In the words of John Lennon, 'I had a smoke and I went into a dream'—later finding that it had contained opiated hashish! The next thing I remember, in between the giggling from all of us, was that I was finding it increasingly difficult to sit up straight in my chair. Suddenly, and seemingly out of nowhere, there appeared above the wall, as if by magic, a tiny baby in the midst of us. It had obviously come from the beach below and was bobbing around on what looked like a stick. It took a little while for us to figure out that this child was actually tied to what looked like a thick bamboo pole. In its hand was a collection tin, again accompanied by that imploring expression. How was this strange image being achieved, we wondered? When we finally got over our shock and managed to peer down over the wall, we could see that a ten-foot pole was literally being balanced on the chin of the baby's father, while he too held an imploring grin, with his hand stretched out. You could not make this up. That became forever known as the 'baby on a stick' incident. A small boy was standing next to him playing an improvised fiddle he'd made—quite expertly, I might add. I needed to lie down.

The first show was in an open-air venue in front of about 5,000 eager music fans. While there were that many inside the venue, there must have been almost as many outside the place, too, just swarming around. With a population in excess of one billion, any kind of public affair in India is guaranteed to create large crowd numbers. John Sherry and I had our Super-8 movie cameras with us, desperately trying to capture it all. During the soundcheck, the musical equipment was pretty substandard, and the PA a little under-powered, but no matter, we were prepared to improvise, and Penny Gibbons, who was along to help out, was enlisted to run the lighting console. I say 'console', but really this consisted of a plywood panel at the side of the stage containing a number of very old switches that activated the stage lights. Essentially, lights were switched on and off along with the dynamics of the music, but each time she hit something it was accompanied by a spark and a yelp or scream from Miss Gibbons. In front of the stage there were crash barriers made of bamboo that were still being assembled as we stormed into the first song.

Being accustomed to a rich tradition of instrumental music based on ragas, our blues-based, guitar-dominated riffing soon gained the approval of the crowd. As Laurie took a solo, the heads and arms would all move in his direction, accompanied by 'ahs' and 'oohs', and then over to me when it was my turn. It was pretty inspiring, actually, and big fun. We played two nights there.

A few nights later we were to be found down south, in Madras, at the university. This would be an altogether more formal event, where the first few rows of the audience consisted of local dignitaries and faculty members dressed as if they were at the opera. The students were seated behind them. After a song or two the older people at the front realised that this was not their cup of tea and uncomfortably made their exit. The students immediately and eagerly filled their places. My guess is that the elders had been there to vet us, to see if we were going to be a corrupting influence on the students.

* * *

These two shows had been something of an exploratory mission for us on the Indian subcontinent, and we were eager to return. We got our wish a little over a year later, in February of 1983, and we were back in Bombay again. This time a more extensive tour was planned, with more cities on the schedule like Poona, Madras once more, and then Bangalore. Another act from New York was to be our touring companion. I was overjoyed to find out that Richie Havens, together with a couple of accompanists, would be on the whole tour with us.

It was an unlikely pairing in some ways: Wishbone with its electric folk-influenced British rock together with the kaftan-wearing unplugged hero of Woodstock. But pretty soon we became friends, and during downtimes I spent a lot of time just hanging with Richie, absorbing his take on life. He'd often come down to breakfast wearing a large hooded garment. I felt he wanted to be a little incognito. I joked with him that with his height and beard alone, that would be impossible. He must also have been about the only black person in India at the time. He was a free thinker, that's for sure—a New Yorker, a philosopher, and a true troubadour with his history, and that very unorthodox way of singing and playing.

Restaurants are actually few and far between in India but a very excellent place was found and a meal planned for our party. I'd requested to hear some

Indian singing—I was fascinated by the traditional classical style, especially the high-pitched female singing I'd only heard in snatches being piped in to Indian restaurants in Westbourne Grove or somewhere else in London. We had a fantastic recital at dinner and then someone suggested to Richie that he get up and sing. Since he invariably carried his Guild acoustic guitar around with him, he proceeded to dive into his own version of Fleetwood Mac's 'Landslide'. It was incredible. The force of his personality and amazingly personal guitar style grabbed everyone's attention. *This is going to be a fun tour*, I thought, and so it was.

We played a great show in Bombay, at the same venue as before, and afterward our hosts suggested we do a little night-time stroll around the red-light district, after we had enquired if there were one. The idea being that there would be no partaking but, as in London's Soho, some colourful sights to be seen. I had no idea that such a thing might exist in India, but we were all game to simply view it from a distance. Our entourage, including Richie and his band and our tour guides, parked our cars and entered the area known as Kamathipura, which at that time housed upwards of 50,000 of what today we call sex workers, and yes, no doubt, traffickers.

By now it was late so there were not too many regular folks on the brightly lit main street, with its garishly painted houses and hovels, which were two and three stories high. What was shocking was that there were women and girls of every age group, every size, every ethnicity literally hanging out of the windows and lounging in the doorways with that guileless stare and lack of self-consciousness that you often get in India. The lights, the colours … it was wall-to-wall women and girls, some decorated in the most elaborate, sexual, and exotic ways with crazy-coloured saris, bells, makeup, silver nose-chains, piercings, hennaed hair; you name it. And they were all now staring suspiciously, it seemed, at our group, as we nervously walked not on the sidewalk but down the middle of the street. Richie had his hood over his head. He and his band, of course, were familiar with Times Square, New York's den of iniquity, as it had been in the 70s, as were we with Soho, of course. We also knew the Reeperbahn in Hamburg. These were the places where the rock clubs and theatres were to be found. But nothing could prepare us for this overwhelming display of truly scary wantonness.

There was a level of murmuring and low conversation as we ran the gauntlet, and then an eerie kind of high-pitched warbling started to emanate from the collective throats of the hookers. Now we were truly scared. They were mocking us, laughing at our pathetic presence on their turf. This was female energy on a massive scale. The shrieking and warbling got louder until at one point, a wretched, toothless old hag of a woman, at least seventy or eighty years of age, dressed in a filthy sari, scurried out alone to meet us, reaching out to grab one of our party and hustle him back with her into one of the hovels, no doubt. The poor victim she was about to select was the cutest and prettiest of us all, Laurie Wisefield. Shock horror.

By now the cacophonous crescendo had reached fever pitch. These women were all laughing at us now—literally hundreds of them. What to do? Run away. Yes, that's what we had to do. There was nothing else for it. A riot was about to ensue. Laurie was not about to have engaged with any of it, of that I'm sure, and if we had stood our ground there would have been an onslaught. This was a truly medieval scene and one of the freakiest things I'd ever seen. You didn't need to be high on hash to get the full impact of it all. Even 'Streets Of Shame', the song we subsequently wrote about the experience, couldn't capture this. It was something else.

* * *

After Bombay we moved on to Poona by road. This was hardcore driving on narrow uneven roads up into the hill area, taking around six hours in tiny cars with vintage 40s suspension. That is to say, leaf springs. It was exhausting and very hot. We stopped after an hour or two at a kind of shack by the roadside—there were no service stations as we knew them at home in the USA or England, obviously, but as we entered there was the sound of music playing on a record player. It was Led Zeppelin's 'Kashmir'. This was too much. Had someone planned it? Either way, the moment was perfect.

We slaked our thirst with something called Limca—a nationally popular lemon-flavoured soda—and carried on our way. Every so often we'd see the remains of accidents and broken down trucks or cars by the roadside. There was no real system of vehicle recovery, and in truly fatalistic Indian style, the survivors of these wrecks would simply camp out by their vehicle and put their faith in the gods that someone would stop and help them. Some truck drivers, fearful of having their loads looted, looked to me to have been stranded like this for days. Where were they going to go anyway—walk out of there? In fact, we all stopped at one point and helped pull a man from his overturned truck.

That whole journey was like a movie. You take for granted in the West just how easy it is to move around a continent by car, but this was travel on a completely different scale. We played the show there, and then got to do the whole journey back again the next day in order to make a pre-arranged flight out to Madras, the hotter-than-hell city in southern India. Upon our arrival there, a day of sightseeing was planned, and we were to view some amazing Hindu shrines consisting of giant boulders with multiple and intricate carvings all over them. The place had a strong atmosphere that seemed quite otherworldly, having been developed in the seventh century. On the way back to our hotel we stopped at a crocodile farm, where we were allowed to witness feeding time. It looked like parts of wild pigs were the food of choice. At the end of all this, while the smaller crocs were absorbed, the keepers suddenly changed the calls they were making and this incredible giant beast lumbered out of the mud. I'd never seen a crocodile so large. It was perhaps fifteen or possibly twenty feet in length. The entire hind quarters of a pig was heaved over the wall to where the croc arrived below us. It opened its jaws and gulped down the butt end of this pig in one go, as if it were merely a light snack.

The city itself was quite different from Bombay, more low-rise and spread out. The streets were dusty and had a far more rural feeling than Bombay, which I always think of as the New York of India, it being very urban, congested, intense. On the way to our hotel, the car in which we were travelling had to swerve sideways as an ox pulling a cartload of vegetables pulled out in front of us. Our car made contact with the cart in a glancing blow, narrowly missing the animal and driver. The cart's contents were spilled all over the road. Our driver did not stop—why would he? This was, it seemed, all quite normal. Any drive in India is an adventure. You never know what you will encounter.

In the cities, everything is sold out in the open, directly on the streets.

You might pass through an area where only dried fish are sold, out there in the baking sun, right on the pavement. Then there might be a region for obtaining coal. Little boys guard their giant piles of coal, black with dust because they literally live and sleep on these piles. Down by the river will be the laundry: hundreds of women scrubbing all kinds of clothing, linen from the hotels, men's shirts, and then all of it laid out on the rocks to dry. I was later to ponder why the 'white' bed linen in the hotels had a grey look to it.

I remember one time speeding through a city by taxi. I believe it was Calcutta, where large parts of the city had no electricity at all at the time. That's scary enough, but at one point my driver simply turned off the lights of the car.

'Whoa, what are you doing, sir?' I screamed.

With that diffident Indian wobble of the head, he turned to me and smiled, 'I do this to save electricity in the car, sahib!'

'Save electricity?' I said, in a high voice. 'But the car makes its own. It has an alternator!!!' No matter, we drove on like that in the shadows until he was satisfied that we could switch the lights on again.

The show in Madras was great—an open-air affair again, with the audience swaying back and forth to the music and particularly loving the guitar solos. This was a true inspiration for Laurie and me, to know that our work was being paid such close attention. Next on the agenda was a trip to Bangalore. This very sedate city with lots of Victorian architecture, multiple statues of the venerable former British monarch, all set in beautiful park spaces, had a calming effect on us. It transpired that the police chief there was a big fan of Wishbone Ash and insisted, together with his men, on personally escorting us to the concert, which was thronged by the usual chaotic mass of people outside. I noticed that our policemen carried these stout, six-foot-long poles or staves. As we walked into the venue, anyone who was in the way would receive a strategically placed clout on the backside or back, or even a whack on the head. I immediately asked our chief to stop this. It was quite upsetting. The police really knew how to wield those things. He smiled obligingly as if to say, 'What's up with you? English pussy.' Everything would be fine as long as I introduced him onstage during our performance, which of course I duly did.

There was one very interesting incident backstage in Madras. Other than the fact that it was my birthday, a couple of visiting Americans got word to us that they'd like to meet with the band. We said it would be OK and that we would see them backstage, and that they would be welcome at our hotel. They were nice guys, very clean-cut and respectful. They had an amazing story, too. They'd been set ashore from a ship owned by the Children of God—the very same religious group that Jeremy Spencer had gone off with after quitting Fleetwood Mac in Hollywood all those years ago, only two weeks before we lost Ted Turner to an LSD-fuelled weekend in the desert at Joshua Tree. These young Americans had been living and working alongside Jeremy, which totally fascinated me as a decade or so had passed since I'd heard anything of his whereabouts. The mission these guys had been on was to broadcast God's word from the ship's radio transmitter to anyone in India, I guess, who would listen.

I kept my cynicism in check and someone proceeded to roll some pretty strong hash spliffs, with which these young chaps had no problem partaking. Suddenly, in the midst of this pleasant stoned haze, there was a loud thud in the middle of the room. One of the two, who'd been standing, leaning against the door frame, simply passed out on his feet and fell like a sack of potatoes into the middle of the room, going down, thankfully, onto the carpet. After the shock of this we revived him with some water and promptly ceased the smoking. I believe that he and his buddy were actually starving or possibly dehydrated, and it was lack of food—plus, obviously, the hash and tobacco—that caused him to pass out.

We eventually flew back to England where we had a couple of commitments. A live recording was scheduled at the Marquee Club as part of the club's twenty-fifth anniversary. Then we headed over to Ireland and once again, just as had happened in St Louis years earlier, we had our equipment truck with all our gear on board stolen during the early hours of the morning. We were in Dublin. Luckily, this time the police were able to locate the truck. It had been abandoned by the thieves. We were relieved to find all our equipment still intact inside it.

* * *

By the time of our third visit to India, in 1985, Mervyn Spence was in the band. We advised him of all the various inoculations that he'd need against typhoid, diphtheria, and so on, and in addition he'd need to start the regimen of malaria tablets. Up until that point, on our prior trips, we'd avoided getting too many stomach upsets. The thing was to avoid drinking tap water, but of course there was always the risk of eating salads, which might have been washed in contaminated water.

As was by now our custom, we landed in Bombay and played the usual sold-out show there, taking great delight in watching Merv's reactions as India gradually worked its magic on him. Our old friend and promoter Vikram lived in a very nice part of the city where the houses were situated in walled compounds. He very kindly threw a banquet for us. As I explained, having grown up in London, where there are Indian and Pakistani restaurants on every street, it was curious to find there simply was not this same restaurant culture in India at that time. That being said, exceptional cuisine was most definitely thriving in the food served in people's homes. It was a truly incredible feast and Vikram seemed to have servants for everything. I was astonished to see that there was even a gatekeeper, possibly one of the untouchables—those at the very bottom of the caste system—a man wearing a hooded cloak who lived in what looked like a wooden dog kennel next to the compound's entrance, and whose sole job was to open and close the large wooded gates for any cars entering and exiting. At our hotel previously we'd numbly watched teams of women, arranged in lines like tea-pickers, weeding the lawns, one weed at a time. There was, in India, a job for everyone, it seemed.

On December 15 1985 we headed up to Goa. I was personally excited to visit this place because it had been spoken of as a mythical place on the hippie trail by my fellow travellers in Morocco, all those years before. It was a former Portuguese colony, and we were delighted to see quite different Christian architecture and an altogether more laid-back atmosphere around the hotel that was found for us on the beach. The people there also had a different look. Some even had dark red hair. I enjoyed going walking in order to absorb the flavour of the place. Weirdly, down by the beach, as I walked by them, a group of musicians were singing and playing what sounded like sea shanties.

Our show was a kind of homespun affair on a makeshift stage and it was fun to have a goodly number of Europeans in the audience, along with the native Goans. Later, relaxing back at the hotel, I asked some of the different hippies I met how life was for them there, perhaps ever the romantic, thinking of saving the place as a post-band bolthole. In actual fact, joining us there was my brother Len. He'd surprised the hell out of me with a phone call in Bombay earlier.

'Where are you calling from, Len? I didn't expect to hear from you while in India.'

'I'm in the hotel lobby. Do you have a spare bed?'

Len then travelled with us on the tour and his help was most welcome. After that he decided to stay on in India for a few months and literally befriended a man with an elephant, helping him secure work for the animal.

We headed back to Bombay before our flight down to Madras. At breakfast, some members of our group were complaining of upset stomachs but Mervyn was nowhere to be found. Steve visited him in his room and reported back that he was delirious and in a terrible state and had had all sorts of 'accidents' in the night, the evidence of which was plain in the room. It was on another level. A doctor was immediately called, and it was announced that there was no way our singer was going to be fit enough to travel with us.

The rest of us caught a flight on to the next city on our schedule. We had always enjoyed our visits to Madras. We were staying outside town at a place called Fisherman's Cove, and our luxury hotel was situated on the longest beach I've ever seen. It was endless. Our entire crew arranged ourselves on loungers around the pool. All of us, to a man, had got upset stomachs, and we were alternately groaning and laughing as, one by one, each of us made hasty exits to our rooms for some relief from whatever it was that had taken over our feeble European constitutions.

Once we were feeling a little better, Steve and I decided to go walkabout and headed to the beach. There was nothing there except little fishing villages dotted along the coast and simply miles and miles of perfect white sand bordering the vast Indian Ocean. After a couple of miles, walking in the hot sun, we were greeted by some tiny, very skinny men dressed simply in loincloths and turbans. They looked to be Tamils and were smiling broadly at us as one of them pulled a small package from the folds of his turban, offering us each a beedie, which was a kind of Indian cigarette. They were going out on a little fishing expedition in their dugout canoe, and it was conveyed to us by sign language that they would like us to join them. This was too great a chance to pass up so Steve and I squeezed ourselves into the flimsy little craft with its outrider. Our new friends started to paddle us out into the vast expanse. It was as if we were transported back to the Stone Age. Our hosts fascinated us—as we probably did them. They looked like Indian pirates, flashing broad grins all the time while paddling us out into the great unknown. What were we thinking?

After returning us safely back onto the beach, our rowers were still all smiles as we watched, far off in the distance, a little girl come running toward us. As she got closer, one of the little men let us know that he was related to her in some way. Then the little girl slowed down upon arrival and took on a distinctly unhappy demeanour. She suddenly looked horror-struck and started sobbing in what looked like total fear, judging by the look in her eyes. Our guys were laughing uncontrollably at her. Steve and I were uncomfortable, trying to process these conflicting emotions—the distraught little girl and the laughing Tamils. Pretty soon we understood what was occurring. She had wanted to see what her older brothers were doing with these two strangers but when she got close, she became shocked and scared, never before having seen Europeans with their ghostly white faces and arms. Our appearance had literally shocked her, and she probably feared for the lives of her older brothers. The realisation of this really impacted Steve and me.

The next day, after our show in Madras, we flew up to Calcutta in the north-east part of the subcontinent. The people there looked quite different from the southerners. They seemed way less laid back and busy, busy, busy. Driving from the airport was, again, like nothing I'd ever experienced before. Firstly, the interior of the bus itself seemed to have been completely rebuilt over the years, with everything having been replaced by makeshift parts. Even the original ashtrays, long since destroyed or stolen, had been replaced by new ones fashioned out of hand-beaten Coca-Cola cans. If this was the interior, what was going on with the engine itself? Health and safety regulations? Forget it.

Pretty soon our senses were becoming overwhelmed. We passed by toxic pools of who knows what—quite beautiful, actually—where the water was every colour you can think of: brown, blue green, yellow, red. The whole perimeter of this city of around five million people seemed to be a wasteland, a toxic dump, on a level that I'd never before experienced. Sulphurous smells, rotting garbage—it was like descending into the pit of hell. However, once we arrived at our hotel we found the usual over-the-top luxury, while just beyond us rabid dogs, businessmen and women, rickshaws and beggars all mingled together in the usual Indian chaos.

I decided once again to go walkabout by myself. I don't know why but I was wearing a white shirt. Within twenty minutes it was filthy, just from the pollution in the air. I had the feeling that there was a more aggressive energy around me than I'd encountered before, but then the thought hit me that the brains of these poor folks were being 'fried' by the over-the-top levels of pollution. I was actually becoming fearful about breathing. It was that bad. At one point I saw five unfortunate souls roped together with the lead person ringing a bell. Were they lepers? I didn't hang around to find out but headed back to the environs of the hotel. I'd already witnessed weddings and funeral processions out there on the streets, as well as seeing the results of child mutilations and dead beggars lying literally in the gutter as folks walked by, hands over their mouths and noses. Once more, I decided, I could use a rest.

Our open-air show that night in the oppressive heat was received ecstatically by the crowd although during the soundcheck I'd nervously been eyeing the vultures that were circling above us, riding the thermals. Were they trying to tell us something? Was our precious career all going to end here, in Calcutta? I had to laugh to myself. At least we'd go out in some exotic style.

It was the 21st of December. We needed to be home for Christmas. We made it to the airport only to find that there would be a substantial delay. I seem to remember us managing to get a temporary room somewhere after being told that the wait could be quite a while. Eventually, we got word that a plane was ready. We found hundreds of passengers camping out in the airport with what looked like all their worldly goods spread out around them on the floor. Boarding started, but in no fixed order, and it became apparent that the seat numbers on our boarding passes were of no use whatsoever. It soon dawned on us that this was a free-for-all, and that the only way we'd be getting on a plane home was to fight our way on—which is what we did. All of us made it to the seats, desperate now to be on our way. It was dusk outside.

We took off, and after a refuelling stop somewhere in the Persian Gulf we started to experience what we thought was turbulence. The captain came over the PA to inform us that he'd had to shut down one of the four engines on our 747 and was now dumping fuel! We would be needing to find a place to land! An unscheduled stop in Kuwait was decided upon, and the plane touched down at the brand new airport in Kuwait City.

As our motley crew of passengers filed off the plane and into immigration, we could see that our hosts were none too happy at this turn of events. The Americans and British were separated out to be pushed around and shouted at angrily by security guards wielding automatic weapons and demanding that we all surrender our passports. That was a no-no in our books, and one of the American businessmen obviously felt the same way. He protested at the sight of the women in the group having their handbags forcibly yanked off their shoulders as the authorities began rummaging through them. He was promptly brought to the ground by the butt of a rifle delivered expertly to his knees. Now we were scared. If I did not know it before, I now felt a sharp realisation as to our vulnerability when travelling overseas.

Arrangements were made for us to stay overnight in what was one of the most elaborate Holiday Inns I'd ever been in, situated on the edge of the desert. We were told that on no account should we go outside but that we could use the hotel's facilities and, with that, we were given food vouchers. Things were looking up. Outside, I could see that the only cars being driven in and out of this beautiful hotel were Mercedes and Rolls-Royces. The wealth was plain to see. The Arab men in the lobby (there seemed only to be men) were immaculately groomed in their white robes and headgear. That was all I could tell about our temporary location. After a good night's sleep we were informed that replacement parts had been sent out for our plane, and that we would be on our way before long. We were reacquainted with our passports and were able to continue our journey home.

As with other trips, and especially since it was Christmas, the culture shock on arriving home was intense. We were straight into the feeding frenzy that Christmas has become in the West. I felt disgusted by it all. It seemed pointless, all this forced present-buying, especially after the insane poverty I'd witnessed in India. It was all too much. It would, yet again, take me some time to put all our experiences together again in my mind. That would have to wait though, because a couple weeks after our return, Laurie Wisefield would decide it was time to leave.

CHAPTER 6
WHY DON'T WE?
(1987–89)

Not long after we fired Miles back in 1975, he was presented with the opportunity to work with his brother, Stewart, and his new band The Police. And then he got very entrenched with punk and several American acts that followed in its wake: R.E.M., The Go-Gos, The Bangles. He built a new empire. These bands in many respects suited his personality more than the fairly serious musos from early-70s Britain, where it was all about the music and maybe less so about doing whatever it took to become stars. When we were trying to come up with a name for Wishbone Ash, Miles's suggestions had included Jesus Duck, Marty Mortician & The Coffinettes, and Wonder Warthog & The War Weenies. From these name suggestions you can see that he loved the overblown, crazy side of rock'n'roll. Thus, when the punk thing came along and he was managing various people in that world, it was really interesting for him, and a natural fit.

The Police were the best of both worlds: ersatz punks, talented musos who managed to connect with the public in a big way through great songs and reggae-style grooves, courtesy of Stewart's drumming. I knew Stewart quite well by this time. Pauline and I had been to the reception when he married Curved Air's Sonja Kristina, and they'd visited our house. I'd been really pleased for him and the band's success because I'd seen how hard he'd worked to achieve it all. I'd been to see The Police in New York when they were trying to make it, borrowing a friend's Chevrolet Camaro to drive there. Stupidly, I'd only just returned from the UK and had been up for twenty-four hours. On the way home after the show, I fell asleep at the wheel, not too far from where I live these days, and had a very close call—a collision with another vehicle in the early hours of the morning.

The other driver and I were both extremely lucky to have made it out alive. Naturally, a court case followed some weeks later, at which time I had to travel back to Connecticut from Florida, where we were recording. I had good representation, and the judge was lenient with me.

By 1987, Miles's period with R.E.M. and The Bangles et al was all coming to an end. So what did he do? He looked back on his career and he said, 'Hey, I worked with some fantastic bands in the 70s—let me call all my old buddies up …' He had a label called IRS Records at the time and he had this great idea—which we only found out after the event—to build his label catalogue up with a load more titles, increasing its value greatly, but artificially, in a relatively short time, so that he could then sell it. He subsequently did, to EMI, for something like £42 million: capitalism in its purest and most beautiful form!

Around April of that year, Miles contacted Steve and me, independently, and he also contacted Martin Turner. He didn't contact Ted because he couldn't find him. He had this master plan of recording a bunch of instrumental albums using all the great guitar players he'd been associated with in the 70s. He had created a new label, No Speak, for the purpose. It was presented as a project: 'Get together, guys. Do a reformed album— but it's going to be instrumental.' So that was a bit odd, but it was great to be back with the guy who always put the wind under our wings. It was another adventure. When the three of us did finally come together and met at his family home in St John's Wood it was agreed that it wouldn't be a permanent reformation, just a one-off project. I think Steve and I were pretty firm on that point because we'd already invested a number of years with just the two of us as Wishbone Ash, with additional players brought in on a contractual basis. We'd managed ourselves and the band's good name through the crisis of bankruptcy, and we obviously didn't want to throw any of that away.

There was always an easygoing feeling with Miles. I think we all got the fact that he was primarily interested in himself: a benevolent dictator who could create things and put people together along the way, producing events and situations by the sheer force of his personality. I don't think anyone was pulling any wool over anyone else's eyes. We always knew that working with

Miles was always about Miles. But it was better to be associated with him than not.

Happily, despite our acrimonious parting a few years earlier, the vibe with Martin was great. He was ready and we were ready. He's a contrary character and, in my view, is prone to saying dumb things. There was so much of that going on in the period leading up to his leaving in 1980. He'd be purposely perverse in discussions, often ending up arguing against a specific point that he'd made himself fifteen minutes earlier. I'd come to realise that this was all a kind of smokescreen to gain or retain control and appear relevant. But there didn't seem to be so much of this going on at this point in time, perhaps as a result of the reality of the situation. That is to say, he needed the work, as did we.

One of the other appeals for Martin in the reformation project was that he had a small recording studio in the basement of Miles's offices in Portobello Road, and the idea was that we could start the project there in order to keep costs down. As far as I could see, not much had been produced from his studio for many years. Martin's younger brother Kim Turner was co-manager of The Police along with Miles Copeland and had probably helped look out for his older brother in this way. So Martin had a strong connection with Miles—albeit an arms-length connection by now. But this would be an opportunity to really produce something worthwhile from the recording studio, keeping it all in the family, so to speak.

I flew in to London and we got down to work in earnest on a new album, *Nouveau Calls*, and it was really, really great to work with Martin again. There was no real angst. He was living a particular life and was happy with it, and if there was any bitterness that his solo career hadn't worked out he kept it pretty well hidden. Wishbone Ash had been a pretty special part of all of our lives and rekindling that was probably the real motivation. It just keeps pulling you back.

I had lots of unused ideas and Martin also had lots of unused ideas and outtake ideas from his solo project. Steve was the man in the middle, but it was really Martin and me as a double act—and there was magic there. It was fantastic. He was in a studio that he was used to, and he got material he could really sink his teeth into, something he could 'produce'—finally something that was tangible. There was even a song on the album called 'Tangible Evidence'. As far as I could see, he'd been faffing around for the previous few years. But he'd probably have said the same about Steve and me, because he wouldn't have had any awareness of what we'd been doing all over the world. The biggest thing he'd done, and which he kept going on about, was an album by Roy Hollingworth, his mate in East Sheen who used to write for the *Melody Maker*. That seemed to be the main thing he'd done in seven years, as far as I could see, though of course there may well have been numerous other projects that hadn't come to fruition. Either way, this instrumental album was a project that was guaranteed to be released and that had a lot of communal energy behind it. It was a kind of rebirth for both Martin and for Steve and me, and hopefully it would be a rebirth for the entity known as Wishbone Ash—if only we could bring Ted to the party.

Thus far we were recording an album as a trio. Where was Ted? It took us a while to find him. I'd found out he was living in a small apartment across the parking lot from the Roxy on Sunset Strip, Los Angeles. It fell to me—as it had years before with Laurie—to fly, this time not to New York but to Los Angeles, and root Ted out of his hidey-hole. He'd been out of the professional music scene for years, and he was unsure about whether he should get back into it or not. He had this vague project called the World Man Band with a chap called Michael espousing various new-age ideals but nothing actually being produced commercially. When I arrived there after the long flight, they both spoke of various concepts and philosophies and were especially fond of the writings of Buckminster Fuller, even showing me a Fuller-style geodesic dome dwelling that they had at their disposal, complete with a motley assortment of gear, located up in one of the canyons. Eventually, I convinced him to come to London and join up with the rest of us for the instrumental project. I left with the understanding that Ted would follow on, once he'd put his house in order. Weeks later, we were deep into the recording of *Nouveau Calls*—in fact we were almost finished—and there was still no sign of Ted. Finally he arrived, but right at the very end of production. We made time for him to add a few bits of guitar, enough to give credence to the concept that this truly was a reunion of the first Wishbone Ash: Andy Powell, Ted Turner, Martin Turner, and Steve Upton.

We had William Orbit do additional production work on the album, much to Martin's annoyance. Miles felt that the music needed a bit more finesse, a bit more groove and track sweetening, and William did do a great job, I thought. His main tools of the trade were several AMS samplers (the very same unit we'd taken out on the road with us years before), which he used to great effect, adding micro-beats and percussion elements—all very current and of the moment. True, the guitars could have been mixed louder by Martin or given more beef in the EQ department but it was, after all, an 80s record. Martin handled that side of the production, and there were certainly no issues in the volume department where the bass was concerned. It was front and centre again, and to be fair to Martin he did a good job of the complex task of handling the various keyboard elements, samples, and loops, all of which were fast becoming the new tools of the trade in the recording studio. Together, we managed to come up with some great melodies and some classic Wishbone Ash riffage, and once again, dare I say it, we had produced some cool new music, relevant to the times.

Nouveau Calls (Steve's pun for 'no vocals') was released in December 1987, at which point Wishbone Ash were on tour in Russia and Lithuania. 'Which-bone Ash?' you may ask. Well, it was me and Steve with Andy Pyle on bass and Jamie Crompton on second guitar, fulfilling the last of the dates we had committed to before the offer from Miles had come along.

Our instrumental album was very warmly received but obviously did not set the charts alight, being seen by the old fans of the band as something of a side project. This was the era of new-age music, and instrumental music was faring very well at the time, with labels like Windham Hill making waves among more mature audiences. While we'd all approached the album as a one-off project, there was a natural moment in the New Year of 1988 where it felt right to continue. There were no more dates on the books with Andy Pyle and Jamie Crompton, and both generously bowed out to allow a full-scale reunion of Wishbone Ash Mk I. Jamie (after an unexpected swansong tour with his own band in Russia) would go into the musical instrument business, heading up artist relations for Gibson in New York and, later on, Fender in the UK; Andy joined Gary Moore and contributed to his phenomenal success around the 1990 album *Still Got The Blues*.

Meanwhile, Steve Upton was having marital problems. This had all come very much to the surface when we were playing the dates in the Soviet Union. It was a very strange time, seeing Steve go into a state of almost complete shutdown and undergo a change in personality. He went into a deep, dark place, retreating into his shell. James would often put his arm around him and encourage him not to bottle it up. I just tried to give him his space. We could all see what he was putting himself through, and it was very distressing. He'd be at the soundchecks and playing the gigs, joining us for meals, but to all intents and purposes, Steve—'the Colonel,' as our tour manager, Phil Griggs had christened him—was not in the room.

We played numerous dates in St Petersburg in one venue alone, a large ice rink, and later moved on to Moscow for one date. It was cold, brutally cold even by Russian standards. This was all in the days of Perestroika or Glasnost, the end of the Soviet Union. The Neva River was frozen solid, with blocks of ice piling up against the shore by the Hermitage museum. We got as much out of being there as we could, sightseeing and such, but the food in the hotel was really awful. It sounds ridiculous but the only palatable thing that was in plentiful supply was caviar—and, of course, the vodka was excellent. That place was a vast tourist-style hotel with an elderly babushka on each floor, sitting on a dais, recording when you entered your room and when you left it. Phone calls were definitely monitored and our interpreters were, we later found out, junior members of the KGB. They were very bright people and spoke excellent English.

On one coach trip, I sat next to a young lady who saw me reading a *Rolling Stone* magazine that I'd brought with me. Looking sideways at an advert for Winston cigarettes depicting Americans with vacuous Colgate smiles grinning into the camera, she asked, 'Is it real, that people in America'—she spat the word—'are always so happy, or is it all an act?'

'Well, it is a bit phony in this advert,' I said, 'but for the most part, life in America can be fun.' She looked away, obviously perceiving it to be a government plot, not in the slightest bit convinced.

On another occasion, I got into a deep and truly fascinating conversation about politics with another of our 'interpreters'. I invited him up to my room so that we could continue talking while partaking of shots of vodka.

He was OK about that, but once we got to my hotel floor, under the watchful gaze of our designated babushka, he became extremely nervous. Inside the room, he was glancing up to the ceiling, trying, no doubt, to make out a microphone or camera. He clammed right up. I found these kinds of glimpses into the paranoid Russian experience fascinating.

We had also committed to a few shows in South Africa during May 1987, along with the band Nazareth, at the Sun City casino complex. This was controversial at the time because of the imminent end of apartheid, but we made it a condition of our contract that the shows were to be open to all ethnic groups. In the UK, however, both bands walked into a firestorm of protest—we were even being blacklisted by the Musicians' Union and the UN, along with the main focus of the press's attention, Elton John, who had also gone to South Africa. In reality, the MU had never done anything for me—they were a joke in many respects—and my view was that, of course, music knows no boundaries. This was to be proved so when during the soundcheck we found ourselves being serenaded by the black stagehands who were all smiles as they sang their a cappella songs. Later, after the main concert, we partied like there was no tomorrow in the mixed-race staff bar of the casino, with all the workers rocking up a storm with the Naz. There had been a few black faces among the mostly moneyed and white crowd at the actual concert but that was mostly due to the location and prohibitive economics of actually getting to the place.

As a side note, we did the obligatory dawn photo safari out into the bush with the Nazareth boys, and that was pretty spectacular in terms of wildlife watching, though we weren't prepared for just how cold it gets out there before the sun comes up.

* * *

On February 27 1988, the first Wishbone Ash became the current Wishbone Ash at a concert in Folkestone—the first date in a long UK tour, swiftly followed by a long European tour. Ted, who had gone back to America, had his return delayed and missed our rehearsals, so the first half of the shows on the British tour featured myself, Martin, Steve, and Jamie, with Ted coming on, dressed in all white and waving peace signs, for the second half, which featured the older numbers he was intrinsically familiar with. The sixth date, in London, was recorded for broadcast by BBC Radio 1. We were, it seemed, in danger of being popular again.

We started working on what was to be our second reunion recording, *Here To Hear*, in the middle of the year. This time, vocals were allowed, and all four of us contributed from the start. We'd have the album completed in October, but it would have to wait until June 1989 for release. I'm a bit hazy about why this was but it was probably because in between, in November 1988 and then again in May 1989, Ted and I were taking part onstage (and Martin offstage) in Miles's latest wheeze: another traveling circus, this time called Night of the Guitar.

Miles had rounded up nine veteran guitar players, most of whom had by now recorded something for his No Speak label—either a full album or an exclusive track for his themed compilation *Guitar Speak*. The line-up for the British tour, in November, would be Ted and me (performing together), Leslie West from Mountain, Alvin Lee from Ten Years After, Robbie Kreiger from The Doors, and our old friend Pete Haycock from Climax Blues Band, along with Derek Holt on keys and bass, Steve Hunter from Alice Cooper, Randy California from Spirit, and Steve Howe from Yes. We'd all come on and each do a three-song set with a great shared rhythm section, Livingstone Brown on bass with Clive Mayuyu on drums, and then we'd all jam at the end. Miles had boiled the whole Star Truckin' experience down to a lean, manageable, three-hour show with a fraction of the logistics and none of the dodgy Dutch accountants. It was, in a way, a guitar-centric reinvention of the British package tours of the early 60s, where vocal stars of the day would come on for three or four numbers backed by a house band. Since then, the Night of the Guitar concept has been reused and recycled by others, including G3; once again, Miles was ahead of the game. My brother Len had the unenviable job on being a roadie for the tour, looking after and tuning all those guitars.

The shows were really something. Randy California seemed to become the musical director and the main 'voice'—whenever singing was required. Alvin Lee did the odd vocal, too, and we had one: 'The King Will Come', our nod to the past, slotted into our set alongside two of the recent instrumental pieces, 'Real Guitars Have Wings' and 'In The Skin'.

Martin was OK about the whole thing because he was recording the shows—there'd be vinyl and CD releases from it, as well as a two-hour home video—so he was able to put his producer hat on again. Steve, unfortunately, wasn't involved. I don't know how he felt about that, but it can't have been easy for him. Nevertheless, it was getting the Wishbone Ash name back out there, and the show was playing to packed houses.

For the second phase of European dates in May, Phil Manzanera from Roxy Music and Jan Akkerman from Focus replaced a couple of the original team. There was no shortage of guitar players from the 70s who'd perhaps slipped out of the public eye but whose musical chops were in good shape. I don't know if everyone involved was trying to rejuvenate their career, but certainly there were one or two who hadn't been very visible for a while. Whatever the motivations, for all of us it was great fun and, if you listen to the recordings, some really great music was produced.

Some of those involved were more 'rock'n'roll' than others. Top of the list would be Leslie West: you just don't get any more rock than Leslie. He is, despite his best efforts, indestructible. It was a disparate bunch, all right: Steve Howe down with the pixies at one end of the spectrum, Leslie West dancing with the devil at the other. Somewhere in the middle were Ted and me.

It could have been a bit daunting on that front for Ted. He had only made his stage comeback, after many years away, on our British and European tour earlier in the year, but he delivered the goods. Though we only played three songs, Ted donned the white outfit every night and 'became' Ted Turner again. It was as if he was playing a role. When you've been offstage for a number of years you definitely do leave your stage persona behind. But he had had enough experience to know what that character was and he could recreate it, albeit with a new West Coast, new-age twist.

With Miles involved as he was—compering every night and revelling in the over-the-top pantomime aspect of the whole thing—you know it's going to be fun. And with Leslie involved it was always going to be rock'n'roll. The first thing he'd say when he got on the tour bus, looking at the non-white rhythm section, was, 'Jews and blacks at the back of the bus!' His being Jewish would be quick to follow. Miles's girlfriend Adriana (later to become his wife) was also on the tour. She was a beautiful Argentinian with a big handbag, and Leslie would be haranguing her every day: 'What's in the bag, bitch?' He simply did not care.

There were times when we were touring in Italy by rail and there'd be great arguments on the platform about which train we were supposed to get on. Leslie would go, 'This is the train …' to which the entire entourage would say, 'No, Leslie, you're wrong.' No one else would get on, the train would start moving off, and there would be Leslie West, drifting off into the sunset with this huge hold-all he carried, including his mini Steinberger guitar inside it. Eventually he'd reluctantly throw the bag from the train before jumping off himself—a heavyset guy landing on his face on the platform. I remember blood everywhere, Leslie screaming and then, later that night, making it onstage with a broken nose, his head bandaged up like something out of the civil war. Things like that happened night after night. He and Jan Akkerman butted heads a lot. He would always call Jan a 'Gypsy Jew', as if he wasn't *really* Jewish like Leslie. Alvin Lee took a lot of heat for having made his career on Woodstock. Mountain had been there too but had not been selected for the actual movie. This was a big thorn in Leslie's side, and he let Alvin know it. He would just needle everybody, find their Achilles' heel—a nightmare, but also hugely entertaining.

Shortly after the European leg of the Night of the Guitar adventure, in July '89, the original Wishbone Ash regrouped for our first US dates in this particular format since 1974, prefaced by a couple of shows in Brazil. We shared the bill with some of the other IRS artists, including Leslie West. He and I went down from New York to Rio de Janeiro to do those first shows, and when we got to Rio Leslie didn't have his papers in order. Passport control put us in a holding room for an hour—during which time Leslie figured out the only way to get through was to get distraught, so he started blubbering. The Brazilian officials just couldn't deal with this grown man crying and freaking out. And sure enough they let us through, happy to get rid of him, no doubt. It's an education being around Leslie West, but after a while you're happy to leave school.

* * *

Things back in Britain were progressing fairly well. *Here To Hear* was released in the Summer of 1989 (June in America, ahead of the US dates; August in Europe). Wishbone Ash embarked on a substantial tour of English town halls and theatres in September and October, followed almost immediately by a similarly substantial tour of Germany. Further British and European dates followed in the first quarter of 1990.

It was around this time that I had a supposedly brilliant idea. I still had my house in Buckinghamshire, Ivy Lane Farm. I was living in the States and already renting the farmhouse out to the PepsiCo corporation—so why not rent it to the band? We could produce some records there, using the modest advances we were getting from Miles's label to create a studio. We had already got back together; why not get back to getting it together in the country? Martin had a studio-load of equipment at home, so we joined forces. The idea was that Martin and I, specifically, would be partners in this—which was fatal. We dived head first into the idea that we could run this as a commercial studio operation in the country—which is a bit like building a big pit and pouring money into it. Aside from the logistical question marks on the enterprise, we were probably the most ill-suited business partners you could ever find. But we gave it a good shot.

I look back on that period around 1990 as a bit of a blur. We were trying to pull together the touring side of things, to capitalise on the renewed flurry of interest around the reunion, and I was also doing about twelve other things, often at the same time. I was managing the fan club; I was running a house with a revolving bunch of musicians, cooking meals for anything from four to eight people a night; I was starting to handle the band's bills; I was running a furniture business with a former publicist, Rod Lynton, who was also living at the house … I had fingers in so many pies but I was starting to 'manage' things, learning a myriad of new skills, becoming more responsible in general. I was working harder than I'd ever worked in my life, with a whole other actual family life going on in the States with my kids, bills, commitments. I certainly did not appreciate at the time just how much was Pauline's commitment in aiding this whole experiment. She must have been amazingly strong to endure what I was throwing at her.

By the middle of the year we were working on what would be the third of our reunion albums, *Strange Affair*, and it would turn out to be an apposite title. Back home on the farm on Ivy Lane, Great Brickhill, Steve got to work in the vegetable garden which seemed to ground him and get him out of his manic state for a while. We were fending for ourselves. It was almost like a commune, except it was driven not by the idea of 'dropping out' but rather by maximising our resources, including this farmhouse and its land, to commercial and pragmatic ends. We'd jokingly refer to each other as we passed by in the way of monks in a monastery: 'Good morning, Brother Martin,' and so on. I had a lot of energy—though God knows how. I was living in America but commuting to the UK for long periods of time. I thought of it all as synergy rather than mission creep. Ivy Lane Farm was a big house and I needed to keep it going. I was just trying to do the most with the least, putting all my assets to work. Also, having spent a lot of time in America, with its 'can-do' culture, I was trying to bring some of that back to my bandmates. That was the way I saw it.

Steve was there full-time; Ted was coming and going a lot as he always did; Martin was happy in the engine room, the control room, crafting the sounds as they went down on the Otari 24-track machine. Curiously, he was not so driven creatively. Perhaps he'd worked out a lot of the demons that had driven his songwriting in the late 70s. He definitely seemed much more content in his new relationship, with kids coming along at fairly regular intervals. But I felt newly responsible because it was under my roof that we were doing all this. I think perhaps the other guys in the band at this time thought that I was taking over—which was exactly the criticism we'd levelled at Martin before he left, years earlier. I'm sure I was a bit evangelical about all the 'can-do' stuff, which might have become a bit wearying to others—particularly to Steve, who had his own troubles to deal with—but we were all, I believe, pushing at the same door. The thing is, as is always the case, somebody generally emerges as a leader, and on this occasion it was me. I saw what needed to be done and I'd do it: if supplies were needed, I'd fetch them. But generally speaking, we all pulled our weight, despite getting back to luxuriating somewhat in taking too much time over things.

The problem was, with everything else that was going on I don't think there was a vast amount of music being written. We'd sit around the kitchen table at night, sometimes picking up a guitar if there was time. One of my songs for *Strange Affair*—'Wings Of Desire', about our experience being at the Berlin Wall during its demise—was written in this way with Rod Lynton, but I don't think the music came fast and furious, as it had with *Nouveau Calls*. I was bringing in outside writers a little bit. Andy Pyle helped out in that regard. The lyrics to the song 'Strange Affair' were written mostly by him with a little help from me, and that became probably the 'big song' from that album, the one that has had the longest afterlife in our live shows. It's a real example of how musicians 'produce' each other, and how a song can change radically. Andy had played me an old demo of the song, which without being too unkind was in the style of Roger Whitaker—that's the only way I can describe it—but once I got hold of it and brought forth a new arrangement, turning the groove into a shuffle, adding a twin lead section, it became more of a rock/blues song. In retrospect, however, we should have ditched the sequencer I'd suggested and played it more the way we'd do it later in a live context.

The 80s production values were still being adhered to but we were now looking the 90s in the eye. That was all to change before too long, but not before we had some fun bringing in what later became Gary Moore's Midnight Horn Section to add some sweetening on that track and another song of mine, 'Dream Train', with Robbie France drumming up a storm. Robbie is sadly no longer with us, but I credit him as being a real mentor and inspiration to my young son Aynsley, who was already a drummer of two years' experience at the tender age of eight! He still plays the original hi-hats Robbie gave him around that time. Of course, he also cut his teeth on all the Steve Upton parts to our songs, playing along to our early records at home, but it was this direct interaction with Robbie that truly fired his imagination in a hands-on way.

In July 1990, Steve Upton left Wishbone Ash. He had been having a hard time during the recording of the album because the drum booth was in a barn, away from the main house. We ran recording lines out to it but he was isolated physically as well as psychologically, and I think he found that difficult in a way that he hadn't at any other time except perhaps during the *Raw To The Bone* sessions. He swore that there was a time lag in the sound because there was so much cabling involved—which was simply not possible.

He couldn't fit in with the grooves we were laying down. Things at home in Surrey had finally come to a head. It was all going horribly wrong for him. Steve would bottle things up a lot and one day the cork just blew out.

I remember him walking into the kitchen saying, 'I'm going.' He had his big Jaguar V12 E-type parked out in the yard. As he walked determinedly through the farm kitchen toward the car, I said, 'What's going on?' In what was clearly a very symbolic gesture he gave me the red ledger in which he always kept everything immaculately ordered, always using an italic pen. In fact he thrust it into my arms. That was it. He left, and I was not to see him again until only very recently—in court, sad to say. It was extraordinary— extraordinary from a man who had shown such a sense of responsibility in everything he did, from keeping the books to time-keeping to driving us for all those years to looking out for our general welfare and everything else. He never formally dissolved anything—he just left. Everyone was gobsmacked. This man who had been a few years older than me, and who had never known his own father, had actually been something of a role model and father figure to me especially, just as Miles Copeland had been to him. But now he simply upped and left. I called Steve several times after this and on one particular occasion attempted to meet with him but he simply closed the door on all of us.

This 'father figure' archetype was something I often pondered in the band. It had been a strong theme. Ted and I had been the babies in the band, while Martin and especially Steve had been our elders or seniors, setting examples, sometimes good and sometimes bad; Miles in turn had been the big daddy to all of us, even though he had his own issues and private relationships to work through. A three- or four-year age difference is a big deal when you yourself are only nineteen. Steve leaving was a line in the sand that broke the spell and allowed me in particular to cast off these constrictive and by now irrelevant bonds. I was to revisit the father theme a couple of years later in the lyric I wrote to the song 'Mountainside', which appeared on the album *Illuminations*, and again in the song 'Tales Of The Wise'.

I should have seen the signs. Steve was deeply unhappy. He was smoking a lot of hash and drinking a lot of Cognac in his room on his own at night. In hindsight, it was all there to see. I knew he'd already had problems playing on albums before as a drummer because the whole role of drums in rock music changed massively in the 80s. Drummers now had to play in perfect time. Drum machines had made this huge leap forward—you never really knew if it was a real player or a machine on the recordings. And that wasn't Steve's style. His sense of time would move a lot—it had a freedom to it that we can now all recognise as being a great thing, a unique style and feel. But the whole record-making industry had become so rigid about drums. Steve must have felt as though every facet of his life was going wrong. Still to this day I don't really know what the full story was. At best, my theories are just that: my theories.

Miles was consumed with other projects, but around the time of Steve's exit he bought Chateau de Marouaette in the south of France. He needed someone to manage the extensive grounds and called me up, aware that my younger brother Len was a trained horticulturist who had studied alongside Britain's most famous garden expert, Alan Titchmarsh.

'Do you think Len would do it?' he asked.

'I don't think so. I don't think this is for Len. But I know who *could* do it—Steve Upton.'

'Yeah, I've thought about Steve. I'm worried about him. Would you recommend him?'

'Well, he's been at my house here for a while—we've got a couple of acres and he's been doing estate management in a way, growing vegetables and so on. He's a man of the earth. He likes growing things, and he's managed the band's day-to-day affairs meticulously for years.'

'You think he could do it?'

'Yes, I'd personally endorse him for that. It could be the saving of him.'

'Yeah, I think I will call him.'

I didn't know how long it was going to last, but it was a place for Steve to go. As far as I know he spent many I hope happy years at the chateau and may even still be there.

Nevertheless, as seismic and profound as Steve's leaving was, and whatever we could or should have done to help him, we were committed to delivering a record. He'd actually reneged on his contractual commitment to do that, leaving us in the lurch. We ended up getting Ray Weston and

Robbie France in to finish the album, and we soldiered on as we always did. Robbie joined us for a tour of Britain at the end of the year and then Ray joined permanently. They were two very different players, and that was actually only a good thing. It opened the music up and showed me that anything was possible. For a brief period we brought in this contact of Ted's, Hana Cunningham, as a kind of manager. Not a good idea. Like in the movie *Spinal Tap* where the band leader's girlfriend tries to get in on record production, uttering the famous phrase 'More Dobly, please', Hana was completely out of her depth, knowing nothing of the music business.

I didn't want to take over the band's management—I still just wanted to be a band member—but I was already in a way managing lots of things by default: the house, the budget, the album recording. I had the energy for all of this. I was already the manager and producer in all but name, although I was probably in denial about it.

Strange Affair, the third and last of the 'reunion albums', was released in April 1991 and really was a strange affair in every sense. For most of that year, which included our first trip to Japan since the 70s, Wishbone Ash comprised Ted, Martin, Ray Weston, and me. Ray was someone who'd originally played with Martin during his solo phase. I got on really well with him. He had a good feel for the band, knew the band's music really well, so it was a natural fit. This was around the time Miles was stepping back. I don't know when he sold IRS to EMI, but EMI started distributing the label in 1990. (I believe IRS folded as a distinct brand in 1996.)

It felt to me, after the third reunion album and Steve's departure, that a phase was coming to an end. I think there was a similar feeling amongst all three of the original members. And at that point—in October 1991 to be precise—I had a second confrontation with Martin—not at anyone's house but over the phone this time.

Ted and I had pretty much conspired together that we wanted the band to carry on but without Martin. So it fell to me, of course, to call him. I can't remember if we felt he was losing interest or wondered if he was serious enough about touring. But that wasn't at the heart of our decision. He just did not seem to have any fire left in his belly. On a personal level I never really got on with Martin. If things were not going according to his agenda he could be really patronising. We were never friends. Neither of us ever looked out for each other in the way that Steve and I had. Thinking back, I can barely count on the fingers of one hand the number of times he actually called me about anything in all the years we worked together. It was always me calling him.

Wishbone Ash, for me, was a long-term career, and if at all possible you want to be involved with people you can get along with. It was very much a grown-up decision: it's got to be clean cut, it can't be this wishy-washy thing; it can't be, to use one of Martin's favourite phrases, 'Now you see me, now you don't'; it can't be game-playing. And if there was one person who was always playing games, it was Martin. So my feeling at this point was, if Wishbone Ash is going to carry on, and if I'm going to carry on with Wishbone Ash, it ain't going to be with Martin.

I called him up, with Ted's backing, and said something to the effect of, 'We're going to carry on … and you're not.' This time it really was actually quite brutal, but it happens that way sometimes. Martin seemed to take it on board without much protest. I remember thinking that in order to fire someone, that person has to buy into the fact that they are being fired. That, at the time, was exactly what he did. That's the way I remember it. The really unfortunate thing was that all this actually took place on Martin's birthday. Sadly, I never realised this at the time.

In many ways, Miles had formed the band. It wasn't a bunch of existing friends. We did push forward this fake 'band of brothers' thing a bit, and certainly in America people seemed to think Martin and Ted were brothers because of the shared surname. Steve and I were the two blond guys; Martin and Ted were darker. There's always some contrivance in marketing bands, and after a while you often grow into those roles—you become a band and work on a collective image. But for me the band's name, the entity of the band, was always bigger than the sum of its collective parts. Some people are 'band people'—team players, like the guys I'm with now. And I didn't see that in Martin at the end of the 80s. I didn't get that feeling. 'Well, you know,' he'd often say, 'I'm really a producer.' There seemed to be this need to put himself apart from or above the rest of us.

On one occasion, which must have been in the middle of 1991, he said to me, in his latter-day 'mockney' accent, having ditched the Devonshire burr a long time ago, 'Look, you know Andy, me old mate, rock's dead, innit? It's gone.' I thought this was a bit strange, not least because rocker Bryan Adams was at number 1 in the charts with 'Everything I Do' at that point. But in Martin's head, rock was a thing of the past. For me, Wishbone Ash is bigger than any individual. I was taking a mature look at it all in deciding that we had to move on without Martin, and in time I believe I was proved right. Martin didn't take it well but he didn't put up any fight. He was ambivalent, it seemed.

There will, I'm sure, be people reading this who'll see me as the bad guy here, people who'll think we didn't have enough cause to cut Martin out of the band's future. It's unlikely I can say anything else that will convince them otherwise. I could draw attention to Martin's walkout in 1980 and the fact that the reunion was only ever meant to be a short-term exercise—a self-contained project within what Steve and I were doing as the residual keepers of the flame. But ultimately it's like this: if you're in a workplace that has a lot of issues for you, people you struggle to get on with, game-playing from colleagues, a lack of certainty that's constantly nagging away at you and likely to affect your company's long-term prospects, would you not finally do something about it? Would you not leave and go somewhere else, where other peoples' issues aren't dragging you down—or, if you're in a position to do so, would you not find a way of removing the individual who's at the root of the issues, and then transfer them to another branch or choose not to renew their contract when it's up?

People have a rose-tinted idea about bands but one thing they are, which one can never get away from, is a workplace with a small set of individuals within it. And, inevitably, the time will come when those individuals will have exhausted their capacity to work together in a positive, pleasurable, and productive way. That's simply what happened between Martin and me, and at the time Ted agreed that we would be better off returning him to the world of producing.

* * *

The whole Wishbone Ash reunion, the No Speak label, the Night of the Guitar tours—they were all part of the swansong of Miles Copeland in the music business. He cashed out. We didn't realise at the time that we were part of that process. But all power to him—it gave us a four-year boot up the backside and produced three more albums.

Andy Pyle came back in on bass and, with Ray Weston on drums, Ted and I soldiered on for another two years, up to December 1993. I'd already been co-writing with Andy so it was a natural thing. As a bass player he was nothing like Martin but I knew it could work, despite him having little respect for Ray, as it turned out. A veteran of so many bands like The Kinks and Rod Stewart and so on, Andy would often refer to Ray as 'the boy.' It was not the best relationship for a rhythm section but I was largely oblivious to these inter-band tensions. Andy prided himself on his punctuality and general professionalism. He'd always be there with his vintage Fender bass in hand, together with a small gig bag—a perfectly self-contained if somewhat aloof individual. One great story involving Andy was on the occasion of some tour dates in California. We were on our way to Carmel, an exquisite little enclave on the beach where the town's mayor at that time was Clint Eastwood. He was also the owner of a well-known local tavern called the Hog's Breath Inn. We were joking with each other on the way there about how amazing it would be to actually bump into Clint during our day off in Carmel and were determined to visit the Hog's Breath, not really believing for a minute that it might come to pass.

Well, we got to the place after checking into the Inn at Carmel, a wonderful old-world-style hotel, and ordered a round of beers. It was nice enough and the ambience was relaxing. Suddenly the conversation level in the bar seemed to rise excitedly. We looked around and there, larger than life, accompanied by his equally large assistant, was Clint himself. He loped up to the bar—his bar—and hunched down, cowboy style, propping himself up on his elbows, looking like a feature in one of his famous westerns. We couldn't believe it. The level of female excitement in the place could now hardly be contained but it was still pretty respectful.

'I'm going to introduce myself to him,' Andy said.

We were like, 'Nooooo, don't blow it, Andy.' But before we could contain him, he's standing next to Clint, seemingly in deep conversation, and they are sharing a round of beers. After a while, Clint and his sidekick decide to leave, and Andy is walking out the door with them, his trusty Fender Precision bass guitar slung over his shoulder. We're all agog at this point.

The next morning as we rendezvoused at the tour bus, Andy was there, prompt as usual, bass and gig bag in place, looking right as rain. We eagerly asked him where he had gone with Clint. It turned out they'd all gone back to the homestead and sat up all night playing songs—British music-hall songs like 'My Old Man Said Follow The Van', 'Knees Up Mother Brown', and so on. Clint, a fair piano player himself, apparently knew all this stuff, and Andy happily accompanied him on bass. We asked how he'd managed to introduce himself to Clint and apparently he'd simply said, 'Hello, my name is Andy Pyle and I come from Tring in England.' To this, Clint had replied, 'Well, I only know one other Pyle and that would be the TV character known as Gomer Pyle.' After that, it was plain sailing, apparently, and now Andy has a unique story to tell of hanging out for an evening at home with one of Hollywood's biggest actors and directors.

The reunion boost had certainly begun to wane by now but there was still a lot of work in both the US and Europe. In a way, the will and momentum to carry on was buoyed by the fact that work was being offered. It's the old thing: a tour comes in, you look at it and think, *Mmm ...* These opportunities are strong motivators.

In January 1992 we recorded *The Ash Live In Chicago*, which was, as it said on the tin, a live album recorded in Chicago. Well, actually the location was in the greater Chicago metropolitan area, in a place called something I no longer remember. Coincidentally, this would be Ted's last album as a member of the band. It would be released by the cynically named Permanent Records in Britain and then released again and again and again by everyone and his dog—possibly the worst contract we ever signed. I'd naively presented it to the rest of the band members before really checking things out in detail. Other artists on the label, like Donovan, would be victims to the same practice. I'd known the owner as the guy who had promoted us at Hammersmith Odeon and now he had a record label. None of us got paid for the subsequent licensing of that disc and, even worse, the guys held me accountable for it. I was getting a taste of what Miles had gone through with the Star Truckin' deal: being held accountable by the very guys I was trying to do something for. That was another big lesson. The worst thing about these kinds of lessons is that they involve music that goes on for all time, so you are reminded of the situation over and over again.

Ted was living in Chicago, I was in Connecticut. I don't think Ted was doing much music of his own volition, even though he had a recording setup that had been bought for him by a mutual friend, Fred Wornock, owner of the Beaumont Bar & Grill on Halstead in Chicago, where we were later to stage a fan club convention, US-style. By that time I was writing songs with Roger Filgate and we were meeting on a weekly basis—because we were neighbours and mates—in Connecticut. I introduced Roger to Ted. We both flew out to Chicago with the idea that we would put a studio album together. Roger had been doing a little bit of crewing for us on an American tour, once famously losing an entire rented drum set that had been poorly secured to the roof of a van. He was obviously not cut out for crewing. The idea started to evolve that Roger would become one of the writers, which was a much better use of his talents. It was not the case that Roger was going to be a third guitar player or anything like that. We had this one song, 'On Your Own', which later ended up on *Illuminations*, and Ted had these lyrics, 'Hanging By My Fingernails'—which should have told us something.

I think 'On Your Own' was the only thing we worked on as a trio, although Ted did come out to Connecticut to play with us under the joint assumed name Tossed Salad in the barn that was serving as our demo studio. It was on the occasion of a garden party hosted by the owner, local artist Don Messer. I think it was during this period that Ted stayed with Pauline and me at our Connecticut home and, weirdly, we got into chopping down trees on my property to expose the view of the valley. I remember Ted really going for that, and of course it was a great help. Shortly after that he sent me a letter saying that he was resigning from the band, and, by the way, he didn't like the way that I was handling the finances …

In retrospect, maybe I just wasn't communicating enough about the band finances to Ted. I was doing a lot and he wasn't, and the balance just wasn't right for him. If we had had a third-party manager handling the business, the equilibrium might have been restored, but I think the geography, and probably the different approaches to life and to the band as a career, would have taken their natural toll in the end. I was, by now, not averse to using my own money to bankroll various travel arrangements and projects on behalf of the band—something I doubted anyone else was prepared to do.

If it seems that I was taking on all the weight of keeping the good ship Wishbone afloat, it was not without the help of certain individuals who, while not directly investing, were acting as mentors and guiding me in a solid direction forward. Chief among them was Leon Tsilis, our one-time promotions man at MCA. We'd always kept in touch through the years, since he was personally invested in many of our releases at the label, having been with us in the studio during recording and then later galvanising his team in the field to promote the band. He had, like us, also logged a lot of road miles.

Leon was becoming enthralled with the idea of the internet and the new possibilities it offered the music business and, being a keen programmer, was about to give the band the greatest gift of all: our own website. This debuted in 1994, making us one of the first bands to have one, and it was to be a game-changer, acting as a one-stop information source for everything to do with our long career, as well as a key place to find out about new events soon to take place.

As Leon ramped up his new activities as a programmer and web designer, my oldest son, Richard, was doing the same, having been born into the Nintendo generation and gaining his inspiration from the new digital world that way. He was always nagging us to buy our first Apple Mac, back in the day. Now he set about revamping the site, working alongside Leon for a while until his own business started to really take off. These days, Joe Crabtree and I make small updates to our website, but the original format has served us extremely well.

In the meantime, our last gig had been in Vienna on December 20 1993. A whole year and more would pass before any entity known as Wishbone Ash would once more grace a stage anywhere in the world. I stared out of a window in Connecticut and pondered the chances of the phoenix ever rising again.

OTHER PEOPLE'S MUSIC

People are always asking me, 'Was life on the road and recording in all these interesting and sometimes exotic places in the 70s quite as rock'n'roll as one would have you believe?' If it's an open-minded person asking the question, I'll usually answer, 'Actually, yes, it was.'

When you're wrapped up in your own thing, criss-crossing continents with a load of ambition, you don't always have time to see everything else that's going on in the music world around you. The party is the thing. That was certainly the case in the 70s. Aside from shared bills and festivals, I didn't always get a chance to hear what my peers were up to. Even with the *Melody Maker* poll-winners concert at the Oval in 1971, where we received an award for having the Top British Album, we arrived late and missed the ceremony. Jack Bruce was there; Rod Stewart was there in a beautiful Lamborghini car. Oh, the glamour of it all! And where were we? Getting dazed and confused, courtesy of our tour manager Rod Lynton, who himself was stoned out of his box, lost on the streets of London. We missed our presentation and were thereby perceived to have snubbed the press and bitten the hand that was feeding us.

The truth is, fans and collectors of 70s rock, then and now, sometimes have a fuller picture of that world than I do, and I was there—physically, at least. But having said that, I've always tried to be a keen listener to other people's music. Sometimes your own thing becomes all-consuming, or you lose the 'fan' side of interest in music. Thankfully I've always had it: I'm still a fan. I can get really excited about a new artist or new music if it is brave and individualistic.

Even in the frenzy of Wishbone Ash activity in the 70s, I still managed to see and hear a lot of other artists. Some amazing future stars opened for us along the way, and now and again I got a chance to see someone else's show as a paying customer as well. The funny thing is, if people ask me today, 'Do you remember playing Bristol in 1972?' I might, with the best will in the world, have to disappoint them. But at the same time, I could tell them all about seeing, say, Little Feat at the Hammersmith Odeon in London around that time. The memories of being a fan and a performer are stashed in two different compartments in the mind.

Thinking back to the bands that had an impact on me, whether musically or in terms of what I could learn from them in a performing sense, these are some of my most memorable gigs from the past six decades, both as a punter in the audience or from the side of the stage as an onlooker. As you run through the names of all these amazing artists, there's something to learn from all of them. If you wanted to hear the best guitar playing in the world, there was Hendrix, Clapton, Peter Green. If vocal harmonies were your bag, try The Hollies. Hammond Organ? It doesn't get any better than Keith Emerson. Songwriting? Try Paul McCartney. Stagecraft? The Who, KISS, Alice Cooper. My generation was satiated—we had it all as audiences, and I still have to pinch myself because I was living it too, often in the eye of the musical storm. It was thrilling.

* * *

In 1959, I was standing at my cousin's wedding as a nine-year-old, watching the guitarist in the wedding band. He was playing a giant red guitar. It was a Gibson, I believe: a semi-acoustic model, double cutaway. It was the colour and the shininess that got me. These things were meant to be noticed. We take all this flashiness for granted these days. Everything is like that in rock'n'roll now, but when I saw this musical instrument up close at that time it was like an artefact from another planet. I was captivated. Vox amplifiers, the twang and the volume: it hit me like a revelation.

In the 60s, as a young musician learning the craft I can vividly recall Geno Washington, The Small Faces, The Birds, The Creation, The Action, Steampacket, Graham Bond, Amen Corner, Alexis Korner, Gary Farr & The T-Bones, The High Numbers, and Spencer Davis.

Between the ages of fourteen and eighteen, my weekends were all about working hard and then going to hear and experience the music of the day while learning how to carry myself among my peers. You were allowed to work all hours at age fourteen and for me, after that on a Saturday night it was a trip by train or bus to Watford, where our stomping ground was the Watford Trade Hall. There were all these great acts: the cream of British R&B during the 60s played there. People danced or moved to the music, everyone smoked. The atmosphere was electric and we soaked it all in. The beatnik Graham Bond Organisation and the odd spectacle of Graham with his black clothes and slicked down hair and Fu Man Chu moustache, backed by Ginger Baker, Dick Heckstall-Smith, and Jack Bruce. Who knew he would, years later, fall in front of a tube train on the London Underground? Mind the gap, indeed.

I recall the young prodigy Steve Winwood in The Spencer Davis Group. He was no older than we were, yet had a voice from the Delta. How could he sing that way, like a black man? Was he possessed? We didn't know. We just raved to 'Gimme Some Lovin'' and 'Keep On Running'. Having a rave-up was genuinely how we described our musical adventures, particularly if it involved dancing. There were pills around and beer, of course. The girls drank rum and blackcurrant and that was about it. There was often a menace in the air. Mod violence spawned by jealousy, if someone had a particularly nice suit or a particularly attractive girl on an arm. Where did they get the money? A frequently used phrase was 'Who are you screwing?'—meaning not who were you having sex with but who are you staring at. You kept your eyes averted unless you wanted to challenge. I once made the mistake of staring and was taken outside the dance hall and threatened with a knife. These were the kinds of chaps who would take great pleasure in stubbing their cigarettes out on your forehead if you displeased them.

My mates and I spent all the money we made in our weekend jobs on sharp clothes. We were all desperately trying to look and act older than we were. You had to have attitude, a furrowed brow, a slight sneer. That was really your protection. Later on, I became a big fan of more foppish bands like The Birds (the English Birds), a heavier act with a young Ron Wood playing bass, along with The Creation and their song 'Makin' Time'. Things were getting musically heavier, while the image portrayed from the stage was becoming more fey and flamboyant. A particular favourite of mine was The Action. All these London bands—including, of course, The High Numbers—were driven by heavy rhythm guitar. I loved that. The power chord ruled, though it was not known as such in those days.

* * *

Nineteen sixty-seven was a particularly important year. It was the Summer of Love, after all. It was going full force in San Francisco, of course, and elements of it all were filtering across the Atlantic. I spent the summer going to rock festivals, culminating in the Windsor Jazz & Blues Festival. Undoubtedly this was the fullest musical awakening for me. It was pretty clear to me that music was the game I wanted to be in. How could anything stack up to the euphoria created by these bands in the audiences that I was a part of? Only one answer: my own band, or least one that I was an equal part of.

I was in the audience at Cream's first gig. I remember Eric Clapton striding through the audience, wearing beads, Indian clothes, and a wild Afro. He did indeed look like a god—as the graffiti around London was proclaiming at the time. When Peter Green's Fleetwood Mac finished their set in the tent stage at the same festival I was in the front row and, at the tender age of seventeen, defied the security to leap up onstage and personally drag him back on for an encore. He was laughing in the euphoria, and they did exactly that. What a band! It was the same with The Nice. Keith Emerson was stabbing knives into his Hammond organ, manhandling it all over the stage while playing their magnum opus, 'America'. It was amazing stuff—all this new music being played by virtuosos, the best that their generation of white musicians had to offer, and it was all right here in our backyard for our exclusive enjoyment.

I was lucky enough to see Jimi Hendrix live on two occasions: once at an open air concert at Woburn Abbey, one of Britain's venerable stately homes, and the other time at London's Royal Festival Hall. On that occasion, I remember Hendrix had all his Marshall cabinets laid down on their backs, pointing up at the ceiling. This was obviously to help with the sound separation in the venue, which is more attuned to classical recitals. It was a strange atmosphere of youth culture meeting 'the Establishment', and there was Jimi at the centre of it all, in all his finery.

I remember at one point a young female audience member got up out of her seat to go the ladies' room or something. Jimi stopped the band and using his wah-wah pedal created a soundtrack to her shimmying down the stairs. It was funny and endearing, and it broke the tension—a spontaneous inspiration which was pure Jimi. He very definitely responded to whatever was going on around him, like the time he ditched his planned song selection on the *Happening For Lulu* TV show, jumping straight into 'Sunshine Of Your Love' by Cream instead.

* * *

In the UK, we were finagling ourselves onto bills with Yes, Fleetwood Mac, Deep Purple, and Colosseum, as well as having other acts doing the same with us, like Tyrannosaurus Rex and Skid Row, the latter featuring a wild young guitar player, Gary Moore. The mentality if you were a guitar player then was much like it is now: a kind of gunslinger mentality. You needed balls and a lot of front if you were going to stand out from the large number of great players that were appearing on the scene. Very quickly I realised that trial by fire was the only way to get noticed—after all, I'd been playing since I was eleven years of age, for God's sake, so why not put myself to the test at any opportunity? That's how I approached playing live with Wishbone Ash: it was do or die. I'm sure we all felt like this. My solos were starting to gain attention on our early records and, most importantly, I had my own sound, the vibrato and the ecstatic way of playing. I had mojo. I felt it. I couldn't control it. It was my soul, my voice coming to the fore.

Pretty soon I had the opportunity to do something that would prove very crucial in getting Wishbone Ash established as a band on the global stage. We got the opportunity to open a show at Dunstable Civic in England for Deep Purple. I wasn't particularly a fan of Purple; I'd found them a bit contrived when they'd appeared at the Windsor Jazz & Blues festival all wearing identical purple shirts with frills down the front. I mean, could anyone imagine Cream and Eric Clapton doing that, or being told to do that by a manager? Cream had a flamboyant style, but it was a style of their own. Purple did not. They had a bloody good guitar player and singer, though, and they had already had a US Top 10 hit with a great song, 'Hush'.

Around four in the afternoon, Ritchie Blackmore was onstage, trying out his gear by himself. It's the usual thing: a guitar player is making so much noise, checking this amp and that amp, that the rest of the band were staying out of earshot in the dressing room. He had one slot in the set that required him to dispense with the Marshalls and plug in to a Vox A.C.30 that would be wheeled onstage. During all this preparation, I slipped behind my gear and plugged in my SG Special. Ritchie would play a lick and then make an adjustment to the amp controls ... except that he'd hear a version of his guitar lick coming back to him. Looking round, he'd see me there cheekily starting a musical conversation with him. Everyone says that Ritchie is a difficult man but all credit to him, he got into the game and we had a great time. I don't know if he remembers it or not, but later in the evening he checked out our set and asked if we had a recording contract. I answered in the negative and he said he'd recommend us to their producer Derek Lawrence.

This was a huge deal. Miles followed up with Derek, who gave him the name of a certain Don Shane out on the West Coast. Don was the head of Decca Records. Miles made all the various overtures to him, and not too long afterwards we all got to meet Don in the States when he attended one of our shows. At any rate, we signed with the label. It was a very, very good deal for us. Unlike a lot of British bands who would sign in London to a subsidiary of an American label, or even a home-grown indie like Chrysalis, we were going right to the mountain—and the mountain came to us. Having an American manager at this point was golden. Miles talked the talk and walked the walk with these guys. We were in business.

* * *

Pretty soon we were touring the States. Endlessly. We were being exposed to all these great American acts and immersing ourselves in the wider culture, and our music was being played on the newly burgeoning FM radio stations. John Peel, an early champion of ours back in England on the BBC, knew all about this, since he'd done a long stint in Texas with his own radio show during the 60s before moving back home. The musical freedom was amazing. It was simply intoxicating. Youth culture ruled. We'd got off to a shaky start with the touring but pretty soon we'd be sharing bills with midwestern rockers like Bob Seger, REO Speedwagon, and Kansas. The Doobie Brothers thrilled me, and then we'd tour through the South and Texas, joining bands like The Allman Brothers, Wet Willie, Black Oak Arkansas, and of course ZZ Top, who at that time were like a college band with short, preppie haircuts, no stage presence but killer blues grooves. Their guitar player, Billy Gibbons, had a beautiful late-50s Les Paul. They'd open for us now but later on we'd be opening for them and the whole thing had changed. Nudie suits, rhinestones, ten-gallon hats—but no beards yet.

One act that opened for us was Grin, from Baltimore, fronted by a great guitar player by the name of Nils Lofgren. He had a great Stratocaster tone and his voice was cool; great songs, too. I immediately became a fan and bought his records. Nils was a former gymnast, and he'd have a small trampoline set up onstage and do these flips in the middle of playing a guitar solo. Beat that! These Americans certainly knew stagecraft. Later he was to join another act that opened for us, Bruce Springsteen. Yes: Bruce opened for Wishbone Ash. As I remember it, he and his E-Street crew just seemed like a gutsy bar band. Never in a million years would I have thought they'd have what it took to stand out from the crowd.

One really amazing tour we played was opening for Alice Cooper. He had two pretty good guitar players, Dick Wagner and Steve Hunter. Alice (or Vince, as we called him) was super nice to us, a real gentleman. His show was amazing and we lapped it up each night. He had total control of these huge arenas. Sure, we'd known acts like Screaming Lord Sutch in the UK with his macabre antics, and then there was dear old Arthur Brown, the first real heavy metal singer, whose 1968 hit 'Fire' was a presage of what was to come. But Alice took it all and simply put it on steroids, with lighting effects, big stage props, and a great band. Pretty soon, we noticed more twin-lead guitar ideas coming into their music. That was cool, too.

When we hit the West Coast, we'd be booked at the Fillmore West. Just walking into that place was amazing. There was so much weed being smoked that you could not see through it across the audience, and pretty soon you'd be stoned on it all yourself. Acts like Harvey Mandel, Poco, and the Siegel-Schwall Band opened for us. When we hit the stage with 'Blind Eye' it was as if the whole crowd received an electric shock. Our form of dynamic rock, with all its light and shade, really woke the hippies up. It was great.

During the summers we often played state fairs and often, just like today, there would be blues bands on the bills. We got to see many of them close up because blues was not really mainstream at this time and again, like heavy metal and theatrical rock, you could not have predicted how big it would become again. Albert Collins, BB King, and John Lee Hooker were all there for the watching and learning. We were getting a great further education in music.

* * *

Back in London, between tours we were doing a lot of socialising. Miles's middle brother, Ian, had left the army after his stint in Vietnam and was in London partying like there was no tomorrow, while working up a position for himself in the booking agency Miles and John Sherry had formed called Pytheon Productions/JSA. Pretty soon, Ian took over from Ed Bicknell as chief booker. Ed had really discovered us and later had Dire Straits dumped in his lap after no one really knew what to do with them. He became their manager, and the rest is history. He'd been the only actual representative from the agency who'd come to hear us at Miles's basement rehearsal space at his home in Marlborough Place, St John's Wood.

Ian moved into this amazing house in Hampstead, London, which was shaped like an ocean liner sitting on a hill. Also sharing the apartment was Al Stewart's manager, Luke O'Reilly. Living in the flat below were Errol Brown and some of the guys from Hot Chocolate. Pauline and I were often there. Ian was a toker and knew how to throw the most amazing parties. The music was always key to it all. Great sounds. It was through Ian that I discovered The Isley Brothers and studied James Brown in depth.

One night Robert Palmer called by. I think he'd just been to New Orleans, recording with this band he told me about called Little Feat. We'd met Robert before when he was in Vinegar Joe with Elkie Brooks, touring with us in the

States. This Little Feat music completely took hold of me. I wanted more of their swampy groove. Pretty soon, Allen Toussaint was in the picture, and Dr John, The Night Tripper, but Robert had sussed it out before anyone in London, and he'd actually got the Feat to back him up on his solo debut, *Sneaking Sally Through The Alley*. I was a paying customer when Little Feat played their legendary show at Hammersmith Odeon, our favourite London venue, and I became a fan for life. I loved everything about them—the drums of Richie Hayward, Bill Payne's keyboards, Lowell George's slide playing, and most of all his songwriting. This was the real deal.

Years earlier, we'd had a Scottish Band called Glencoe open for us on an early UK tour. They were great. They'd be part of the London scene and Ted, in particular, was friends with them. I believe they were stablemates at the booking agency. In fact, their keyboard player, Graham Maitland, now sadly deceased, was to join us on Fender Rhodes on American tours, which a lot of British fans are unaware of. Wishbone Ash with keyboards: who knew? I sold Onnie McIntyre of The Average White Band a great black Telecaster that I believe his bandmate Hamish Stewart later acquired. He still plays it to this day, or at least he did when I saw him in Paul McCartney's band years later.

During the latter half of the 70s, a lot of the acts I've just mentioned were really getting into their stride, cutting great deals with the labels, and we'd once again be joining them on shows. One such band was Aerosmith, who were getting hit singles and had really ratcheted up their stagecraft. Steven Tyler, who had been a sulky lead singer in the early days, had transformed himself into a frontman par excellence, as had Bruce Springsteen; ZZ Top, in particular, had their presentation down like no one else. We joined one of their tours in Texas at that point and were amazed to see this whole travelling menagerie backstage, including a buffalo and a bald eagle.

Flashiness and stage antics had always been a part of the blues but these bands took it to new heights of swagger, spectacle, and wit. Laurie and I took it all on board. While we'd dabbled in spectacle on our *Number The Brave* tour, with its giant set, props, staircases, and raised walkways, the Americans were beating us at our own game. Only The Greatest Rock'n'Roll Band On Earth, Britain's Rolling Stones, did it better.

ZZ's take on the blues definitely had a musical impact on our album *Twin Barrels Burning*. You can hear their influence on songs like 'Engine Overheat'. Not much English Pastoral in that one. That album, along with *Raw To The Bone* featuring Mervyn Spence on bass and vocals, revealed a much more muscular, heavy side of Wishbone Ash. It was all a long way from the feel of *Argus*, which I still felt was our true direction, and so did the fans. But a new generation of rock fans were coming of age, and they did not want any ambiguity or subtlety.

Around this time Cliff Williams, Laurie's mate from his first band, Home, had gone to auditions in London. He'd wanted to be in a country-rock act but now had to settle with being offered a job in a heavy rock band with a couple of diminutive Australian brothers in a band called AC/DC. They would also soon be taking the rock spectacle to new heights. All of this was feeding into the mix of what we were doing at this time. It was the zeitgeist, but somehow I didn't feel all that comfortable with it. We were behind the curve, whereas during the early 70s we'd been ahead of the curve, influencing bands like Thin Lizzy, Judas Priest, and Iron Maiden—yet to come of age but soon to be at the forefront of the New Wave of British Heavy Metal.

* * *

Wishbone's line-up changed around quite a bit during the 80s. Music itself was becoming self-conscious and reconstituting itself. On the one hand, you had all these new young rock acts wanting to outdo the guitar-based bands that had influenced them, and then you had the hipper outfits like The Fixx, Level 42, Nik Kershaw—all still rock but with a sheen of sophistication about them, not least in the new digital technology that they were harnessing on record and using to present their live shows. I don't think we fitted into either camp at this time, despite dabbling with metal and playing shows with acts like Ted Nugent and Metallica. We were out of step with the times, and the albums we produced reflected this.

It was a blessing in a way that the original band did reform and produce those three albums on IRS Records because it gave me breathing space—a chance to live a little and to think about the bigger picture.

There's nothing like having an on-going recording contract. Throughout history, artists have benefitted from patronage, and we had that for a while before we imploded again.

Of late, as I've entered my mature years, my taste in rock music has erred firmly toward song-based material, often by bands working the Americana seam. Much of this stems from when I'm at home. There are few really good rock radio stations in the North East and those that do play rock tend to be so hopelessly stuck in the past that I simply can't tune in. (If I hear one more Zeppelin tune on the radio I'll go crazy.) So I tune in to college radio stations. Most of the hipper jocks who used to be on FM stations now work for WFUV out of New York and their blend is distinctly white alt.rock and Americana, plus the occasional track by older artists like John Hiatt and Neil Young.

This all tends to frame my tastes when I'm home and don't wish to search too hard on the internet. I also listen to radio stations from Canada, as I find the French vocal approach very soothing. I'm looking to be soothed, I guess. Bands like Arcade Fire have recently kicked me out of my stupor, and we went to see them perform last summer in Bridgeport, Connecticut. My son Aynsley, who lives in Brooklyn, turns me on to new music, including his friends in bands like MGMT and Lucius.

Some of this white-bread, music-college spawn can bland you out, though, and before long I'm straight back to the blues. I always come back to Little Feat or Frank Zappa or something. I know it's the same for the other members of the band. When it comes to rock, it's hard to top what went down back in the 50s, 60s, and 70s.

CHAPTER 7

HARD TIMES
(1994–99)

The end of 1993 marked a point in time where the band consisted of me, a co-writer, and a creed of positivity with which to sustain us. All the other members had left, sometimes with unfinished work in progress and personal commitments, both financial and creative, discarded in the name of self-preservation. One could be forgiven for conjuring up an image of me standing like a captain on the bridge of a sinking ship, watching as even the rats were scurrying off into the swirling seas of anonymity.

On paper—especially if that piece of paper contains a Wishbone Ash gig list—it might seem as if nothing much happened during 1994. Had I given up the ghost? Not at all. Over the next couple of years the rebirth of Wishbone Ash was certainly a work in progress, but simultaneously lots of stuff was happening in my home life.

It was a period of flux and transition. Even the idea of the '90s' sounded futuristic if you were born in the 50s. It was coming up to the end of a millennium. There was a feeling in the air that anything could happen, and there was a need to get it together. For me it was extremely liberating, because at that point I was in my mid forties: I was still young but I could see I was getting older. I saw a great bumper sticker at the time that said 'Jesus Is Coming—Get Busy' and I just thought, 'Wow—yes!'

To me, the old Wishbone Ash was a distant memory, whereas I was still feeling creative, I still wanted to play guitar—I *needed* to be doing it. The fan base needed us to be doing it, and I would receive numerous requests and encouragement from those quarters. Where I live, we have a famous local venue called the Georgetown Saloon. Back in the 50s and 60s it had been a country & western bar. Living around Westport and Weston in the 70s we'd sometimes come out to this place, which really was out in the boondocks. Local musicians other than myself would stop by and play—guys like Ritchie Blackmore, José Feliciano, even Keith Richards, who would leave his Weston lair in the appropriately named Devil's Den and pop into the club. So in the 90s I was doing open-mic stuff there, keeping my hand in.

One day, I got chatting about music with my insurance agent, Mike Mindel. He said he was a keyboard player and that he was putting a blues band together to be called The Sure Thing. *Oh God*, I thought, *that's so hokey*, but nonetheless I started going down to his place in Fishkill, New York, once a week to rehearse with what turned out to be a great blues band. I met some exciting players there, and there was a whole scene going on there that I hadn't plugged into before.

Having taken on so much of the management of Wishbone Ash in recent years, it was fun to just be a musician again—turning up with my guitar, playing, going home. I made it clear right from the start that the now-renamed Blue Law was to be a side project for me, and that my life with Wishbone Ash would always take precedence. They completely understood this since they, in common with all musicians, had day jobs, other bands, and so on. Our singer Jon Moorehead, for example, worked for an advertising firm, and our bass player, Al Payson, was a studio engineer by day.

I love being in bands and realised that I was missing the whole camaraderie, male-bonding aspect of it, and the music didn't hurt either. It was the same for all of us. Initially, they hit me with thirty-six songs to learn. *What?* I thought *This is work!* After a while there were a couple of gigs a week and then even more, in clubs all up and down the Hudson River. We played three sets a night. I thought I was a road warrior after twenty-five years in a global rock band, but three sets a night? What is *this*? It was hardcore—and at the end of it I'd even get the 'pleasure' of driving home at one o'clock in the morning.

I made a good friend in Al who, these days, plays bass with José Feliciano. As a side note, Al even stood in for Bob Skeat occasionally at Wishbone festival dates. Back in those days, Al managed a studio for a well-known veteran jazz vibes player, Don Elliott. There had been a whole artistic scene in Westport in the 50s and 60s, centred around the actor Paul Newman. I started to meet local musicians and to play gigs in their world. Blue Law was a seven-piece band with horns, with Mike Mindel on a doubtless comprehensively insured organ, and it was great fun, great camaraderie. I loved the music, plus I was playing my old '52 Telecaster every night. It really was back to basics: guitar, amp, back of the car, off to the gig. Most importantly, if this was to be something of a wilderness moment for the good ship Wishbone, I was keeping my chops up.

At the same time, life was getting very busy at home. Pauline and I decided to sell Ivy Lane Farm and buy the house we'd been renting in Connecticut. We had already decided that Pauline, a teacher by profession, would stay at home during the boys' early years. This was especially important now as they all entered the American school system, which we were both unfamiliar with. However, with a growing interest in New England, the area where we were now living, Pauline sought and was offered a part-time position at New Pond Farm, a rural-studies educational facility in our town.

Many a morning found me tramping through snowy woods to help her light fires and prepare for classes about Native Americans, or help set the tree taps for maple sugaring—a wonderful winter pursuit. I was a stranger in a strange land, and I was loving it. When Pauline was offered a permanent teaching position at a local private school I was more than happy to step into her snow boots for a few hours a week. I gamely learned a whole new set of skills, and it was fantastic for me for a while. Again, I made it abundantly clear that I was a musician, and that my profession and work would take precedence, but as long as they could accept my frequent flying trips, I'd love to give it a try.

This was an idyllic time for us, a two-year period of stability full of adventure for the kids and an appreciation of nature. We were getting to know the area and its history, which was so much more accessible and immediate than that of our own. I think this immersion for me in music, and in the culture and history of the old town that we'd found ourselves living in, was truly what we'd been looking for as a family. Without getting too romantic, one is never far away from the old New England traditions in the countryside here, the story of the pilgrims and their tough colonisation of this part of the world. There was just so much to learn. Our town had been named after John Read, who obtained an early grant for land constituting part of the new town. During the war against the British, General Putnam and the Revolutionary Army had actually camped in our town in the winter of 1778–79. The only battle in the state of Connecticut had taken place in Ridgefield, the town next to ours, with Benedict Arnold himself fighting on the side of the Continental Army. The original resident of the town was Chief Chickens Warrups, or Sam Mohawk, as he was sometimes known. As new immigrants ourselves—though not in any way comparing ourselves to those pilgrims of old—it somehow got me really thinking about our immigration to America and the commitment we'd made. We decided to become fully-fledged American citizens.

This gorgeous 250-year-old farm, where I found myself working part-time, had been bought in the 50s by an actress, Carmen Mathews, and I loved the idea of helping out on it. Country life was exactly what I needed at the time. I learned to drive a tractor, bale hay, milk cows, and tackle every kind of farm job you can imagine—and, in addition, I was able to give the kids that visited the farm on school trips very real experiences concerning the natural world and where the food on their tables actually came from. It was truly alarming how little these children knew about the food culture in their country, so it all felt like a very worthy cause. To the kids I became known as Farmer Andy. I was up each day at dawn, doing rock interviews, organising band travel, hustling gigs in the UK, where the time difference worked in my favour, via email and phone, and returning back home after my farm chores at lunchtime in my pick-up truck to communicate with our American agents and labels. I was doing all of this, working harder than I've ever worked in my life, and I was absolutely loving it—no, I was thriving on it all. I was playing evenings in the blues band, being a dad on weekends, mending fences on the farm, cleaning out pigpens, tending to a massive Belgian dray horse, playing open nights at the Saloon, and learning all about the newly important internet.

With three young boys with very active lives to keep organised, whatever they had going on—swimming, theatre productions, football on a Saturday, and of course music lessons—life was hardly dull. It was full on, 24/7, for both Pauline and me, and we loved it. I even became a chaperone on Friday-night school trips to our local ski mountain. Never again: after a few hours skiing, I'm ready to relax, but those kids were ready to party. The bus trips home were uncomfortable, let me tell you. If you've ever had a ride on one of those yellow bone-shaking American school buses full of kids on a sugar high, you'll know exactly what I mean.

* * *

This was an extremely creative and busy time—a wonderful period, a renaissance. It showed me that there is more to life than just being a whingeing musician. That being said, at the same time I was formulating ideas with my neighbour, Roger Filgate, for some kind of forthcoming Wishbone Ash album project.

I'd met Roger when he was working in a local music store, one of four gifted brothers who'd all been brought up single-handedly by their redoubtable mother, the renowned concert pianist Agatha Filgate. I took him on as a crewmember first, during the last months of Ted's tenure. We'd hang out and play guitar together. My youngest son Lawrence took up piano lessons with Aggie, who would often give wonderful musical soirées in her large, bright conservatory full of cosy couches, overlooking a lake and featuring two amazing old Steinway pianos. Visiting Russian virtuosos would perform, tea and cakes would be served, and the Filgate brothers would lighten things up with a Beatles rendition or two, before older brother Wit blew your mind with a banjo piece, complete with mid-song de-tunings. Downtime for Roger and me would involve little fishing expeditions by canoe out on the lake where I would get to understand and experience the blissful summertime in Connecticut, which reaches a peak in mid August, when it seems that the natural world is abuzz with activity: lily pads, bullfrogs, turtles, fish, birds. This place was really getting to me, and I was forming bonds with the countryside that have had a lasting, permanent impact.

We enlisted the help of Tony Kishman, from Tucson, Arizona—a huge fan of the band with whom I'd kept in touch throughout the years. He was always picking my brains about songwriting and recording. By that time he'd done an album in England with Chris Neil—coincidentally, the same guy who had produced Dollar's 'I Want To Hold Your Hand' back in 1979, its groove very similar to Wishbone's version of 'Come On'. Tony was both a singer and a writer. I told him I wanted to go down the route of getting a dedicated singer—namely him—into the band. By way of preparation, Roger and I did a couple of exploratory recordings at Active Studios in New York City with a session guy on bass and Rob Hazard, a Connecticut native, on drums. Tony is actually a fine musician—he plays bass, guitar, and piano—and he eventually came on board as both bassist and vocalist in a live context, with Roger and me on guitars and (on Mervyn Spence's recommendation) a third American, London resident Mike Sturgis, on drums. Before we knew it we had a new band. Mike was an incredible player and all-round great guy with a sunny but direct Wisconsin disposition. He'd toured the world with A-Ha and also played in Asia—but not any version featuring John Wetton.

At one point, before Mike was involved, Tony came down to Connecticut and we played as a trio, with Roger, at a garden party held by a friend, artist/painter Don Messer, who owns a fabulous and huge New England barn. Ted flew in from Chicago and it was a lot of fun. Subsequently this 200-year-old barn became a substitute work studio for Roger and me to write what became the *Illuminations* album. After Ted baled on us, Roger and I set up a demo studio on the upper level where we could throw open the huge upper shutters. Pigeons would fly in and out as we recorded our ideas. Another location we used was an old converted stable block in Norwalk, Connecticut, which had been a feed supplier and a hatchery for some kind of fowl. Not the healthiest of environments, but we took what we could get. I particularly remember us getting into the monster riff in the song 'Mountainside', which had Roger working the Taurus bass pedals and Rob Hazard on drum duties. I'd constructed the lyric while working in the fields at the farm. They came together in one single outpouring, and I memorised them as I worked. Inspired by Steve Upton's battle with fatherhood, the song had, and still has to this day, bags of commitment in every way.

* * *

Shortly after this latest incarnation of Wishbone Ash had been more or less forged we started to get offers of work overseas. As a performing entity, Wishbone Ash was reborn. To be precise, it was reborn for our UK fans at the end of March 1995 at a Leisure Centre in Rotherham, South Yorkshire. This was a venue utilised by the Classic Rock Society in the UK and run by two former police officers, Andy Yates and Martin Hudson. We were very warmly received by an audience that had been mourning the disappearance of lead guitar in rock music of late. We took this as a good sign for the future.

One week later, we found ourselves at a small club in Geneva, recording a live album on digital multitrack while at the same time producing a live TV show performance in a brand new, state-of-the-art, high-definition video format. Once again we were ahead of the competition when it came to using the latest technology. Released almost exactly a year later on our agent Martin Looby's Hengest Records label, *Live In Geneva* contained no new songs but unveiled a whole new sound. And it would mark the start of a whole new chapter for Wishbone Ash.

Toward the end of 1995 there was a point where Tony couldn't make a particular tour in the UK. I was still on speaking terms with Martin Turner so I called him up and asked if he was interested in filling in for Tony, which he was happy to do. It might seem curious that Martin was up for this, given that we'd asked him to leave only a few years earlier. But when he was asked to leave there was no big fight about it—it was really more of a mutual understanding. He wasn't really taking band life seriously, and he didn't really 'believe' at that point. He thought rock music was dying, having picked up on some kind of general feeling in the business. It was getting extremely hard to market 'rock music' as we knew it.

So, with all that in mind, it was very good of him to fill in for Tony at pretty short notice, but it was understood that it was on a contractual basis— it wasn't another reunion. Things did, inevitably, get a bit fuzzy among the fans and in the media. The first thing we did in Britain was Tommy Vance's cable TV show, *The Bridge*, on VH-1. Martin and I were interviewed, and the four of us played a song from *Argus* ('Leaf And Stream') and a song from the still forthcoming *Illuminations* ('The Ring'). Any viewer—and you can see it online—would come away with the impression that Martin and I were both very much still in the band.

Martin didn't make it particularly easy, though. We would turn up at his house in Southfields, near Wimbledon, having agreed to meet at two o'clock for pick-up, and he'd keep us waiting out there in the car for forty-five minutes while he was 'finishing me lunch'. He'd make sure we really paid for his time. You could never get past the ego with him. But at the same time it must have been awkward for him because he was having to eat humble pie, in a way. There were new people involved, there was new music to play. He was not calling the shots. Mike Sturgis in particular was not willing to take his shit, and nor was our agent. I remember a rehearsal session in Putney, his locale, where as usual he arrived late, making some lame excuse about taking his son to a football match. He went straight into berating Mike about what he defined as a 'snotty' snare-drum sound (whatever that meant). Mike was not about to listen to this nonsense as Steve had so patiently done years before, and simply said, in his very direct but polite Midwestern way, while looking down his nose, arching an eyebrow, 'Excuse me?' It spoke volumes, and M.T. was put in his place.

Illuminations was still a work in progress at that point, but during that tour we did try to see if Martin could become a part of the recording process. To explain the thinking behind my strangely inclusive approach is to put the situation in context. I was very mindful of the respect that I wanted to pay Martin, and I was trying to produce an album that would resonate with the fans. Why not open things up to ex-members, just as I had when Ted had started out being involved in the early writing for *Illuminations*, especially someone as important to the DNA of the Ash as Martin?

It didn't work out. We booked a session at John Sherry's new studio by the Thames. Martin came down, having travelled just a few miles from his home while we'd flown over from the States. He arrived with Gary Carter in tow. It was all very awkward, and it was obvious that Gary was fully in Martin's thrall. Martin was grandstanding in front of us all, and young Gary in particular. We watched as he grappled unsuccessfully with the bass parts that we were hitting him with. I believe the song was 'Top Of The World'. Martin was waffling on about having pulled the bass out from under his staircase, having not played it for years. He was actually boasting about this. Roger looked on at his one-time idol, mouth widening in disbelief at what was going on here. He'd imagined Martin would be the epitome of professionalism, not some bumbling oaf. John Sherry, who'd set up the session and was now keen to try to find a new deal for the band he'd managed, was understandably nonplussed. Personally, I was mightily miffed, and this only confirmed my feelings through the years that no real serious involvement with Martin would ever be possible again.

* * *

Live In Geneva, recorded a year before, slipped out in March 1996. John Sherry once again bowed out. Sadly, events overcame him. He'd contracted cancer, and was to pass away in an unbelievably short period of time. John had been our agent and later our manager through good times and the bad, but mostly he had been a good friend and confidante to me, often displaying the patience of a saint. He went to extreme lengths to accommodate equally extreme egos. He had done something unheard of in the business: he had managed to get us re-signed to a major label, MCA Records, that had previously dropped us. Quite a feat. His was a sad loss.

Under the auspices of a new manager, Martin Looby, *Geneva* was a terrific recording of a live performance by the full new version of Wishbone Ash: Roger Filgate, Tony Kishman, Mike Sturgis, and me. The French TV film of the show was broadcast but never released on home video, although a bootleg version of the album did later appear. Just as had happened with 1980's *Live In Chicago* recording, we were duped and double dealt, this time by a German outfit that released the album on multiple occasions.

A couple of months later I toured the UK and Ireland with Blue Law, promoting our album, *Gonna Getcha*, which was also released on Hengest in the UK. Later on, we would play a couple of festivals in Holland and Belgium. At our London show at the Bottom Line, Miles Copeland of all people turned up, with Martin. Miles came into the dressing room and roughhoused with me but Martin stayed away. He was there simply to observe. Ironically, a few years later he was to use a British blues band as his means to get to grips with bass-playing again and plot his course trying to reinvent himself.

* * *

Back in Connecticut that summer, at Unicorn Studios, where we had started recording *Illuminations* in earnest, it became apparent that Tony could only come in for brief periods of time. He was still doing the Beatles tribute show, which he's always done, and it got to the point where it was difficult to juggle the two. Mind you, he didn't need much time in the studio, recording all the vocals for the album in a mere two days. Tony was the singer; he was playing bass by default but he's not really a 'rock' bass player, more of a pop bass player. Roger had worked out the bass parts already, so I said, 'Why don't you just do it? You know the kind of sound we're after. We'll figure out how to do it live later.'

Roger was a huge fan of Chris Squire—I'm a moderate fan—so he wanted to use a Rickenbacker bass like Chris. So much for sorting out the bass problem.

I also wanted to have good production values, so I enlisted the help of John Etchells, the famous engineer, who had worked with George Harrison, Queen, Pet Shop Boys, and Sham 69. John said, 'Yeah, I'll do it for a small amount of money. My wife'll come out and we'll have a bit of a holiday and I'll record the drums.' So that's what we did. John recorded all the basic tracks, with Mike Sturgis joining the party. At last we were getting somewhere.

Aside from Tony's musical moonlighting, we had two problems standing in the way of a full-scale rebirth of Wishbone Ash as a recording entity: firstly, the funds to record something to the standard I felt we needed to, and secondly, a record label to take us on.

I'm a big fan of National Public Radio when I'm home in the States, and one day I heard an interview with a female folk singer. She was talking about how she'd put the word out to her friends and followers and had actually self-funded an album. I thought it a great idea. This kind of thing didn't really have a name at that time—it was long before the likes of Kickstarter and PledgeMusic, which are now almost standard mechanisms for would-be recording artists (new or long-established) with a reasonable following of keen supporters to circumvent the need for bank loans or record labels.

Marillion are often cited as the first 'name' act to record and release an album through fan-funding, which they did very successfully with *Anoraknophobia* in 2001, but Wishbone Ash were there in 1995–96, in the very earliest days of the internet, doing exactly the same thing with what was to become *Illuminations*. I'd done all this work over the years with Wishbone

Ash fanzines and I'd always kept in touch with fans. Maybe it's time, I thought, to get the fans involved. So that's what we did. I put the word out through the fanzines and also through our website. Before long we'd raised something like $20,000. I naively said to everyone, 'We'll give you a 15 percent return on anything you invest.' These days, people don't give anything except perhaps free concert tickets, a round of golf with your favourite star, or dinner with the band! But, actually, we were able to do that: pay John Etchells, pay the studio, give everyone a return, and list everybody's name on the album itself. We were back in business again, and it was truly exciting.

The label that took us on was HTD—it stood for something, though nobody at the time found out what it actually was. It was run from a garage in leafy, suburban Bexleyheath, Kent, belonging to one Barry Riddington, along with his business associate Malcolm Holmes. Barry and Malcolm are great characters. (It was Gary Carter who introduced me to them—I was still on good terms with him at that point and I do owe him a debt of gratitude there.) Only recently, in researching this book, I asked Barry what the letters stood for, and he laughingly told me the story. He and his partner had had a similar problem to us in thinking up a name for their new venture. In desperation they'd simply settled on the name Henry The Duck, disguising it with the first letters of each word to give it some gravitas.

I called Barry from America one day before my farm duties and we hit it off immediately. Barry went to great lengths to say that theirs was only a small label, but I liked the cut of his jib and I knew he had a basic idea of the rock world. He'd had some involvement with Uriah Heep, The Groundhogs, and people who used to be in Caravan, although he was more clearly in the folk world, really, working with the likes of the Albion Band, Fairport Convention, and various offshoots from that particularly luxuriant tree of British folk-rock.

Wishbone Ash definitely had some folk leanings and folk roots, with Fairport Convention especially being an influence of mine during the *Argus* period. *This feels nice*, I thought. *These fellows are not your typical rock'n'roll hustlers. They go down the pub, they drink beer, they sign and record music for Morris dancers. That kind of goes with the feeling I've got right now, living in Connecticut, visiting harvest festivals and pottering about in the country …*

The planets probably aligned the day Barry and Malcolm actually found a man *called* beer to sign—Phil Beer, a solo alumnus of the Albion Band (as most people in British folk tend to be). It all felt very benign to me and I got on very well with Barry. It was the same feeling when I met Malcolm. They have a certain image—dressing in leather jackets and cowboy hats and looking quite scary, like members of Lemmy's band—but they're the gentlest souls you could ever meet. I realised that I'd found a home, and so it proved to be. We went on to release many records with them, including studio albums, acoustic projects, and live compilations.

Barry became something of a mentor for me and would always act as a sounding board. Even today, whenever I'm in England we make a point of going to dinner together and shooting the breeze. And even though he's quite a bit younger than me I call him Uncle Barry.

It was a great period, the 90s, having all these foils to bounce off. HTD became a safe home for Wishbone Ash, which was exactly what was needed. The fact that these were real people—people you could call up at any time day or night to run an idea by—was invaluable. I was part of a team again. It really reminded me of how Wishbone Ash had started out. Barry would never shy away from telling me if I was shinning up the wrong tree but he really did stick with Wishbone through thick and thin.

The label subsequently morphed into Talking Elephant, after Barry and Malcolm sold some assets to Sanctuary Records and rebranded. In recent years we've moved on, working with labels in Germany, for example. With the German economy soaring above that of the UK, and with Barry's blessing, I've gone where the best opportunities are, in terms of both money and marketing. Barry's a physical-product man at heart: he's in the business of CDs, with only minimal investment in downloading and that kind of thing. But never say never—the door to that garage in Bexleyheath is always open.

* * *

Illuminations was released on HTD in October 1996 to coincide with a two-month UK tour. Once again, Tony Kishman could only make a handful of the dates, so Martin gamely stood in again.

Being an Anglophile, Roger got on well with Martin at first. Before the tour we went to visit him at his home and he invited us to the British Airways pantomime of all things, as he was mixing the live sound. It was somewhere near Wimbledon, and it was a scream. Literally. The campness was off the scale. Martin was absolutely loving this whole vibe. Once the after-show party had run its course, we went back to his house and played him the *Illuminations* album. He was a bit offhand about it—'Oh, that sounds like a bit of a posh record'—but it *was* posh. It was a big Anglo-American production. We'd thrown the kitchen sink at it, all the bells and whistles. But he put it down nonetheless.

Illuminations was as good a classic-rock album as we could make, a powerful record, and we were very proud of it. We toured on the back of it … and then nothing happened. Roger in particular really thought this was going to get some great reviews and, yes, we did get a few reviews, but it didn't sell outside of our immediate fan base and didn't ignite anything in the business. Nothing changed at all. I thought, particularly in Britain, that it would be an event. Certainly, our fans thought, *Wow! This is more than we expected.* And I'm sure our peers in other bands thought we'd done a good job, but nothing changed. It was another time when things were changing around us; dance music was coming to the fore, and as usual we were at odds with the moment. But then, unexpectedly, the 'moment' came looking for us.

I don't know quite how it happened, but the producer Mike Bennett got in touch with me and said, 'Look, I'm doing these dance albums with The Fall, Kim Fowley, and others, and I'm working with a label that is doing these kind of things, if you fancy it as a bit of a side project.' And he talked me into it.

Fuck it, I thought, *why not?* My kids were playing dance music around the house all day long and it was driving me crazy, but I 'got' it. I'd loved Tamla Motown back in the day, I'd been to dance clubs in the 60s, and on Wishbone tours in Europe in the 70s and 80s we'd always go clubbing afterwards. So I got the whole dance thing. And I thought, *Well, Illuminations has done nothing, why not do this: do a complete 180-degree turn?*

It was reactionary, sure, but it was also in the spirit of throwing everything against the wall. At the same time I made things as clear as possible to anyone who would listen that it was strictly a side project for the band. We weren't abandoning our dyed-in-the-wool musical style on a permanent basis. So I went along and started mixing Ash samples into this album that would be credited to Wishbone Ash and called *Trance Visionary*. We had these amazing techno grooves but we needed something to anchor it in the bass area so we brought in Bob Skeat. Wishbone had played the Town & Country in London some time before that and the opening act, fronted by our old crew guy Ashley Griggs, brother of Phil the soundman, had Bob on bass. I'd watched him playing and really liked his tonal approach, the lines he was laying down, and most importantly, the man could groove with the best of 'em. I think he may, even then, have been wearing his now legendary cap. Coincidentally, Mike Bennett knew Bob, too—in fact, Bob had actually assisted in repairing some of Martin's bass parts on the *Live Timeline* album that had been released prior to the the trance albums, and was probably the main catalyst in my involvement with Mike. It might have been a bit of karma—Bob would join Wishbone Ash as a permanent member not long after this and at the time of writing, seventeen years later, he's still here. And so is his cap.

Trance Visionary came out early in 1998, and a second dance album, *Psychic Terrorism*, followed a few months later. It was a liberating experience. In PR terms it might have been daring to use the name Wishbone Ash on these albums, but in real terms it wasn't: there was no business; we were doing nothing in the marketplace. Zilch. What did we have to lose? The brand name needed to be in the public eye, one way or another, and we were getting traction in quite different outlets as a result—shaking things up, so to speak.

I felt it was like sticking two fingers up at the music business—flicking them a Flying V, if you will. We'd just done an amazing record that took blood, sweat, tears, and two or three years of toil to produce. We'd done everything that we could possibly do with that album, and it had zero impact. So why not do a couple of dance albums?

In the summer of '98, in between the two releases, we tried to tour with the idea. We did one show in Camden Town and about five people came along! I got flak from the hardcore fans—'*What* are you doing?'—but it was only ever a side project. It did get us into some dance charts and dance clubs, and it did provide some kind of lateral promotion of the band's name. There was a new generation coming along: they didn't give a crap about screaming guitars but they did like beats. And now, for the first time, my youngest son would actually talk to me about my band's music! (Lawrence, an exceptional visual artist, gradually softened his approach to our music and later went on to design posters, DVD covers, and even the cover of the *Bona Fide* album, but that was still some years off.)

Dance music was big in Europe at that point in time. I took the flak for our foray into that idiom, but of course we were still touring as Wishbone Ash. We hadn't become a dance act. We had, though, become an all-British band again.

* * *

Despite the impression I might have given above—that every time a tour came in, Tony Kishman couldn't do it—Tony did actually do a fair amount of road work with Wishbone Ash during the two and a half years he was involved, spanning 1995–97. By the end of 1997, however, he was getting offers he couldn't refuse related to the Beatle-themed shows to which he still owns the rights. And while he really loved the music of Wishbone Ash, he was a single parent and he had to work. So that was that. But we had had an amazing time on the road together.

In fact, Tony was one of the funniest guys I've ever toured with. I loved his irreverence. We'd laugh our way through tours with a nonstop stream of abuse. We'd listen to comedy cassettes in the car and generally keep things light-hearted. It was the era of the Jerky Boys and being a boys club, as all bands inevitable are—even the girl bands—we thought this stuff was a hoot. It definitely got us through some pretty rough shows playing for Welsh rugby clubs, workingmen's social clubs, and East German border towns. Our merchandising lady, Carol Farnworth, even got in on the act, calling everyone 'Buttnut', while Mike Sturgis became 'Mike De Rookie' and so on. When Tony came to London, on our first UK tour together, we stayed at a favourite old rock'n'roll hotel near Marble Arch called the Columbia. Tony would play the 'American abroad' everywhere he went: he used to be a chain smoker, he liked his burgers, and he'd drink Dr Pepper constantly—it had to be on the rider at all the gigs. He would fly from Tucson to London via Rome, because at that point Alitalia was the only airline that would still allow you to smoke on the plane.

After waking up jetlagged from one such journey and arriving just in the nick of time for breakfast, he came face to face with the battle-axe of a woman running the dining room.

'What do YOU want?'

'Err ... the full English ... please.'

The breakfast service had ended by the time she came back ten minutes later and slammed his food down at the table, took one look at Tony, and said, 'There yer go—good enough fer the likes a' you!'

Poor old Tony. Welcome to Great Britain, indeed. Events like that would surround him wherever he went, and we laughed about that one for days. But he loved Britain and he loved British music, had a real feel for it. He'd get a total kick out of the quaint but funny names of places we'd pass through on tour, like Puddletown or Nether Wallop. I have very fond memories of working with him. Just as it was with Jamie all those years before, he helped me see touring in a fun and different way.

Roger Filgate decided to move on shortly after. I don't think he got over his disillusionment over *Illuminations*' relative failure, and the touring could be tough. He'd not spent years doing this as a way of life, and he was also rearranging his life in Connecticut, working on his teaching career and production work in the studio he had at his mother's large house. He did play guitar, I believe, in Tony's band later on, which took him to far-flung countries like the Philippines. But Roger and I have remained friends, and in fact he continues to be a part of the Wishbone Ash family—he contributed a terrific song, 'Strange How Things Come Back Around', to our 2014 album *Blue Horizon*.

After that, it was a no-brainer to ask Bob Skeat to join on bass, and Bob in turn recommended Mark Birch on guitar. Bob at that point was like any other pro musician in London, working with many different hats in many different outfits. He'd been Gilbert O'Sullivan's bass player for some time, as well as working with the guys from FM and also Toyah Wilcox's band, to name but three very different acts. Both his dad and his uncle were

RIGHT Mum and Dad, courting in the 40s.
BELOW Me aged five.

LEFT One of my first professional gigs, at the Ovaltine works social in Kings Langley, Hertfordshire, with friends John Cleeve, Johnny Carlisle, and Richard Larman.
TOP With cousins Eddie, John, Mike, Barry, and Carol and my brother Len. **ABOVE** With Barry and Mike, and my homemade guitar, at a family wedding in the mid 60s.

LEFT Steve Upton cooking crabs to celebrate Ted Turner's twenty-first in Wildwood, New Jersey, August 1971. **BELOW LEFT** Pauline and me in Austin, Texas, 1971. **RIGHT** Goofing around backstage in the 70s.
BELOW Receiving gold discs for *Argus* and silver discs for *Wishbone Four*. The presentation was made by TV personality Janet Webb after our Christmas concert at Alexandra Palace, London, December 22 1973.

ABOVE Family support: Mum; Pauline's parents, Vera and Jack, and her sister, Rosemary; Pauline; and our son, Richard, at Hemel Hempstead Pavilion, February 1980. **RIGHT** Trevor Bolder, Laurie Wisefield, Steve Upton, and me c. 1982. **BELOW** In Memphis with two newly acquired 50s Korina Flying Vs. **OPPOSITE** Me and the V.

ABOVE With Ted at the Berlin Wall, 1989.
BELOW LEFT Onstage during the early 80s
with a vintage Gretsch guitar.
OPPOSITE Braving the cold in Red Square,
Moscow, December 1987.

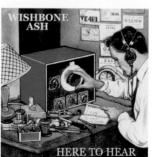

HERE TO HEAR

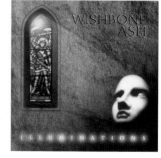

LEFT Me, Steve, Andy Pyle, and Jamie Crompton, 1986. **ABOVE** Loyal crew Daniel Vetter and Chris Boast. **BELOW** Equipment transport, Indian style, December 1981.

andy powell
wishbone ash

LEFT In an acoustic mood (*courtesy of Richard Powell*). **ABOVE** Checking lyrics with the Mudster at Le Triton, Paris, May 2015. **BELOW** Roger Filgate, Martin Turner, Mike Sturgis, and me in the mid 90s.

Wishbone Ash Fanclub,
PO Box 58, Matlock,
Derbyshire DE4 5ZX

www.wishboneash.com

LEFT Bob Skeat, Ben Granfelt, Ray Weston, and me in 2002.
ABOVE The Warrior—you never know when he'll turn up.
RIGHT With Ray, Bob, and Mark Birch in the late 90s.

ABOVE Lawrence, Richard, Aynsley, and me at the wedding of Aynsley and Tara in Tuscany, June 2014.
RIGHT Taking time out at Sherwood Island, Westport, Connecticut.

pro musicians, his dad being a sax player who had played loads of London sessions with 60s pop stars and had even been a member of the hugely popular Billy Cotton Band. He'd also made a solo album with the Bolshoi Symphony. So Bob was brought up in that world—and, coincidentally, on the same street in Ealing as Pete and Simon Townshend, whose dad was also a professional dance-band musician. Bob is one of the most professional gigging musicians I've ever met. He understands that you have to be ready at a moment's notice to sling your bass over your back, jump in the car, and do a gig. And that was exactly what I needed.

Mark was also a really musical guy, a fabulous find and a lovely person. He never had pretensions of being a virtuoso player in the way that perhaps Ted had seen himself, but he was so much more in so many ways—very musical, with a really beautiful voice. It was a pleasure to meet him. He and Bob had played in a 60s party band called Mike Fab Gear, doing a lot of university balls. They had this great freewheeling vibe where music could be fun while at the same time a privileged thing to be fortunate enough to do. So I felt that, yes, I could definitely play with Mark. Mark played a Fender Stratocaster, which I liked—it was a nice foil to my Gibson—plus he could sing like an angel. He would take lead vocals on a couple of things, ballads like 'Persephone' and 'Everybody Needs A Friend'. He added a certain gravitas to the performance of those kinds of songs. In addition, I could hit him with anything on the guitar and he could handle it:

'Right, you're going to solo for twenty minutes on "Phoenix" …'

'Oh? OK.'

There was a transitional period of a few months but shortly after Tony and Roger had left, Mike Sturgis moved on, too. Married life, settling down, and the offer of a full-time teaching post at the Academy of Contemporary Music in Guildford beckoned. Ray Weston, a Wishbone veteran from 1990–93, during the last days of the 'reunion era' of Wishbone Ash, came back in and reclaimed his place on the drum stool. Suddenly Wishbone Ash was a 100 percent British band again. It was another big change to get my head around.

It's a strange thing: I find it easy these days to be a dual citizen. It did take a lot of practise, mind you, but by then I could slip effortlessly between two cultures. I was living in America, deeply entrenched in American society—I understood the jokes, understood the politics, and in Blue Law I got to hang out with New Yorkers. I could discern between a Boston accent and someone from Portland, Maine. I'd been to more states than the average American but I could effortlessly flick the switch and be an Englishman once more. A lot of Americans are salesmen of themselves or, should I say, their talents, like mini business entities; British people are no less that way but they often hide it under cosiness, camaraderie, and self-deprecation, so you have to switch gears and switch hats to accommodate that. There was a little bit of mental readjustment in getting involved with Bob, Mark, and Ray, but it was refreshing—all adding to the rich tapestry of life.

* * *

Mark Birch never made what you might call an 'album proper' with Wishbone Ash, although he was with us for a good couple of years. He did some great work on various video and sound recordings, but this period did nonetheless see a number of other cultural artefacts, some very much of the moment, produced under the Wishbone banner.

'Unplugged' albums were a big thing in the late 90s and early 2000s. Did Wishbone Ash make one? Of course we did! *Bare Bones*, released through HTD in 1999, comprised mostly rearrangements of classic Ash material for the format, plus a couple of new songs. 'You Won't Take Me Down' was one that hinted at what might have been, with Mark's moody vocals to the fore. His voice was very well suited to ballads, and he turned in some lovely work on that album—the only one he would make with the band. One of those rearrangements, Mark's take on the *Wishbone Four* song 'Everybody Needs A Friend', would be his song of choice when he reappeared with us ten years down the line for our 40th Anniversary Concert (which was filmed for DVD release).

Early in 1999, during an American tour, we participated in two podcasts of live concerts—long before the word 'podcast' had been coined. One was from the Whisky A Go Go in Los Angeles and the other from the House Of Blues in Chicago. A few months earlier, in 1998, The Pretty Things had garnered a lot of publicity, and a career revival, with a daring attempt at a video stream of their performance of their 1968 rock opera *S.F. Sorrow* live from Abbey Road Studios, with Arthur Brown and Dave Gilmour guesting. Technical gremlins meant it never reached anyone but the in-studio audience at the time, though it's since appeared on DVD. Similarly, The Who were talked into a supposed video podcast from a Las Vegas casino in October 1999, which either didn't work or was a con from the start. Either way, it too subsequently appeared on DVD, as *The Vegas Job*. This was still very much the pioneer days of the internet, and while a few clued-in people—including old-stagers like ourselves, the Pretties, and The Who—could definitely see the huge potential of it in the music world, it took a while for the technology to catch up and the public to embrace it.

The show at the Whisky was fun. I remember Mick Fleetwood being in the audience, and someone from The Beach Boys was there too. We met all kinds of interesting people. It was a week of anniversary celebrations for the venue, and it was somewhere we'd often played back in the early days. For old times' sake, I reserved us rooms at that famous rock'n'roll hotel, the Hyatt House, or the Riot House as it used to be known, and I decided to rent a Chevrolet Camaro convertible to take the band on a tour of Sunset Strip and Beverly Hills. It was a classic California day when we pulled off the road into a gas station and I started to pump gas into the tank. We were all crushed into it, I paid the attendant, and we set off again—but stupidly with the gas pump still attached to the car. I'd forgotten to take the nozzle out of the thing. I felt something stretching and managed to stop before we trailed the pump along Sunset Strip with a frantic gas station owner running behind us. So much for my fast-car, rock-star cool.

Alongside virtual product like internet broadcasts, DVDs were growing in popularity. The first of several official Wishbone Ash releases in the new format would be our *30th Anniversary Concert*, staged in London with guests like Laurie Wisefield and Claire Hamill in 2000 and released the following year. My eighteen-year-old son Aynsley joined the band on drums for the song 'No Joke'. Tommy Vance was the master of ceremonies.

Embracing new possibilities like internet broadcasts never bothered me. I never got hung up about the technology. If the worst comes to the worst you can always put a guitar on and play to people. Everything else—

podcasting, DVDs, putting dance grooves around your music, whatever it is—is just a medium between you and the listener. The rest is just work and the often not-so-simple execution of it.

The work ethic itself goes back to my teenage years. To this day I still play open-mic nights near where I live—two or three songs to see if I sink or swim. Sometimes I do sink but mostly I swim. It's the same with the band. To me, a band is left with no credibility if it can't ride with the waves and adapt to the times—and I've seen Wishbone Ash adapt so many times that one could say that this is probably one of our greatest attributes. There have been so many people pass through the band but, to me, it's only ever had any validity if it could hold its own against anyone, and that's what I've always tried to do with it. If you do a festival, you could be on there with Mahavishnu Orchestra or Bananarama—you walk onstage and you play 'Phoenix', however bizarre the bill is. We'd done that time and again, so why couldn't we do a dance album? Why couldn't I simultaneously be in a blues band? Why couldn't we do live concert broadcasts? It's all just music.

So why did Mark leave? It was partially the boot-camp fatigue again. I think I ground the band into the dust. I worked them like there was no tomorrow, on tours of America that would have made your hair turn white.

On one occasion I remember traveling overnight in an ice storm in Arkansas. We pulled over at one point and Ray got out of the vehicle and promptly slipped over on the half an inch coating of ice that was on the road surface, over which we had just been flying at 70mph. Later on, there'd be storms and tornadoes and all kinds of unhelpful weather situations that one might expect if one was foolhardy or bloody-minded enough to tour across a rugged continent in the middle of winter. The distances between dates were extreme, often entailing eight- or ten-hour drives. In and around all of that we'd be dashing across the Atlantic for a couple of European festivals somewhere and back again. It was like a military operation—all of the time!

But we were all just trying to survive, taking work and opportunities wherever we could. Certainly our date sheets became the envy of other bands in our position, although of course they did not see the extreme toll all this was taking on us and our families. On one tour, for example, I invited along a teenager by the name of Chris Boast. As a drummer himself, his parents had previously brought him along to a UK show of ours with a request that if there were any openings in the music business, could I please keep Chris in mind. Well, what better opportunity than a nationwide tour of the USA by van and trailer? After a couple of weeks on the road, Chris and I could be found under the van, high up a mountain pass in Oregon, during a massive snowstorm, attempting to attach snow chains in order to make it over the pass for our show that evening. This was touring the hard way, no doubt about it. Chris still credits me with opening his eyes to the world in some weird way and still, to this day, joins us on the odd European tour as driver and backline tech.

There was a bit of a parallel between Mark and Tony Kishman, both being single fathers of daughters. Mark needed to spend time with his daughter, Harriet, and was also planning to remarry. He couldn't carry on being this itinerant musician, flying all over the place earning not very much money with his personal life going to hell. That's often the case with musicians. Mark was getting really interested in computers and programming. I saw a real passion there. He wanted to invest himself in areas that were going to give him more stability—and he was quite right. For the work we were doing, I was OK: I was earning a little bit from royalties, I could get by. But to base your whole income on gigging was tough. So I didn't hold it against Mark when he decided to cut his hair and leave the band.

Somehow, Wishbone Ash had managed to slip, largely unnoticed by the dinosaur hunters and tastemakers of the world, into the twenty-first century. We'd doffed our cap to the past with that anniversary concert in London and we'd trodden water well enough with an unplugged album of old songs in new clothes—a rather tight corset, if the cover art is to be believed.

Did we have anything new to say? And, more importantly, where was I going to find another guitar player?

GUITARS

Collecting musical instruments, specifically guitars, is an addiction as intense as any other. Walking into a music store is like walking into a candy store as a kid, with all the brightly coloured jars of sugary sweets. It's that same thrill that you might have experienced as a child, seeing all these incredible shapes and colours—metal flake, exotic woods, flamed maple, sunbursts ... every hue under the sun, in fact. For the record, I *was* an addict but I'm cured now—although, as every former addict well knows, one is always in recovery. I have an incurable sweet tooth as well, by the way, and have not been able to curb that addiction.

Keeping a small number of essential instruments for my craft, that's a different thing. Each of those has a specific job to do other than indulging my covetousness.

I first got the bug as a nine-year-old while attending my cousin Carol's wedding in Dagenham. She had always been my conduit to rock'n'roll, ever since I first heard the hiccuping vocals of Buddy Holly on her Dansette record player. Finally she left her teenage pursuits behind and her wedding to Jack Rivers, a rock'n'roll name if ever there was one, was announced. On the big day there was a beat group at the reception, all in sharp suits, and the guitarist, as mentioned earlier, had a blood-red semi-acoustic Gibson strapped across his body. Even today I can remember just standing there in awe, watching as this incredibly exotic musical instrument from what seemed like another planet shone in the lights, while my eardrums were being assaulted by the twang and thump of the sounds coming out of his Vox amplifier. This was very powerful mojo.

Later, I'd pore over music catalogues and make little trips to local music stores just to ogle the admittedly poorer British versions of American instruments, which were streets ahead in style and design of what was coming out of the UK at that time. That was until a salmon pink Fender Stratocaster appeared in the window of our local music shop. It was an impossibly fantastical amalgam of sensuous curves and colour. I marvelled at how the wood of the body could be carved into those body-hugging contours, at the mechanics of the new-fangled tremolo system and the scrolled headstock with tuners aligned on one side for ease of operation. Even the way the amplifier cord jack plug entered the body was sexy.

There was no way in hell I'd ever be able to afford to own one, and it was the same for my mates who were also getting the bug. A neighbour of mine, Bob Moreton, decided to build a copy of a white Strat, and very fine it turned out to be. We were both good artists and adept with our hands and it was he who inspired me to have a go at making my own. I must have been about twelve years old. The new grammar school I was attending had a woodworking studio, and I'd love those classes—the smell of wood dust, the feel of the shavings—as I got to grips with using a plane and spoke shave while building a table lamp and, later on, a coffee table. Guitar building was not going to be accepted here, though. We were concentrating on things that were deemed useful to society. I had other plans.

My uncle Jim managed a timber suppliers and wood yard in Brentwood, and it was he who obtained for me some fabulous maple wood to build a guitar neck. He was supplying builders of bowling alleys—another American idea—and the lanes were constructed from planks of strong American maple wood, perfect for carving into a guitar neck. We also found a great lump of mahogany for the body of the guitar. I set about mapping out the design for that as best as I could, basing my ideas on that Fender Stratocaster, working out the shape from memory. The wood was rough-hewn into shape out in our tiny shed, while the rest of the work was actually done on the dining room table. The dust and mess must have been unbelievable, and I can't believe now that my mother let me do this, but that's where my first guitar was built. She was a mother of boys, though, and she also really liked the modern rock'n'roll music, just like me and my younger brother. Dad helped with some of the brass metalwork, which he had chromium-plated at work, and I was in business. I later built a Les Paul-shaped guitar and learned a lot about how the different constructions of these two key instrument styles affected tone and playability. To this day, these two basic types of guitar construction rule the rock world: either guitars with bolt-on necks, like Fender instruments, or the more traditional construction featuring glued-on necks, as featured in the Gibson range of instruments, which harked back to an earlier era of jazz and dance bands.

There's nothing better than learning how to actually make or build the instrument that you will eventually play, as our son Aynsley later learned. He was already a very skilled drummer, having started playing at age six. He found out about making drums, African-style, when, as a student at Berklee School of Music in Boston, he enrolled in a month-long course in Ghana to study African drumming. The kids there are selected by the tribe to have the privilege and honour of being trained as drummers at around the same age Aynsley was when he started playing. The history of the tribe is somehow told through drumming. Those boys must first kill the animal and skin its hide, then cure and dry it before stretching it across the carved tree trunk that they have already cut down and hollowed out. It is only once they've done all of this that they will begin their lifelong journey to become accomplished drummers.

With my homemade guitars I felt that I'd paid some of my dues. I did not acquire my first actual Gibson guitar until I'd been in Wishbone Ash for a number of months. It was an all-mahogany SG Special, finished in a faded burgundy, with a fixed tailpiece and two P90 single-coil pickups. Up until that point I'd played my homemade 'Les Powell,' the second guitar that I made. I began to feel that I needed a guitar with a little more output. I'd play the SG strapped high up on my chest and it had a rather unstable neck that you could bend to create vibrato effects when chording. Without using any pedals the guitar was powerful enough to overdrive amplifiers like the Laney sixty-watt thing that I'd bought on credit.

There is so much information about guitar technology out there these days but, essentially, nothing that much has changed in that area in fifty or sixty years. Guitars and amps are basically the same now as back then. I was finding things out first-hand by getting out on the road and developing a style based on whatever I could get my hands on at the time. Not long after, in America, I obtained two vintage Fender Concert combo amps, which I used exclusively in the studio for their clear, warm tone, both perfectly complementing the Gibson. I also picked up a vintage 1959 tweed-covered Fender Bassman combo, which I still use to this day, though mostly in the studio. The circuitry of the Bassman amplifier, incidentally, was what British amp manufacturer Jim Marshall based his original Marshall Plexi fifty-watt amp head on.

It would be a year or two before we arrived in the States and started combing the pawnshops for the instruments that we could only have dreamed of as kids, and to our surprise we'd often find them at knock-down prices, the rock'n'roll fad having faded from the next American generation's consciousness. Even as late as 1974, when Laurie Wisefield mentioned to me that he too would like to go on one of these pawnshop excursions, we found him an incredible 1954 Fender Stratocaster—an even earlier prototype model of the salmon-pink one that had arrived like an alien presence in my local shop in Hemel Hempstead around 1960—for a mere $300! I myself also picked up a mint '54 Strat for around the same amount, and later we each found a vintage Telecaster.

These instruments had serious mojo—they were genuine mid-century artefacts of American ingenuity, perfectly embodying the flavour and spirit of the times. They were early mass-produced instruments, finished by hand and exhibiting real playability. Now we literally were kids in a candy shop. Those instruments began to make their presence felt on our recordings, on songs like 'Lorelei' and 'Come In From The Rain'. They were simply begging to be played rather than languishing in dusty pawnshops. This fact, that we were actually getting these instruments on our recordings, made the whole collecting obsession even more exciting and even more meaningful.

Ted and I, before Laurie's arrival in the band, had already made connections with a group of young enthusiasts and dealers on the first tours. These guys—Paul Hamer and Jol Dantzig in Chicago, together with Pete Alenov in St Paul, Ed Seelig in St Louis, and Robert Johnson in Memphis—would turn up at our soundchecks, driving big old American V8 clunkers their cars of choice. You could stash, out of sight, securely, half a dozen primo axes in the trunks of these monsters, and we'd have our choice of them to try out later in the show or backstage.

Often, if I purchased a nice Flying V model or Ted picked up a Les Paul, Ed or Paul Hamer would throw in a vintage Gibson mandolin or lap-steel guitar at a giveaway price, as an incentive. It appeared that you couldn't give these things away sometimes. I still have my circa-1919 Gibson A4 mandolin that Paul found for me in this way. Ed started the Silver Strings music store in St Louis on the back of all this trading, supplying guys like Johnny Winter. Paul Hamer with Jol Dantzig started building guitars at the new Hamer Guitar Company, making custom models for us and Rick Nielsen of Cheap Trick. We were all learning about the almost-forgotten techniques that Gibson and Fender had pioneered. The companies themselves certainly were not aware of this underground boom in guitar collecting, still believing that they should forge ahead with new—and, we thought, substandard—models. There were no widely used Gibson or Fender Custom Shops that all came later, inspired from the ground up by enthusiasts like these guys and musicians like us.

I met another music fan and player around this time who was making a name for himself in the pickup-manufacturing business. Larry DiMarzio was our gracious host on Staten Island, where he lived not far from the renowned Mandolin Brothers, one of the few pro vintage-instrument dealers in America at that time, along perhaps with Nashville's George Gruhn. Larry, a 1959 Les Paul Standard owner himself, had studied the genius of the humbucking pickup design that Gibson's Seth Lover is credited with inventing. He was manufacturing a beefier version of the same idea in a tiny workshop on the island. He showed us around the unassuming place and then casually mentioned that the odd guitar would come through his hands that he would trade or sell. After showing me his Les Paul, he pulled out a 1952 Fender Telecaster that he had purchased from Roy Buchanan, the virtuoso from Arkansas and later Virginia who could do things with this clunky guitar that no one else was doing at the time. My eyes widened on seeing it, because I knew that this was from the first years of manufacture. Larry let me have that one for $300, which seemed to be the magical figure for Fenders at that time. No one really wanted them.

Ted had certainly scored several models of Les Paul, by now his favourite guitar, having graduated from the single-pickup, double-cutaway Les Paul Junior he'd first played. You can really hear the P90 pickups to great effect on our early recordings: tone for days. He was also obtaining vintage 50s Stratocasters, and the Fender sound made its presence felt on our recordings of songs like 'Blowin' Free' and 'The Pilgrim'. Ted—like myself, I like to think—could always coax out of those two very different guitars the very essence of what they were built for. (Much later on, I too was to acquire a Les Paul, and one of my greatest treasures is Les's own signature on the scratch plate, which I obtained from him at the end of one of his legendary shows at the Iridium Club in New York. He was in his nineties at that point but still playing great.)

Around the spring of 1972 I got word that the Orange shop in London had a couple of mid-60s Gibson Flying Vs for sale. They had come over from the USA, still in their Gibson cardboard packing cases, brand new, unplayed, but already five years old. Seemingly no one in the States was interested so Cliff Cooper, the owner of the store, imported them to the UK. I immediately set off from my flat in Sumatra Road, West Hampstead, determined to take a look at these two rarities. I'd never set eyes on an actual Flying V until now.

We had started to use Orange equipment at Ted's suggestion, since our idols Fleetwood Mac were using it too, so we were familiar with Orange. Sitting in the shop I tried first one guitar and then the other. I tried them acoustically. They both had a very resonant sound even before being plugged into an amplifier, but one seemed to have the edge in tone and sustain over the other. After plugging it into one of the OR100 amps, I was sold. The thing sounded amazing. I immediately felt I'd found my instrument. We bonded. The guitar had a cool Vibrola system and the whammy bar fell naturally into the palm of my hand. There was no question; I had to have it. Somehow the magical figure of £300 was found, and I carried my new instrument home on the Tube to my tiny bedsit. I lay on the single bed of my miserable little room that night, staring at the guitar I'd lovingly propped up on a chair in order to get the best view of it, marvelling at how I'd been able to obtain such a thing. It was the beginning of a relationship with something made of wood and steel that I'd wear on my shoulder for the next forty-plus years, and that would be my weapon of choice as I'd start to stride the world's stages.

The Orange backline came along not long after this. We bought a selection of 100-watt heads and even 200-watt heads, together with separate reverb units. The German designer, Walter Mathias, actually had a factory in Huddersfield, Yorkshire. The cabinets we used would, in time, be upgraded with JBL K120 speakers, making our rigs the cleanest-sounding units around. They were also unbelievably heavy. It required a lot of accuracy in the playing because there was not much distortion in the sound—which, as a lot of guitar players will know, can mask mistakes. When I think back on our poor road crew, the Hobbit and Chris Runciman, having to lug this stuff across stages all over the world, on and off trucks, I feel for them. None of us were big guys, including the crew, but they bulked up pretty quickly.

I was not using the Orange gear in the studio, however. I found that I did not need all that volume, and I liked the way my two Concert amps broke up nicely when driven a little harder. In fact, those four ten-inch Jensen speakers in each unit had a really musical tone. Sometimes I'd record with one amp set on full bass and no treble, with the other miked up alongside it with the exact opposite settings on the tone controls—that is to say, full treble and no bass. By combining the close-miked sound from each amp and then carefully placing ambient mikes in the room at a distance, I produced a fat sound that I could solo with or play rhythm parts when overdubbing. Remember, we were not using any overdrive pedals in those days. The tone and feedback had to come from the fingers, the guitar, and the amps.

It would be an understatement to say that we were on the road a lot in the States in the early 70s, first with Ted up to 1974 and later with Laurie. Almost by default we would all gather ever-increasing collections of guitars and basses, and I have to say the quality was always primo. Pretty soon I became the proud owner of a 1959 Korina wood Flying V. This guitar was in mint condition and quite an extraordinary find. I used it on the *New England* album and, unbelievably, having paid around $2,000 for it—a fortune in those days—would carry it around on the road in its original case. One would never do that now, simply because that guitar, of which only ninety-eight were ever made, in the years 1958 and 1959, would be worth around $250,000! A couple of other 1967-vintage models arrived shortly thereafter. Not many of these had been made either, but they cost less money so I snagged them while I could. One was a tobacco sunburst finish and one was what we called champagne-pink metallic in finish. All these guitars were in excellent condition and had great playability, but none equalled the original model I'd bought at the Orange shop.

In between all of this, Fender guitars would come to our notice, and almost without trying, I had amassed a collection of Stratocasters from virtually every one of the classic years from 1954 through to 1963. My favourite was a 1956 fixed-bridge model in ice-blue metal flake with plenty of mid-range in the pickups and a big old fat neck. It had obviously been a player's guitar so it had that infused into it, with a nice patina of wear throughout.

Firebirds were also interesting to Ted and me, and at one point we thought we'd like to present ourselves both playing these, along with the similarly shaped Thunderbird bass that Martin was now using. Miles saw me playing my beautiful white Firebird VII, with its three pickups and gold hardware, and freaked out.

'You can't stop playing the V!' he stressed. 'That's your image—you are in every music paper around the world playing that instrument!'

Miles was nothing if not market and image-conscious. I sheepishly resigned myself to this executive order—not that it was a hardship. The V suited my style more than any other guitar, and I loved it, so eventually the white Firebird was sold to Stephen Stills, who was known for those instruments himself and already had a goodly collection of them. Fred Renz, a great American friend of mine who had been present during the *New England* sessions, later coined the phrase, 'Without the V it cannot be.' Fred was a good friend of our road manager at the time, Tom Hagan, who also used to work for Stills. The story goes that Steve Stills used to be the Hagans' lawn boy back in the days when Tom's mother would hire him to mow the lawn for the family, but now the tables had turned and Tom was working for him.

Steve Stills also bought from me an incredible double-neck, semi-acoustic Gibson from the 50s. It was a mandolin and six-string guitar combination that I loved but that was really more of a collector's item finished in black lacquer, like a Les Paul Custom, with ivory binding and three 'Patent Applied For' humbuckers.

By the end of the 70s, Pauline and I had decided to upgrade to a large country house and found a converted granary and stable block as part of a farm complex. Like a lot of musicians I'd always dreamed of having my own recording studio, and there was initially a happy pooling of resources, during the late-80s Wishbone Ash reunion period, that would see Martin install all his recording equipment there and me finally see this house work as both a family home and a music-production facility. To pay for this great leap forward necessitated the raising of some finances. It came down to this: the studio or the guitar collection. I rationalised selling off most of the guitar collection in the sense that I could not play all the instruments all the time and that unless I was going to run some kind of travelling collection in the way that Steve Howe does these days, many of them would simply have to go.

Rudolf Schenker of Scorpions—a big Flying V fan, along with his brother Michael—bought at least three of my collection of Vs, and I think these can be viewed on his website. Some interesting people turned up through word of mouth to view pieces from the collection. One gentleman, a stonemason whose work took him high up in cathedrals and the like, bought the metal-flake Strat. That one was a real player and I was sorry to let it go. The 1954 model was sold for a lot of money in what I can only describe as an encounter much like a drug deal—or more accurately an arms deal. This person flew in his private airplane to acquire the instrument, meeting me in the countryside on a remote airstrip in the dead of night. He brought along a guitar expert who, after dismantling the instrument and satisfying his boss that it was indeed a 1954 Strat, gave the OK for the handover of a wad of cash, which would in due course go into financing Ivy Lane Farm.

I was already indulging my love of hanging out in woodshops with the likes of a certain Ray Cooper from Berkhamsted in Hertfordshire, who made me a great Strat-style instrument that I'd used to great effect on songs like 'Underground' and 'Open Road'. It had a compressor built into the body and could produce these very modern sounds that were really in tune with the 80s. He built me a fabulous Telecaster-style guitar body using ash wood that had come from the ancient bar top of the Red Lion pub in Berkhamsted, which was being demolished at the time. I'd also had a Flying V-style guitar made for me in the late 70s by Sam Li, who had a workshop in Gerrard Street in Soho's China Town. Sam was an inscrutable guy who a lot of us pro players would use to repair instruments that had got broken on the road. When this occurred he had a real ability to keep you on edge by saying very little at the inspection, and then for weeks after, until you finally would get to see a perfectly restored instrument. He was the best. He definitely made you feel stupid for allowing an accident to occur to a precious guitar. He was very in-demand, too, so you would have to wait weeks—it didn't matter who you were.

Years earlier, a Soho violin-case maker made an incredible case for my original Flying V, which I'd use to carry the instrument by hand all over the world. I remember one security guy down south asking me if it was a giant snake catcher. In fact, the guitar itself had actually once been used by me to pin down a human-sized snake—an over-zealous Russian security guard at one of our Leningrad concerts. He was wading into the crowd, beating kids. Both Trevor Bolder and I used our instruments as weapons on that occasion. The V could be useful in more ways than one.

In the 90s I had the great good fortune to meet another private luthier, Kevin Chilcott, who lived with his wife Lyn and their three delightful daughters in Llangeadog, Wales. Kevin was a fan of Wishbone Ash and it turned out that it had been his avowed ambition to make me his version of a Flying V. We met, and I laid out my ideas for how a variation on the theme could be produced, complete with a piezo pickup system, in addition to the regular magnetic pickups, so that I could obtain acoustic guitar sounds from it as well. The first prototype he called 'Problem Child', because we'd encountered issues mostly to do with my impractical demands concerning the finish and so on. But finally two other beautiful guitars made from aged Honduras mahogany arrived, and to this day I still play them, keeping one in the States and one in the UK. They have ebony fingerboards and are real workhorses, very solidly built in order to stand up to the rigours of the road. Several fans of my guitar playing have subsequently had replica instruments of the Andy Powell series of Vs made by Kevin, and I believe they are all supremely happy with their babies. Sadly, for health reasons Kevin no longer builds instruments, but I'm supremely grateful to him and to Lyn, who aided and abetted all the projects he undertook for me.

Most recently, another in the line of great luthiers that I've had the pleasure to work with is Jon Case who, aside from being a fan, is another full-time luthier with an avowed ambition to build a V for me. He has come up with his own version of this concept, the JV1, also featuring this time a Fishman piezo system as opposed to the L.R. Baggs setup on the Chilcott Vs. The tremolo system is a Wilkinson, and the body of the guitar has an incredible layer of buckeye burl wood forming the front of the instrument.

I keep a nucleus of player's guitars in my arsenal of instruments: the 1952 Buchanan Tele is still integral, and has appeared on pretty much every recording I've ever made. It's an incredible instrument, recently re-fretted by German pickup guru Andreas Kloppmann, who himself rates it as one of the finest Telecasters he's ever seen. My original 1967 V still makes appearances on recordings, and recently I've been working with the Duesenberg company from Hanover, Germany, who make a great line of real rock'n'roll guitars that sound great both in the studio as well as onstage. They feature a similar construction to Gretsch guitars. I owned a great 1959 6120 model once and regretted selling that one. These Duesenbergs have great sounding pickups along the same lines as those found in the early Gretsches.

Every guitar player should own at least one Fender Stratocaster. It was the electric guitar that first inspired me. I have a $400 Jimmie Vaughan model Mexican Strat that is an excellent value-for-money modern instrument, not too dissimilar to the original 1954 model I once owned. And, just for good luck, I purchased, at over £4,000, a Fender Custom Shop fifty-year reissue of the 54 Strat. I like it, but I can honestly say that it is no better an instrument than the $400 Mexican Strat.

That's the way guitar collecting goes. It can be like playing the stock market. If I still had my original collection of instruments from the 70s, it would perhaps be worth a couple of million. But I've no real regrets. I've had the great pleasure of playing them all, onstage and on record, and that means more to me in real terms than stashing them in cupboards or under beds. Great guitars need to be played. If left idle, they lose their vibrancy—and, I like to think, their soul. The very act of the constant vibration of playing seems to do something to the molecules in the wood itself, realigning them and bringing everything alive, so to speak. And then there is the wear on the fingerboards, the sweat and toil that all adds up to the guitar being your greatest friend. It sounds romantic, but I've been so grateful to have my trusty V in hand on some alien festival stage in a foreign country: sometimes I'll look down on this old friend and see my own fingers dancing across the fret board and—this can be dangerous—wonder at the gift of music and all those years of working the craft, as I'm transported in the middle of a guitar solo. Real guitars do indeed have wings.

CHAPTER 8

DRIVING A WEDGE

(2000–07)

We get a lot of applications from bands asking to open a show when we're on tour—usually a local act at what to them would be a local venue. In a way, it was a support slot to Deep Purple on one gig back in 1970 that began our career, so we're always happy to give people a platform if we can—you never know what impact it might have, even in the reduced world of today's music business.

Sometimes, though, particularly in Germany, where we tour religiously every January and February, we get bands asking to play support for the entire tour. While Mark Birch was still holding down the second-guitar role we had such an application from a band from Finland called The Guitar Slingers. I'd always been aware of guitar players in Scandinavia—a lot of good rock and also a lot of good pop music has emanated from that region over many years, and a lot of good production work as well. Consequently, despite their having one of the corniest names I'd heard, The Guitar Slingers came on the tour. Even weirder than the name, though, was the fact that there only was one guitar in the band, slung by a man called Ben Granfelt.

We were touring Germany quite prudently by then, not wasting any money and not careering around like archetypal rockers. Rebalancing the image, these guys turned up in a Nightliner bus. We were sleeping in nice hotels, possibly even drinking cocoa and snoozing off to the shipping forecast on Radio 4 LW; they were partying on the bus.

Thus we trundled around Germany together, and we all became friends. They were just such a laugh. We had a great time on the road: we got something from them and I think they got something from touring with us. A couple of the guys had previously been in The Leningrad Cowboys, a large-scale band full of Elvis impersonators with huge wigs and winkle-picker shoes. They were a big deal in Finland. Ben had been the guitar player in the Cowboys and, for all the absurdity of their stage personas, he was a really tasty player.

In due course, as I've mentioned above, Mark tendered his resignation after I'd dragged him around one too many extreme American tours. He wanted to settle down, and he'd earned his honourable discharge from the Academy of Wishbone Ash. I was mulling over what to do about replacing Mark when it came into my mind that I should give Ben a call:

'Hey Ben, the guitar slot in Wishbone Ash is vacant—whaddaya think?'

'Yeah, that would be really great! Count me in!'

There was no hesitation at all. And thus started another phase of the band: the Finnish phase. We'd had an American phase with Roger, Tony, and Mike; we'd reverted back to a British phase with Mark, Bob, and Ray; and now here was a whole other culture. Actually, it was a culture within a culture: Ben would often say, 'Well, you know, I'm not strictly Finnish. I'm a Swedish Finn.' You learn something new every day.

On one level, it didn't matter where he was from. With the advent of the internet, everything really had become global and the great thing about rock'n'roll is that it's no big deal if you're working with someone from Tucson, Arizona, or someone from Helsinki, Finland—you're all plugged into the same influences and the same lifestyle.

When The Guitar Slingers toured with us they'd brought their own soundman, Pete Knuutinen, and we were able to pick Pete up ourselves for odd tours after that. In due course, we would co-opt another Finn into mixing an album, *Bona Fide*, the first blast of twenty-first-century Ash on record. So while it may have seemed as though there was simply one Finn in the band with three Brits, the change was subtler and deeper than that. I was getting Ben, I was getting a live sound mixer, and I would also be getting a studio sound mixer.

Onstage, for me, it felt totally refreshed. Ben was using Engl amps, from Germany, and getting a much more compressed guitar sound. I never went down that amplification route myself, but it made for an interesting pairing. We would have proximity limiters on the vocal microphone, so we were starting to isolate the stage volume. This was something that all the players in Finland were used to. I realised that while we all shared, as I've said, the same rock'n'roll influences, they had 'learned' rock music in a different way from those of us in Britain or America. Finland was just about on the touring map in the late 60s and 70s, though it was still fairly exotic and not somewhere you routinely visited. To a great extent, the way the Finns received music from British and American bands was on the radio, whereas we in Britain, certainly, had heard lots more of it live, in clubs and at festivals. That affects how one then goes on to make music. If you're keenly aware of it in a live context, you're going to play it really loud. In Finland, and in Scandinavia in general, they can produce what sounds like a very loud sound but in a very controlled manner.

Wishbone Ash suddenly started to up its game because of this Finnish influence and the various technical adjustments that improved our stage sound. I'm sure our fans noticed around this time that *something* had changed but they probably couldn't put their finger on what it was. I put a lot of thought into this at the time. Suddenly, to coin a phrase, we were a Finnish product.

Having made the connection with Uncle Barry at HTD we now had an album deal on the table, plus a label that we could record for, so we started to work toward our new album, *Bona Fide*. Ben would have a huge input into the album, contributing six of the songs. When somebody like Ben comes into a band like Wishbone Ash you've got years of accumulated ideas meeting a vehicle within which they can be let loose. It was the same when Mervyn Spence joined in the 80s. That's one of the bonuses when you change members of a band—it refreshes it in so many ways.

Ben was a fan of the band: he knew the songs and, in fact, he'd already been in a twin-lead-guitar band years before with one Muddy Manninen, who was, unbeknown to us all at the time, his Wishbone successor in waiting. That band was called Gringos Locos and, amazingly, they had recorded an album for Atlantic Records with Tom Dowd as producer around the same time that we'd recorded *Locked In*.

All the other guitarists in Wishbone Ash had brought something unique and valuable to the table—different personalities, different ideas, different creative and technical approaches, and a different dynamic, naturally, in the twin-guitar partnership with me. One of the areas where Ben differed most keenly with his two immediate predecessors, Mark Birch and Roger Filgate, was in road experience. He already had a good idea of what being in a professional band was all about and the various demands it made. The Leningrad Cowboys had toured everywhere and performed some really big gigs, including one in Helsinki with the entire Red Army Choir as backing vocalists. Ben had stamina, too—he's a martial arts expert. When we went to Brazil he'd already been out there independently to study martial arts. Often, we'd go to a bar for lunch and he'd go off and do some training.

With all this in his modus operandi, a lot of things became very easy when Ben joined the band. His physical energy, his showmanship, his writing— they all raised everyone's game. One other impact was that it pushed me even further into the vocal area, into unashamedly being the band's main vocalist, because I felt I had material now that I could get to grips with. It was a new century and, with no disrespect to the members of the previous few years, it felt like a newly rebooted Wishbone Ash, ready and willing to take it on.

* * *

We recorded *Bona Fide* in a studio that Uncle Barry knew, near a farm down in Kent. We stayed in a little motel down there and somehow, despite the bucolic-sounding environment, we got a high-energy album out of the experience. Released in 2002, *Bona Fide* would be the only Wishbone Ash studio set between our 1999 acoustic album, *Bare Bones*, and 2006. You might alter that analysis to say it would be our only studio album proper in the ten years between *Illuminations* in 1996 and 2006. It was a time for Wishbone Ash to stake our claim anew as a vibrant and creative entity, and we wouldn't be wasting the opportunity. *Bona Fide* would be an album to define an era for us, and we were giving everything we could to make it right.

Players, studio, production techniques, what mood people are in, the weather—it all plays a part. But the foundation of any album is the material you choose to present. If the songs are no good, or if the spirit behind them is wrong or the writing half-baked, all you end up doing is creating a record—literally, a record—of your mediocrity or lack of focus at that particular moment in time. We'd already had *Locked In*; we weren't going to do that again.

The opening track, 'Almighty Blues', written by Ben, is an exquisitely controlled explosion of energy. It would be a big stage number for us for many years. I produced the track, adding the twin-guitar stamp and some high-energy soloing and so on. Ben had everything else nailed down. Some of the other songs were trickier, because we were recording in the year of 9/11. For any artist, the dilemma was to either choose to ignore this momentous event or to somehow address it. We chose the latter in songs like the successful 'Ancient Remedy' and the even more ambitious 'Come Rain Come Shine'. I think we scored big on cuts like 'Faith, Hope And Love' and also 'Changing Tracks'. There was soloing aplenty from both Ben and me, while Bob and Ray upped their energy levels considerably on the album. The fans lapped it up.

Bona Fide would have seemed to long-term Ash listeners, like our recently revamped stage sound, both familiar and new. It is undeniably 'Wishbone Ash' yet it doesn't quite sound like a typical British or American rock album. Partly that's because, while all the recording was done in England, engineered by Rob Williams and assisted by Rob Spickett, it was mixed in Finland.

Ben had been working with one Magnus Axberg, an engineer in Helsinki, and he said, 'I really trust this guy's work, especially with vocals and guitars. Would you mind if we took it up there and let him mix it?'

By this time I had noticed the production quality and techniques from a lot of people coming out Scandinavia but I was really nervous about letting go of the reins. It would be a first for me to not be in the studio during the mixing sessions. There's absolutely no reason new ideas in studio production can't originate in what some might assume to be some kind of backwater in Scandinavia and travel from there around the world. Whatever one might think of ABBA, their production sound was, and remains, unique—and it translated very successfully to a large part of the wider world. Another more recent band from that part of the world of whom I'm a huge fan is The Cardigans, and I particularly like their production.

So we gave Ben's recommendation a go, and we got the benefit of that.

I really enjoyed what they did with the vocals, particularly. I think we spent about £20,000 on the album, and a lot of that was on the production. Rob Williams was quite disappointed that he didn't get a crack at the final mixes—it would have sounded very different, a lot more English, less processed. But I was happy. As far as I was concerned, *Bona Fide* was an album for the new millennium. We had somebody from another planet— Ben from the planet Finland—and it was a new era: 'anything goes'.

It was a fresh start in every sense of the word. Touring became a lot of fun. Ben was very garrulous, and the fans loved him. They still talk about him. They loved the energy that he brought. They could see I was getting a kick up the pants, guitar-wise. Fair enough, there was a lot of drinking going on—Ben was as serious about that as he was about his fitness—but we became an even more upbeat, positive rock'n'roll band. I really enjoyed having Ben shoulder some of the relentless positive energy that I'd always employed in the different incarnations of the band, because sometimes it can take its toll on you physically. Having Ben's upbeat energy in the mix definitely gave me some respite from this constant aspect of keeping the good ship Wishbone Ash ploughing forward, ever onward.

* * *

Ben Granfelt, Bob Skeat, Ray Weston, and I made a good team at the time—one that lasted about four years. To the casual observer it may have seemed that Ben and Ray were the rakish personalities in that band, while I was out there at the front, captaining the ship. But, as is often the case, the quiet fellow in the background is the one with a firm grip on the rudder.

Bob Skeat's contribution to Wishbone Ash cannot be underestimated. At the time of writing, he's been in the band for nearly eighteen years— almost as long as Steve Upton was a member, and longer than anyone else at any time, bar myself. You wouldn't keep someone on side for that length of time unless he was delivering the goods musically and was easy to get along with, and Bob ticks both of those boxes. He's always been the most musical guy in the band, and it really helps if your bass player is that way because they're the person underpinning the music.

Aside from his great musicality, Bob's a great diffuser of tension. He's so schooled in the life of a professional musician that he realises you can't fight it—you've just got to go with the flow. He's superbly well adapted to the demands of the lifestyle and is also very, very disciplined. Somehow, Bob's always smiling. He seems to just float through. He never throws a wobbler, though he *might* come down to a hotel reception once in a while and express his views robustly if the internet's not working in his room or the taps are dripping. It'll be something small like that, but it isn't often.

On another level, though, Bob is very, very important to the band because he's been someone the other members can all go to individually with various gripes and grumbles and he'll dissipate all the angst. I joke with him that he's our first lieutenant, but his 'rank' is really much higher. He's got a great sense of humour, so whatever the problem is it always seems less so after a chat with Bob. In fact, you might say 'Bob's your uncle'—which will probably mean nothing to anyone unfamiliar with the rich lexicon of English clichés and euphemisms.

There were points where Ray and Ben clashed and the dynamic there was a bit different to any minor clashes between Ray and me. I think it was a question of egos. Ray could see that Ben was somewhat of an ascending star, while Ray had been in the band quite a while and was going through his own problems, which were starting to come to the fore a bit. Ben was the opposite: very gung-ho, very positive. It was an alpha male thing. Ray was a ladies' man, had a certain swagger in his step, and maybe Ben was taking some of that focus of attention now. There were times when it would flare up. To be honest, I was oblivious to it a lot of the time but Bob would often clue me in: 'Oh, bit of tension there …'

There was one time when I think Ray was challenging Ben physically, making fun of his martial arts. And of course, as with anyone who studies martial arts, they never unleash it on anyone else, even in jest. Funnily enough, years before, Miles Copeland was the same—he was a black belt in judo. The rest of us would always try and provoke him. There'd be three or four of us on his back, roughhousing in hotel rooms on the road, just to see if he'd ever use his judo, and he never did. That was the kind of situation that was going on between Ben and Ray. One time I came out of a venue and saw the two of them literally rolling around in the dirt. I think Ray had taken it one step too far—a Wishbone clash—but even then, Ben still didn't unleash his weaponry.

So there was always this taunting going on, but that's a part of the dynamic of any band. Perhaps in this case, though, it hinted at something of more consequence. Ray was basically a lovely guy and he and I had some really fun times on the road together—much of the time it was just a laugh. He'd leave the band in 2006, and in these later years, when he'd been in the band a long time, he'd be in the back of the van, just groaning, lying down. I could see he was starting to become lost at sea.

One day we stopped at a layby for a bit of a breather on the road. I'd noticed that Ray was reading quite a lot of self-help books, often by Deepak Chopra—who could make a lot of sense.

There was Ray, in this layby, standing by a bush. He wasn't having a pee; he was just standing there.

'Ray, what's going on? Why are you standing by that bush?'

'Oh, Deepak says I need to be in nature for at least twenty minutes a day.'

So Ray's standing by this bush, 'in nature'. I don't think this is what Deepak meant, exactly—I think he was talking about a walk in the country. But the best Ray could do, as an itinerant musician, was stop in a layby and look at some shrubbery.

* * *

In hindsight, Ray was coming to a kind of natural end for his time as a hard-touring musician. It was Ben, though, who would leave first, and for similar reasons. In the four years we were together we did a lot of live work around the world, probably close to 500 shows, all on the back of that one album, *Bona Fide*. It had legs. We were still of the mindset that an album like that could create some kind of waves in the rock world. While it did among the fan community and the venues we were playing in, it didn't really change anything, career-wise, for any of us. It was difficult to see where we could take it on from there.

There was a feeling with Ben that maybe he'd expected more out of his involvement with Wishbone Ash in commercial terms. There were also, as had been the case with Mark Birch, domestic issues that were occurring alongside the amount of touring we were doing, and which were really impacting him in a big way.

I remember we played a show one night in Chester while he was going through a breakup. I'd seen this so many times with different members of the band. There's so much travel involved in being in a band that relationships almost inevitably suffer. Even Pauline and I, married now for forty-three years, have had to surf those waves. But there we were in Chester, about to go onstage, and Ben was literally falling apart. It was heartbreaking.

Ben did end up getting divorced and then not too long after that he found a young lady, Jona, and became engaged to her. He remarried and became a father. He was also heavily involved with the Engl amp company and started importing and retailing their products to build up a livelihood outside of the band. This was all within the tenure of his time in Wishbone Ash, and so all of that played into his eventual decision to quit the band. He simply needed to be with his new family in Helsinki.

I was very sorry to see Ben leave because we worked well as a team. But it wouldn't necessarily be true to say there was a great second album waiting to emerge that was suddenly dashed by his departure. The way I view it is that this incarnation of Wishbone Ash lasted pretty much the right amount of time.

Ben gave an enormous amount to the band. He pushed me into being a vocalist, fair and square, and the energy he brought was tremendous. There was never any hanging around in the studio—he got on with the job. He remains one of the most efficient studio musicians I know. He'd come in with all the sounds, the effects, the pedals ready to go. He'd already 'produced' his sound before he walked into the room. A true pro. But the greatest gift Ben gave me was his replacement—and an individual of greater contrast it would be hard to imagine.

Shortly after playing his valedictory gig as a member of Wishbone Ash, Ben rang me in Connecticut one day and asked, 'Well, what are you going to do?'

'I'm going to go down that road again, Ben: go to London and start auditioning guitar players.'

'Well, look, by all means have the auditions. But I would like to put forward the guy I played with in Gringos Locos all those years ago. I know his style would fit perfectly for Wishbone. Why don't you at least see him at the auditions?'

And that was Muddy Manninen. If this were a fairy tale or a Hollywood movie, I'd be able to say that Muddy breezed into the auditions, our eyes met, bluebirds sang, and immediately I knew the whole thing was sorted out. Nothing could have been further from the truth.

We eventually got round to holding the auditions at Ritz Studios in Putney. It's a well-known rehearsal studio, built underneath the railway arches in Putney High Street, and I'd always liked the sound of the rooms. Unusually, the studios are set up with a window looking through to a kitchen/waiting area—a detail that will become relevant in due course.

All sorts of people came down there by word of mouth. Ray had a good address book—he'd played with many people in London—and had put the word out. It was a fairly formal process. Personally, I hate auditions. It's the worst way you can meet someone. People were lined up in a waiting room, coming in cold and playing through some prearranged songs. It's a far cry from hanging out with someone on the road, watching them from the side of the stage and getting to know their personality and their musicianship in a natural environment, as had been the case with Ben.

I remember speaking to Phil Palmer one time after he'd auditioned for Eric Clapton's band. You lined up, you walked in, and it generally turned out you weren't even auditioning with the maestro himself—it's his backing band, and in due course somebody does or doesn't put you on a shortlist. In this case, however, Eric was actually there, and Phil told me, 'I started to play and it suddenly hit me that all the licks I was playing were Eric's!' The guy's been around so long you can't help having some of his moves in your arsenal, but poor Phil had come face to face with the man and was coming over like a tribute act. He still got the gig, though.

I'm not sure that I would be so forgiving, if that's even the right word. The refreshing thing with Ben was that he had his own lexicon of riffs and licks, but at this audition for his replacement I'd have some of these guys coming in and playing my own licks back to me, and I'm thinking, *Oh God, no, no, no…* I'm sure it's meant to be flattering, or at least ingratiating, but it's just depressing. If I want to hear someone playing like that I can do so onstage every night, and he's standing in my shoes.

After a whole day of this sort of thing I was putting one guy through the mill and at the same time looking through the interior window at this other fellow, very gauche, very awkward, clinging to a Les Paul Junior and looking distinctly uncomfortable and distinctively, well, Finnish. *Gosh*, I thought, *this must be Muddy ...*

He came into the audition room, plugged in his guitar, and immediately it was a total fit, hand in glove. His vibrato synched up with mine, his guitar tone was in the same area as mine. We smiled at each other because we both knew it was working. Bob and Ray were there and they too could see it immediately.

I think Muddy was the last to audition that day. I told him I'd let him know. His musicality was fantastic, but I remember having these serious reservations because of his reserved character. But ultimately I decided the musical 'fit' was too good to pass up. We'd had one Finn in the band before and it had worked, plus Ben had spoken highly of Muddy and had worked with him in a professional band before. We'd give it a go.

Where Ben had been an extrovert onstage and loved the limelight, Muddy was the opposite. It became even more apparent, actually, after he joined the band. I had to change my game massively to compensate. He was a muso, pure and simple, and he still is—though, in a way, that somewhat aloof aspect he so effortlessly projects has become a kind of personality in itself. Fans have grown to know and love him for it. It's a win-win situation.

While Muddy didn't have any desire to become a limelight-hogger, what he did have was a vast musical knowledge. His mother was a keen record collector, and Muddy's the same. I've always thought that if he hadn't been in a rock band he could have been a musicologist, somebody teaching popular culture in a university—engaging with it quite happily from the comfort of a book-lined seminar room with a great valve hi-fi and turntable in the corner. His knowledge of music history is better than anyone I know. He listens to music all day long.

'What are you listening to?' I'll ask.

'Frank Sinatra.'

What?!

Periodically he'll get into a whole trip on Cab Calloway or Juicy Luicy or Moby Grape or someone equally left-field. Typically, over breakfast on the road, he might momentarily remove his earphones and ask, 'Did you ever play with Quintessence, back in the day?'

'Err, yeah, I think we did …'

As Muddy told me later, even though he could speak English well there were lots of things about the English culture and use of language in his early days with us that he would miss. It later became apparent to me that it was a nightmare for him to meet people, not least fans after a show. By this time we had become a very open and engaging band, always available to glad-hand fans and chat to people. With Ben in the band we had done our first fan-club cruises: package vacations in the Caribbean, where it's all about giving the fans total access. Ben was a natural at that stuff but I don't think we could have done that immediately with Muddy. He's better now but at that time he would have found it very difficult to engage fully with all the schmoozing—with becoming a 'personality' in any obvious sense of the word. But it was no problem, really; it just meant a bit of a rebalancing of the band dynamic.

Unfortunately, a bit more rebalancing was on the horizon. Not long after Muddy joined we recorded a new album, *Clan Destiny*—which I'll talk more about in a couple of chapters' time—which was to be Ray Weston's last.

For all the inspirational reading and nature-contemplating that Ray had been doing of late, he was obviously conflicted. Being in a band doing the level of touring that we were was clearly no longer good for his well-being. For a start, he was becoming obsessed with death. With his Scottish accent there was a certain morbid humour to it, like Private Frazer in *Dad's Army*: 'We're doomed, DOOMED, ah tell ye!'

Bob's eyes would roll every time: *Oh boy, we're talking about death again* … Eventually I had a one-to-one with Ray. Something had to give. He wasn't living in London any more. London was burying him: he'd been a musician, playing in a large number of bands and in studios; he'd done the London thing and it was time for a change. He was giving California a try. I think in a way I pre-empted the inevitable and brought it to the surface. Sure enough, he did move on: he met a wonderful girl and moved permanently to California, started a new life out there, and, as far as I know, he's extremely happy.

* * *

It was 2007. As I look back now, a whole new chapter—to my mind, the very best to date—was starting in the Wishbone Ash story with the arrival of Joe Crabtree as our new drummer. In hindsight, Joe completed the jigsaw. Wishbone Ash, in this form, became once again greater than the sum of its parts, as I believe had been the case with the very first line-up at its best.

To date, we've delivered a series of albums that I regard as among our best—*The Power Of Eternity* (2008), *Elegant Stealth* (2011), and *Blue Horizon* (2014)—along with some fabulous concert performances, some of them filmed for DVD release. We have a small but perfectly formed support network of sound and road crew, website, PR, and merchandising associates around us, and some of the best and most loyal fans in the business. But that loyalty would be sorely tested during this whole period. Just as the good ship Wishbone was beginning at last to steer a steady course and find a fair wind to sail with, something was playing out that would have the effect of seriously endangering the buoyancy.

In 2005, Martin Turner—'founder member and original creative force' behind the band, as his publicity material was declaring—started running an entity called Martin Turner's Wishbone Ash. The market couldn't stand it and, ultimately, neither could I. After seven years of attrition, of trying to be accommodating, trying to be pragmatic, trying to find some way in which we could all work around it—and finding that Martin and those advising him had no apparent interest in compromise—I was left with no option but to take him to court. Wishbone Ash added its tuppence worth (actually, a bloody sight more than that) to the ensuing trade mark dispute case in London, September 2013.

The next chapter is my record of and reflection on that sorry episode. After that, we can all get back to a more positive subject: music.

CHAPTER 9
TANGIBLE EVIDENCE
(2008–13)

On October 29 2004, Martin Turner and his wife came along to a show we were doing in Surrey. Looking back, it's possible that this was when Martin got the idea to create a version of the band himself. Sometime after that, he told me on the phone that he wanted to get back into playing music. He'd had this aborted solo career after he left Wishbone Ash in 1980, and by this point I think he realised that with Wishbone Ash he had been involved in something that was really quite special. Plenty of people were telling him as much. Enough years had gone by where he wanted to start playing that music again—which was great, and on a personal level I was delighted to hear it.

Near the end of 2005, he suggested he use the name 'Wishbone featuring Martin Turner' or 'Martin Turner's Wishbone', and I was cautiously relaxed about it. 'Well, you've got to be careful,' I said, 'because, you know, we've never ceased to be a band since you've left and we've got various business contracts in place and a lot of tours booked and we don't want anything to upset the apple cart.'

I was quite clear about it, and on that basis we came to what you might call a 'gentleman's agreement'. But, for whatever reason, it didn't take long to unravel. When it came to pass that his new vehicle was to go on the road as 'Martin Turner's Wishbone Ash', that's when people I was working with started saying, 'Wow, you can't have this, Andy—you can't have two bands out there with the same name.' And so, naturally, I made our objections felt.

By this time Martin had been introduced to his new manager, Martin Darvill. As a man with many hats, managing myself and juggling all the many things that go into keeping a band on the road, at this stage I still hadn't cottoned on that these people had a very specific agenda, which was building up to a coup d'état. I was a man running a modest corner shop, with a loyal and long-standing customer base, too busy just getting by to notice that all these people in supermarket trucks weren't just circling around the area on a works outing. They wanted my business.

Martin's comeback trail had coalesced by 2007 into a real 'them and us' situation. They had started a website that was strikingly similar to our own. Our site had proved very, very successful—since we started it, in 1995, it had become a tremendous resource in connecting with fans and keeping people up to date with news and our current music and touring activity. We'd registered the domain name wishboneash.com in March 1998. As it later transpired in court, Martin had subsequently found wishboneash. co.uk to be unoccupied and registered it for himself three months later, though it would be a while before he used it. If Martin wanted to use it as a place for historical information on the band and his role in it, that was no problem at all—it was when it became a promotional tool for his current activities—given that the only proper noun in the URL was 'Wishbone Ash'—that it crossed the line.

Funnily enough, the fact that we were using a dot-com site in itself became a focus for disparagement among some on Martin's forum—this bogus argument that we were a US band running a US website. It wasn't a US website, it was a global website; and we weren't a US band, we were *the* band, operating worldwide, with one person who happened to collect his mail in the US and three others in Europe. Spats about pointless minutiae like this would become wearying over the next few years.

With a website in place, Martin started to rally people to his camp; our band became known as 'the dark side'. There was a lot of extremely volatile to-ing and fro-ing between the two sites: fans turning on other fans and people nobly, if vainly, getting involved to defend my position—because by and large I wasn't keen to go down that route. There's just no point in slinging mud online and creating a quasi-permanent legacy of petulant commentary. There's no dignity in it, and after a while nobody takes you seriously.

As the decade rolled on, Martin's band were beginning to have a material effect on Wishbone Ash's ability to function. He was trying to get into the German market and had an aggressive agent who would simply study the dates that we were doing and then contact the same venues and promoters, offering to undercut us—and on many occasions he succeeded. Consequently, the first foray into a legal confrontation was in Germany at a venue called the Post Halle in Bavaria. We said to the venue, 'Look, you're booking a band and you are calling it "Wishbone Ash" and you're sending out flyers all around Bavaria saying "Wishbone Ash is playing the Post Halle in Wurtsburg"—and you can't do it.' Given the modern German tradition of respect for the law, the venue backed down immediately, once it was explained to them that we had legal registration of the name Wishbone Ash. We had gone through a German lawyer and sent them what's called a 'cease and desist' letter, after which they ceased and desisted. This was the same procedure that Steve Upton had employed years earlier, when Ted had tried to usurp our position with *his* bogus band, simply assuming he could purloin the name Wishbone Ash. It would have taken a lot of legwork to have had to do that with every booking, but thankfully the word soon got around in Germany, and a lot of other clubs that were thinking of booking Martin's Wishbone Ash backed off.

So we had saved the German market, which was a start. Now came the UK.

Back in Blighty, some of the weaker promoters, keen to make a quick buck, were booking Martin into venues for, in some cases, a third of our fees—places where we had worked long and hard over fifteen-to-twenty years to build an audience. I immediately ceased working with those promoters. What choice did I have? But that, of course, compromised the amount of work that we could do in the UK, along with the building of credible tours, which we had always managed to do. We weren't weekend warriors, throwing a few amps in our cars and doing forays into the provinces. These tours took a lot of organisation, but now they were being seriously curtailed. We had become used to doing two UK tours a year—and, more importantly, the fans had come to expect it. Now, suddenly, we found that it was only possible to do one. Eventually, enough promoters—the good guys—were saying to me, 'Andy, you've really got to sort this out because it's not doing the name any good—the brand is being sold down the river.'

However misty-eyed a band's fans might be, those bands that provide the soundtrack to their lives are brands like any other—from football clubs to baked beans. And where there's a brand it has to be protected. In this day and age, however brutal and myth-busting that may be to hear, and however contrary to the notion of rock'n'roll as a world of free spirits and outlaws it may be, it really is that simple. I'll stick it to the man with as much gusto as the next person, but I still pay my taxes, drive within the speed limit, and help old ladies across roads if they require it. And I have a feeling most people are exactly the same.

I had had the trade mark 'Wishbone Ash' registered in 1998—the impetus being the discovery that somebody in the UK was operating a clothing company called Wishbone Ash—and I'd been religiously paying trade mark dues, protecting the name from people with various products over the years. We had to come to arrangements with people from a company marketing a cartoon dog to another marketing a device designed to keep earphone cords in place. They all liked the ring of the words 'Ash' and 'Wishbone'.

All of that was really good for the band's former members, because it kept the name Wishbone Ash intact and solid, with obvious consequences for the continuance of residual income streams. In addition, I'd waited eight years before registering the name, in which time there'd been no activity by any former members to protect and further the brand name. Not one of them had raised a hand objecting or called me to say, 'Oi, we don't like you carrying on the name of the band all these years and releasing albums and so on …' None of them had pushed the idea that we'd disbanded because, in fact, we had not. They'd all left in a piecemeal fashion, one after another, during different years and phases. It was all agreed and well documented among the fans and in the press alike.

There was a huge upsurge of tribute bands during the 90s—acts cheekily grabbing these bigger bands' names and in some cases duping the public. It was a kind of Wild West period all over again, except the pioneers had done all the hard work finding the gold-bearing rock in the 60s and 70s, and now everyone and his dog was free to come along, put on a wig, come up with a wacky variation on a name, and start working the seam. Everyone thought it was a huge hoot—especially in Britain—but it was wreaking havoc with the business. As far as I know, there was never a Wishbone Cash-in or a Blowin' Freeloaders, but there didn't need to be: Martin had come along and, in respect of his fees, the pub-sized venues he was tending to play, and his easy accessibility to punters around Britain any other weekend, he had effectively cornered that market himself, even making cheesy jokes about the names he'd considered and publishing an article on his website titled 'What's in a name?'

Joking aside, there was an interesting precedent during 1990–91, when Johnny Fean, former lead guitarist and co-vocalist with Celtic-rock band Horslips—who operated between 1972–80 and were a particularly popular live draw in Ireland—fronted an act called The Spirit Of Horslips. He was effectively an original member operating his own tribute band, and doing so with the relaxed approval of his former colleagues, who were all following paths outside of music at that time. Nobody was being conned. In fact, it's a bonus for any fan going to see a tribute band and finding it's fronted by one of the tributes. If he'd called the band 'Horslips', coming back after a ten-year gap with only himself and hired hands in the line-up, I'd imagine people would have felt cheated. As it transpired, the full Horslips reunited in a blaze of glory in the mid 2000s for occasional gigs and live albums on an ongoing basis, and now everyone's a winner. The point being: if Martin had wanted to do something like that it would have been fine by me, but I completely understand that he would have felt uncomfortable embracing that 'tribute band' flag so obviously. What I don't understand is why he seemingly had a problem with using a clear, descriptive name that would have celebrated the music but avoided all the confusion.

Eventually, the gentlemanly exchanges in trying to resolve this thing went out the window. I'd started to receive phone calls not from Martin Turner but from Martin Darvill, and I found them intimidating. He had clearly been talking to all of the former Wishbone Ash members from the 70s and they had, apparently, all come to the conclusion that now was a good time for a reunion. The plan was a short UK tour and a concert at the Hammersmith Apollo. I was an inconvenient thorn in their side at that point because I'd never left the band—I'd just continued. The existing

Wishbone Ash—*the* Wishbone Ash—had relationships with agents and record labels; we'd done tons of work all over the world, and the fans were behind us. It wasn't a business in limbo, looking for a buyer. There may have been vacancies in the entertainment continuum labelled 'The Beatles' or 'Pink Floyd' or 'The Dudley Moore Trio', but the plot of ground marked 'Wishbone Ash' was already occupied; the deeds were in order and the mortgage payments were up to date. The occupants had no wish to move on.

Nevertheless, with all his other ducks in a row, Darvill came calling with this plan for a reunion. While Darvill was someone I disliked and wished to avoid, I wasn't actually against the idea of the four of us—Martin, Ted, Steve, and myself—playing together again. As the popular music business evolves and the textbook continues to be written as new circumstances arise, usually with the pen of pragmatism, there are always ways and means to square what might at first appear to be a circle. In 2008 and again in 2011, the five original members of Pentangle regrouped for limited concerts and TV appearances in the context of short sabbaticals for the other members of 'Jacqui McShee's Pentangle'. The latter group was a touring and recording entity the singer had been fronting since inheriting the name, with the blessing of all concerned, in the mid 90s—the other originals having dropped out one by one in the fifteen years following a 1982 reunion. It was all perfectly amicable. Perhaps even closer to the Ash model, the 'classic' 70s line-up of Status Quo regrouped for a couple of short tours in 2013–14— John Coghlan and Alan Lancaster momentarily burying whatever hatchets there were with Quo lifers Francis Rossi and Rick Parfitt, all with the active endorsement of the current Status Quo rhythm section. Again, everyone seemed perfectly happy about the arrangement. There was no loser in either case, and the fans were the winners. Everyone had their cake and ate it.

The key differences with the Wishbone Ash scenario, of course, was the presence of Martin Darvill as would-be impresario, and the dysfunction in communications between the supposed creative participants from the get-go. I found it weird that not one of these guys who had shared the band with me in the 70s had ever called me up about this reunion idea. Not one call. There was no human element to it.

Throughout this whole sorry episode I was criticised for being some kind of business-oriented power freak by people in the Turner/Darvill camp. But my ethos for running a band is this: yes, it's got to have elements of very tough business, so that we get the best deal possible to keep the ship afloat, but it's also got to have this huge fun factor to it and a good lifestyle factor. And, not least, it mustn't forget the fans. At the time of writing, we've run about twenty fan club conventions all around the world. The fan community to me was massively important—and this 'Martin Turner's Wishbone Ash' situation and the idea of a reunion cash-in was just dumping all over it.

We could certainly have done something similar to the Status Quo solution in a limited way, but you don't initiate a wonderful, feel-good event like that unless there's genuine positivity behind it. That being said, I've always been a very easygoing, inclusive person, and despite the fact that all of this came as a kind of ultimatum, I was still at that point fairly open to possibilities. The problem was that Darvill had inserted himself very firmly in the middle.

There had been very little contact between the three other original members and myself in recent years—and probably also very little contact between themselves. There had been periods in the 90s, for example, where I'd been playing in France near where Steve Upton was living, running Miles Copeland's chateau—I'd be only 10km away but when I'd call him up he'd tell me he had 'another appointment'. I'd call him as well as Martin Turner periodically about royalty issues, though, which was fine. As for Ted, he was somewhere in Arizona. Ted was always an errant soul—no one could ever get in touch with him, or at least not easily. Laurie Wisefield and I were in communication at various points, and I'd seen him socially, if briefly, over the years at gigs he was doing with Tina Turner and suchlike. I suppose it's not that different to a situation where school or college friends are part of an intensive social circle for a period but eventually grow up, change, move on, find new circles of friends, become different people. Where bands differ is that, having created 'product' that has a long commercial afterlife, there remains a residual business connection, which can endure and require periodic attention long after personal relations have cooled or are extinguished.

Still, you might well wonder why Laurie was involved in all this. I wondered that too. He was apparently there as a potential rabbit in the conjurer's hat. I was told in no uncertain terms that the ex-members would like me on board with this reunion but if I didn't want to be on board, there was always another 70s guitarist from Wishbone Ash: they would have a four-piece band either way. And at that point, Darvill said that they were going to do this with or without me, and if I wanted to do it they would give me £30,000 in cash.

That was the big carrot. 'Well, I'll consider it,' I replied, 'but at this stage of my life, I'm not doing everything just for cash. I don't think this is necessarily a good deal for the promoters … and I'm a bit pissed off that you didn't have the good manners to ask me rather than tell me. In fact, you have no legal right to negotiate for anything under the name Wishbone Ash.'

At the very least it was disrespectful. I had kept the name going in the dark years, out there treading the boards in all sorts of places aside from regular tours of the UK, America, and Western Europe, and all the ex-members had continued to receive regular income as a result—mechanical and publishing royalties from a shared back catalogue that was being kept buoyant by current activity, PRS concert repertoire income from vintage songs continuing to be played live all over the world. But now, having been goaded by a third party, they had decided it was time to slaughter the fatted calf, throw a banquet in Hammersmith, pull some lapsed fans out of the woodwork, and gorge like there's no tomorrow. And that's exactly what would have happened: there would have *been* no tomorrow—it was a cash-in based purely on the lure of cash, a short-termist enterprise with two people in Steve and Ted who hadn't played professionally in over twenty years, another in Martin Turner who couldn't be bothered to talk to me on the phone, and a middleman waiting in the wings to push Laurie Wisefield onstage in the very likely event that such an ill-starred reheating of the soufflé might collapse in mistrust, acrimony, or a basic lack of any real ability to play to a professional standard. To my mind, it had all the ingredients of a sell-out (in both senses) and a fiasco.

The whole thing had been presented to me by Darvill as a fait accompli, with the suggestion that, if I decided to pursue legal recourse, I'd not only lose the case but quite possibly lose my house. For me, really, that was the last straw. I saw red.

We already had our own fortieth anniversary thing in mind, which was a concert at the Shepherd's Bush Empire, due to be filmed for DVD. I just went ahead and booked a date in June 2009. I put it out in the press that I would love to invite the original members to join us onstage.

There was an element of taking the fight to the enemy in that press statement, but the truth is I wouldn't have minded if we'd all got together—a good-spirited one-off jog down memory lane in a controlled environment where everyone could shine for a moment, share in the revenues, and give pleasure to a lot of people. It might have cleared the air—and, after all, in purely musical terms, Wishbone Ash is the shared heritage of everyone who's ever been in it. Martin, however, saw that as me being disrespectful to him, as if I was saying, 'Come along and be bit-part players in my band.'

Prior to all this, Darvill had turned up in person in New Jersey, to a little place we were playing, where I'd met him for the first time—or so I thought. It was then that he told me, as I've mentioned earlier, that he'd come to my home as a kid and I'd signed a guitar for him. But the way he did it was so odd and intimidating, sidling up to me, whispering in my ear, before any other introductory chat.

I've been in your house …

What sort of person does that? What other instinct would any sane person have to that kind of thing other than one of defence? Nevertheless, he's managed to build a kind of empire with a stable of bands from a certain era and I suspect he's done so because musicians, especially guys from the 70s, are used to having big amounts of money dangled in front of them; they are used to somebody sorting their lives out and managing them, and when I say managing them, I'm talking about changing their nappies. That works for a lot of people. He must have thought I was one of them.

* * *

In 2008, Steve Upton, Martin Turner, and David (Ted) Turner applied to OHIM—The Office for Harmonization in the Internal Market, the people who look after Trade Marks in Europe—for the name 'Wishbone Ash'. I heard about it in November of that year and registered my objection. In May 2010, OHIM ruled in my favour. But that was only the opening skirmish at law.

I engaged the British law firm Walker Morris, and in due course I initiated a kind of summit, at their office in Leeds, with the two Martins. It seemed to me that the pair of them treated the whole thing as a bit of a joke. They were on their way to a football match in Leeds and this meeting seemed to be just something to do on the way. There was a moment of light relief in the meeting when Martin T. wanted to record the whole thing but couldn't make his gadget work—a so-called producer who couldn't find the 'on' button on a digital voice recorder!

In general terms, as a punter, when you see something advertised as 'Mike Pender's Searchers' or 'Eric Burdon's Animals', you understand that it's going to be that person plus some other guys. But it can also feel pretty tawdry. It is implicit, if a construction like that is being used, that somewhere out there, someone else is running a vestigial version of the same band. As a fan you can't help feeling things must have got a bit desperate—that something you might once have loved has been carved up in acrimony and the carcass, or in some cases a distant echo of it, is subsequently being trawled around the country for a last-gasp effort to squeeze some cash out of the thing.

Funnily enough, along these very lines, Martin Darvill held up as a beacon of positivity the recent saga of Barclay James Harvest, a soft-prog band of our era, as a win-win situation: a benchmark for the Cloud Cuckoo Land successes awaiting a 'double Wishbone Ash' scenario. Following a sabbatical or a falling out of some sort in 1998, one of the BJH guys, John Lees, released an album entitled *Barclay James Harvest Through The Eyes Of John Lees*. That then became, however implausibly, the name of his touring band. Worse, John then roped in another original Harvester, Woolly Wolstenholme, and fans would be confronted with publicity material encouraging them to attend something called Barclay James Harvest Through The Eyes Of John Lees Featuring Former Founder Member Woolly Wolstenholme. I mean, really—in the annals of rock, has there ever been a band name less compelling or more absurd? And in what way can someone be a 'former founder member'? They either are or they aren't. You can't take a sabbatical from having been a founder member of something. At that point Les Holroyd, another Barclay-as-was former/founder alumnus, launched Barclay James Harvest Featuring Les Holroyd and, perhaps inevitably, rounded up the only other former/founder member, Mel Pritchard. While Les had the sense not to bill his act as Barclay James Harvest Featuring Les Holroyd And Also Featuring Mel Pritchard, he did go on the road as Barclay James Harvest Featuring Les Holroyd With The City Of Prague Philharmonic Orchestra. It's almost as if the whole thing was a memory test for fans ('former founder fans' included) or an attempt to find the cumular limit of what is possible to fit on a T-shirt.

Darvill said something to the effect that if Barclay James Harvest can do great business with Les Holroyd and John Lees operating their own versions, what was the problem? 'But Martin,' I replied, 'do you not realise how tawdry that looks and sounds? If you think Wishbone Ash are going to go down that road you're really mistaken. This is a forty-year-old band with a great cachet. Those guys you're representing won't know it now but it's actually worth it to them in the long run to keep this thing intact.' Aside from which, as far as I was aware, from what promoters were telling me, the two Barclay James Harvesters currently on the road were gathering in corn of appropriately reduced volume to what would have been the case were John and Les operating the same vehicle—combined Harvesters, if you will.

At one point during the meeting, when it was clear that nothing of any value was being agreed, my lawyers suggested we take some time out and think about the options, to see whether there was some kind of agreement we could come to. I was trying to be pragmatic; I wasn't trying to restrain Martin from playing music. That he'd decided to pick up the bass again, and play the music of Wishbone Ash, wasn't an issue. I thought it was a good thing. But to blatantly try and grab back the name, fifteen or more years after he'd left, was ridiculous.

This ridiculousness seemed perfectly obvious to me, and I was hoping—if it came to it—that the law would agree. But I was also hoping, if at all possible, to avoid taking it to court. The huge expense and disruption that was sure to entail is not to be taken lightly. I can only assume that the two Martins thought I lacked the will or the resources to do so.

In the meantime, our 'thrash it out' summit turned out to be just a fumbling, bumbling, inconsequential meeting that was extremely expensive to set up and, as it appeared to my lawyers and me, not taken remotely seriously by the other side. I realised then that they had no intention of changing the name of Martin Turner's Wishbone Ash. You had a manager who was independently well set up and who was stroking the ego of somebody who simply didn't realise what the business had become and now had nothing to lose. The two of them were like a double act. Without his namesake, I don't believe that Martin would have had the balls. As it was, they were just 'having a laugh'. It appeared to be all about needling me. And it was working.

* * *

Shortly after that meeting, in May 2012, we issued a communication saying we were going to try and get the case tried in court. We decided to use the Intellectual Property Enterprise Court (formerly the Patents County Court) because this was basically an argument about a trade mark and the ownership thereof. It was time to lance the boil.

Anyone who's seen the Beatles-spoofing film *The Rutles: All You Need Is Cash* (1978) will no doubt recall the terrific scene where Michael Palin, playing a business representative of The Rutles in their death throes, stands outside the offices of 'Rutle Corps', casually reeling off a list of people he's going to sue that day—as a stream of furtive individuals can be seen in the background, walking out of the place with office supplies, items of furniture, and stuffed gorillas. It's a great satire of the business end of music, because there's enough of a ring of truth about it. In fact, anyone who has read Peter Doggett's *You Never Give Me Your Money: The Battle For The Soul Of The Beatles* (2010) will be stunned (shocked and stunned) to find out just how much truth there was to it. The Beatles' cooling personal relations and complex business affairs at the end of the 60s generated such a colossal afterlife of litigations—at one point, as Peter discovers, they literally sued themselves, just as Palin's character had supposedly spoofed—that one finds it incredible that any of them had the mental space to continue creating music and maintaining a positive outlook over the subsequent twenty-odd years.

From my own limited experience, the only way to deal with this is to compartmentalise it: hire lawyers and put the necessary time into supplying them with whatever information is required (or, if you're a Beatle, hire someone to do the information digging for you) but regard it all as a separate entity to the day-to-day running of your ongoing career.

If I was going to prove that Wishbone Ash had, in the eyes of the law, devolved to my ownership, I needed to find documentation to support the claim. For the whole summer before the trial date, Pauline and I became Wishbone archaeologists. I have storage units in the UK and in the States wherein lurk the artefacts of our entire business, going back nearly forty-five years. Many times in the past, Pauline had told me, 'Andy, get rid of this crap—do we really need it?' Well, it turned out we did.

Among all the detritus we found Ted Turner's handwritten resignation letter from 1974, complete with spelling mistakes. The whole process was like breathing in the dust of the 70s, without the fun of having a trip in the TARDIS. It was utter drudgery, soul-destroying at times. Despite being in a band that's forty-six years old, I live pretty much in the present: I like being in the present, and I like to think in the present. That being said, now and again we did find the odd interesting surprise and things that I had completely forgotten about—contracts from shows that would cause you to do a double-take: 'Wow, you're kidding me—we actually made ten grand back in 1972 for a show in Boise, Idaho? *We* certainly didn't *see* ten grand!'

Trawling through this stuff, I'd forgotten that the 80s was the era of faxes. So there'd be all of these faxes that had all but faded—built-in obsolescence. And then you'd go back to the 70s and find ledgers and other paperwork, all handwritten, largely by Steve Upton. In those days he was the road manager, so he notated stuff in painstaking form. It looks like something from the age of Dickens.

We were particularly keen to find Steve Upton's 'cease and desist' letter to Ted Turner, from the time in 1983 when Ted was briefly running a bogus 'Wishbone Ash' in Texas. I knew he'd used a law firm in New York City—

Grubman, Indursky & Schindler, which subsequently became one of the biggest music-business law firms in the world—but at that time they were just our little lawyers. I rang them up.

'Can you guys dig around and see if you can find this cease-and-desist letter?' I asked.

'We'll get back to you in a couple of weeks,' they replied. 'We've got storage units ourselves …'

Sure enough, they came back in a couple of weeks: they'd tried but they just couldn't find it. Luckily, though, they had found a letter from Steve requesting it. Thus, after three months of crate-digging, when we walked into the court room that September morning, I was pretty confident that, for anything they could throw at us, I could say, 'Ah, well, I'll think you'll find that this proves …'

* * *

I'm lucky to be a naturally positive person, but I can understand those who might find themselves consumed with the trauma of being involved in a legal action. These things don't happen quickly. Between filing the 'Infringement of Trade Mark' claim in May 2012 and having our day in court (two days, as it transpired) in September 2013, there was over a year's worth of preparation and anxiety, with about seven years of mounting attrition before that.

Pauline, in particular, found the whole thing a horrendous experience. She went through a long period of hating the internet, having to keep up with what was going on at Martin Turner's website. Being kept informed was a necessary evil, but there were some vicious people posting there.

I kept a very low profile during all of this online warfare, and to an extent so did Martin, although he did keep posting a lot of what at the time were referred to as 'clarification statements'. It became a running joke among a lot of fans on our website: *Not another clarification statement*— which often turned out to be a clarification of a clarification. Once you start doing that, you are totally damned if you do, damned if you don't. So I was wise to keep quiet. The time would come.

The stress continued, however. There were times when Pauline would wake at six in the morning and go and sit on the porch and write letters. None of them were ever going to be sent but it was a kind of coping mechanism: getting down on paper all the injustice and exasperation that was clogging the mind. All the while, this vision of losing our home was ever-present.

Eventually we became stoic about it all. Years before, we had been burgled. When the police came they said, 'You'll go through a whole range of emotions: you will be scared, upset, and the very last emotion you will get to is anger.' And that's pretty similar to the rollercoaster of emotions when something like this happens: it feels like your whole life is being burgled on a daily basis with the possibility that one day they'll stop chipping away and just come for your home. It was a violation.

It was heartening during this period to find out who your friends are, and to be reassured that their number was great. My current band colleagues, Bob Skeat, Muddy Manninen, and Joe Crabtree were first among the faithful, sharing the load as much as they could. In purely legal terms they are all 'subcontractors' rather than part of an 'equal partnership'—that's been the case with every new member since Laurie Wisefield left in 1985—but that employment status hides a much bigger picture. All three have bought into being long-term members of this band. At the time of writing they've been members for eighteen, eleven, and eight years, respectively—and that eight-year period as a four-piece alone is longer than any other Wishbone Ash incarnation. They've put their heart and souls on the line in creating the music and spending time convening with the fans. They're invested in it, not just monetarily, but on a personal and familial basis.

Aside from those in my immediate circle, the majority of the fans that kept the faith with the band were completely in sync with what we'd been doing. Most people saw common sense. Aside from a hard core of very long-standing supporters, we have fans now around the world, particularly in Germany, who are in their thirties and forties—people who simply weren't around when we were playing the town halls of Great Britain back in the early 70s. They had become fans of *this* band. Bob Skeat means more to them than Martin Turner; Martin is a distant memory.

Of course, every band member in every band has their own coterie of fans, and there were lots of people who particularly loved Martin's songwriting and his singing and his persona, and a Martin Turner comeback would have pulled those people out of the woodwork—people who wouldn't necessarily have been interested in the band as it had developed in the years after his departure. These people saw it very much in black-and-white: Martin was the original bass player, therefore Martin should be allowed to share the name.

* * *

On Thursday September 19 2013, the four founder members of Wishbone Ash donned uniforms of sobriety and turned up in court, the latest in a long line of sorry music-business litigations that everyone else can read about in a brief news item on page twelve of the London *Times* or the Washington *Post* and think, 'Dear oh dear, what a shower ...'

It's funny: no one would think that about intellectual-property disputes between those who manufacture goods or provide services, but when it involves musical artists, the gut reaction is to think of words like 'gold-diggers', 'has-beens', 'whingers'—be it Mike Love claiming the authorship of this or that line in Brian Wilson songs written half a century ago or a steady trickle of rival versions of Bucks Fizz, Saxon, The Animals, Barclay James Harvest, Showaddywaddy, Sham 69, Racey, and whoever else. I suppose it's because music is based on emotional connection—when people see something tawdry happening to a name they associate with something intangibly bigger and more resonant to their lives—even their lives in the past—than competing brands of toilet tissue or hamburgers, it feels like a betrayal. It's slightly illogical, but I understand it completely. I would feel the same—and when it came to my own band, I most certainly *did* feel the same.

I ended up sitting at the back of the court simply because Pauline was sitting there and I wanted to sit with her. I didn't actually give it any thought, and I didn't know what the protocol was—that this was like an American-style court where you sat on benches and you could sit with your counsel.

There are six fans with whom we communicate on a regular basis, and it was wonderful to see that they had all turned up there for the duration of the case to give moral support. Carolyn and Chris Wright, Simon Atkinson, Colin Hargreaves, and witnesses Keith Fox and Guy Roberts joined us for lunch each day. The interesting thing here was that some of these six had never actually seen the original band. They were curious to see what the guys were like. There are quite a lot of fans like that now. Conversely, I had a woman turn up in Toronto recently with an original fan-club membership card—an original fan who'd never had the opportunity to see the band back in the day but who had followed the music from a distance ever since. The richness and diversity of the fan community really is the lifeblood of Wishbone Ash—and, I would imagine, the same is true of most bands and artists with decades on the clock. It doesn't surprise me that the likes of Neil Diamond and Cliff Richard, however critically panned their careers may have been (even if Neil's almost fashionable these days), have an extremely hard-core element to their fan bases.

Curiously, none of the original guys in Wishbone Ash—at least, as far as I'm aware—had ever really invested any time outside of the band in getting involved with the fan community. We had invited Martin along to a fan-club convention once; he came along, sang some songs, and left with a kind of a bitter taste in his mouth because we hadn't done all the songs we had said we were going to do. I think that Martin expected to just come back and be a conquering hero, but it wasn't like that, because he'd not really invested any time with the fans. You can't leave something for twenty years and then suddenly expect it's just all going to be the way it was when you'd left. But I think that sense of entitlement was common to all the guys who came to court from the original band: they just assumed that the judge was going to take their view of the world as it was. It was extremely naïve.

Ten witnesses, including myself, took the stand on day one for my claim; Martin and his witnesses appeared on day two.

I was up first. I had thought a lot beforehand about the kinds of things I might be asked, but all of that goes out the window when you get on the stand. It's a discombobulating environment: you just have to speak the truth as you know it. Being first on, and not knowing the protocols, I was probably far more concise than I could have been. Others in the witness box after me at least had an idea of how the process worked. Certainly, the loquaciousness Martin Turner displayed as the last witness of all would suggest that by that point the once unfamiliar and imposing scenario had entered the realms of a chinwag down at the golf club. I daresay any dispassionate observer to both days would come away thinking I was Mr Serious and Martin was a clown.

The judge, Douglas Campbell, is a man in his mid forties with extraordinary credentials: first class honours at Oxford University in chemistry, top distinction in law at City University, proficient in Japanese, a brown belt in karate, and governor of the Contemporary Dance Trust in his spare time, when he wasn't advising governments on intellectual property matters or dealing with old rockers who've thrown the rattle out of the pram. He was engaged and inscrutable throughout, never letting on if he was familiar with any of the music, although I did get the feeling that he at least knew *who* we were, the type of band that we were, and the period that we were from. I think he had a good sense of what bands meant in those days and what they mean now. Certainly, the historical preamble in his published judgment would give Pete Frame and his *Rock Family Trees* a run for their money in terms of clarity and accuracy—and all in plain English, too.

Presenting my case was relatively simple. It was based around two central issues: Martin's use of 'Martin Turner's Wishbone Ash' as the name of his band, and his use of the domain name wishboneash.co.uk—specifically, using it to promote the activities of Martin Turner's Wishbone Ash as opposed to it being purely a resource for historical information. Key to establishing whether the trade mark had been infringed was whether there was a likelihood of public confusion over the two entities trading as 'Wishbone Ash', and also whether the 'goodwill' associated with the band's reputation in the marketplace resided with me at the time of application, and whether that application was made for reasons other than a malicious disenfranchising of any previous members who had an active interest at that time in maintaining the brand themselves.

Martin's barrister, Madeleine Heal, was pretty robust in her style, but she seemed not to be totally conversant in some of the details of the band's history, or the music business in general. At one point she seemed to get mixed up between the album *Illuminations* and the boxed set *Distillation*. I had to gently interject to point this out. Later, Ms Heal and I had a lengthy exchange about the relative sales figures for albums released at different points in the band's career, during which she seemed in my view to be suggesting that our more recent work was of lesser importance because it had sold in smaller quantities. After I had established that our most recent album at the time, *Elegant Stealth*, had sold in the region of 25,000 copies, by comparison to *Argus*'s sales in excess of 800,000, the conversation turned to *New England*, released in 1976, by which point, I noted, sales of the band's albums had begun to wane significantly.

> HEAL: So, if the sales for *Argus* were 800,000, were the sales for *New England* 500,000?
> POWELL: No, I'd probably say a third of that, maybe.
> HEAL: About 250,000?
> POWELL: Maybe, yes.
> HEAL: Around there.
> POWELL: Possibly, worldwide.
> HEAL: Worldwide, but certainly a very great deal more than 25,000 which *Elegant Stealth* has sold?
> POWELL: Yes, absolutely. That goes for every band of that era. The sales of discs now are—for example, the latest David Bowie CD, which reached number 1 in the US charts, it did that on sales of 94,000 CDs, and Mick Jagger, one of the biggest rock stars in the world, he produced a solo album a few years ago and I think he sold 900 copies in the UK. So, the sale of actual hard discs has just plummeted. You know, our business has been decimated in the last few years as far as the sale of discs; you know, everything is downloaded now.

Next up was Guy Roberts, a company director who has been a fan of the band right from the very beginning, and who has been a constant help with all sorts of things: merchandising, the website, almost all of the fan club conventions we've ever done. He was calm and clear about the things he remembered, including Martin's apparent lack of interest in the band at the time. He affirmed for the court part of his written statement:

> I invited Martin in for a cup of tea and we had a conversation. During the conversation we got talking about Wishbone Ash and Martin said to me, 'I don't know why Andy still bothers but if it wasn't for him Wishbone Ash would have died years ago.' It appeared that he couldn't believe that Andy had actually carried the band on.

There was, in retrospect, quite an amusing moment when Ms Heal, who was trying at length to establish what effect Wishbone Ash's continued existence had on interest in its back catalogue, brought up The Beatles.

HEAL: And the Beatles have now completely disappeared, have they?
ROBERTS: Two of them have.

Shortly after Guy, Martin Looby, my agent from the early 90s, and Andy Nye, my current agent, gave evidence. They were phenomenal. Andy had a mass of relevant facts and figures at his fingertips. He could graphically demonstrate how Martin's operation had usurped certain venues in which we had been building up an audience over many years. Martin Looby could testify about Martin Turner asking him in the mid 90s if he could help him with a solo career.

We had invited Martin to play on the *Illuminations* album in 1994. We even went to a recording studio with him—and it was a disaster. Martin physically couldn't play the bass and awkwardly bragged how he hadn't picked it up in years, it having been stashed under the stairs at his home. Bass playing and singing were out of his range of abilities at that time, because if you haven't been performing frequently, you can't suddenly go into a studio and do it. He did, however, fill in for us on bass during a tour after the album had come out, on a temporary basis, and had been perfectly happy with that arrangement. So there were lots of things like that which made it clear that I had made overtures to Martin, tried to be inclusive, but that he was of the mindset that he couldn't understand why I still continued as Wishbone Ash. It was, in his mind, a waste of time.

We had a really fabulous witness in Nicola Bowden, manager of the Mick Jagger Centre in Dartford, Kent. She took the stand and said that if she books a band under the name Wishbone Ash, she expects it to be Wishbone Ash as it is legally known.

> HEAL: [Mrs Bowden] if you understood that a band called Martin Turner's Wishbone Ash was more likely to fill the Mick Jagger Centre than a band called Wishbone Ash that had Andy Powell playing, you would choose Martin Turner's Wishbone Ash, would you not?
> BOWDEN: No, I would choose through research the name that gives the stronger opinion of the original line up. We have many acts, from The Animals, The Troggs, many bands that have been around for many years, but each time it's only ever one band. You wouldn't have The Troggs with another name in front of it, you wouldn't have The Animals preceded by the name of another artist. You would have the main name; you wouldn't have George Michael with another name. You would have the band name, you would have the product.

It had turned out that the last time we'd played there, Martin's agent had cannily booked 'Martin Turner's Wishbone Ash' into a club down the road around the same time—obviously hoping to tempt people away. Explaining that she regularly rebooks acts at two year intervals, and that this routinely delivers successful shows, she continued:

> We went from 599 to 383 [ticket sales] in two years. In the whole two years, no other act that I've booked had the massive decrease in ticket sales. Our profile hadn't changed and Andy Powell's profile hadn't changed. There was no other reason why the ticket sales could have been so low apart … from Martin Turner performing in the same area in the same time…

Nicola's view was simple: if you book a band, you book the genuine legal entity. And she couldn't be budged from that.

We went to great lengths to get our webmaster, Leon Tsilis, into the process, as well as Kate Goldsmith, our US publicist. They had to jump through a lot of hoops because they were in the States, so gave evidence by video link. They had to go to a lawyer's office to do it, but there were various technical issues. Leon ended up using his iPad.

As well as being our webmaster, Leon was a US regional promotions person, and had been head of A&R for MCA back in the glory days. He was a straight-talker then and now. His testimony was amazing not only because of his forthright style but because it was on a big flat-screen TV in the courtroom. At one point he leant forward so that his face dominated the screen and said, 'The other members had all quit, and in this country, when you quit something, you quit.'

The court just went *woooooaaaaaah*—here was this huge disembodied face on this screen staring at everybody. It was so powerful. It was like something out of a movie—*Just cut the crap, these guys all quit the fucking band!* When it came time for my counsel to wrap things up on the second day, he said, 'May it please your Honour, this is, in my respectful submission, a pretty simple case. The thing to remember here, I think, is that as Leon Tsilis put it yesterday, "Once you quit, you quit."' It was quite the moment.

Kate Goldsmith gave some first-hand evidence about the way Martin's band was being marketed in the States, and the confusion it was causing. Keith Fox, one of our fans from Yorkshire and a serving police detective, gave similar first-hand evidence of confusion he was aware of closer to home, and also expressed views about the musical quality of Martin's act. Joe Crabtree, our current drummer, gave written evidence of how one of his drum students had seen posters in Spain for Martin's band, with Martin's name in tiny font, and how the student believed it to be the band featuring his tutor.

I think Martin's side were rather taken aback at just how strong our witnesses were. There was no waffling or irrelevancy: one after the other, they gave a clear, concise presentation of pertinent facts and figures. At the end of that first day, I felt very good about the way things were going down. My legal team weren't leaping up and down shouting, 'It's in the bag!' but they were very confident, very prepared, and very business-like. At this point, at least, there were no negatives. What would the second day bring?

* * *

Among the portents of better fortune as we began day two was the happy news that Martin Darvill was not there. Gary Carter, whose witness statements included all sorts of issues he had with me, didn't attend either—which, I feel sure, saved the court a complete waste of its time. Laurie Wisefield had turned up to observe the proceedings, supporting Martin. It felt as if someone had decided that, if a load of former members of Wishbone Ash showed up in court, the judge would think, 'Gosh, you guys are obviously all a team here, and Andy Powell's the odd one out, so he loses.'

Three of the remaining five from Martin's team from whom the judge was to hear were, of course, Steve Upton, Ted Turner, and Martin himself. I felt sad when I saw them all take the stand, one by one—sadness and pity for them, for the name of the band, for all that we had done together. There seemed to me to be a large element of desperation and befuddlement in the way they were trying to represent themselves—and a complete detachment from the modern world.

My career has had a beginning, a rise, a peak, and then a decline, a long tail, and then a bit of a rise again—enough to feel that I've withstood everything that the game has thrown at me. I felt, however, that my ex bandmates were disconnected—certainly from the nature of the modern music business—and I thought that was a shame. I had this feeling that, even if the opportunity ever presented itself, there was no way I could sit down in a room and successfully explain to them what the band means to the fans currently, what we have gone through together and all of its recent history, because they just wouldn't get it.

Steve's cross-examination, in the transcript, reads like something from a 50s British courtroom comedy, rife with confusion and misunderstandings and interventions and discussions involving the judge and both barristers. Part of the confusion came from Wishbone Ash having two former members known to the court as 'Mr Turner', but much of it came from Steve's constant use of legal terms like 'asset' and 'goodwill'. There seemed to be a disconnect between what Steve understood these concepts to be and what the court did. At one point, Mr Recorder Campbell tried to hammer home the point:

> CAMPBELL: You are using words like 'asset' and 'partnership' and 'goodwill' and these may not even have been concepts that you were discussing back in the 1970s. Now, were you answering the questions on the basis of your current understanding of the position or how you thought it was at the time?
> UPTON: Well, at the time we were aware that we had a partnership. We were aware that we had goodwill created by that partnership and when one person left, which was Ted Turner, we had a new partnership and used the asset, the goodwill, Wishbone Ash, with a new partnership.

And so it went on. Later, my counsel, Mr Harris, had a lengthy exchange with Steve about Ted's use of the name Wishbone Ash in 1983, which had prompted Steve to send him a cease-and-desist letter, after which Ted 'duly stopped' using the name.

> HARRIS: So logically Martin Turner would be doing the same thing under Martin Turner's Wishbone Ash wouldn't he?
> UPTON: Well, I don't know that Ted Turner went out as Ted Turner's Wishbone Ash. He went out as Wishbone Ash, which is very different from Martin Turner's Wishbone Ash.
> HARRIS: But the central part of the name is undoubtedly Wishbone Ash, isn't it?
> UPTON: Of which Martin Turner has a right—as an asset of the original band and the goodwill, he has a right to that.
> HARRIS: I suggest to you that in fact it would cause just as much confusion as any other form of use of Wishbone Ash.
> UPTON: I don't know. Do I answer that? You're suggesting it to me.

Well, if Wishbone Ash as Martin Turner's Wishbone Ash is going out, he's specifically stating what it is.

CAMPBELL: Mr Upton, perhaps I can try and short circuit this. I think what Mr Harris is suggesting is that if you go back to 1983 you wrote all these cease-and-desist letters to Ted Turner and you have explained that the reason you did that was because you experienced a lot of confusion at venues. Promoters were unhappy that they were having one band and then the other. Now, what Mr Harris is exploring with you is doesn't the same thing happen when you have Martin Turner doing—as Mr Harris would have it—doing the same thing. OK?

Wrapping up his cross-examination, my counsel asked Steve whether there could have been any reason, in 1994, for me to think that he had any objection to my continuing to perform and record as Wishbone Ash.

UPTON: I don't know what he would assume.

HARRIS: But you knew at the time he was continuing with Wishbone Ash?

UPTON: At which time?

HARRIS: 1994.

UPTON: I had very little contact with him then so I really didn't know what he was up to.

Well, he surely must have known what I was 'up to', because he was continuing to earn royalties from all the live work that was going on through the years. All the ex-members are in the PRS (Performing Right Society), and all the work I've been doing—thousands of gigs, all over the planet—has been generating a steady income on an annual basis for us all.

I had been with Steve in the band when it was just him and me: after Martin and Laurie left, we *were* Wishbone Ash. There were a number of years where we both had young families and were both struggling financially. We managed to skirt bankruptcy, we paid off the debts, we worked bloody hard in far-flung places together to do that; we went through a lot of angst and grief together, but all of that was now by the by. I had counted on Steve as a friend. I thought we *were* friends. But it was greatly apparent to me in court that we were not friends and we never would be again. That contributed to the overwhelming melancholy of the experience.

Steve leaving the band back in 1990 had coincided with a marriage breakup. I think he left the band a really bitter man but bitter not just about the band but about many, many things. It's a matter of great sorrow to me that somehow I became wrapped up in his mind with what was obviously a period of his life that he associated with anger and regret. For many years after that, I'd found it odd that Steve had denied even the fact that I'd helped him, when he left the band, to get a job at my recommendation, running Miles's estate. Now, he seemed to me to be embarrassed and ashamed to even be in court; some friends saw him sitting outside the courtroom with his head in his hands. I felt sorry for Steve—he just didn't belong there.

Ted's performance in the witness box seemed like an exercise in vagueness. Here was a man staring at the ceiling, perhaps hoping to find there something to say that might be in some way relevant. Like Steve, he looked as if he didn't really want to be there. It was noticeable that Steve kept disappearing from the room, and when the proceedings were over he literally ran out of the court. I don't think that any of them looked as though they were in the same band or that they were in any real sense 'together'.

Martin's booking agent, Don McKay, tried to explain in his evidence that he absolutely couldn't see that if the words 'Wishbone Ash' appeared on a poster in bigger font than the words 'Martin Turner' that this might in any way mislead the public. Even he conceded, though, that a handful of times per year—despite his agency specifying that the qualifier 'Martin Turner's' be used—promoters would ignore this and simply bill the act 'Wishbone Ash'. Oddly, both Don and later Martin, under cross examination, tried to argue from two standpoints that seemed to have a built-in absurdity. They felt that adding the qualifying words 'Martin Turner' to 'Wishbone Ash' was important because of Martin's reputation as the 'creative force' from the band's glory days, and because of his subsequent reputation as a solo artist … and yet it was simultaneously crucial to use the words 'Wishbone

Ash' because that meant people might actually turn up. Did Martin have a reputation on his own merits, or was it just hubris?

Hana Cunningham, an ex-girlfriend of Ted's who presented herself as our 'manager' from a brief period in the early 90s between Steve leaving and then Ted leaving for the second and final time, had nothing to say that was relevant. Her presence seemed to revolve around vague and half-baked attempts to besmirch my character, which had no foundation whatsoever. She said that I had borrowed some money from her to buy a house; when she was asked how much money it was, she couldn't remember. At one point in her testimony, there came another drily amusing intervention from Mr Recorder Campbell:

CAMPBELL (TO CUNNINGHAM): Do you have a clear recollection?
HEAL: The answer is either yes or no.
CAMPBELL: I wonder which it is going to be?

In the end she just walked off the stand in embarrassment and stormed out, never to be seen again. Everybody was left wondering, *What was that about?*

Finally, at the end of the day, Martin Turner presented himself to the court. And no doubt felt that the court would melt like ice cream before his raffish charm and ribaldry. It didn't.

One of the basic rules of appearing in court is respecting it. I certainly don't wear a suit every day, but there are occasions when formal dress is appropriate. One contribution Martin made when he got in the witness box—having opted to stand up throughout, when everyone except Ted and him had been happy to remain seated—was to explain to the judge and my counsel that 'this is not my normal attire', which felt, to me, disrespectful. It set the tone for a kind of sneering, swaggering disparagement and demeanour throughout what was to be a long and rambling testimony. Just like the meeting in Leeds, Martin seemed to be treating the whole process as a bit of a joke. And I don't think that was lost on the judge.

It also became clear during the questioning that Gary Carter had been writing some of Martin's online statements, after my counsel, Mr Harris, quoted a line from Martin's website: 'Disagreements over group policy and musical direction led to Martin reluctantly resigning from the band in 1980.'

TURNER: Well, that is not accurate.

HARRIS: But this document is endorsed by you.

TURNER: Well, it may have been but I certainly didn't write it.

Setting aside the sheer import of the thing, and the fact that it was costing huge sums of money, Pauline and I found a kind of gallows humour in that second day. It was great entertainment, almost like a movie—you could have filmed the whole thing. We kept looking at one another: *Did he really say that?*

In many respects there was always this tension and conflict between Martin and me. We have never been friends, only bandmates who shared common goals for a time. And creatively we were able, for that time, to find a dynamic that worked—we could play off each other, and we produced some great work, for which we can both be proud. This kind of thing is not uncommon in bands. People have said the same for years about Jagger and Richards in The Rolling Stones, Lennon and McCartney in The Beatles, Townshend and Daltrey in The Who. Sometimes you need a bit of grit to create a pearl. The trick is sustaining the kind of partnership which, on purely social terms, would ordinarily never last. In the early days, our first manager, Miles Copeland, managed all of this in a very astute way. Miles would never allow Martin to speak to the press, for instance, because most of what came out of his mouth was off-message. He was a contrarian. I suppose he tried to be the John Lennon of Wishbone Ash. But we can't all be that smart.

To my mind, Miles had created the band out of nothing, and it became something significant only under his influence, his positivity, and his drive. With his involvement gone our paths inevitably diverged. There were a lot of artists in the 60s and 70s who saw their managers as father figures, just like Brian Epstein was with The Beatles at the beginning, and Miles was like that in some ways for these guys. He was like that for me, too, until I grew up. There was something very endearing and inspiring about him. In the early days it was 'all for one, one for all'. We were all young men and we were all going into this world together. Now, however, none of us, as far as I know, approached Miles to be a witness. I don't know why that was. I wonder what he would have made of it all?

Martin, given his soapbox, went to great lengths to tell the court that he was an artist while I was a businessman. I don't think that washed, on either count, for a minute. Firstly, if he wished to establish credentials as an artist, where was the evidence? The claim could hardly be substantiated outside of his Wishbone Ash career, because there simply isn't a body of work. Secondly, in trying to label me a businessman he was apparently assuming that everyone would boo, hiss, and point their fingers—immediately identifying me as a pantomime villain, a caricature philistine smoking a fat cigar, guzzling steaks and counting piles of cash while the truly creative people, like him, were out there rocking and sticking it to the man. Martin evidently thought 'the man' was me.

For a start, this whole stance was an embarrassing anachronism; more importantly, this was a case that was not *about* creativity—it wasn't, for instance, about plagiarism or disputes over publishing credits—but *about* business: his and mine. It was irrelevant which one of us reckoned ourselves to have more cred as a flag waver for the values of the 60s counterculture.

Am I a businessman? Not in any pejorative sense; not if it has those emotionally charged little speech marks around it. What I am is a working musician—an artist with a body of work—and I run a business. It's called Wishbone Ash. Martin, Steve, and Ted used to run it with me. We were *all* businessmen. And then there was just me. And I kept running the business.

In Martin's mind, a musician cannot be a businessman, which is both out of touch with and disrespectful to every professional musician on the planet. Today's musicians have to be self-promoters. The infrastructure of the professional music world has changed beyond all recognition within the space of a generation. The vast majority of professional musicians operate as cottage industries now: self-reliant, savvy sole-traders or limited companies or legal partnerships, where once they would have been a gang of free-spirited gunslingers periodically underwritten by fat advances from a label or a publisher, or a stipend from a patron or manager—overgrown teenagers given a license to career around the world as semi-salaried spokesmen for alternative lifestyles. These days, no matter your level of talent, if you don't have a grip on deal-making, taxes, insurance, multi-platform communications, publicity, endorsements, travel arrangements, and any number of other wheels that need to be oiled on a regular basis, you will almost certainly not be able to build or sustain a viable career in music.

With Martin, there was a clear sense of entitlement. You do need a lot of ego to get up there in front of a band and to sing your songs, but that same ego can also be your greatest undoing. I believe Martin to be an example of what happens when ego gets out of control. Swaggering around onstage is one thing, but in a court of law it was incongruous, inappropriate, and frankly embarrassing. He was the kingpin of a trio of disparate individuals who had presented themselves in a twenty-first-century courtroom like visitors beamed in direct from a half-remembered past: two befuddled backwoodsmen and someone occupying a space that brought to mind Norma Desmond from *Sunset Boulevard*; three people who didn't even belong together anymore, and who, it seemed to me, couldn't really understand what it was they were fighting for.

* * *

In amongst all the flimflam it would have been easy for a casual observer sitting in on those two days in court, certainly during the second day, to have lost track of what it was all about. The crux of the matter was that I had applied, in good faith, for a trade mark for the band's name way back in 1998. That trade mark was granted in 2000.

One of the interesting things about the detail of that trade mark is that it encompasses 'entertainment services by stage production and cabaret'. Thus, were I ever to appear under the banner of Wishbone Ash wearing a velvet suit and playing medleys of Barry Manilow hits in a Yorkshire workingman's club or a third-rate lounge bar in Las Vegas, I would—aside from being quite clearly at an advanced stage of a career-death situation—be entirely protected from people ripping off my act. Whether anyone would wish to do so is a different question. On the other hand, the trade mark specifically does not grant exclusivity in the event of Wishbone Ash producing a children's television series. Which is one of two reasons why the world has never seen a show called *Thomas The Tank Engine Meets Wishbone Ash*.

These hypothetical byways aside, we had the trade mark, and that was really all there was to say about it. We had done our best to explain the background, to argue infringement, and to provide evidence of public confusion and impact on trading linked to Martin's use of the name. We could only get on with life and wait for the judgment, which was due in a matter of weeks.

* * *

Rock music and litigation are fairly regular bedfellows. The fast and loose nature of the business during its first twenty or thirty years in particular, from Elvis Presley's first record to Status Quo's first Farewell Tour, left plenty of ragged edges, dropped balls, and papered-over cracks, all ready for the legal profession to scrutinise forensically in the years following. Some of the better-known early cases had been concerned with the authorship of songs—George Harrison vs The Chiffons ('My Sweet Lord'); John Lennon vs Chuck Berry ('Come Together'); various people versus Led Zeppelin (none of those came to court, but one or two publishing credits were quietly altered).

Cases concerned with the ownership of band names are a more recent development. Numerous other trade mark disputes had been cited in our court case, and several would return for an encore in the eventual written judgment. Among them were issues involving people selling washroom products, energy drinks, and chocolate rabbits. One case that kept coming up was a particularly complex one involving the company that runs the Orient Express and the associated Hotel Cipriani in Venice against a man called Giuseppe Cipriani who operated a restaurant in London (a dispute in which my legal team acted for the successful party). It's far too mind-boggling to try to summarise the ins and outs of that one here, but it seemed to be pretty significant in the case law.

Back in a world that was a bit easier to understand, a handful of previous band-name disputes that had ended up in court were cited: Bucks

Fizz, Frankie Goes To Hollywood, The Animals, Saxon. By coincidence, the latest round in the Animals saga was taking place the very same month as the Wishbone Ash hearing. One of the key aspects to it—an appeal by singer Eric Burdon against a previous judgment affirming drummer John Steel's ownership of the trade mark (as of 2004)—was its exploration of the nature of 'goodwill' in the brand of a supposedly ephemeral musical act.

The original Animals had enjoyed the last of several reunions in 1983. For twenty-odd years after that, various line-ups of bands appeared with the word 'Animals' in the name (Eric Burdon & The New Animals; Eric Burdon & The Animals; The Animals II; The Animals & Friends), fronted by either John Steel or Eric Burdon. Some of them, inevitably, ended up on venue posters as just 'The Animals', which confused people. Burdon objected to Steel in 2005, and the thing got to court in 2008. The judge on that occasion decided that the 'goodwill' in the name had long since run out by that point, and consequently any of the 'last men standing' (a legally understood term that crops up in the judgments of many of these sorts of cases, including my own) from the 1983 reunion was eligible to trademark the name for themselves. Which is exactly what John Steel had done.

One gets the impression that the judge in that hearing had been somewhat exasperated by Burdon and his representatives. In his judgment, he wrote:

> The opponent seems to contend that he is, at least in his own mind, a rock and roll legend whose mere existence serves to keep the goodwill in the original band alive. He is I am afraid mistaken. His counsel described him as 'the charismatic lead singer and songwriter who has captivated the hearts and imagination of generations upon generations of teenagers the world over' and also stated that 'no one remembers the drummer'. As to the former, this was not borne out by the evidence provided and with regard to the latter I trust that she does not encounter Ringo.

The reference to Ringo wasn't quite as fatuous as it seemed (or as the judge had intended it to be). John Steel's group, The Animals & Friends, is a similar outfit to Ringo Starr & His All-Starr Band: a loose assemblage of various vintage musicians with a hit or two to play, working within a group based around a drummer who needed them as much as they needed him. One suspects, though, that Ringo's act plays bigger venues than the Spotted Dog in Willesden—scene of 'The Spotted Dog incident', as referenced in Eric Burdon's appeal judgment of September 2013. The publican of said premises, back in 2006, had booked The Animals (Burdon's band name that month) and ended up with The Animals & Friends (Steel's), and he wasn't happy about it. It had been an administrative error: astoundingly, both acts were represented by the same agency.

The 2013 appeal judge (whose views on whether Burdon was or remained a 'legend' were not recorded) ruled that goodwill in the name had not, in fact, run out when Steel applied to register the trade mark: a truth to which the constant stream of Animals CD reissues, clips in retro TV shows, and appearances in magazine lists of the 60s' greatest this or that would surely attest. The goodwill, he felt, rested with no individual member, hence neither Steel nor Burdon could trademark the name.

'Goodwill' was something that came up a lot in our case: the intangible but nonetheless crucial concept that, in terms of musical acts, a reputation with commercial currency attaches to that act which endures for an indefinable period after that particular act has ceased to be active. Martin, Ted, and Steve seemed to believe that any goodwill in Wishbone Ash's brand was wholly traceable back to the first line-up, in which they had been a part (although Ted, under cross-examination, conceded that the goodwill when he left in 1974 passed on entirely to the new line-up with Laurie Wisefield); my view was that the entity had never ceased, and consequently said goodwill was being constantly refreshed with new performances and recordings.

The Animals' case involved a band that had stopped entirely (after the 1983 reunion), unlike Wishbone Ash, with versions reappearing by stealth in the years subsequent to that. The Saxon case—Byford vs Oliver and Dawson, 2003—was referred to a lot by both sides in the Wishbone Ash case and was different again. This time, two former members had registered the trade mark for the name while the band (long without them) played on, to borrow an appropriate phrase.

Saxon had been going since the mid 70s: Steven Dawson and Graham Oliver had left in 1985 and 1995 respectively; Biff Byford, the frontman, carried on throughout, as he does to this day. In 1999, with Saxon still active, Oliver and Dawson applied for a trade mark in the name and, remarkably, were given it. The Trade Mark Registrar had decided that any of the original members had a right to register the name and Dawson and Oliver were simply the guys who had got there first. The judge in 2003 ruled that the trade mark had been applied for in bad faith, and consequently Biff was able to carry on rocking in the ever-evolving saga of Saxon thereafter.

The judge in the Byford case, however, had actually created new case law—which was cited in the 2013 Animals judgment and also, as it would transpire, in our own—which seemed to have unresolved potential consequences. His judgment, in explicitly linking the goodwill in a band to the informal partnership that created it, effectively implied that in bands that are or were such a partnership (as most bands of our era were, with nothing on paper), the name cannot be used in the event of one member of that partnership leaving.

In practical terms, of course, virtually the only bands of our era of any consequence to have observed this principle—stopping entirely when one member leaves (or dies)—are Led Zeppelin and The Beatles. Or, at least, that was the case with The Beatles as the world knows them: John, Paul, George, and Ringo.

Poor old Pete Best, The Beatles' drummer between 1960–62, had to live not only with the ignominy of being sacked from the band on the cusp of their EMI recording career and world domination but also with his very name becoming a byword for any early member of a subsequently successful band who missed the boat. I wonder what would have happened had he taken The Beatles to court in the 60s? Funnily enough, he ran a band called Pete Best & The All Stars for a while after his sacking—a coincidental pre-echo of Ringo's own post-Beatles outfit. He also released an album in the USA at the height of Beatlemania called *Best Of The Beatles*. Pete finally had a payday from his Beatles association with the release of *Anthology 1* in 1995 and has since returned to music as a kind of retirement hobby, running his own Pete Best Band. The funny thing is, he has a second drummer in the line-up, his brother Roag. This opens up a whole cupboard of amusing possibilities: if Roag is ever sacked, does that mean he becomes the 'Pete Best' of the band? And what would that make the actual Pete Best, who would still be in the band? Taking the hypotheticals to their ultimate point, if Pete outlives both Paul and Ringo, would there be anything stopping him, if he wished, from performing as Pete Best's Beatles with whomever else he chose? I doubt if he would wish to—he seems at peace with his lot now—but it's an interesting question. A version of The Quarry Men—the 1956–60 pre-Beatles skiffle group that included John, Paul, and George in its ranks—reformed in 1997 under that name, featuring five original members, and continues to tour. It's a great example of the textbook of rock continuing to be written.

Roger Waters spent a long time being seriously annoyed that the Beatles/Zeppelin principle hadn't applied to the remaining members of Pink Floyd when he decided to leave the band in 1982. However, he recently revealed on TV, during an interview on *The South Bank Show*, that he had been misguided in his pursuit of the Pink Floyd name after he'd quit the band and the rest of them had simply decided to carry on. As for everyone else, we tended to muddle through, evolve, get new people in, and keep Pete Frame in business. Sometimes it might be a pretty threadbare afterlife: the current version of Dr Hook is 'Dr Hook Featuring Ray "Eyepatch" Sawyer'. If you really need to hear 'Sylvia's Mother' sung by the man who played maracas on it, this is the show for you.

If I were to win the Wishbone Ash case, Mr Recorder Douglas Campbell would have to add to case law and create a precedent—a new interpretation—for what happens vis-à-vis the goodwill attached to an old-school 'partnership' band when people leave one after the other and it devolves down to one guy: the last man standing.

Not all vintage bands in these multiple-version situations go down the legal route. The financial implications are not to be sneezed at. The two Barclay James Harvests, for instance, have—at the time of writing—fought shy of sorting it out in court. It's only a guess, but I would imagine that their previous experience of the law is putting them off. In 1985 a musical arranger, Robert John Godfrey, who had worked on a couple of their early albums in the 70s, sought redress against all four BJH members (John, Les, Woolly, and Mel), alleging that he was essentially a fifth member and had co-written a number of their songs, and as such was entitled to substantial recompense. When it came to court in 1995 the judge ruled that he had a reasonable claim around the co-authorship of six songs but kicked out any notion of being owed a share of the band's subsequent success based on this 'fifth member' suggestion. The case was apparently both stressful and expensive, and I can understand why John and Les aren't rushing to repeat it. Still, at the very least, that judge back in 1995 did manage to protect mankind from any possibility of a future entity called 'Robert John Godfrey's Barclay James Harvest'.

All this goes to show that where there's a musical brand that has some level of resonance with the public, and some level of ongoing commercial viability, questions of brand ownership will continue to be relevant—and solutions to the consequences of complex membership histories and cooled personal relations will continue to be sought. These days, it would be a very foolish band indeed that didn't have something on paper from the outset covering these issues. But there are more than enough active survivors from the glory days still kicking around to ensure that cases like Powell vs Turner keep having to be heard to help fix the leaky plumbing of long ago.

* * *

The result of the case was due on October 24 2013. The court days had come during a tough period for us: we had a friend's funeral, then two days in court, and then a tour starting almost immediately after that. When the result came through we were heading toward a show in Kendal, in England's Lake District. The recollection is vivid because to get there we were driving across moors and had no phone signal at all—with the knowledge that a call from our lawyers was imminent. We were very tense. We pulled in to get some diesel, and then the phone rang. It transpired that the only reception for miles and miles around was at that petrol station. And, by chance, that was where we were the very moment the lawyers happened to phone.

'You've won,' they said.

It had been a long four or five weeks to wait but at the end of that second day my feelings were that if the case did not go our way, something must be seriously wrong with the legal system. I was really hopeful but resolved at the same time.

In the event we were awarded costs and then began preparing for a damages hearing, for which we produced a very detailed analysis of Martin's activities and how they had negatively impacted our own. It was a massive amount of work—we had to produce a spreadsheet of eight years of gigs Martin did in order to justify our claim, including information on his fees, as well as what shows we could have done had he not been on the scene, what shows of ours had been gazumped, what shows of ours were impacted, what shows we were prevented from going back to because he had undersold the band to such a degree that the credibility of the name was shot. It was totally forensic—a daunting project taken on by our loyal agent Andy Nye. In the end, however, we did not proceed with the damages hearing, as Martin had entered bankruptcy.

The full judgment is available online, but in a nutshell, having heard all the evidence and explored at length a wide variety of previous judgments, Recorder Campbell had come to the following conclusion:

> I am in no doubt that the use of [the name] Martin Turner's Wishbone Ash involves a clear likelihood of confusion with the registered mark.

I had needed to show only one of three possible kinds of injury, known in the law as 'dilution', 'tarnishing', and 'free riding'. The judge was satisfied that two of these three were established: dilution (wherein the market is diluted as a result of the confusion) and free riding (wherein the rival has essentially prospered on the coattails of the claimant's brand). Tarnishing is where the reputation of a brand is diminished by the appearance of poor-quality bogus versions of that brand. This was the judge's view on the matter:

> It was suggested that the Defendant's band was of lesser musical quality than the Claimant's band; that it cheapened the brand by

playing smaller venues and/or for reduced prices; and that it had harmed relations with promoters. I am sure that the Claimant sincerely believes in these complaints but they were strongly disputed by the Defendant and were not substantiated by the evidence. I reject that part of the Claimant's case.

Earlier in his judgment, Recorder Campbell had commented thus on Andy Nye's evidence:

In Mr Nye's view, the fact that the Claimant's band was still producing new material was a key factor in its being able to continue touring, and that if the band had merely played the original songs that would not have been possible. I do not agree … the Defendant's band does not play any new songs, yet has toured for many years.

Establishing whether one performing entity is of a lower standard than another is, I'll agree, a difficult proposition. If it were simply a matter of comparing two recordings, the evidence is there in aspic, ready to be mulled over by trained musicologists for as long as they require, but live performance takes place in the moment, and appreciation of it to a great extent a matter of subjective opinion. Beauty is the ear of the be-hearer. I can certainly appreciate, and accept, the judge's ruling on this aspect, though the question of whether a vintage act can successfully tour over an extended or indefinite period of years is an interesting one.

On the one hand, an act like The Rolling Stones can seemingly tour on an ever-ongoing basis playing only old material because they're a special case: they are so wrapped up in mythology (be it of their own making or others') as 'the greatest rock'n'roll band in the world' and have such huge personalities in Jagger and Richards, whose reach extends way beyond pure music fans, that they can almost be guaranteed sell-out stadiums any time they choose to regroup. They are an event—a kind of 'bucket list' experience rather than a simple live music show. Intriguingly, almost nobody on earth is interested in them recording or performing new material—and with hours of classics to choose from, they don't need to. The very fact that Jagger, as

I pointed out in evidence, can release a new solo album and sell fewer than 1,000 copies of it in his home country—while stadiums full of people are simultaneously ecstatic at paying hundreds of pounds to see him perform old songs under the Rolling Stones banner—surely demonstrates the point. You might also be able to make the case for The Who being in that bracket as well, although Townshend is too restless a writer to be happy without some kind of new project on the go and odd new songs dropped into the set—but seeing The Who in the twenty-first century, selling out huge arenas, is still largely an oldies show. Paul McCartney could very easily play oldies sets from here on in, but again he's a restless creative—and more prolific than Townshend at releasing new stuff. You feel that it must be a matter of pride for him to keep pushing new albums and singles and working the media.

Those two or three exceptions aside, though, I'm firmly of the view that peddling classic material alone is a template for diminishing returns. The way we appreciate albums as listeners may have changed radically from the 70s, when buying a new record was an event and listening time for it was more dedicated than it can possibly be today—where everything is instant and fast moving, and so many other distractions are available—but core fans of any working band or artist want to, expect to, and deserve to hear something new on a regular basis. If I were to perform the whole of *Argus* as a tour set, it would be a great tour the first time out; second time out, there'd be fewer people; third time, fewer still. Aside from core fans, the media and promoters need to see that an act is still creating new work for its credibility and currency to remain, which of course affects the fees that can be negotiated for performances. And finally, as musicians, we need to have the goal of periodically working on something new to sustain our own interest and self-belief.

Eventually, if you stop creating new work, your audience will simply drift away. A case in point is the American singer-songwriter and solo bluesman Chris Smither, who had a popular and acclaimed career in 1969–72, releasing two albums and giving Bonnie Raitt her signature song, 'Love Me Like A Man'. He then boozed for twelve years on the road as his audience gradually moved on. He only resurrected his career when he stopped drinking and started writing and recording new music again in the mid 80s. Chris is currently a major figure in the roots music world, and he would tell you without any doubt in his mind that it was the new music, not his lifestyle changes, that brought the punters back.

As for Wishbone Ash, we'll respectfully agree to differ with the judge on this one: we'll continue delivering new music and continue refreshing the oldies part of the set. All the original band members have a lot to be proud of from those 70s records, but if I left it at that, I have a feeling that the scenario I mentioned earlier, with the velvet suit and the lounge bars, might become a little too plausible.

Mr Recorder Campbell went on to say:

> Given the Defendant's case that the qualifier is sufficiently strong to prevent confusion with 'Wishbone Ash' arising in the first place, it is difficult see why the words 'Martin Turner' are not strong enough to use as a name for his band. The Defendant's logic was that people were coming to see him because he was widely recognised as the creative force behind the original Wishbone Ash, hence using his name should attract those people.
>
> I find that the Defendant's use of Martin Turner's Wishbone Ash was without due cause, as was the use of the domain name to market his band.

And finally, the judge rejected outright Martin's counterclaim to see my accounts from 1969 to the present and obtain a share of all profits based on the share of goodwill that resulted from his contribution to the original band. He rejected this manoeuvre on the basis that: (a) it was a bit late in the day, given that he hadn't sought anything in the near forty years since the demise of the original band; (b) I was the sole owner of the goodwill since 1998; and (c) based on the logic of the Byford vs Oliver judgment, he was the wrong person to even be making the claim—it could only come from an Administrator on the dissolution of the 'partnership'—and, if it did, we'd need to see Martin's accounts too.

I won't lie: the judgment made me extremely proud to be British. And it made me feel extremely proud of the team that had put the case together.

Martin Turner believes, as he says in his promotional material, that he's 'the original founding member and key creative force of Wishbone Ash'. Whatever his contribution to Wishbone Ash, and whatever his creative force may be, the real tragedy is that not once in this whole process were he and I able to sit down in a room, one-on-one, and thrash this out—which we could have done easily.

You can still go to Martin's website and find a small number of people posting there who enjoy complaining about it. That's up to them, but I can't suddenly change my life or erase bits of it to please a few hundred people. What I've found when I travel around is that most humans want to help other humans—that's the basic modus operandi of people. If something's positive, they'll get on board with it. But there'll always be curmudgeons and conspiracy theorists. It's a different world, and I'm glad I have no part of it.

I enjoy the old albums as much as anyone. They're little vignettes, but they're from another century, for God's sake. I listen to an old recording of a song like 'Blind Eye', on vinyl, and I think, *My God, that's just brilliant.* It's the coming together of a number of forces at that particular moment in time, which can't be recreated. But taking the decision to lance the boil of what Martin was doing was inevitable, because I felt that we had something *current* to protect. Not only my livelihood but the livelihoods of my fellow band members, Bob, Muddy, and Joe; the reputation of the band name; and not least the body of work that we've made in the last ten-to-fifteen years. We don't make new albums for the hell of it—we do the best we can every time and we put heart and soul into it and hope people enjoy it just as much as the records we made in the past. To me, that was worth protecting. Bringing it to court wasn't a matter of ego, it was about dignity.

Right now, I seem to be a star in the legal world, appearing more regularly in legal publications than I do in the music press! But I'm not bitter about the whole experience. I wish it hadn't happened, of course, but I'm not gnashing my teeth about it or re-running old arguments in my head. I don't have any bitterness. But I don't like being bullied. I'll stand up to that, as anyone would.

There's a line in the sand now. Promoters know what the score is with the name 'Wishbone Ash'. That means more to me than anything else from that whole experience. It showed people that this is a life—a career and a brand that's worth fighting for. And even though Martin was a very important, intrinsic element of that brand he did of his own volition, in the first instance, leave it—and so did all the others. It goes on in the business world all the time: a business gets started, then the company gets sold to someone else. In the music instrument business, for example, Gibson Guitars was owned in the 80s by a company from Ecuador. People don't generally know that. Currently, it's owned by a man of Polish origin.

* * *

Not long before we received the judgment up there on the hills around Kendal, Pauline and I were in the States, in a shoe store, and we noticed a big chrome sign—a wishbone in a circle, virtually our current logo, accompanied by the words 'Wishbone Shoes'. There's no way they could have come up with that logo without seeing ours. So, as wearying as it may be, I may have to jump into the fray again.

'What can you tell us about this?' we asked the sales assistant.

'Oh, I've got four pairs of Wishbone Shoes myself. They've been going for years. They're great shoes …'

ROAD WORKS

We've often been associated with the term 'prog rock', largely because journalists often find it difficult to categorise us as a band—and these days there is always the need to categorise everything. To me, 'prog rock' sounds endlessly boring. It's like some sexless, sixth-form version of rock'n'roll—something cerebral and not at all anything that might give rise to the crazier, sexier, fun side of music, unless you count the druggy influences that have played a role in the music of the Pink Floyd or Porcupine Tree, for example.

Early on, there was a distinct line in the sand concerning drugs in our career. Miles Copeland was vehemently anti-drug; so was Steve Upton and, to a lesser extent, Martin Turner. All three of my bandmates were cigarette smokers, though. I'd smoked hashish in Morocco, but I could take it or leave it. On arriving in London, Ted was pretty enamoured with the smoking scene, and naturally our road crew lapped it up—in most cases, our conduit to consumption was through the crew. Musicians would not wish to be seen doing the dodgy business of actually buying the stuff. I can tell you, though, that in my experience, anyone who says that pot is not a gateway drug has just got it wrong. And so it proved to be in our band. Then again, the peer pressure and the times we lived through made it very hard to stand on the outside of the drug culture. It became such a thing that, years later, I was actually astonished to hear from promoters that they had assessed us as a band of 'heads', and that it was seen as a prerequisite to have the necessary drugs on board at venues we'd play at, just to keep us happy. In my mind, we were only ever dabbling in the bloody stuff.

The labels were no better than the promoters in this regard, because those were the days of equal opportunity employment. It was mandatory to have on your team at least one woman, one black person, a Hispanic, and, of course, a hippie. Hippies were seen as a disadvantaged group in their own right. That might sound funny but in our case one Jeffrey Dengrove, the stoner to end all stoners, was assigned to us on American tours to cover promotion and PR as we made our way across the United States. I can see him now with that leather shoulder bag full of delights to keep us sedated or uplifted, as the case may be, paid for, no doubt, out of our promotions budget. In other words, as a cost to be debited against our large recording advance.

I can honestly say that aside from promoting circuitous THC-infused conversations or fits of giggles when we'd visit restaurants, the whole thing was a monumental waste of time, quite literally, in terms of the recording process. In the case of our road crew, it actually interrupted one US tour, resulting in at least one member of our crew—definitely Kevin Harrington and quite possibly Mark Emery—being deported after a hotel-room bust. It was unfortunate for Kevin because he'd been back in the hotel asleep at the time, minding his own business while the rest of the crew were out partying at a nightclub, when they'd been intercepted by law enforcement officials who demanded to be taken back to the crew's hotel in order make a search.

Criteria Studios in Florida, where we recorded several albums, was the worst place to be if you wished to avoid the drug scene. It was all pervasive, as can be seen by the albums that were produced there: Joe Walsh, CSN, The Bee Gees, The Allman Brothers, Derek & The Dominos ... none of these guys were doing drugs, right? We were no exception. Before the advent of digital tuners, I can remember us spending hours simply trying to tune the guitars before we even played a note together, while suffering the mildly hallucinatory effects of Jamaican weed. Certainly, cocaine-fuelled guitar solos were in evidence on those sessions, and at other studios, too. I remember spending hours moving my amplifier all over the building in order to achieve some kind of ambience in the guitar sound and, on at least a couple of occasions, I'd be standing on the MCI recording console, holding the guitar up to the very expensive playback system, cranked at full volume in the small control room—anything to try to achieve the feel and energy of playing live in a concert hall. These excursions were undoubtedly drug-dependent and would have given things a certain edge, no doubt.

Hallucinogens rarely had their impact on our recorded catalogue or general band career except to say that there was a moment in time that Martin used to mention, concerning a particularly bad acid trip that he underwent in London, where he describes a kind of lightning-bolt impact on his psyche around the time of *Argus* or *Wishbone Four*. He never seemed quite the same after that. Similarly, Steve Upton went through a major personality change after doing a 180-degree shift in his attitude to drugs, subsequent to helping out a photographer friend on a shoot and partaking of the weed. Something of an epiphany ensued and he fell completely under the spell of the stuff to the point of growing it, eating it, and generally living the life of a pothead of refined tastes.

All of this was difficult to handle for our management, agents, and anyone who had to deal with us in a professional way. We'd met all the notorious groupies of the day, too—The Butter Queen, The Plaster Casters, Miss Connie Hamzy—at various shows in Texas and Los Angeles, and we'd had our well-documented chaotic showcase in front of the MCA/Decca brass at the Whisky A Go Go almost upended by Ted Turner's similarly well-documented three-day disappearance in the desert at Joshua Tree while tripping on LSD. The LA rock scene was turning weird around this time and the original late 60s hippie euphoria was being replaced by a scarier vibe. The bubble burst after the Manson murders, and by the time we hit town in the early 70s the mood was decidedly different from the West Coast cool which had inspired bands like CSNY—bands that were only now inspiring some of our own musical repertoire in songs like 'Blowin' Free'.

We used to like a drink, too; that old rock'n'roll favourite, Scotch and Coke, was our drink of choice. Scotch whisky still finds its way on to our touring rider, although I'm about the only one who drinks it. Old habits die hard, but these days I prefer a nice single malt, sipped quietly by the fireside. Beer was a thing, too, but more as a thirst quencher. It never caused any major issues except for one time during our first visit to Washington DC, when we were pulled over by a police cruiser right outside the White House. We simply had not realised what a huge deal it was in America to have open cans of beer—or any alcoholic beverage—in a car. To us, American beer was like weak pee anyway—we viewed it as a kind of soft drink. The officer ordered us out of the vehicle, right within view of the president's residence, and slammed us up against the side of his cruiser. Being as we were so young, and foreign to boot, he made allowances and let us off with a stern warning after Miles in his Brooks Brothers attire explained in an obviously American accent, 'Officer, this an English pop group'—as if that alone designated us as clueless. It was a close call, but there were other times where we were not so lucky.

* * *

In the early days, we'd fly from gig to gig on these huge tours of the US, travelling on domestic carriers, playing one-night stands in Des Moines or Duluth. My geography of the United States in particular was extremely sketchy at that time: I knew that New York was on the East Coast and LA was on the West, but the rest of it barely registered. It wasn't until much later that I got a handle on it all. We'd make do with very little sleep, and I have a lot of memories of running to airport gates to make flights. We were always late and in a hurry, having partied to the wee hours after a show somewhere. The main function of our tour managers was to wake us up and to get us to the airport. I remember a lot of times we'd simply screech to a halt at, say, Houston airport and run to the gate, leaving the rental car in the road for the company to come and collect it.

There was very little airport security in those days, if any at all. We often travelled with a full backline of British equipment, which would need to somehow get on the plane with us, courtesy of our dedicated crew. The crew would somehow be at the airport before us and our tour manager, whether it be Mel Baister of Mal Ross, would be bribing the freight handlers with $100 bills to stuff this massively heavy artillery onto the planes. We had all these powerful amplifiers and speakers made by Orange. They weighed more than any other equipment you could buy because we loaded the cabinets with upgraded JBL K120 speakers. I can't believe how our road crew carried these things.

Once we made it onto on the plane, we'd slump into our seats and commence smoking and drinking, as everyone did on airplanes those days, ready for the next soundcheck and show later that afternoon. Mostly the flights were city-to-city hops. This would go on for weeks. I remember all kinds of dodgy landings in snowstorms or escaping hurricanes, being diverted miles out of our way, horrendous air turbulence (which latterly seems to have disappeared), and much, much worse things to do with the glamorous world of flying.

When you are young and cocksure, you are totally oblivious of how close danger can be at hand when flying around the world. Flying itself is—or was—often a harrowing experience. Some of the pilots we encountered, particularly in the South, were real characters. On one occasion, after touching down in our turbo prop and going into a sideways slide, we heard the disembodied voice of the captain over the intercom: 'That was a close call' followed by 'We're heading back out like gang-busters here, y'all!' On another occasion, the pilot let us know, while chuckling to himself, that a particular manoeuvre would not have been possible in a larger jet.

Then there was the time we looked out of the window of our 747 after departing London Heathrow and saw flames licking around the engine cowling. We were forced to land in Ireland instead of continuing on to the US. There was the time when we were flying out of Yugoslavia. We'd all been anxiously waiting for Martin to join us on the plane so that the cabin door could be secured for take off. Finally, our errant bass player joined the rest of the passengers, the last person to board the plane. Mart had long been a member of the 'white knuckle club' and had a distinct aversion to flying, which was rough if you had to do it for a living. We went through the usual pre-flight routine and the plane shot down the runway, heading into a steep climb as it took off. At the very peak of this climb all hell broke loose as lights flashed on and off and the sounds of a warning buzzer filled the cabin. Apparently the cabin door had not been secured properly, thereby preventing proper pressurization—to say nothing of any other dangers. The pilot immediately put the plane into a steep dive back to the runway. That was truly disconcerting for all the passengers and no doubt for Martin in particular, who grimly held onto the arms of the seat as we went through the whole take-off procedure for a second time.

* * *

One of the advantages of international travel is that you sometimes find yourself in the eye of a storm caused by atmospheric or political conditions, which could be a shock to a bunch of guys brought up in the benign, liberal, nanny state of Great Britain in the 60s. My first shock in this regard came before I joined Wishbone Ash, when I was kicked by a jackbooted fascist Spanish policeman for sitting on the steps of a monument, while dressed in hippie garb sporting long blonde hair, which I was very proud of at the time.

That was in 1969. Only recently, in 2015, we played a small town in Belgium called Verviers. It was a great show, the first date on our European tour. The very next day, we left for Germany. Just days later, we saw footage on TV of Verviers in complete turmoil as police were seen to be raiding a terrorist cell right there in the town.

Years earlier, we saw the threat to freedom directly in Northern Ireland. On more than one occasion, when travelling from the South into the North, there would be no alternative but to go through armed checkpoints on the country roads near the border. The way it worked was that a couple of tense soldiers—the ones who'd obviously drawn the short straws—would come up to the car to study your passports and so on, fingers very much on the triggers of their automatic weapons. Others in their platoon would be positioned in ditches, observing the whole procedure, fingers also on triggers. The checkpoints themselves would be repositioned on a daily basis. It made us all aware of just how vulnerable we were.

This was really scarily serious for all of us. We were just mere minstrels coming to this fair land to play our songs to the people, and here we were in the middle of a war zone. It was made abundantly clear to us by our driver, a rambunctious fellow who described how he'd watched as his brand new Mercedes minibus had exploded after terrorists tossed a grenade into it. Thankfully, he and his passengers had been told to get out before these guys—whom he described as being very 'wired' after a day of such hits—threw the grenade. This, apparently, had been their last gesture of the day; the British Army was closing in on them.

Being in Berlin in 1989, first two weeks prior to the fall of the Wall and then a week or so after it actually started to come down, was hugely exciting. I was inspired to write a couple of songs, 'Chimes Of Freedom' and 'Wings Of Desire', the latter of which made it on to the album *Bare Bones*. Having toured Germany for so many years and gone through the crazy border patrol in East Berlin, travelling the 'corridor', seeing the plight of these 'other' Germans, it was fascinating to now be able to meet some of them and hear their side of the story.

The fall of the Wall was generally viewed as a liberation but much of their familiar past was eradicated overnight—place names, identity documents, currency. That's the side you don't hear about. No nation other than Germany, in my experience, could have pulled off such a massive overhaul of infrastructure in such a short time. Prior to the Wall coming down you'd travel in the East and it was a time warp—the smell of coal fires, cobblestone streets, food scarcities, cheap cigarettes, farmers tilling the fields with horse and plough. Overnight, it seemed, after unification, buildings were power-washed and repaired, and gleaming new autobahns spidered out across the fields. You'd see these quirky little family units picnicking on super highways, seemingly oblivious to the Porsches and Mercedes flying by. They'd be sitting beside their Trabants—sad little cars with body panels made of plywood—that they'd saved up to buy over the course of decades.

Back in the dark days of communism we'd balked at having to stay on the Berlin corridor road, figuring we knew better. Again with Rod Lynton at the wheel, we decided to take a side road through a village, just to check things out. Within minutes of our deviation we were surrounded by very irate, gun-wielding soldiers with German shepherd dogs and firmly escorted back to the main road. Many bands travelled that road made of concrete slabs, and I can still recall the spine-jolting journey as you clunked along it. We did it dozens of times. In the old days you'd see Russian officers partying in their oversized caps and jackboots. It was colourful and threatening at the same time. Berlin had some of the craziest nightclubs I've ever been to—seeing live sex onstage was not uncommon, but then you'd be able to juxtapose that with a visit to some tearoom, where a string ensemble would be playing in a genteel manner while you sipped your drink.

Berlin was then, and still is, a city of contrasts. More recently, we had around 20,000 euros worth of equipment stolen from a van parked outside our hotel there, in what appeared to be a very safe street. We'd played a show at a club in the city called Quasimodo's and left the vehicle for no more than three or four hours on the street. A gang had very professionally drilled off the lock—which they did microscopically, so that we didn't notice until we reached the next city, hundreds of miles away—and made off with some nice instruments, including a favourite Les Paul of Muddy's. Since the theft had taken place only 60km from the Czech border, the assumption by the police, when we made the report, was that the goods would be long gone toward Eastern Europe, and that there would not be much chance of retrieving the precious Les Paul and the rest of the items that had gone missing. I hope someone is making some nice music somewhere with those guitars.

We've been robbed several times, in fact. I remember Ted Turner always being robbed from whichever flat he rented; perhaps he was too trusting with visitors? In 1972 we had an entire truck taken from a hotel car park in St Louis, with all our custom Orange equipment and guitars on board. We were devastated. Luckily, I'd taken my precious Gibson '67 Flying V with me to my hotel room, so that survived. We never did see the rest of it again until, strangely, in early 2005. The rumour at the time was that the heist was somehow connected to our promoter in St Louis, or that it had been an inside job in some way. It was just too convenient. At any rate, we really depended on our stage setup and customised Orange gear, which was the backbone of our sound, and we felt that there was no other option but to simply cancel the tour and return home. We'd lost everything, and it was pointless trying to replace it with makeshift gear from the States. That's how precious we were about our live sound in those days.

What happened much, much later on was that odd bits of information would turn up here and there about the stolen equipment. It turned out that no one had else in the US had the same stuff, and in addition we'd had it all branded with our logo, deep into the actual wood. So it was very difficult for the thieves to 'fence'. Someone said that Joe Perry from Aerosmith had ended up with an amp or two. It was all rumour until many years later, after a return show to St Louis, during an audience meet-and-greet session, a strange guy came up to me and told me that he had bought one of my amps and really felt bad about it. He did not have the amp with him but pressed a wad of two-dollar bills into my hand, saying that he would at some point return with the amp, which he said he would donate back to me despite having bought it.

Sure enough, the next time we played in town, he turned up with yet more of these unusual, brand new two-dollar bills—some kind of compensation, I guess. I thought the guy was slightly nuts but the third time we hit town, he arrived with a sad remnant of one of my favourite amplifiers that had been so badly bastardised and mutilated that it broke my heart. I took it from him, though, and have recently been trying to restore it as a memento of that time. It still sounds great.

Another great benefit of touring the world is making friends in different countries and seeing life through their eyes as you get to know them. You hear stories of how our music might have helped them as students in some far flung university, or how soldiers or sailors in foreign warzones had our music with them to inspire or comfort, or how it might have fostered friendships with others. All of this is a huge honour, and I take it pretty seriously. In fact, it's part of the impetus to carry on and keep the band together, and is an example of how, as Hilary Clinton might say, it takes a village to produce a band and its music.

* * *

One of the best travel adventures we ever undertook was the world tour of 1974, just after Laurie Wisefield joined the band. Ted was off in the Peruvian mountains on a donkey, but we were having our own adventures visiting Hawaii, Australia, New Zealand, and Japan. We were on a fifty-date American tour, and instead of going home for Christmas, Miles chartered this fabulous vintage motor yacht built in the 30s. We cruised down to Key West in Florida, where we avoided the cold weather back home and had a ball with our families for a couple of days, water-skiing, fishing, and jamming under the stars on the back deck of this fabulous vessel, with its state rooms and old-world finery. From there we played more US and Canadian dates before boarding a plane in frozen Edmonton en route to sunny Honolulu.

Finally, we were able to get some real rest and relaxation, with time off to go to the beach and play at being tourists. One of the first things we did was convince a catamaran rental company that we were all sailors. The crew and band got several Hobie Cats and headed out into the surf, which was running at about six feet—which is a lot when you're in a small sailboat. For the first few minutes we were flying in these things, but then one by one we all capsized and, after fruitless attempts to right our crafts, had to be rescued by an irate owner of the business. Rock'n'roll comes to town.

We met a couple of rogues on Waikiki beach who were running a rickshaw ride business, and before long, after they discovered that we were in a famous band, a limo was produced from somewhere in order to tour the island. One of these guys kept going on about Thai stick and temple balls, and how we should try these super-potent blends of grass, which of course we did. Things got whacky. Much later on—several months on in fact—we found out that at least one of these fellows was either on parole or on the run. He turned up in London, visiting Martin at his flat in St Quintin Avenue, where Martin gave him a bed for the night and was repaid by having his rather fine Nikon SLR camera purloined. He only realised this after the chap—Dave was his name—had gone on his merry way.

We had one date in paradise, at the University of Hawaii, before heading on to Australasia. It was a tour like no other, and visiting all these different places really turned your head around. In Japan we were treated like a teenybopper band with screaming girls meeting us at Tokyo airport. Laurie—or 'Lolly', as they would scream at him—was the favourite, and it took a real security job to keep the fans from invading our hotels. They were truly ingenious, using fire escapes and all manner of ploys to get to where we were. One morning I came down to breakfast and there was the actor Richard Kiel, a giant of a man at seven-foot-two who played Jaws in the James Bond movies, sitting there in the breakfast room. He was hardly inconspicuous, but acted as normal as anything.

I remember arriving in Australia, jetlagged, but being whisked straight into a press conference, complete with TV cameras. It must have always been a big deal when foreign acts visited Oz in those days. The first question I was asked was, 'How d'ya like Australia, Andy?' Blearily, I answered, 'I'm not sure—I only just arrived. It seems nice.' In fact, of far more interest to the press than our arrival was that of The Osmonds, who were staying at the same hotel as us in Sydney. Pauline was thrilled by this, and even got to share an elevator ride with Donny himself.

We had some great shows there, plus some useful downtime, which Pauline and I used to join up with an old school friend, Suzanne, and her husband Bob. We hired a car and travelled out into the outback with them and our tour manager, Russell, dodging kangaroos along the way. After that we hiked into the Blue Mountains, which was amazing: abandoned mining camps, eucalyptus forests, kangaroos, parrots, and all kinds of wildlife, including a giant lizard they call a goanna that walked lazily through our campsite one night.

From there, we went on to New Zealand, where we played Wellington, Christchurch, and Auckland. We had a couple of days off beforehand, so Pauline and I decided to get a small charter flight down to the South Island to visit the town of Dunedin, where I had some long lost relatives. I particularly wanted to see my Uncle Bill, who by now was in his seventies. He'd been my father's oldest living brother, but dad had never met him because Bill had left Britain as a teenager, before my dad was even born, he being the youngest of the six brothers and sisters. I'd heard stories of Bill around the dining table while growing up. I was not sure if he'd stowed away on a ship or lied about his age to obtain a working passage or what it was all about, but at any rate he'd left home, much to his mother's distress, at the tender age of fifteen, marrying out there and producing a large family while becoming a sheep farmer. What else?

We went up to the door of his modest bungalow, which was opened after a pause by a carbon copy of my father, complete with the Powell signature bald pate, same posture, same smile and blue eyes. It was as if I'd known him all my life. Incredible. Over lunch we heard tales of his life and were introduced to his family, and then after an emotional departure we set off back to join our rock'n'roll tour. It was all of great interest to my English family, and I like to think that Pauline and I were instrumental in Uncle Bill's arrival in the UK several years later for a truly emotional reunion. My father himself couldn't believe it, and the tears of joy flowed freely.

The whole tour would leave incredible memories and impressions on all the band members. We would travel far afield in later years but at the age we were at that time, the impressions and adventures were so vivid, as they are when in your early twenties. We went out in a flourish in Auckland at the Western Springs Stadium on March 15, where we played an open-air concert. Steve Upton's custom of late had been to leave his drum stool and take over proceedings on the mic, to give us all a break. He'd taken to wearing these cut-off denim overalls and rainbow-striped socks, giving him a hint of the clownish demeanour of Robin Williams in *Mork & Mindy*.

Steve would get the audience in an even better mood by doing a riff on smoking a spliff, miming the actions as he went on. This always went down fabulously in the States, where people were quite open to all that at the time. Not so, though, in staid old New Zealand, which was quite behind the times, and where the police and authorities took a dim view of this kind of brazen public encouragement. The final straw came when Steve announced from the centre of the stage that we were about to play 'F.U.B.B.', which had been so titled as a result of our drug-infused recording sessions in Miami. It was an acronym for 'Fucked Up Beyond Belief'.

On his utterance of the dreaded F-word, the wheels were put in motion to forcibly take Steve from the stage. To be fair, the police waited until the end of the concert, possibly fearing a riot, but down to the local jail he went, in handcuffs. This was all pretty exciting. With one word he had assured us of headlines around the world—not least in the British *Daily Mail*—and I'm sure it shocked the life out of his mother when she read of his escapades. Knowing Steve as I did, it was all very much out of character, but it was great in a way that he'd been so risqué.

CHAPTER 10

BLUE HORIZON
(2007–PRESENT)

Back in 2002, Jethro Tull released a live DVD entitled *Living With The Past*, a knowing nod to their 1969 hit single 'Living In The Past'. Tull-meister Ian Anderson was good at those hostage-to-fortune titles: 'Too Old To Rock'n'Roll' (from 1976) is hard to beat. But he always had his tongue firmly in his cheek and a winning way to keep the show on the road, adapting to new times and circumstances with new music while also keeping the faithful on board with deluxe remasters and 'classic album' shows.

In many regards, Wishbone Ash have followed a similar path. As was expressed robustly during the court case, I passionately believe in Wishbone Ash creating new music. I'm equally passionate that when the band does so, there is often evidence of a thread of DNA linking it back to the best of what was produced back in the day. I'm not interested in writing or recording thinly veiled copies of 'Living Proof' or 'The King Will Come', or anything else from the back catalogue, but there will be a sound and a spirit that we can draw from and tap into while crafting new work that resonates with people in the here and now.

One downside of having such a long history, with the greatest commercial successes and greatest public awareness at the beginning of our career, is that— outside of the core fan base, which has followed all the twists and turns—an impression can be formed that the current Wishbone Ash is 'Andy Powell plus some other guys', the implication being that, unless there are more of the 'name' players from the 70s involved, it somehow can't possibly be any good. Who are these 'some other guys', though? Are they people I've just bumped into in pub bands and co-opted into this tour or that? Of course not!

Even during the tough times in the 80s, we never settled for mediocrity.

Players were always found with personality and quality, with something exciting to bring to the table in terms of their energy and musicianship. Even the short-term alumni of Wishbone Ash cannot be doubted in this assessment. To give one example, John Wetton, a 'name' musician, lasted one album and no live shows: I didn't click with his personality, but his playing was superb. To give another, Phil Palmer, a pro sideman and a musician's musician, stepped up to the plate at a week's notice and single-handedly saved some dates.

In the calmer and more predictable waters of the new millennium, Wishbone Ash has become a firmly established, solid, and viable commercial entity. To imagine that I'd take my eye off the ball and start working with mediocre players is bizarre. Casual students of 70s rock may not have heard of Muddy Manninen, Bob Skeat, or Joe Crabtree—not least because Joe, for one, wasn't even born in the 70s—but take it from me: there are no passengers here, no dead weight. Setting aside the magic of the first years of the original band, I'd argue that the current Wishbone Ash is the best Wishbone Ash there has been.

If that sounds like hubris or marketing, or the ramblings of a dotard, all I can suggest is this: listen to the music, watch the live DVDs, check out the evidence.

* * *

I view the 'modern phase' of Wishbone Ash as beginning with *Bona Fide* in 2002 and gathering a further head of steam with Muddy Manninen joining in time for *Clan Destiny* in 2006. Our first concert DVD of this modern era was *Live At The Spirit Of '66*, filmed in the venue of that name in Verviers, Belgium, in February 2006, two months before *Clan Destiny* was released. Ray Weston was still in the band but it was early days for Muddy Manninen on second guitar. None of this mattered, though, because everyone played a blinder.

A typical Wishbone Ash live set from these past fifteen years or so is roughly two thirds 1970–96 material, from *Wishbone Ash* to *Illuminations*, and one third 'modern era' material, from *Bona Fide* onward. The sixteen-song set on *Live At The Spirit Of '66* is a fair example: two songs from *Bona Fide*, three from the forthcoming *Clan Destiny*, and eleven from the seventeen albums up to *Illuminations*. The ratio on the set captured on our next DVD, *Live In Hamburg* (2007), is similar: eighteen songs, five of them from the current album, *Clan Destiny*; one from *Bona Fide*; and twelve from all the previous albums, many of these different selections from those heard on the *Spirit Of '66* set.

That two-thirds/one-third ratio feels right. And barring maybe three or four 'signature songs' that people probably have a right to expect, we have the freedom to shake up the oldies part of that ratio on a regular basis. As I've explained previously, I very much live in the present, but I'm proud of the Wishbone Ash legacy and always respectful of what fans want to hear when they come and see us. And, happily, we've found a way to keep it interesting and refreshed for all concerned. A couple of times in recent years, like Jethro Tull—and like many of our British rock peers—we've based tours around whole 'classic albums': *Argus* in 2007 and *Live Dates* in 2014. Even then, though, we bookended those sets with some of our most recent songs. It's all about paying respect to our heritage but not being a slave to it.

So, these recent songs, you might be wondering: are they any good? And who's writing them? Fair questions both. You can surely guess my answer to the first. The answer to the second is a bit more involved. Let me explain.

In the early days, and certainly for the first couple of albums, Wishbone Ash was a band with a sound in search of songs. It's now a band with songs, with something to sing about, *and* with a sound. We're older and wiser but we still seek to tap into and deliver the euphoria we found when the planets first aligned for us back around *Argus*. I'll explain also that I always use the term 'we' because a band, though a singular entity, is made up of pluralities. It matters not to me that the current 'we' is different to the original 'we'. The concept of this band and many bands is that a band can only exist if the 'we' aspect, the team aspect, is always to the fore—just like sports teams, actually. Indeed, it's been my experience that when it ceases to be that way, the band can be seen to be standing on shaky ground.

A team also needs a leader. It took me a while to realise this and even longer to move, reluctantly, into that position. It took only a little while longer to find that I could actually enjoy this, even finding creativity in it, despite the obvious pressures of responsibility. The gamesmanship and navigational skills required to keep this musical entity viable and vital take a lot of energy. As a side note, I rarely find card games, gambling, or board games relaxing. My theory is that my everyday existence requires such a lot of these skills that I need some very different kind of stress-buster when relaxing.

Back to the early days …

The way I look at it is this: by the time the original band recorded *Argus*, we had three years of intense living under our belts. In a collective sense, we were able to just spew all this out. It was the four of us bearing our collective soul—a band that lived and breathed together. We were also reading a lot of news as well as mythology and philosophy, all of which became topics of conversation in vans driving home from gigs. All of that played into *Argus*.

After that we were, in some respects, spent. The success of *Argus* had surprised us and left us self-conscious. We needed time to assimilate all of this, to get things in perspective. Ted's solution was to quit the band. Martin stepped into the breach in the mid 70s and started writing about his experiences—which, by then, weren't our joint experiences. We could play fantastic embellishments to that music—and some of it is music I'm still happy to have been a part of, and still happy to perform onstage—but it wasn't so much a collective production. We were all living different lives. We weren't able to completely buy into Martin's vision.

Nowadays, to me, it's the best of all worlds. In the band as it is now, there's a team. All of us are able to bring something to the table, which gives everyone a sense of gratification.

Over the past few years the team, in creative terms, has grown outwards to include not only the four band members but also all of my sons, a few friends, and some fellow travellers. A close perusal of the writing credits on the five albums from *Bona Fide* on will reveal those regular collaborators: my son Aynsley Powell; my friend Ian Harris; former member Roger Filgate; and fellow road warrior, guitarist, and fiddler Pat McManus. Pauline even chips in with lyrics sometimes.

Where lyrics are concerned, Ian Harris is the most prolific of this inner circle, and a very old friend indeed. He was introduced to me by Roger Dean, a fashion and fabric designer I went to school with, who made lots of the threads I wore onstage in the 70s. I remember one time when he and Pauline took off to John Lewis's fabric department in Oxford Street, returning with a roll of green velvet with pink spots. I was flabbergasted, but Roger proceeded to produce the most amazing double-breasted suit for me, which I loved. I had met Ian in that context. Ian's wife Maggie was Roger's model, and we all hit it off immediately. He has an encyclopaedic knowledge of rock and is the same age as me; he had been a mod and had seen all the same bands as I had in the 60s. In short, Ian was much more in sync with me culturally than some of the actual members of the band I helped form back in 1969. The London sense of humour, for example, is a million miles away from the yokel laughs of Devon and Cornwall. No offence to my West Country brethren, but when the phrase 'Get yer handbag off my plough' results in paroxysms of guffaws, you really have to be from that part of the United Kingdom to get it.

By the 90s I was becoming the de facto vocalist in Wishbone Ash, even though I'd always resisted it. I'd also done a bit of recording in New York, one time with a producer called Kashif, who'd worked with Whitney Houston. I'd been introduced to him by our old tour manager Russell Sidelsky, who was himself moving up the ladder with Kashif, Cher, and later the Def Jam label. I'd seen the way black artists were running things. It was a communal approach, it being impossible to do everything on your own. These guys had little production houses on the go. No sooner would they get some traction with a hit than they'd open it up to their circle and get everyone on board, thereby becoming even more productive. It got me thinking: *I don't have to be precious. All I have to do is keep to the fore the ethos and sound of the band. Why not bring in my old buddy Ian on lyrics? Why not bring in a session player here or there if we need it?* I admired and was inspired by this production-house technique. This communal approach was how we'd originally thought of Wishbone Ash, but we had lost that after Ted quit.

Beginning with one co-write on *Bona Fide* in 2002, Ian has now collaborated, in an elegantly stealthy manner, on six songs on 2014's *Blue Horizon*. This takes a weight off my shoulders and allows me to concentrate on the production of the albums, to create something from the raw materials in front of me. At this stage, I've done everything I ever felt I needed to prove as far as being in a band is concerned. It's not about notching up credits on songs for the sake of it. Opening things up to others is a win-win situation.

Creating the songs on Wishbone Ash records has consequently become a truly fluid, collaborative affair once more. On *Bona Fide*, it was a simple split: Ben Granfelt contributed fully half of the songs, I wrote three, and we co-wrote the remaining two together, with Ian Harris providing lyrics for one of them. When Muddy joined, in time for *Clan Destiny* in 2006, things started spreading out a bit: Muddy contributed one; I had three, one of them co-written with Aynsley; three more came from outside writers; and all the band members collaborated on the remaining five, with Ian Harris providing lyrics for one of them. The subsequent albums have all seen a myriad of collaborations between myself, Muddy, Bob Skeat, Joe Crabtree, Ian, and Aynsley, plus a couple of songs from Pat McManus and one, on *Blue Horizon* (2014), from Roger Filgate. Indeed, the lead track on *Blue Horizon*, 'Take It Back', was a solo composition by Aynsley.

Aynsley, like Ian, has grown up listening to the band—in his case, literally from being a toddler while we were rehearsing or recording. As a result he's also got a really defined sense of what constitutes 'the sound' of Wishbone Ash. I still think it's important to follow the mission we adhered to in the early 70s. My aim has been to reconnect with what it's like to be in a so-called band of brothers—to produce band-centric songs and to keep the joy and euphoria intact in the playing, while continuing to display the high production values that Wishbone Ash have always been known for.

There's far more stability now in camp Wishbone, more *joie de vivre*. And without wishing to blow my own trumpet, I believe a lot of that comes from me: I'm able to infuse the band with that. I'm good at bands: forming them, working them, and making them productive and happy. Another point to consider is that, when you're twenty-two or twenty-three, as we were when *Argus* came out, how much life have you lived? What have you got to say? It's remarkable that we were able to fashion something of depth and meaning at all, as young as we were. But now, song-wise, I've got this whole life behind me that I can tap into. It seems much more natural for me to be writing songs from the standpoint of an older person than it did when I was in my twenties.

While it's fair to say that my writing contributions on the most recent couple of albums have been almost entirely collaborative and ensemble-based, my writing as an individual was possibly at a peak on *The Power Of*

Eternity. Certainly, I'm very proud of the songs I wrote on that album, and on *Clan Destiny* too.

The overriding theme in my writing has always been self-questioning: 'What's it all about, Alfie?' I'm a great closet philosopher. In addition to that, relationship songs are my forte. 'In Crisis', from *The Power Of Eternity*, was written from the heart, actually on the back of a brown paper bag, while crossing the Delaware Bridge at rush hour. The words 'Are You In Crisis?', flashing on a sign across the lanes, resonated with my dark mood at the time. Strength in adversity is another recurring theme. People think that the older you get, the more you know, but it's actually the less you know—or the more you realise that there is so much you don't know. You surrender. And when you surrender, you start producing songs. You become a conduit.

It's become increasingly apparent to me that some guitar players picked up the instrument in the first place because they weren't comfortable singing their own songs. Or, to put it another way, using an instrument is an alternative to using the greatest gift of all: the human voice. This thing around your neck can be an artifice. It's been an amazing revelation to me to find a way to tap into the truth as I know it and give voice to it in songs. I'm so grateful to the band for allowing me to figure this out. I'd also credit Eric Clapton, because I saw Eric go from being a guitarist to a writer and singer of songs. When people who play guitar give vent to their own voice, it turns out to be pretty nice. Peter Green and Gary Moore come to mind, too, though Jeff Beck's an exception to the rule. After years as a reluctant singer, I'm happy with my voice now.

Having said that, I don't need any kudos from critics these days. The only critics that matter to me now are the audiences who come out to our gigs, come rain or shine. An audience can tell if a song has verity. When you tap into something that you did or that occurred to you and sing your song about it, there's nothing more powerful.

* * *

The current Wishbone Ash is in a good place. It's an extended family. Attention will inevitably always focus on the two incarnations from the 70s, from the time when Wishbone Ash were gracing the album charts and receiving regular media coverage. During those years there were four other guys (including Laurie) and me, and maybe some people still draw an inference from the fact that when we all met again in court, forty-odd years adrift from the triumphs of our youth, it was those four other guys ranged against me. But that's not the full picture.

As I count it, seventeen other people have come through the ranks of Wishbone Ash since then, and I have remained on very cordial terms with almost all of them after we parted ways. One consequence of the court case that I haven't mentioned so far, which caused me some distress, was finding that Ray Weston had allowed the financial fallout from the *Live In Chicago*/Permanent Records situation back in 1992 to fester. Although we'd parted on good terms in 2006 and had seen each other since, it appeared that he still had a gripe that somehow some money had gone missing and I was responsible for it. And so, seemingly solicited by the Martin Turner camp, he wrote a statement about this particular issue to cast doubt on my character. The judge ignored it because it simply wasn't relevant, but on a deeper level it was relevant to me.

Ray, I thought, *are you serious?* I've never contacted him about it, but I was angry. I have great memories of fun on the road with Ray, so it was very disappointing.

I've observed so many bands over the years. You'd encounter them on the road, where the overall atmosphere was pretty negative—sometimes very aggressive, sometimes bullying, sometimes just depressing. We've had elements of that in Wishbone. There were times, during the period when Laurie was in the band, where people would not dare to come backstage after the show because we would be bitching every night—'You were too loud', 'You were hogging the limelight', and so on. I saw Martin almost break his hand on a table top while arguing with Steve. Steve would often goad Martin, and you could goad Martin very easily. So I'd had some times like that with Wishbone but I'd come to the conclusion that if I was going to stay in the band, I wanted a happy band, and in later years it became just that. That's why it was so disappointing that it ended the way it did with Ray.

I sincerely hope and believe that the days of falling out with people in the band are over. Partly it's down to character; partly it's down to the external circumstances you have to live and work through, like skirting bankruptcy over a long period and getting stiffed by record labels. These were part of our lot, and I guess that same sort of thing has been part of the lot of so many of our peers. The ones still here, still touring, still making music, are the ones who didn't crack, or who at least didn't crack completely, under those kind of pressures.

In recent years, everything in Wishbone Ash has been so much more mature—a natural consequence of age and experience. It really has become a big new family, an extended family where you might see the cousins every once in a while, like Ben Granfelt, Mark Birch, and Mervyn Spence guesting on the 40th Anniversary concert, or Roger Filgate contributing to *Blue Horizon*, or the likes of Jamie Crompton, Phil Palmer, Tony Kishman, and Mike Sturgis just keeping in touch.

We go our own ways, do our own things, but we can get along like normal people—like people who worked together for a time and shared a few ups and downs and a few laughs along the way. Most people reading this book will have colleagues and friends they worked with for a couple of years maybe twenty or thirty years ago. It's easy to drift apart but, actually, there's no reason you can't stay in touch or at least reconnect every so often with such people. Bands are no different. Well, they can be—but they don't have to be!

The current Wishbone Ash has been together, at the time of writing, for nearly eight years. That's the longest period of time together for *any* line-up of the band. It's also been one of the most productive line-ups: three studio albums (*The Power Of Eternity*; *Elegant Stealth*; *Blue Horizon*), three DVDs (*Live In Hamburg*; *40th Anniversary Concert*; *This Is Wishbone Ash*), three live albums (*Road Works Vols. 1–3*). A fourth concert film, documenting a series of theatre shows in Paris, will be available, all being well, by the time this book is published in the autumn of 2015, by which time I'm sure we'll be thinking about another studio album.

So what has made this unit so stable? Well, the foundation stone is certainly Bob Skeat. If we're off the road and I don't call Bob for a month, I always know that when we do connect next we'll be able to carry on from where we left off.

Muddy is the polar opposite to Bob. Maybe it's a Finnish thing; maybe it's to do with the cold dark winters up there, but he never wastes time on small talk—or *any* talk. It sounds weird but we'll actually communicate post-tour more comfortably by email, but nevertheless I'm one of his biggest admirers. Muddy's a total Anglophile in his cultural tastes and has, in fact, recently moved to Britain. One of the reasons Ian Harris and Muddy have hit it off is in a shared interest in English history and music, plus a wacky sense of humour. For all his apparent Nordic gloom, Muddy has a particularly refined sense of the absurd. He loves the ridiculousness of Monty Python and the strains of Roger Miller singing 'I'm A Nut' can often be heard in the dressing room after a show.

Muddy is serious about his music, though. He's brought a distinctive, rather 'weird gothic' songwriting aspect to the band. 'The Raven' on *Clan Destiny* and 'Dancing With The Shadows' on *The Power Of Eternity*, for instance, are pure Muddy. There's his dark Finnish soul right there. I'm older than Muddy by many years, but I still think I'm far more in the present and far less rooted in the past than he is. It's a luxury to go through life with that retro-centric focus, but it's great that we have one member of the band who can indulge that luxury and draw from it. If there's one thing Britain's always been good at, it's talented eccentrics. So perhaps Muddy will fit right in.

Muddy and I will clash from time to time—quite frequently, in fact—but we get it out of the way very quickly because we realise that we're both very sensitive souls. We'll often second-guess each other. We co-wrote on *The Power Of Eternity*, which was interesting. The way it works for us is that he'll produce me and I'll produce him. We've both got enough respect for the raw essence of an idea so we give each other enough of a chance to flesh it out individually and then we come back and refine it together. There's a certain intensity there, and I think Wishbone Ash fans want that.

Aside from our different personalities, Muddy does a lot more conscious listening to music than I do, and that feeds into his writing. With me, if there are any musical hints to other artists' styles, it's more subconscious. I'll occasionally say when we're working on something together, 'Oh, that middle eight sounds a bit Stones-y—shall we scrap it or keep it?' Muddy and the others are usually less bothered than I would be about these occasional spillings-over from the box of influences. There is, after all, very little that is new under the sun, in music.

Muddy has heart and soul—you've just got to dig deep to get it. And, crucially, he's in it for the long haul. 'You're not going to get rid of me that easily!' he'll say laughingly. And I'm always very glad to hear it.

Purely from my perspective, there's a bit of a blessing and a curse in always playing with another guitar player. Sometimes you think, *Oh, wouldn't it be nice just to have the freedom to play solo in a band?* But the other side of it—the blessing to counteract the curse—is that you've always got a new guitar teacher or sparring partner to pit yourself against, to inspire you. It never gets complacent. I never need to go for guitar lessons: there's always someone there! I'm sure it's been the same for my various partners—all seven of them.

I've written already about the huge, often under-appreciated impact Bob Skeat has on the well-being and forward movement of Wishbone Ash. He has an ability to cement everything and make it real and to sanction the musical correctness of any new idea. He's a consummate musician and, if required, he's going to get up there and vamp away on jazz, folk, blues, or whatever it is. If Bob has to go and play party music one night, he'll go and do it; if he's asked to sit in with the pit band in a West End musical, he can do it. That's partly the nature of being a bass player, but Muddy and Joe are the same way. That's the point we're all getting to in our lives. If it turns out there's a global bossa nova revival in the offing, Wishbone Ash could go out there and play 'Girl From Ipanema' with the best of 'em. As a musician, you're always still open to influences, using the language of music to find a dialogue with anyone who is participating.

When Ray left us in 2006 I asked Mike Sturgis, who'd been with us in the 90s, if he could recommend any drummers. And just as Mervyn Spence had recommended Mike Sturgis, Mike Sturgis recommended Joe Crabtree. The power of the Wishbone family! 'He's the closest to my style that I've met in recent years,' Mike said. 'If you like my style, I'd recommend Joe …' So I called Joe and we brought him in on *The Power Of Eternity*, purely on that recommendation. What he brings to the band in addition to his musicality and prodigiously accurate chops are his organisational and computer skills—he's a whiz at that stuff. He's enabled me to computerise our whole business. Everything has become a spreadsheet.

We have a huge database of information now. If I say, 'What set did we play in Hamburg in 2005?' it's there at the click of a mouse. Which at least means people in Hamburg (or wherever else) don't hear the same set twice. Joe's been a huge resource to the band in that way, a fantastic asset, and to cap it all he's a genuinely nice guy. Joe was looking around for something to sink his teeth into in the music game during the mid 2000s. He had done a few gigs with David Cross from King Crimson, and he'd played full-time with the English prog-rock band Pendragon. So he'd seen a smattering of what it's like to be in a touring band. But he's really thrived in Wishbone Ash. We can throw any kind of music at him and he will translate it and make it work. And that's amazing. It wasn't always the case in the early days, with Steve Upton. Steve had his own idiosyncratic style that would either fit the music or wouldn't. I remember Martin, in particular, would spend a lot of intensive time with him, trying to make a part work, mimicking tom fills and spitting out kick-drum patterns verbally. It was often quite funny to watch. With Joe, he can take the music and give it legs, and that's massive. He's also extremely calm and controlled, and I rarely see him get rattled.

On the subject of Steve, I'll never forget that before we got Nelson 'Flaco' Padron to play the conga part on 'F.U.B.B.', we gave Steve a try on the track. We were in Criteria Studios, Miami, with Bill Szymczyk. We ran the track for him and Bill isolated the conga part in the control room as Steve attempted to lay it down. I say 'attempted' because, in addition to the strangely camp dance he was doing around the drums, there was this stream of guttural grunts and noises that were obviously going to destroy the recording of whatever part he was coming up with. He'd never played these kind of drums before, and they require a very specific technique of the hands—cupping them, using the fingertips, and so on. The rest of us were in tears, literally on the floor in the control room—at dear old Steve's expense, of course. Needless to say, a new round of respect for Latin drumming was forged once we heard Flaco do his thing. This merciless piss-taking was never far from the surface in those days, and Steve would have been the first to have found someone else's weak spot and exploit it. Man, we were cruel to each other, but these cruelties were great tension-busters.

These days, with Joe's involvement, we're a production entity in and of ourselves. A lot of the barriers that made recording awkward and lumpy in the past have been removed by the internet and electronics. The technology now means you can create magic. The trick of it is to retain that live feeling there in the room and to harness the electronics to deliver a great result. Joe is a child of that era. Like my own kids, he's only known this world of magic. He loves making magic, and I think that's how Joe sees the creation of music. And I love that passion about him.

So when you put these four forces together in a studio, you really have got a prodigious amount of talent. And we can have a laugh, too. The way of being in the modern Wishbone Ash was wonderfully captured in the French-made 2013 'rockumentary' *This Is Wishbone Ash*. If you want to know what makes us tick—who oils the clock, who winds the hands, which one's the cuckoo—that's the place to go. The title might, on the surface, be a nod to *This Is Spinal Tap* (who could resist?) but it also says a couple of things that are subtle but crucial in a real-world context: '*This* Is Wishbone Ash'—not any other band that might operate with the name; and 'This *Is* Wishbone Ash'—it really is how we are and how we create music that carries on from the earliest days and builds something new on those foundations, again and again.

* * *

When you're working on an album there's often a front-runner—a song that seems to define the flavour of an album and will end up almost naturally as the opening track. Ben's 'Almighty Blues', on *Bona Fide*, was a no-brainer—a huge, ebullient stage song. 'Eyes Wide Open', on *Clan Destiny*, was largely one of Aynsley's, with lyrics by me, and another great one to play onstage.

Should a listener be wondering if 'Eyes Wide Open' was a commentary on the constant headache of the Martin Turner situation that was in full swing at the time—well, they might be right. Ditto 'Slime Time' on the same album. There are, I suspect, a number of songs that have been drawn from that particular well of inspiration and emotions, releasing pressure, like opening a valve. Things that go on in one's life inevitably give one pause for thought, and to an extent it all comes out in songs. A lot of it is pretty oblique: I might have taken inspiration from one set of circumstances, happening specifically to me, but I want the listener to be able to relate the phrases and ideas I'm using to their own lives.

If I'm talking about an 'open season on my life' by 'clowns and reformers' in 'Eyes Wide Open', I can be confident that a fair number of people listening will be fighting rear-guard actions themselves against their own set of clowns and double-dealers in their own lives and workplaces. Venting a universally applicable spleen is a lot more useful than whingeing in song about one or two named individuals. The most specific song in that regard might be 'All There Is To Say' on *Blue Horizon*, but you'd never really know the real inspiration without being told—or maybe you would, but none of this should get in the way of the song. The joy of creating and working within a team is an undeniable pleasure, and that feeling never leaves you.

Muddy and Ian Harris's 'The Power', the opening track on *The Power Of Eternity*, is a celebration of the positive. And it really rocks. It's a kind of mission statement. A good band has always got a 'mojo' about it, and 'the power' is just another phrase that sheds light on that mojo, in my mind. All of us could really get behind that idea. It's a song of affirmation about what we are. I've had many conversations with Ian where I've talked about the power of music, and different elements of power or mojo that different bands have had. I remember when we both used to be fans of Arthur Brown in the late 60s: Arthur was one of the first true 'rock' singers (as opposed to rock'n'roll). So many people copped his operatic style and ran with it. Ian Gillan's had an entire career with Arthur's voice. I had the good fortune of playing with Arthur not so long ago, in Austria. He's still got a name in Europe, and rightly so—he's an incredible character and singer. Someone like that has a literal 'power'. When I read Ian's lyrics and tweaked them a little, even though I hadn't written the song I could really sing it and make it my own. You become a part of it and it becomes a part of you.

To me, the most fantastic thing, which was there in the original classified ad for members of what would become 'Wishbone Ash', was the positivity. That for me has always been associated with the band. It's been a creed to live by. One's life is precious. You're not going to want to continually fail with your life. You're going to want to wake up every morning and think 'I'm a success', even though you might be going through a period where it doesn't feel that successful. 'Hope springs eternal', to quote one of my songs.

The band is, for me, now, like an abstract entity—an altar, a confessional. I think it's like that for the others in the band, too, otherwise they wouldn't keep on doing it. We all view it as a very precious thing that has a life of its own, and all we do is add to it. We bring gifts to the altar, we nourish it, we nurture it, and it gives back to us tenfold. That's very much the way I see it. It transcends anything the greater music business might think about us. We're really operating outside of the so-called music business now, creating our own opportunities to interact with the people who want to hear us.

In the wider world, people still associate the name Wishbone Ash with four or five particular individuals from the 70s—I know that, I accept that, and, beyond writing this book, there's nothing I can do to change that perception. But it was apparent to me in court, with regard to the other guys from the first line-up, that they really had no idea what kind of career Wishbone had in the present. They seemed to think I was running a tribute band—just out there earning a living. I even read one quote from Ted Turner about how he did not wish to deprive me of my livelihood but that, really, the band's name should reside with the original members. How considerate of him. They didn't equate it with artistry, with me having the same kind of philosophy about being in the band as I had when I was twenty-one, all this by virtue of never having quit the band. It was sad to hear this, but it was an eye-opener. We all are, after all, products of the lives we have led.

To me, there's no difference between being in the band now or in 1970. Every time I help to create a new body of work under the banner of Wishbone Ash I've *got* to have the same outlook. It hasn't always been as easy—there have been many obstacles along the way—but it *has* to have a sense of occasion about it, a sense of euphoria. The band has been my sustenance, like tapping into a life force. To me, it is the gift that keeps on giving. It *is* 'the power'. It's a beacon of positivity in my life and, in however great or small a way, in the lives of others, too. And I'll keep the beast alive as long as I can, as long as feels right.

WISHBONE ASH AT THE BBC
BY COLIN HARPER

We've researched this appendix by bringing together information from several sources: the BBC Written Archives Centre (WAC) in Caversham; the BBC Sound Archive database; legendary sleeve designer Phil Smee's collection of BBC Transcription Discs; the BBC Worldwide printed catalogue of available syndication material; Ken Garner's *In Session Tonight* (BBC Books, 1993) and *The Peel Sessions* (BBC Books, 2007); the BBC's Project Genome online digitisation of *Radio Times*; and various Wishbone Ash fan sites, bootleg information sites, and other online resources.

Information gathered for us by my friend Hannah Lawrence from the BBC Written Archives Centre material has provided the backbone to this appendix, but no BBC-related source is ever quite complete, hence the need to piece the jigsaw together from several. Even then, the odd anomaly will persist (like the 1977 Glasgow Apollo concert). There may yet be missing information or something we've got wrong— particularly in the matter of working out what was broadcast on UK *In Concerts* and what appeared on the often divergent US syndication discs—but we think this digest of Wishbone Ash's adventures at the BBC is pretty close to the truth.

The official CDs on which BBC recordings of Wishbone Ash appear, to date, are: *BBC Radio 1 Live In Concert* (Windsong, 1991); *Live At The BBC* (Band Of Joy, 1995), reissued as *On Air* (Strange

Fruit, 1999); *Live Timeline* (Receiver, 1997); *Distillation* (Repertoire, 1997); *Tracks* (Talking Elephant, 2002); and the second disc of *Argus: Deluxe Edition* (Universal, 2007). The broadcast versions of the two 1971 *Old Grey Whistle Test* tracks appear on the DVD *Phoenix Rising* (Classic Rock Legends, 2004).

THE BROADCASTS

All the shows listed below were on BBC Radio 1 unless noted. Correspondence quoted is sourced from the BBC Written Archives Centre.

Sounds Of The Seventies
Rec: 6/8/70
TX: 19/8/70
Presenter: Bob Harris
Producer: Jeff Griffin
Engineer: Phil Stannard
Studio: Paris Theatre, London
Tracks: *Errors Of My Way* / *Phoenix* / *Blind Eye*
Note: 'Blind Eye' was recorded but never broadcast. Bob's other session guests that week were Tyrannosaurus Rex.

Early in June 1970, Wishbone Ash were booked for a 'Trial Broadcast' through the BBC's Light Entertainment Bookings department. A document extant at WAC from this time, from Miles Copeland, provided the BBC with information on the band for their files. The band's agent ('pending authorisation', which meant that the band members had to confirm this in due course) is given as Myles [sic] A. Copeland, 21 Marlborough Place, London, NW8.

A note dated June 23 from one Mary Ramode to Jeff Griffin, at the 'audition unit', confirmed that Wishbone Ash had been engaged to appear in 'Sounds Of The Seventies (Bob Harris)' and were to record a session from 3pm to 6:30pm on August 6 at Studio Paris [Paris Theatre] on Lower Regent Street, London. The note goes on to say that this is to be treated as a trial broadcast, in lieu of an audition: 'Will you please ensure that a copy of the recording [is sent to the Audition Unit] immediately, so that it may be submitted to the production panel for an early decision. A personal report from the producer in charge is also necessary.'

On July 3 a contract from Light Entertainment is signed regarding the session. The producer is confirmed as Jeff Griffin and the fee is £40—which no doubt came in very handy at the time. On July 9 the members of Wishbone Ash wrote to Patrick Newman, the Light Entertainment Booking Manager at the BBC, appending their four signatures, with that authorisation they were looking for: 'This is to confirm that all members of Wishbone Ash are under management contract to Miles A Copeland III … and that in future all contracts [with the BBC] should be signed by him.'

Newman's assistant, one Marjory Lipscomb, wrote back via Miles on July 24, acknowledging the above letter: 'Perhaps you would kindly clear up one thing for me, and that is how do Wishbone Ash want their cheques to be made out; should they be made payable to you or to the group? This is not clear from the authority received.'

Had the band passed the audition? The powers that be (or were) were keen to find out: twice during August and September 1970, Margaret Gibbs of the Audition Unit wrote to Jeff Griffin asking for both the tape of the broadcast and his report on the band's worth so that it might be put before the 'Production Panel'. Eventually, Griffin either gives in or gets around to it. The Production Panel listened to the tape at some point, probably late in October (their report was stamped 'received 29/10/70 by Light Entertainment Bookings'). They had this to say:

Audition report (as referenced above) on Wishbone Ash, with feedback from the named producers.

Jeff Griffin: 'An exciting new group featuring two lead guitarists, bass and drums. They use original material—one of these 'Phoenix' being a really outstanding composition and performance. Their vocal work is pretty good but their strength really lies in their arrangements and instrumental ability.' PASS

John Walters: 'A very competent 4 piece progressive group which could develop into a major talent.' PASS

Bernie Andrews: 'One of the few new groups in 1970 to offer something really original and worthwhile on the progressive scene. The two guitarists work very well and the whole band sounds very together.' PASS

On November 10, Marjory Lipscomb, Assistant to the Light Entertainment Booking Manager, wrote to Miles Copeland, giving him the good news: 'We are pleased to confirm that their performance received favourable reports and that their name has been added to the list of those available for broadcasting generally.' A copy of the audition report, albeit with the comments as anonymous, was enclosed. The letter confirms that the songs performed were 'Errors Of My Way' and 'Blind Eye'—though Griffin had referred to 'Phoenix'. Ken Garner's book *In Session Tonight*, based on extensive research, including 'Programme as Broadcast' files at WAC, lists all three tracks as having been recorded but 'Blind Eye' as having not been broadcast. One assumes Marjory was only partially informed when writing her letter.

The copy of the letter held at WAC contains this further typed comment from Doreen Davies, who was Chief Producer and later Head of Music at Radio 1:

YES—Doreen Davies 9.11.70
Excellent lead singer. Well-rehearsed and they sound experienced. Not too way-out—a thick exciting sound, first-rate musicians. Harmonies good in choral work. Progressive programmes only.

John Peel's Sunday Concert
Rec: 19/11/70, 9–10:30pm
TX: 29/11/70; repeated 2/12/70
Presenter: John Peel
Producer: Jeff Griffin
Location: Paris Studio, London
Tracks: *Vas Dis / Phoenix / Where Were You Tomorrow*
Note: This was a one-hour show that Peel fronted during 1970–71, none of which survive at source. Wishbone Ash shared the bill with The Faces, who performed five songs. A poor quality off-air copy apparently exists. The contract for the show was issued on October 30. The fee was £48. The repeat on Wednesday December 2 was, confusingly, under the *Sounds Of The Seventies* banner. 'Vas Dis' and 'Phoenix' appear on *Live Timeline*.

Disco 2 (BBC2 TV)
Rec: 2/12/70
TX: 5/12/70
Presenter: Mike Harding
Producer: Granville Jenkins
Tracks: *Queen Of Torture / Errors Of My Way*
Note: Very few episodes of this BBC2 predecessor to *The Old Grey Whistle Test* survive—and this isn't one of them. According to its *Radio Times* billing, this edition also featured James Taylor, filmed 'on a recent trip to Britain', and 'Wishbone Ash, a new four-piece group whose music is described by John Peel as 'original, exciting and beautifully played'. Wishbone Ash probably played two or three songs live in the studio.

A contract from Television (Light Entertainment) was signed on November 24 for the programme, the performance to be recorded 3pm on December 2 at Television Centre. The fee was £50, with the band's contact address as follows: Scope International, 27 Dryden Chambers, 119 Oxford Street, London, W1. (Miles Copeland isn't mentioned by name but that was his management company at this time.)

The Peel endorsement above actually came from an interview he gave to *Melody Maker* a couple of months earlier, where he said, 'I heard Wishbone Ash for the first time, and haven't been so impressed with a relatively new band for a long time. Their music is original, exciting and beautifully played.'

Wishbone Ash had already performed

on Peel's Sunday Concert and would go on to do three studio sessions for his regular evening programme, *Top Gear*, which was rebranded as *John Peel* after 1975. During one of his programmes for the British Forces Broadcasting Service in 1992, he apparently mentioned Wishbone Ash as one of his favourite bands from the 70s and went on to play 'Time Was', for old time's sake.

Sounds Of The Seventies

Rec: 1/1/71, 8–11:30pm
TX: 11/1/71; repeated 15/2/71
Presenter: Bob Harris
Producer: John Muir
Engineer: John White
Studio: Maida Vale, Studio 5
Tracks: *Queen Of Torture / Errors Of My Way / Vas Dis / Lullaby*
Note: The contract was issued on December 8. The fee was £40. 'Lullaby' was only broadcast on the repeat date. Bob's other session guests that week were the blues duo Mark-Almond; on the repeat it was Mythica.

Sounds Of The Seventies

Rec: 21/4/71, 2:30–6pm
TX: 29/4/71; repeated 27/5/71?
Presenter: Stuart Henry
Producer: Malcolm Brown
Engineers: Mike Harding, Mike Franks
Studio: Maida Vale, Studio 4
Tracks: *Blind Eye / Lullaby / Phoenix*
Note: The contract was issued on March 15. The fee was £40. Beggar's Opera were Stuart's other session guests. Based on *Radio Times* information, the session was probably repeated on May 27, when Wishbone Ash shared the programme with a Hawkwind session. 'Blind Eye' and 'Lullaby' appear on *Live At The BBC*.

Top Gear

Rec: 5/7/71, 2:30–6pm and 7–11pm
TX: 10/7/71
Presenter: John Peel
Producer: Peter Harwood
Engineer: John Walters
Studio: Playhouse, Northumberland Avenue, London
Tracks: *Jail Bait / The Pilgrim / Lady Whiskey / Lullaby*
Note: The contract was issued on June 21. For whatever reason, the band got to enjoy the luxury of longer recording time here—most BBC sessions in the 70s were standard three-hour affairs. The contract also specifies that the broadcast will be on July 10, with a repeat on another date TBC. Presumably it *was* repeated, but the information as to when remains elusive. The fee, as usual, was £40. (Two contracts for this session were issued in error, the second one being cancelled.) 'The Pilgrim' appears on *Live At The BBC*.

On September 28 an internal memo was circulated around various departments (including Light Entertainment Bookings, Programme Accounts, and the Tax Unit) to confirm that Myles [sic] Copeland was Wishbone Ash's agent.

The Old Grey Whistle Test (BBC2 TV)

Rec: 12/10/71
TX: 12/10/71
Presenter: Richard Williams
Producer: Michael Appleton
Tracks: *Vas Dis / Jail Bait*
Note: While only two tracks were broadcast, just over twenty-six minutes of audio-visual footage of Wishbone Ash working on the tracks survives at source: two complete takes of each song plus an incomplete take of 'Jail Bait'. The contract for the show,

from Television (Light Entertainment), was signed on September 24. The fee was £55. Lindisfarne were the other live band featured that night. Audio from the broadcast takes appears on *Live At The BBC*; audio and video appears on the *Phoenix Rising* DVD.

Sounds Of The Seventies
Rec: 18/10/71, 6:30–10pm
TX: 1/11/71; repeated 13/12/71?
Presenter: Bob Harris
Producer: Pete Dauncey
Engineer: Adrian Revill
Studio: Studio 1, Transcription Service, Kensington House, Shepherd's Bush
Tracks: *Jail Bait / The Pilgrim / Lullaby*
Note: A contract issued on September 28 states that the session was to be recorded on October 11 from 7–10:30pm in Kensington House, with John Muir as Producer. On October 12 a letter was sent to Myles [sic], presumably after a phone call from him saying the date or time was difficult for the band, confirming that the recording had been moved to October 18. Presumably John Muir now wasn't available, so they got Pete Dauncey instead. The fee was still £40. Other sessions on Bob's show that night came from David Bowie, Stone The Crows, and Dando Shaft. Based on *Radio Times* information, the band's session was probably repeated on December 13 1971; the other sessions on that episode coming from The Strawbs, Roy Harper, and Spyrogyra. 'Jail Bait' appears on *Live At The BBC*. All tracks are extant on Transcription Disc.

A supplementary contract, with a 'special' fee of £10, was issued on September 28 1972 for the use of 'Lullaby' on an edition of *Sounds Of The Seventies* broadcast on October 20, presented by Pete Drummond, and produced by John Muir. Presumably one of them particularly liked this version of the song, for a special contract to be created to allow for its rebroadcast.

Top Gear
Rec: 18/4/72, 2:30–11pm
TX: 25/4/72
Presenter: John Peel
Producer: John Walters
Engineer: ?
Studio: Maida Vale, Studio 4
Tracks: *Blowin' Free / Warrior / The King Will Come*
Note: The contract is issued on 26/3/72; the TX date is TBC. The fee is £40.

Sounds Of The Seventies
Rec: 10/5/72, 2:30–6pm
TX: 18/5/72; repeated 13/7/72?
Presenter: Pete Drummond
Producer: Malcolm Brown
Engineers: Mike Harding, Mike Franks
Studio: Maida Vale, Studio 4
Tracks: *Throw Down The Sword / Warrior / Time Was*
Note: The contract was issued on April 19 1972, stating the session was to be recorded May 3, 2:30–6pm, at Maida Vale 4 with Malcolm Brown. Presumably the date didn't work for the band; a second contract was issued with the revised recording date (as above), though studio and producer remained as was. The fee was £40. Pete's other session guests that night were Al Stewart, prog-rockers Egg, Graham Bond, and Pete Brown. From *Radio Times* information the session was probably repeated on July 13, with the other session guests on that occasion being Al Stewart, Listen, and The High Level Ranters. 'Throw Down The

Sword' appears on *Live At The BBC* and also on *Argus: Deluxe Edition*.

In Concert

Rec: 25/5/72, 9–10:30pm

TX: 3/6/72

Presenter: Bob Harris

Producer: Jeff Griffin

Location: Paris Theatre, London

Tracks: *Time Was / Blowin' Free / Warrior / Throw Down The Sword / The King Will Come / Phoenix*

Note: The contract was issued on May 25 1972. The fee was £40—which seems a bit unfair in hindsight! They certainly got their money's worth: this concert has been rebroadcast in full a few times, on Radio 1 in 1986 and on BBC 6 Music in 2009 and 2013. The full show appears on *BBC Radio 1 Live In Concert* (in mono) and (in stereo, with better mastering) on *Argus: Deluxe Edition* and has also appeared on various bootlegs (see below). Online sources suggest that 'Jail Bait' and 'The Pilgrim' were recorded but not broadcast.

Sounds Of The Seventies

Rec: 31/5/72, 7:30–11pm

TX: 3/7/72; repeated 14/8/72?

Presenter: Bob Harris

Producer: Jeff Griffin

Engineer: ?

Studio: Aeolian Hall, Studio 2

Tracks: *Blowin' Free / Leaf And Stream / The King Will Come / Sometime World*

Note: The contract was issued on May 26, broadcast date TBC. The fee was £40. Wishbone Ash received a letter dated June 21 from a Miss Quinault, 'Assistant Light Entertainment Booking Section', informing them that the broadcast date would be July

3: 'Perhaps you would be good enough to alter your copy of the contract accordingly.' I'm sure they did. Bob's other session guests that night were Ralph McTell, Stealers Wheel, and Paul Williams. The session was probably repeated on August 14, with the other exclusive content providers that night being folk-rock band Trees. 'Blowin' Free' appears on *Argus: Deluxe Edition*.

The Old Grey Whistle Test (BBC2 TV)

Rec: ?

TX: 21/11/72

Presenter: Bob Harris

Track: *Blowin' Free*

Note: This was a promotional film of 'Blowin' Free' shot at Cambridge Corn Exchange by Eyeline Films Ltd. In other words, either the band or the record label provided the *OGWT* with the film to use on the show. It lasted 3:44 (a short version), 1:05 of which survives at the BBC (part of this episode of *OGWT*, as with several early episodes, is missing). However, the same film was undoubtedly the one sent to the Australian Broadcasting Corporation (ABC), which used it for *GTK (Get To Know)*, a black-and-white programme, in which form it survived. This is the version that was sourced for the DVD release *Phoenix Rising*. It's likely the promo was originally filmed in colour, as all of the UK TV stations had adapted to colour by 1972.

Stackridge & Co (BBC West Country TV)

Rec: ?

TX: 5/12/72

Note: This was a BBC regional series, with Wishbone Ash appearing as guests on this episode, which is extant in the BBC Sound Archive. The SA blurb is: 'Alan Read intros music from Stackridge, Dave Evans, Hunt & Turner & Wishbone Ash'. The band probably played one song; the episode's duration is 29:25.

In Concert
Rec: 14/2/74, 9–10:30pm
TX: 23/2/74
Presenter: Alan Black
Producer: Jeff Griffin
Location: Paris Theatre, London
Tracks: *Ballad Of the Beacon / Sometime World / Rock'n'Roll Widow / Blowin' Free / Jail Bait / Time Was / Phoenix*
Note: This was Ted Turner's last performance with Wishbone Ash. A contract was issued on December 20 1973 for this show to be recorded on January 10 for broadcast on January 19. It was noted that the band's management/representation had changed to 'c/o John Sherry Enterprises Ltd'. The 'special' fee offered was £80. That same day, a memo from the Light Entertainment Booking Manager to the Programme Account requested the above contract be cancelled. The following day a Miss Kenney, Light Entertainment Bookings, sent a memo to Jeff Griffin and other departments: 'This is to remind you that Wishbone Ash were not willing to accept the transcription clause covering possible sale of records of their performance for transmission in the USA and its territorial possessions. [Therefore] we have deleted this clause on their contract for the above programme. Will all departments that this affects please make a note of this restriction on the usage of the recording.'
Consequently, as a result of whatever problem the band or their management had with this US syndication aspect, this *In Concert* was never cut to transcription disc.

The recording and broadcasting date were then changed. A new contract was issued on January 11 for February 14, with a rehearsal that afternoon at 3:30pm. The fee was still a 'special' £80. Maybe John Sherry had reckoned it was time the standard £40 was negotiated upwards. Miss Kenney circulated her internal memo again on January 31.

Amazingly, the BBC Sound Archive database suggests that, although it was probably not rebroadcast (unlike the much repeated 1972 concert), this 1974 *In Concert* does survive in master quality on tape. A bootleg CD from a decent FM off-air copy also circulates. Four of the songs performed at this *In Concert*—plus one that wasn't—would be the subject of separate contracts over the course of the next fifteen months to allow their rebroadcast on episodes of *The Alan Freeman Show*. So the full concert certainly existed on master tape at that point in time.

The 'Fluff' episodes were as follows:

Alan Freeman Show
TX: 9/3/74
Tracks: *Blowin' Free / Jail Bait*
Note: The contract for this was issued on March 19 1974. The fee was £20 'special'.

Alan Freeman Show
TX: 23/3/74
Track: *Phoenix*
Note: The contract was issued on March 27 1974. The fee was £20 'special'.

Alan Freeman Show
TX: 23/11/74
Track: *Rock'n'Roll Widow*
Note: The contract was issued on December 9 1974. The fee was £20 'special'.

Alan Freeman Show
TX: 16/8/75
Track: *The King Will Come*
Note: The contract was issued on August 21 1975. The fee was £20 'special'. The contract confirms that this song was recorded at the February 14 1974 *In Concert* performance, although it wasn't part of the February 23 broadcast.

By December 1974, the band's representation had changed from 'John Sherry Enterprises Ltd' to 'Scope International', albeit with the same address. On February 11 1975 a memo was circulated to BBC departments notifying them that their agent details had changed again: from 'Scope International' to 'BTM (Artistes Management Ltd.)'. The memo also confirmed that this is the new name for the previous company. Miles was a man of many clothes—but the band were getting tired of his wardrobe. On 6/4/76 (having fired Miles after the financial issues around the August 1975 Star Truckin' tour) another internal BBC memo was circulated informing departments that monies should now be payable to 'Wishbone Ash' and sent c/o Dick Jordan, 138 Dukes Avenue, N10.

John Peel Show
Rec: 19/11/76
TX: 9/2/77
Location: Apollo Theatre, Glasgow
Tracks: *Runaway* / *The King Will Come* / *Lorelei* / *Mother Of Pearl* / *Blowin' Free*
Note: Occasionally, John's show featured exclusive studio sessions provided by an artist or record company, from their own studios or foreign locations, rather than the norm of having been recorded on BBC premises. One famous example of these would be

a series of sessions, or exclusive mixes of album tracks, supplied by The Who (the first act allowed this leeway) from 1967 onward. A less famous example was Wishbone Ash. Although classified as a studio session in Ken Garner's second book (it's absent from the first) and given an erroneous recording date of January 16 1977, this set was introduced by John as exclusive concert tracks—which they were.

The tracks (running to 29:42) were recorded by Wishbone Ash, independently, at Glasgow's Apollo on November 19 1976. The contract defining the BBC's use of the tracks was issued a few days retrospectively of the broadcast, on February 16 1977. The fee was £75 'special'. The terms were that the band granted the BBC the right to use the material for one broadcast on *The John Peel Show*. It warranted that Wishbone Ash were entitled to supply the recording for this purpose, and that they had obtained any necessary consents. Specifically, the band indemnified the BBC against all claims and expenses arising out of any failure to comply with this. The contract also confirmed that the BBC would ensure that the recording was not used for the BBC's Transcription services. Wishbone Ash were obviously still concerned about overseas syndication.

With this contract the band's representation contact changed (again) to 'John Sherry, NEMS Agency, Nemperor House, 3 Hill Street, London, W1'. Brian Epstein's old company. The contract was signed two days later, and John sent in a letter of authorisation from the band confirming this latest change, noting that cheques for Wishbone Ash should be paid to NEMS: 'This authorisation being duly signed by a member of the group Mr Steven Upton.' The full set at the Glasgow Apollo on November 19 1976 was this:

Jail Bait / Time Was / Blowin' Free / Warrior / The King Will Come / Rest In Peace / Runaway / In All My Dreams / Lorelei / Outward Bound / Bad Weather Blues / Mother Of Pearl / Persephone / It Started In Heaven

Tracks from the concert have appeared on various Wishbone Ash releases, beginning with 'Lorelei' on a free single with the original pressings of the 1978 album *No Smoke Without Fire*. 'Lorelei' and 'Rest In Peace' also feature on *Distillation* (Repertoire, 1997). Other tracks have appeared on the three volumes of *Tracks* on Talking Elephant in the 2000s.

As was the case with the 1974 *In Concert*, *The Alan Freeman Show* was given a second bite of the cherry. The band must have verbally agreed to this in advance because, in spite of the 'one broadcast only' clause of the Peel contract, John Sherry signed contracts for them subsequent to the rebroadcasts of three of the Glasgow Apollo/*John Peel Show* tracks on Alan's programme. The details are as follows:

The Alan Freeman Show
TX: 12/2/77
Track: *The King Will Come*
Note: The contract was issued retrospectively, on May 4 1977. The fee was £18.75 'special'.

The Alan Freeman Show
TX: 16/4/77
Track: *?*
Note: The contract was issued retrospectively, on the same date as above. The fee was £18.75 'special'. Oddly, the contract neglects to specify the track.

The Alan Freeman Show
TX: 17/12/77
Track: *Blowin' Free*
Note: The contract was issued retrospectively, on December 22 1977. The fee was £18.75 'special'.

The David Hamilton Show
TX: 14–18/11/77; repeated 28/11–2/12/77
Tracks: *?*
Note: This was another case of Wishbone Ash being allowed to provide exclusive tracks recorded, as the contract states, in the band's 'own studio in USA'. David fronted a mainstream afternoon show broadcast simultaneously on Radio 1 and 2 at the time. While the tracks aren't specified, the band obviously provided five songs that would be broadcast one per day during the weeks in question. Clearly, the proviso that was stated on their audition panel report back in 1970, that they were for 'progressive programmes only', had worn off by now! The contract was issued on November 4 1977. The fee was £62 for the session, with a repeat fee of £31. John Sherry 'lost or mislaid' the contract but must later have needed it for some reason (tax, possibly), as a replacement copy was requested a few months later, on May 26 1978.

The Old Grey Whistle Test (BBC2 TV)
Rec: late 1977
TX: 11/10/77
Presenter: Bob Harris
Producer: Michael Appleton
Tracks: *Baby Come In From The Rain / Goodbye Baby, Hello Friend*
Note: Colour film of the band performing at Criterion Sound Studios, Miami. The film is extant and BBC records indicate it was

shot by *OGWT* rather than provided by a record company (as often happened). Audio of both tracks appears on *Live At The BBC*.

In Concert
Rec: 17/10/77
TX: ?
Producer: ?
Presenter: Brian Matthew
Location: Apollo Theatre, Glasgow
Tracks: *Blind Eye / Lady Whiskey / Warrior / Throw Down The Sword / Front Page News / Goodbye Baby, Hello Friend / Come In From The Rain / Phoenix / Blowin' Free*
Note: This one's a real mystery. There is not one bit of documentation about it at WAC and no broadcast date can be found via *Radio Times*. And yet it exists, certainly in the form of a BBC Transcription Disc with the above tracks and Brian Matthew's introduction (erroneously stating the venue as London's Rainbow). At this point, Brian was presenting mostly on the BBC World Service, so it's possible that this concert was broadcast only on the World Service, not Radio 1.

Adding to the mystery, a long tape version of the concert must exist because the band licensed 'Sometime World' from this concert, from the BBC, for use on *Distillation* (Repertoire, 1977)—and yet this 1977 *In Concert* is not listed among the Wishbone Ash concerts in BBC Worldwide's own catalogue of *In Concert* broadcasts available for syndication.

The full setlist, sourced from the fan site www.glasgowapollo.com, was this:
Blind Eye / Lady Whiskey / Sometime World / Blowin' Free / The King Will Come / Warrior / Throw Down The Sword / Bad Weather Blues / Runaway / Front Page News / Goodbye Baby, Hello Friend / Jail Bait

In Concert
Rec: 25/10/78
TX: 11/11/78; repeated 11/8/79
Producer: Jeff Griffin
Presenter: Alan Black (on repeat)
Location: Hammersmith Odeon
Tracks: *The King Will Come / You See Red / Front Page News / The Way Of The World / Phoenix / Anger In Harmony / Queen of Torture / Blowin' Free*
Note: The contract was issued on October 31 1978. The fee was £160 'special'. The contract states that payment was to be made to NEMS Agency. The track list is 58:18 in duration.

A letter from John Sherry dated February 19 1979 (after a previous exchange of letters not extant in the WAC file) to a Miss Heritage from Drama and Light Entertainment Booking, confirmed 'Wishbone Productions Inc. London—New York' to now be the name of the band's representation. He confirms that he is still empowered to sign all Wishbone Ash contracts and asks for monies to be paid to 'Wishbone Ash Limited'—asking for the *In Concert* contract to be altered so the outstanding £160 can be paid direct to 'Wishbone Ash Limited'. An internal memo was then circulated advising all relevant departments that John Sherry was no longer with NEMS and that his new address was: John Sherry, Wishbone Ash Ltd, 31 Kings Road, London, SW3. Nine months later, on November 16, another memo told relevant departments that Wishbone Ash could be contacted c/o Phil Banfield, esq., P.A.N., 10 Sutherland Avenue, London, W9.

The Friday Rock Show
TX: 3/8/79
Presenter: Tommy Vance
Producer: Tony Wilson

Note: This was a rebroadcast of some or all of three sessions from the early 70s: *Sounds Of The 70s* (recorded on April 21 1971), *Top Gear* (July 5 1971), and *Sounds Of The 70s* (May 31 1972). A letter between Booking Manager Miss Kenney and Accounting Services dated December 7 1979 suggests the contract was issued to the band retrospectively that month. The fee was £86.40 for each of the three sessions.

Year Of The Child Concert (BBC1 TV)

Rec: 22/11/79
TX: 1/12/79
Producer: Michael Appleton
Location: Wembley Arena
Tracks: *two songs (probably Helpless / Bad Weather Blues)*
Note: 1979 was OXFAM/UNICEF's 'International Year Of The Child'. Wishbone Ash performed at this concert with David Essex, Sky, Gary Numan, The Real Thing, and Cat Stevens (certainly one of the more eclectic bills the band played). This TV show was one hour of highlights produced by *OGWT*'s Michael Appleton. A contract was issued on November 19 1979. The fee was £240. Once again, the band's representation address had changed, and was now 'Wishbone Ash Ltd, 206 Upper Richmond Road, London, SW15'. The TV broadcast survives in the BBC Sound Archive—the two tracks from Sky, for instance, can be found on a CD/DVD edition of their first album released in 2015. This TV-highlights show featured two songs by Wishbone Ash, though they are listed as 'unknown' in the Sound Archive database, whereas everyone else's items are named and timed. From adding these timings, one can infer that Wishbone Ash got roughly

fourteen minutes of airtime, which equates to the combined timings of 'Helpless' (3:50) and 'Bad Weather Blues' (8:55), which we know from the SA information with the radio version of the show (below).

Year Of The Child Concert

Rec: 22/11/79
TX: 2/12/79
Presenter: Andy Peebles
Producer: Jeff Griffin
Location: Wembley Arena
Tracks: *Blowin' Free / Living Proof / Helpless / Bad Weather Blues*
Note: This was a two-hour Radio 1 broadcast from the same event. The contract was issued on November 21; the fee was £120 'special'. John Sherry signed the contract on December 18, reminding the BBC to make cheques payable to 'Wishbone Ash Ltd'. (An undated internal memo circulated, seemingly not long after this, confirming that the band's agent was now Phil Banfield but that monies should be sent to the Upper Richmond Road address and that John Sherry still had permission to sign.) As with the TV version, the radio recording survives at source—all five of Sky's tracks from the radio version of the show are on the 2015 CD/DVD edition of their first album. The set lasted 24:05.

In Concert

Rec: 2/2/80
TX: 1/3/80; repeated 16/8/80
Producer: Jeff Griffin
Presenter: Tommy Vance
Location: Hammersmith Odeon, London
Tracks: *Doctor / Blind Eye / Living Proof / Lifeline / Insomnia / Blowin' Free / Helpless / Jail Bait / Bad Weather Blues / [Too Much Monkey Business]*

Note: This *In Concert* (specified as such on the contract) was broadcast as a one-hour segment within Tommy Vance's three-and-a-half-hour show *Rock On Saturday*. The repeat was also within Tommy's Saturday show. The contract was issued on February 5 1980. The fee was £160 'special'. The BBC Sound Archive, unusually, holds two versions of this concert: one (which the SA database wrongly identifies as 'likely' to be the UK 'Programme as Broadcast') is the 58:39 version that features on the Transcription Discs for US syndication; the other is the 54:05 version above. The situation is further complicated because audio of 'Bad Weather Blues' complete with Radio 1 presenter Tommy Vance's outro voiceover, ending the broadcast, appears on YouTube. 'Bad Weather Blues' does not appear on the first Sound Archive version—and yet a 1:55 version of 'Too Much Monkey Business' (surely an encore number) is listed in the SA database as following 'Bad Weather Blues'. It's possible, of course, that Tommy aired two versions of the show on his two broadcast slots … but why? If all the available material were combined, the length would be 69:39. See below for the US syndicated version.

The Friday Rock Show
TX: 17/4/81
Presenter: Tommy Vance
Producer: Tony Wilson
Note: This was another rebroadcast of an early-70s session; on this occasion it was from *Sounds Of The 70s* (recorded on October 18 1971). On April 28 1981 a BBC memo was circulated stating that Wishbone Ash's 'new' agent was John Sherry at the Kings Road address of before. Phil Banfield's details were to be deleted. A request for a contract was

sent by Miss Kenney to Accounting Services of April 29. The fee was £102.80.

Simon Bates Show
Rec: 17/5/81
TX: 25/5/81; repeated 1/6/81
Producer: Paul Williams
Track: *Get Ready*
Note: On May 21 1981, Dave Brown, Head of Promotion at MCA Records, wrote to Paul Williams at BBC Radio 1: 'A special session was set up by Wishbone Ash on the 17th May for the *Mike Read Show* at which the following musicians were present: Andy Powell, Laurie Wisefield, Steve Upton, Claire Hamill and John Wetton on keyboards. A copy tape of the session is enclosed herewith containing the following title: "Get Ready".'

Someone has crossed out 'Mike Read' and written above it 'Simon Bates', adding the broadcast dates. The contract was issued on May 26, confirming this to be an 'own studio' session and adding the band member names as provided. The fee is £128.50 plus a repeat fee of £64.25. On July 1 John Sherry wrote to one Maggie Gibbs at the BBC, explaining that he'd amended the contract, replacing John Wetton's name with that of Trevor Bolder. As he says, 'It's hard to keep pace nowadays!'

In Concert
Rec: 2/6/81
TX: 4/7/81
Producer: Jeff Griffin
Location: Hammersmith Odeon
Tracks: *The King Will Come / Lady Whiskey / Where Is The Love? / Living Proof / Underground / Warrior / Loaded / Kicks On The Street / Blowin' Free / Get Ready*
Note: The contract was issued on April 29

1981; the fee was £250 'special'. Wishbone Ash on this occasion was Andy Powell, Laurie Wisefield, Claire Hamill, Trevor Bolder, and Steve Upton. The above 58:20 track list is from the 'Programme as Broadcast' information. The Transcription Discs for US syndication added three tracks from the show and dropped five from this UK broadcast.

On May 1 John Sherry wrote to 'the Chief Accountant, BBC Radio Accounts', asking that all cheques for payments are made to 'Wishbone Ash Limited' and sent to the Kings Road address. Presumably all these alternative agency names and addresses that had been floating around had been causing problems.

On April 13 1982 (and again on June 1) an internal memo circulated, headed 'Notification of Obsolete Address', with the following instruction: 'A cheque recently sent to [Wishbone Ash, Upper Richmond Road] has been returned by the Post Office with the following comments: GONE AWAY. We suggest this address is deleted from your records.'

An alternative address (one of the many that the administrative corners of the BBC had accumulated by this time) was suggested: 'J. Sherry Ents., 27 Dryden Chambers, 19 Oxford Street, W1', with the caution to 'please note that this does not represent a direct instruction from the contributor'.

The Friday Rock Show
TX: 2/3/84
Presenter: Tommy Vance
Producer: Tony Wilson
Note: Once again, Tommy was unearthing gems from the vault. This time he repeated three of the four that had previously been

rebroadcast on his show: *Top Gear* (recorded on July 5 1971) and two episodes of *Sounds Of The 70s* (October 18 1971 and May 31 1972). A letter was written on March 12 1984 by Jackie Jenney, Light Entertainment Booking Assistant, to Accounting Services (Radio): 'Please would you arrange for the artist / group to receive a repeat fee for this contribution, payment to be based on a current fee of £136 each session (3).' The contact address she suggested was 'c/o John Sherry (Wishbone Ash Ltd.), Queens Theatre, 51 Shaftesbury Avenue, London, W1V 8BA'.

Five months later, on August 4, Steve Upton (on behalf of the group) wrote, from Grainger's Farm, to the 'Programme Accountant, BBC Radio': 'We recently received a payment from you of £204 in connection with BBC Radio repeat fees for Wishbone Ash. I am writing to ask for the VAT due on this amount and enclose an invoice as appropriate.'

This may not at first seem connected to the *Friday Rock Show* repeated sessions of March 2 1984, but Jackie Jenney had asked for the fee to be £408 (three times £136). Someone had obviously decided to give the band exactly half of that figure.

On September 17, an internal note to Miss Heritage at Light Entertainment (which is amusing, given that Wishbone Ash were on the way to being categorised as a 'Heritage Rock' act) asked her to change the contact info for Wishbone Ash from John Sherry to 'Wishbone Ash Ltd, Grainger's Farm, Brentmoor Road, West End, Woking, Surrey'. The note specifies: 'Delete: John Sherry'.

On May 22 1985, things were changing again. A note to Miss Truscott at Light Entertainment asked her to change the band's contact details from Grainger's Farm to: 'Wishbone Ash c/o David Potts, Tristar Management Ltd, 15–16 Newman Street, London, W1P 3HA'. The note also updated the band's personnel, with Trevor Bolder and Claire Hamill deleted and Mervyn Spence added.

The Friday Rock Show

Rec: 24/5/85, 2:30–6pm and 7:30–11pm
TX: 5/7/85
Presenter: Tommy Vance
Producer: Tony Wilson
Engineer: Dave Dade
Studio: Maida Vale, Studio 5
Tracks: *Cell Of Fame / People In Motion / Love Is Blue / Long Live The Night*
Line-up: Andy Powell, Laurie Wisefield, Mervyn Spence, Steve Upton
Note: The session log, used by Ken Garner in *In Session Tonight*, lists Mervyn as 'Melvin' Spence, although the contract gets it right. The contract was issued on May 22 1985, at which point the broadcast date was TBC. The fee was £360, specified as £180 for each of the two sessions. The fee had certainly gone up since the previous year, when Jackie Jenney's letter had mentioned the standard fee as being £136. Perhaps Tommy and Tony were being generous to the band; perhaps they hoped to get enough material for two different session broadcasts. Either way, this was to be their last studio session for BBC national radio. The tracks ran to 16:52 duration and are retained by BBC Sound Archive, although with a proviso that 'this material must not be used without prior copyright clearance'—the same proviso as one attached in the Sound Archive database to the 1976 Glasgow concert tracks that Wishbone Ash had supplied to the BBC. There seems no reason for that proviso to attach to this session, which was recorded on BBC premises, and for which the band were handsomely paid.

In Concert

Rec: 4/3/88
TX: 9/4/88
Producer: Pete Ritzema
Location: Hammersmith Odeon
Tracks: *Living Proof / Genevieve / The King Will Come / In The Skin / Phoenix / Blowin' Free / Jail Bait / Bad Weather Blues*
Note: Curiously, there is no documentation extant for this broadcast at WAC. However, the 'Programme as Broadcast' is extant in the BBC Sound Archive, with the approximately 51:30 track list above. The show itself occupied a 58:55 slot, so presumably seven minutes of intro and outro speech was involved. Jamie Crompton played second guitar on the first set of this show (from whence come 'Living Proof' and 'Genevieve') which was early in the band's reunion period; Ted Turner came on for the second set. 'In The Skin' is on *Tracks* (Talking Elephant, 2002).

The US syndication, as usual, had a different selection from the show:
Tangible Evidence / Living Proof / Genevieve / No More Lonely Nights / The King Will Come / Throw Down The Sword / Clousseau / In The Skin / Blowin' Free / Jail Bait

The setlist of the complete show was as follows:

Set 1: *Miles Copeland Intro / Tangible Evidence / Living Proof / Genevieve / No More Lonely Nights / Real Guitars Have Wings / Room 602 / Underground*

Set 2: *The King Will Come / Throw Down The Sword / Clousseau / In The Skin / Phoenix / Blowin' Free / Jail Bait / Bad Weather Blues*

Look North (BBC Yorkshire TV)
Rec: ?
TX: 7/11/96
Presenter: Martin Kelner
Note: This was a five-minute presenter-led piece for BBC Yorkshire that included clips from the 1971 *OGWT* and some new clips of the then-current band rehearsing, performing, and being interviewed at Leeds Irish Centre, along with vox pops from fans. The piece was pegged around the presenter being a fan from the 70s who used to see the band live at Leeds as a student, and was now catching up with them again decades later.

BBC SOUND ARCHIVE HOLDINGS

The BBC Sound Archive (which holds only material extant on tape, not Transcription Disc) contains the following Wishbone Ash concert material from radio: 1972 *In Concert*; 1974 *In Concert*; 1976 Glasgow Apollo/*John Peel Show* tracks; 1978 In Concert; 1979 *Year Of The Child* set (radio version); 1980 *In Concert* (two versions); 1981 *In Concert*; 1988 *In Concert*. These are all sourced from the UK 'Programmes as Broadcast', save for one, the 1978 *In Concert*, which has been sourced from Transcription Disc (presumably the tape copy was wiped at some point).

The Sound Archive also contains the following TV material: *OGWT*, 1971 (including outtakes); *OGWT*, 1972 (partial); *Stackridge & Co*, 1972; *OGWT*, 1977; *Year Of The Child*, 1979 (TV version); *Look North* 1996.

The only studio session material in the Sound Archive is the 1985 *Friday Rock Show* session and the six early-70s tracks used on the CD *Live At The BBC* (Band Of Joy, 1995), namely:

'Blind Eye'—*Sounds Of The 70s* (recorded April 21 1971)
'Lullaby'—*Sounds Of The 70s* (April 21 1971)
'The Pilgrim'—*Top Gear* (July 5 1971)
'Jail Bait'—*Sounds Of The 70s* (October 18 1971)
'Blowin' Free'—*Sounds Of The 70s* (May 31 1972)
'Throw Down The Sword'—*Sounds Of The 70s* (May 10 1972)

It appears that these six tracks were added to the Sound Archive as a block in 2000, hence taken from the CD. The CD was clearly a selection of tracks taken from Transcription Discs. From the information in the section below, it's clear there are at least two further BBC studio session tracks from the 70s which have never been released: 'Warrior' and 'The King Will Come', both recorded on April 18 1972 for *Top Gear*.

BBC TRANSCRIPTION DISCS

Transcription Discs in the 60s and 70s involving exclusive pop/rock sessions and concert recordings were cut for two reasons: for reuse on the BBC World Service (principally Brian Matthew's *Top Of The Pops*, not to be confused with the British TV show of the same name); or for syndication to foreign radio stations, principally in America, such as *In Concert* recordings. Often these discs would come with notices to destroy them after a certain date, the contracts with each artist involved having contained information on the number of rebroadcasts and the period within which they were allowed.

The BBC Worldwide catalogue of *In Concert* programmes available for license from other stations lists five discs/programmes for Wishbone Ash, which can be matched to the *In Concerts* the band did for each of the years in question: 1972, 1978, 1980, 1981, and 1988. As explained above, the band declined permission for the 1974 *In Concert* to be syndicated to the USA, hence it was never cut to Transcription Disc. Similarly, they prohibited syndication of the 1976 Glasgow Apollo concert, which was recorded privately by the band for license to *The John Peel Show* in early 1977.

This may well be an incomplete list, but Discs certainly exist of the following:

Top Of The Pops #347

Tracks: *Blind Eye / Lullaby*

Note: These tracks were two of the three recorded for *Sounds Of The 70s* on April 21 1971. Keith Skues, rather than Brian Matthew, presented this episode. Other artists on the disc are Richard Barnes, Osibisa, Julie Felix, Curved Air, and The Sweet.

Top Of The Pops #353

(BBC Transcription Services 128418)

Track: *The Pilgrim*

Note: This track was originally from the July 5 1971 *Top Gear* session. Other artists in the episode are The Hollies, Barclay James Harvest, Family, Bronco, and Rory Gallagher.

Top Of The Pops #367

(BBC Transcription Services 129474-S)

Track: *Jail Bait*

Note: This is from the October 18 1971 *Sounds Of The Seventies* session. Other artists on the disc include The Move, Mary Hopkin, and Peter Sarstedt. The original session was recorded at a Transcription Service studio and both the producer, Pete Dauncey, and

his engineer were dedicated Transcription Service employees. Online sources suggest that another TS Disc exists with the same catalogue number, 367, with all three tracks from the session on one side.

Top Of The Pops #391

Track: *Warrior / The King Will Come*

Note: This was two tracks from the band's *Top Gear* session on April 18 1972. Other artists on the episode were Paul Jones, The Strawbs, and The Johnstons.

Top Of The Pops #397

Tracks: *Blowin' Free / Throw Down The Sword*

Note: This episode/disc information is problematic: the notes with the disc say both tracks were recorded for *Top Gear* on April 18 1972. Ken Garner's research lists only 'Blowin' Free', of those two titles, as having been recorded for that session. Conceivably, 'Throw Down The Sword' was recorded for it but not broadcast on Top Gear. Alternatively, the disc notes could be in error, with 'Blowin' Free' deriving from the May 31 1972 *Sounds Of The 70s* session plus 'Throw Down The Sword' from the May 10 session. That accreditation would fit with the information attributed to the versions on the *Live At The BBC* CD—although exactly where that information came from is unclear. Other artists this episode were Plainsong, David Bowie, and The Move.

In Concert 1972 #18

(BBC-TS CN 1552/S)

Tracks: *Time Was / Blowin' Free / Warrior / Throw Down The Sword / The King Will Come / Phoenix*

Note: The oft-repeated May 25 1972 Paris Theatre recording.

In Concert 1977

Tracks: *Blind Eye / Lady Whiskey / Warrior / Throw Down The Sword / Front Page News / Goodbye Baby, Hello Friend / Come In From The Rain / Phoenix / Blowin' Free*

Note: This is the mysterious October 17 1977 Glasgow Apollo show with the Brian Matthew introduction (see above). One presumes this must exist on Transcription Disc, although it's not in the archive.

In Concert 1978 #187

(BBC-TS CN 3214/S)

Tracks: *The King Will Come / You See Red / Front Page News / The Way Of The World / Phoenix / Anger In Harmony / Queen Of Torture / Blowin' Free*

Note: The Hammersmith Odeon concert from October 25 1978. Online sources suggest there were two versions of this show syndicated, on Transcription Disc, to stations in the USA. One, titled *In Concert*, was the 58:18 content above, which is exactly the same as the UK FM broadcast.

BBC Rock Hour 1978

The King Will Come / Warrior / Errors Of My Way / You See Red / F.U.B.B. / Front Page News / The Way Of The World / Phoenix / Anger In Harmony / Time Was / Runaway / Lady Whiskey / Jail Bait / Queen Of Torture / Blowin' Free

Note: This is an alternative (longer) syndicated version of the Hammersmith show above. It adds 'Warrior', 'Errors Of My Way', 'F.U.B.B.', 'Time Was', 'Runaway', and 'Lady Whiskey'.

In Concert 1980

Tracks: *Doctor / Blind Eye / The Way Of The World / Insomnia / Queen Of Torture / Lifeline / Blowin' Free / Living Proof / Helpless / Jail Bait*

Note: This 58:39 US syndicated version of the February 2 1980 Hammersmith concert differs from the UK FM broadcast version by adding 'The Way Of The World' and 'Queen Of Torture' and excluding 'Bad Weather Blues'.

In Concert 1981

Tracks: *Lady Whiskey / Living Proof / Underground / Warrior / Kicks On The Street / Phoenix / Number The Brave / Helpless*

Note: A version of the June 2 1981 Hammersmith show that's different to the UK FM broadcast. It adds 'Phoenix', 'Number The Brave', and 'Helpless', while excluding 'The King Will Come', 'Where Is The Love?', 'Loaded', 'Blowin' Free', and 'Get Ready'.

BBC Rock Hour 1982

Tracks: *Lady Whiskey / Living Proof / Underground / Warrior / Kicks On The Street / Phoenix / Number The Brave / Helpless*

Note: This has exactly the same tracks as the above *In Concert*, having presumably been repackaged for a US syndicated series called *BBC Rock Hour*.

In Concert 1988

Tracks: *Tangible Evidence / Living Proof / No More Lonely Nights / The King Will Come / Throw Down The Sword / In The Skin / Clousseau / Phoenix / Blowin' Free / Jail Bait*

Note: This is the US syndication version of the March 4 1988 Hammersmith Odeon show, different to the UK FM broadcast.

BOOTLEGS OF BBC BROADCASTS

There are several Wishbone Ash 'Recordings Of Independent Origin' CDs/download albums that feature BBC material. This may not be all of the bootleg CDs out there, but it's a start.

Ted's Last Gig

Tracks: *Ballad Of the Beacon / Sometime World / Rock'n'Roll Widow / Blowin' Free / Jail Bait / Time Was / Phoenix*

Note: Taken from the Radio 1 FM broadcast of the Paris Theatre concert on February 23 1974. This show doesn't survive at source, neither on tape nor Transcription Disc. It was, indeed, Ted's last gig with the band— until the 1988 reunion, of course.

Live In London 1978

Tracks: *The King Will Come / You See Red / Front Page News / The Way Of The World / Phoenix / Anger & Harmony / Queen Of Torture / Blowin' Free*

Note: Taken from the BBC Transcription Disc of the November 25 1978 concert at Hammersmith Odeon.

Hammersmith Odeon 1978

Tracks: *The King Will Come / Warrior / Errors Of My Way / You See Red / F.U.B.B. / Front Page News / The Way Of The World / Phoenix / Anger & Harmony / Time Was / Runaway / Lady Whiskey / Jail Bait / Queen of Torture / Blowin' Free / Bad Weather Blues*

Note: This is a 2CD bootleg containing probably the full set of the above show. The track list is identical to the US BBC Rock Hour Transcription Disc(s).

Glasgow 1977

Tracks: *Blind Eye / Lady Whiskey / Warrior / Throw Down The Sword / Front Page News / Goodbye Baby, Hello Friend / Come In From The Rain / Phoenix / Blowin' Free / [Sometime World]*

Note: This is taken from the hard-to-pin-down broadcast or Transcription Disc, with Brian Matthew's introduction. It omits 'Sometime World' as it appears on the official 4CD *Distillation* (Repertoire, 1997).

In Concert 1980 *and also*
Live In London 1980

Tracks: *Doctor / Blind Eye / The Way Of The World / Insomnia /Queen Of Torture / Lifeline / Living Proof / Blowin' Free / Helpless / Jail Bait*

Note: The February 2 1980 Hammersmith Odeon concert, from the 58:39 Transcription Disc version.

Hammersmith Odeon 1981
and also Playing Free

Tracks: *Where Is The Love? / Living Proof / Underground / Warrior / Kicks On The Street / Phoenix / Number The Brave / Helpless / Blowin' Free / Get Ready / The King Will Come*

Note: From the June 2 1981 Hammersmith Odeon concert. At seventy-five minutes long, this is probably a combination of tracks from the UK FM broadcast and the Transcription Discs. It omits 'Lady Whiskey', which is contained on the two identical BBC Transcription Discs (*In Concert* 1981 and *BBC Rock Hour* 1982) and was also on the UK FM broadcast. At 2:45 it was the shortest track in the set. Maybe the bootleg compiler just didn't like it?

Lady Whiskey

Tracks: *Lady Whiskey / Underground / Warrior / Kicks On The Streets / Phoenix / Number the Brave / Helpless*

Note: This is a 50 minute selection from the June 2 1981 Hammersmith concert. It mirrors the two Transcription Discs for US syndication, save that it omits 'Living Proof'.

Wishbone Ash At The Hammersmith Odeon

Tracks: *Living Proof / Genevieve / The King Will Come / Clousseau / Jail Bait / Phoenix / Blowin' Free / Bad Weather Blues*

Note: This is a version of the March 4 1988 Hammersmith Odeon concert, different to the UK broadcast version by the addition of 'Clousseau' and with 'In The Skin', omitted by virtue of its having been included on the

official CD *Tracks* (Talking Elephant, 2002). Who says bootleggers don't care?

Magic Night At The Hammersmith Odeon

Tracks: *Tangible Evidence / Living Proof / Genevieve / No More Lonely Nights / The King Will Come / Throw Down The Sword / Clousseau / In The Skin / Phoenix / Blowin' Free / Jail Bait*

Note: This is another version of the above Hammersmith show. It mirrors the US syndication Transcription Disc save that it adds 'Phoenix' between 'In The Skin' and 'Blowin' Free'. Presumably, the bootleg derives from the Transcription Disc plus 'Phoenix' taken from the UK FM broadcast. One also presumes they ran out of room to add the only other FM-only track, 'Bad Weather Blues'.

APPENDIX 2
SELECTED DISCOGRAPHY
BY COLIN HARPER

As you might imagine, having been a band for forty-five years, with product released in many territories, on several labels, and then repackaged in various ways including variations of sleeve design, content and even title, the Wishbone Ash discography is a complicated beast. Some years ago Andy collaborated with some serious Ash fans on *The Illustrated Collector's Guide To Wishbone Ash*, and since then numerous discographical resources have appeared online. What we've done here is boil the discography down to the essential elements:

- *the core studio albums*
- *the core live albums (those released as 'current' product by the band)*
- *retrospective releases, including selected compilations featuring significant exclusive content and those live albums which fall into the category of being archive releases*
- *miscellaneous releases featuring Andy (guest appearances and side projects).*

We've added a line or two of information for many of the albums, indicating first and most recent CD reissues, recent heavyweight-vinyl reissues, and the odd other variation in between that might be of interest. Ash fan and serious collector Rainer Frilund very kindly looked over the work and provided several additional bits of information and corrections. Hopefully, this discography will help casual fans and newcomers to make sense of what's out

there. Luckily, a great deal of the band's key releases are, at the time of writing, readily available somewhere in the world (usually the UK, USA, France, or Japan) and hence readily available via worldwide online retailers—or, in the case of a fair selection of items, at the merchandise stall at a Wishbone Ash concert. Every album up to 1991's *Strange Affair* appeared first on vinyl LP; after that, CD was the preferred medium. The band's most recent two studio albums at the time of writing, *Elegant Stealth* and *Blue Horizon*, have appeared near-simultaneously on CD, download, and as 180-gram vinyl.

So who's on that one, then?
There have been twelve record-making versions of Wishbone Ash. There may well have been intermediate line-ups in between, but let's keep it simple! The information below only includes the two guitars, bass, and drums line-up of the band proper at any given time. There have often been guest musicians—keyboards, percussion, violin, backing vocals, and so on—on albums, but purely for clarity, and meaning no disrespect to those wonderful players, what follows below is the core line-up of the band and the span during which they made records:

Wishbone Ash Mk I (1970–74): Andy Powell; Ted Turner; Martin Turner; Steve Upton
Wishbone Ash Mk II (1974–80): Andy

Powell; Laurie Wisefield; Martin Turner; Steve Upton
Wishbone Ash Mk III (1981): Andy Powell; Laurie Wisefield; John Wetton; Steve Upton
Wishbone Ash Mk IV (1982): Andy Powell; Laurie Wisefield; Trevor Bolder; Steve Upton
Wishbone Ash Mk V (1984): Andy Powell; Laurie Wisefield; Mervyn Spence; Steve Upton
Wishbone Ash Mk I (reunion) (1987–89): Andy Powell; Ted Turner; Martin Turner; Steve Upton
Wishbone Ash Mk VI (1991): Andy Powell; Ted Turner; Martin Turner; Robbie France/ Ray Weston
Wishbone Ash Mk VII (1992): Andy Powell; Ted Turner; Andy Pyle; Ray Weston
Wishbone Ash Mk VIII (1995–96): Andy Powell; Roger Filgate; Tony Kishman; Mike Sturgis
Wishbone Ash Mk IX (1997–2001): Andy Powell; Mark Birch; Bob Skeat; Ray Weston
Wishbone Ash Mk X (2002–04): Andy Powell; Ben Granfelt; Bob Skeat; Ray Weston
Wishbone Ash Mk XI (2006): Andy Powell; Muddy Manninen; Bob Skeat; Ray Weston
Wishbone Ash Mk XII (2007–present): Andy Powell; Muddy Manninen; Bob Skeat; Joe Crabtree

STUDIO ALBUMS

Wishbone Ash (MCA, 1970)
Blind Eye / Lady Whisky / Errors Of My Way / Queen Of Torture / Handy / Phoenix
Producer: Derek Lawrence
Personnel: Wishbone Ash Mk I
First released on CD in 1992, in Japan. The most recent CD edition is a 2010 MCA/

Geffen SHM-CD, also in Japan. In 2007, Talking Elephant released *First Light*, effectively a demo run through of this first album retrieved from the sole surviving acetate. It features early versions of all the eventual first LP tracks except for 'Phoenix' but includes three other tracks: 'Roads Of Day To Day', 'Joshua', and 'Alone', the last of which would be resurrected for the band's second album, albeit as an instrumental.

Pilgrimage (MCA, 1971)
Vas Dis / The Pilgrim / Jail Bait / Alone / Lullaby / Valediction / Where Were You Tomorrow (Live)
Producer: Derek Lawrence
Personnel: Wishbone Ash Mk I
First released on CD in 1987, in the UK, with the addition of a live 'Jail Bait' (from the *Live From Memphis* 1972 US promotional LP). The most recent CD edition is a 2010 remaster on SHM-CD, on MCA/Geffen in Japan, featuring the original track list.

Argus (MCA, 1972)
Time Was / Sometime World / Blowin' Free / The King Will Come / Leaf And Stream / Warrior / Throw Down The Sword
Producer: Derek Lawrence
Personnel: Wishbone Ash Mk I
First released on CD in 1991, in Japan, with the addition of the single A-side 'No Easy Road'. In 2002 MCA US released *Argus: Expanded Edition—Remastered & Revisited*, which was in fact a remix by Martin Turner with the addition of all three tracks from the US promo LP *Live From Memphis*: 'Jail Bait', 'The Pilgrim', and 'Phoenix'. In 2007 Universal UK/Europe released a 2CD *Argus: Deluxe Edition* featuring a remaster of the original LP mix plus two of the three *Live From Memphis* tracks ('The Pilgrim'

and 'Phoenix'), the 'No Easy Road' single A-side, a BBC Radio *In Concert* from 1972 and two further BBC Radio session tracks from 1972. The most recent editions of Argus are a 2010 SHM-CD version of the 2CD *Deluxe Edition* and a 2010 single CD SHM-SACD, both from Japan, on MCA/Island and Geffen respectively. A 2010 180-gram vinyl edition is also available from Universal US.

Wishbone Four (MCA, 1973)
So Many Things To Say / Ballad Of The Beacon / No Easy Road / Everybody Needs A Friend / Doctor / Sorrel / Sing Out The Song / Rock 'N' Roll Widow
Producer: Wishbone Ash
Personnel: Wishbone Ash Mk I
First released on CD in 1991, in the UK. The most recent CD edition is an SHM-CD on MCA/Geffen in Japan, 2010.

There's The Rub (MCA, 1974)
Silver Shoes / Don't Come Back / Persephone / Hometown / Lady Jay / F.U.B.B.
Producer: Bill Szymczyk
Personnel: Wishbone Ash Mk II
First released on CD in 1992, in Germany. The most recent CD edition is an SHM-CD on MCA in Japan, 2010.

Locked In (Atlantic, 1975)
Rest In Peace / No Water In The Well / Moonshine / She Was My Best Friend / It Started In Heaven / Half Past Lovin' / Trust In You / Say Goodbye
Producer: Tom Dowd
Personnel: Wishbone Ash Mk II
First released on CD in 1995, in Germany. The most recent CD edition is an SHM-CD on MCA/Geffen in Japan, 2010.

New England (MCA, 1976)
Mother Of Pearl / (In All Of My Dreams) You Rescue Me / Runaway / Lorelei / Outward Bound / Prelude / When You Know Love / Lonely Island / Candlelight
Producer: Howard Albert & Ron Albert
Personnel: Wishbone Ash Mk II
First released on CD by BGO in 1998 as a two-on-one with *Front Page News*. Also released as a two-on-one with *Locked In* by Wounded Bird in the US in 2005. The most recent CD version is an MCA/Geffen SHM-CD from Japan, 2010—unshackled with anything else, for a change.

Front Page News (MCA, 1977)
Front Page News / Midnight Dancer / Goodbye Baby Hello Friend / Surface To Air / 714 / Come In From The Rain / Right Or Wrong / Heart Beat / The Day I Found Your Love / Diamond Jack
Producer: Howard Albert & Ron Albert
Personnel: Wishbone Ash Mk II
First released on CD in 1994, in Germany. The most recent CD edition is an SHM-CD on MCA/Geffen in Japan, 2010.

No Smoke Without Fire (MCA, 1978)
You See Red / Baby The Angels Are Here / Ships In The Sky / Stand And Deliver / Anger In Harmony / Like A Child / The Way Of The World (Part 1) / The Way Of The World (Part 2)
Producer: Derek Lawrence
Personnel: Wishbone Ash Mk II
Originally issued in the UK with a free single: 'Come In From The Rain' b/w 'Lorelei'. Currently available on MCA/Geffen SHM-CD, Japan, 2010, with the single sides added as bonus tracks plus two outtakes and another B-side: 'Firesign', 'Time And Space (Remix)', and 'Bad Weather Blues (Live)'.

Just Testing (MCA, 1980)

Living Proof / Haunting Me / Insomnia / Helpless / Pay The Price / New Rising Star / Master Of Disguise / Lifeline

Producer: John Sherry & Wishbone Ash

Personnel: Wishbone Ash Mk II

First released on CD in 1998 in the UK and Europe, adding both sides of the non-album single 'Come On' backed with 'Fast Johnny', plus period live recordings of 'Blowin' Free' and 'Helpless'. The most recent CD edition is a 2010 SHM-CD edition on MCA/Geffen from Japan (without the bonus tracks).

Number The Brave (MCA, 1981)

Loaded / Where Is The Love / Underground / Kicks On The Street / Open Road / Get Ready / Rainstorm / That's That / Roller Coaster / Number The Brave

Producer: Nigel Gray

Personnel: Wishbone Ash Mk III

First released on CD in 2001, in Japan. The most recent CD edition is an SHM-CD on MCA/Geffen in Japan, 2010.

Twin Barrels Burning (Metronome, 1982)

Engine Overheat / Can't Fight Love / Genevieve / Me And My Guitar / Hold On / Streets Of Shame / No More Lonely Nights / Angels Have Mercy / Wind Up

Producers: Ashley Howe; Nigel Gray; Stuart Epps & Wishbone Ash

Personnel: Wishbone Ash Mk IV

First and only CD release: Castle Communications, UK/Europe, 1993.

Raw To The Bone (Neat, 1984)

Cell Of Fame / People In Motion / Don't Cry / Love Is Blue / Long Live The Night / Rocket In My Pocket / It's Only Love / Don't You

Mess / Dreams (Searching For An Answer) / Perfect Timing

Producer: Nigel Gray

Personnel: Wishbone Ash Mk V

First and only CD release: Castle Communications, UK/Europe, 1993.

Nouveau Calls (IRS, 1987)

Tangible Evidence / Clousseau / Flags Of Convenience / From Soho To Sunset / Arabesque / In The Skin / Something Happening In Room 602 / Johnny Left Home Without It / The Spirit Flies Free / A Rose Is A Rose / Real Guitars Have Wings

Producer: Martin Turner/William Orbit

Personnel: Wishbone Ash Mk I (reunion)

First released on CD by IRS in 1987. Only subsequent CD release: Talking Elephant, UK/Europe, 2003, with bonus track (single B-side): 'T-Bone Shuffle'.

Here To Hear (IRS, 1989)

Cosmic Jazz / Keeper Of The Light / Mental Radio / Walk On Water / Witness To Wonder / Lost Cause In Paradise / Why Don't We / In The Case / Hole In My Heart (Part One) / Hole In My Heart (Part Two)

Producer: Martin Turner

Personnel: Wishbone Ash Mk I (reunion)

First released on CD by IRS in 1989. Most recently available on CD from Talking Elephant, 2003, with the following period bonus tracks: 'Heaven Is', 'Bolan's Monument', 'Duffle Shuffle', and 'Cosmic Jazz (Karaoke Version)'.

Strange Affair (IRS, 1991)

Strange Affair / Wings Of Desire / Renegade / Dream Train / Some Conversation / Say You Will / Rollin' / You / Hard Times / Standing In The Rain

Producer: Martin Turner
Personnel: Wishbone Ash Mk VI
First and only CD release on IRS, 1991. The last Wishbone Ash album to be routinely released on vinyl.

Illuminations (HTD, 1996)
Mountainside / On Your Own / Top Of The World / No Joke / Tales Of The Wise / Another Time / A Thousand Years / The Ring / Comfort Zone / Mystery Man / Wait Out The Storm / The Crack Of Dawn
Producer: Andy Powell & Roger Filgate
Personnel: Wishbone Ash Mk VIII
A 2CD *Deluxe Edition* was released in 2014, adding live performances of eight of the album's tracks plus an audio interview with Andy Powell. (Note: Yes, we've jumped straight from Mk VI to Mk VIII—Wishbone Ash Mk VII recorded only the live album *Live In Chicago*.)

Trance Visionary (Invisible Hands, 1997)
Numerology / Wonderful Stash / Heritage / Interfaze / Powerbright (Black & White Screen) / Remnants of a Paranormal Menagerie / Narcissus Nervosa / Trance Visionary / Flutterby / Banner Headlines / The Loner / Powerbright Volition / Gutterfly / Wronged By Righteousness
Producer: Mike Bennett
Personnel: Wishbone Ash Mk IX

Psychic Terrorism (Invisible Hands, 1998)
Transliteration / Narcissus Stash / Sleep's Eternal Slave / Monochrome / Breaking Out / The Son Of Righteousness / Psychic Terrorism / How Many Times? / Bloodline / Back Page Muse / Powerbright Conclusion
Producer: Mike Bennett
Personnel: Wishbone Ash Mk IX

Bare Bones (Castle, 1999)
Wings Of Desire / Errors Of My Way / Master Of Disguise / You Won't Take Me Down / Love Abuse / (Won't You Give Him) One More Chance / Baby Don't Mind / Living Proof / Hard Times / Strange Affair / Everybody Needs A Friend
Producer: Andy Powell
Personnel: Wishbone Ash Mk IX
An all-acoustic album featuring reworkings of classic material plus new songs. Reissued in the US as DVD-A by Silverline, 2002. Most recently reissued as a 2CD *Deluxe Edition* on Talking Elephant, 2014, adding live performances of six of the album's tracks plus an audio interview with Andy Powell.

Bona Fide (Talking Elephant, 2002)
Almighty Blues / Enigma / Faith, Hope and Love / Ancient Remedy / Changing Tracks / Shoulda, Woulda, Coulda / Bona Fide / Difference In Time / Come Rain, Come Shine / Peace
Producer: Andy Powell
Personnel: Wishbone Ash Mk X
Slipcased *Special Edition* released in 2008 adds the following tracks featuring new member Muddy Manninen: 'Hard On You' (studio), 'Almighty Blues' (live), and 'Tales Of The Wise' (live). The 2CD *Deluxe Edition* released in 2014 adds live performances of six tracks plus an audio interview with Andy.

Clan Destiny (Talking Elephant, 2006)
Eyes Wide Open / Dreams Outta Dust / Healing Ground / Steam Town / Loose Change / Surfing A Slow Wave / Slime Time / Capture The Moment / Your Dog / The Raven / Motherless Child
Producer: Andy Powell
Personnel: Wishbone Ash Mk XI
Reissued by Eagle, 2011.

The Power Of Eternity (Talking Elephant, 2007)
The Power / Driving A Wedge / In Crisis / Dancing With The Shadows / Happiness / Northern Lights / Your Indulgence / Growing Up / Disappearing / Hope Springs Eternal
Producer: Andy Powell & Wishbone Ash
Personnel: Wishbone Ash Mk XII
A 2CD *Deluxe Edition*, released in 2014, added live performances of four of the album's tracks, studio outtakes/alternative versions of six tracks and an audio interview with Andy Powell.

Elegant Stealth (ZYX/Golden Core, 2011)
Reason To Believe / Warm Tears / Man With No Name / Can't Go It Alone / Give It Up / Searching For Satellites / Heavy Weather / Mud-slick / Big Issues / Migrant Worker / Invisible Thread / Reason To Believe (remix / hidden track)
Producer: Andy Powell & Tom Greenwood
Personnel: Wishbone Ash Mk XII
Released in a CD/DVD *Story Behind* edition in 2012, including bonus audio, the 'Reason To Believe' promo video and a documentary on the album. Also released on heavyweight vinyl in 2012.

Blue Horizon (Solid Rockhouse, 2014)
Take It Back / Deep Blues / Strange How Things Come Back Around / Being One / Way Down South / Tally Ho! / Mary Jane / American Century / Blue Horizon / All There Is To Say
Producer: Tom Greenwood, Andy Powell, Joe Crabtree
Personnel: Wishbone Ash Mk XII
Simultaneously released on heavyweight vinyl.

LIVE ALBUMS

Live From Memphis (Decca, 1972)
Jail Bait / The Pilgrim / Phoenix
Personnel: Wishbone Ash Mk I
A US radio promotional LP. Although never issued or reissued commercially as a stand-alone album, all three tracks (thirty-three minutes worth) have appeared on various compilations and expanded versions of albums in the CD era. Still common enough for second-hand originals to turn up for £30–40, it would be nit-picking to exclude it here.

Live Dates (MCA, 1973)
The King Will Come / Warrior / Throw Down The Sword / Rock 'N Roll Widow / Ballad Of The Beacon / Baby What Do You Want Me To Do / The Pilgrim / Blowin' Free / Jail Bait / Lady Whiskey / Phoenix
Personnel: Wishbone Ash Mk I
First released on 2CD by MCA in 1992, adding 'Phoenix' from the *Live From Memphis* promotional LP. Released by MCA/Geffen as SHM-CD in Japan, 2010. Most recent CD reissue is an HDCD from Culture Factory/Universal in France, 2013. Also reissued on heavyweight vinyl by MCA, 2013.

Live In Tokyo (MCA Japan, 1979)
F.U.B.B. / The Way Of The World / You See Red / Jail Bait / Blowin' Free
Personnel: Wishbone Ash Mk II
A Japan-only release, recorded in 1978. First released on CD in Austria, 2010. Most recently released as an SHM-CD by MCA in Japan, 2013.

Live Dates Volume Two (MCA, 1980)
Doctor / Living Proof / Runaway / Helpless / F.U.B.B. / The Way Of The World / Lorelei / Persephone / You Rescue Me / Time Was / Goodbye Baby Hello Friend / No Easy Road
Personnel: Wishbone Ash Mk II
Originally released as a limited edition 2LP, then as a single LP (retaining the first six tracks listed above). Recorded on tour in Britain in 1976–80. Not released in USA. The initial bonus disc was later released as a separate LP in Germany titled *Live Dates Volume Two—Additional Tapes* (1980). First released on 2CD as an SHM-CD by MCA/Geffen in Japan, 2010. Most recently released on 2CD by Culture Factory/Universal in France, 2013.

Hot Ash Live (MCA, 1981)
Blowin' Free / Living Proof / Goodbye Baby Hello Friend / Bad Weather Blues / Doctor / The Way Of The World / Helpless / No Easy Road
Personnel: Wishbone Ash Mk II
This is an edited version of *Live Dates Volume Two* with the addition of two further tracks for the US market. Originally released only in the USA and Italy, then Japan and a couple of other territories the following year. Never available on CD.

Live In Chicago (Virgin/CBH, 1992)
The King Will Come / Strange Affair / Standing In The Rain / Lost Cause In Paradise / Keeper Of The Light / Throw Down The Sword / In The Skin / Why Don't We? / Hard Times / Blowin' Free / Living Proof
Personnel: Wishbone Ash Mk VII
The first Wishbone Ash album to be released solely on CD. Subsequently reissued on CD by various labels under various titles, including *The Ash Live In Chicago, Living Proof—Live In Chicago, Keeper Of The Light*, and *Lost Cause In Paradise.* One German reissue, titled *The King Will Come,* added insult to injury by featuring only Martin Turner and Laurie Wisefield on the cover—neither of whom were on the record. Also reissued as one disc of the 2CD set *Live Affairs* on Music Avenue, Germany, 2006.

Live In Geneva (Hengest, 1995)
The King Will Come / Strange Affair / Throw Down The Sword / In the Skin / Hard Times / Blowin' Free / Keeper Of The Light / Blind Eye / Runaway / Sometime World / Vas Dis
Personnel: Wishbone Ash Mk VIII
Recorded in 1994. Reissued on other labels as *Live At Geneva* and *The Very Best Of Wishbone Ash: The Anniversary Album—Live At Geneva.* Also reissued as one disc of the 2CD set *Live Affairs* on Music Avenue, Germany, 2006. Most recent CD reissue on Angel Air, 2012.

Live Dates 3 (Eagle, 2001)
Come In From The Rain / Living Proof / Persephone / Lifeline / Wings Of Desire / Errors Of My Way / Leaf And Stream / Throw Down The Sword / F.U.B.B. / Phoenix
Personnel: Wishbone Ash Mk IX
Recorded in Paris, 1999.

Almighty Blues—London & Beyond (Classic Rock Productions, 2004)
Almighty Blues / Warrior / Throw Down The Sword / Standing In The Rain / Faith, Hope And Love / Changing Tracks / On Your Own / Come Rain, Come Shine / Ancient Remedy / Time Was / Jail Bait
Personnel: Wishbone Ash Mk X
Recorded at concerts during the *Bona Fide* tour of 2002–03 and released as SACD.

Several tracks are audio from the concert DVD of the same name. Also appeared on CD on Southworld as *Live On Air*.

Live In Hamburg (Golden Core, 2007)
Eyes Wide Open / Healing Ground / The King Will Come / The Warrior / Why Don't We / Dreams Outta Dust / The Raven / Sometime World / Valediction / Sorrel / Capture The Moment / Tales Of The Wise / Almighty Blues / Standing In The Rain / Phoenix / Blind Eye / Ballad Of The Beacon / Blowin' Free
Personnel: Wishbone Ash XII
The audio from the band's DVD of the same name, released as a 2CD in Germany. A nine-track single vinyl LP, *Live In Hamburg*, was also released in 2007 by Golden Core.

Argus 'Then Again' Live (Talking Elephant, 2008)
Intro / Real Guitars Have Wings / Mountainside / Growing Up / Time Was / Sometime World / Blowin' Free / The King Will Come / Leaf And Stream / Warrior / Throw Down The Sword / Way Of The World
Personnel: Wishbone Ash XII
Recorded live in Washington DC, 2008—the whole of *Argus* performed live in sequence, with bookends.

40—Live In London (Golden Core, 2009)
Blind Eye / Runaway / Right Or Wrong / Growing Up / Sometime World / Rainstorm / Way Of The World / Everybody Needs A Friend / The King Will Come / Throw Down The Sword / Cell Of Fame / Almighty Blues / Faith, Hope And Love / Engine Overheat / Phoenix / Jail Bait / Blowin' Free
Personnel: Wishbone Ash XII + guests
A German 2CD release, being the audio from the separately released DVD of the

same name. A combined 2CD+DVD set was also released while an 8-track single vinyl LP called *Live In London* also appeared in 2009 by Golden Core sister label ZYX.

Live At The Grand—Road Works Volume 1 (no label, 2010)
You See Red / The Power / Driving A Wedge / In Crisis / Rock N Roll Widow / Can't Go It Alone / F.U.B.B. / Lady Jay / Lullaby / Jail Bait
Personnel: Wishbone Ash XII
Recorded at The Grand, Clitheroe, UK, October 13 2010. A kind of official bootleg/concert souvenir primarily available for sale at the band's gigs.

Live In Hamburg—Road Works Volume 2 (no label, 2012)
Dreams Outta Dust / Front Page News / In Crisis / The King Will Come / Northern Lights / Disappearing / Reason To Believe / Engine Overheat / Throw Down The Sword / Phoenix
Personnel: Wishbone Ash XII
Recorded at Fabrik, Hamburg, February 21 2011. Another official bootleg tour souvenir.

Live In Germany—Road Works Volume 3 (no label, 2013)
Sometime World / Keeper Of The Light / Faith, Hope And Love / Leaf And Stream / Warrior / The Pilgrim / Healing Ground / Phoenix
Personnel: Wishbone Ash XII
Recorded at various venues in Germany during January and February 2012. A third official bootleg tour souvenir. Yes, there's a pattern developing.

Live At Ashcon 2014—Road Works Volume 4 (no label, 2015)
The King Will Come / Warrior / Throw Down The Sword / Rock 'n Roll Widow / Ballad Of

The Beacon / Baby What You Want Me To Do / The Pilgrim / Blowin' Free / Jail Bait / Lady Whisky / Phoenix
Recorded at Ashcon, November 2014

RETROSPECTIVE RELEASES

BBC Radio 1 Live In Concert (Windsong, 1991)
Blowin' Free / Time Was / Jail Bait / The Pilgrim / Warrior / Throw Down The Sword / The King Will Come / Phoenix
Personnel: Wishbone Ash Mk I
A 1972 BBC concert, subsequently included in the *Argus Deluxe Edition* 2CD set.

Live At The BBC (Band Of Joy, 1995)
Blind Eye / Lullaby / Pilgrim / Jail Bait / Blowin' Free / Throw Down The Sword / Vas Dis / Goodbye Baby Hello Friend / Baby Come In From The Rain
Personnel: Wishbone Ash Mk I & II
A selection of BBC radio session and TV audio from 1971, 1972, and 1977.

Live Timeline (Receiver, 1997)
Lost Cause In Paradise / Standing In The Rain / Strange Affair / The King Will Come / Throw Down The Sword / In The Skin / Why Don't We / Wings Of Desire / Time Was / Living Proof / Blowin' Free / Vas Dis / Where Were You Tomorrow
Personnel: Wishbone Ash Mk VI & I
Recorded live in Nagoya, Japan, on May 23 1991, plus two tracks from a 1970 BBC session.

Distillation (Repertoire, 1997)
Personnel: Most incarnations of Wishbone Ash, 1970–96

Too many tracks to list. A lovingly crafted 4CD set of classic album tracks, non-album singles, remixes, rarities, previously unreleased live, and studio material with a booklet essay from Chris Welch and track notes from Martin Turner and Andy Powell. No longer in print but worth seeking out.

Live In Bristol (Classic Rock Legends, 2002)
Real Guitars Have Wings / The King Will Come / Cosmic Jazz / Keeper Of The Light / Why Don't We? / Blowin' Free / Medley (Blind Eye / Lady Whiskey / Sometime World / Phoenix / Jail Bait)
Personnel: Wishbone Ash Mk I (reunion)
Audio from a 1989 recording for the UK TV series *Bedrock*.

Tracks (Talking Elephant, 2002)
Warrior / The King Will Come / Persephone / Front Page News / Anger In Harmony / Queen Of Torture / You See Red / Lifeline / Living Proof / Insomnia / Number The Brave / No More Lonely Nights / Tangible Evidence / In The Skin / Keeper Of The Light / Why Don't We / Standing In The Rain / Throw Down The Sword / Way Of The World / The Ring / Everybody Needs A Friend / Master Of Disguise / Wings Of Desire / Ballad Of The Beacon / Strange Affair / Outward Bound
Personnel: Various
A 2CD compilation of previously unreleased live tracks. Reissued as *Live History: Tracks Vol.1* by Happinet/Ward in Japan, 2009.

Tracks 2 (Talking Elephant, 2003)
Time Was / Blowin' Free / Lorelei / Errors On My Way / F.U.B.B. / Too Much Monkey Business / Bad Weather Blues / Phoenix / Underground / Cosmic Jazz / No Joke / Real Guitars Have

Wings / Sometime World / Living Proof (Acoustic Version) / Bona Fide / Mountainside / Faith, Hope And Love / Ancient Remedy (Electric Version) / Coulda, Woulda, Shoulda / Mercury Blues / Ancient Remedy (Acoustic Version) / Leaf And Stream / Almighty Blues / Steppin' Out
Personnel: Various
A second 2CD compilation of previously unreleased live tracks. Reissued as *Live History: Tracks Vol.2* by Happinet/Ward in Japan, 2009.

Lost Pearls (Talking Elephant, 2004)
Is Justice Done / Bells Chime / Hard On You / Out On A Limb / Where You Been / Halfway House (Martin Vocal) / Halfway House (Claire Vocal) / Football And Boxing / John Sherry Jam / Too Much Monkey Business (Live) / Night Hawker / Sheriff Of Sherwood (Demo)
Producer: Martin Turner
Personnel: Wishbone Ash MkII + MkIV
A selection of previously unreleased material from 1978 (with one track from 1982). Reissued by Eagle, 2009.

Backbones (Talking Elephant, 2004)
Personnel: Wishbone Ash Mk VIII & X
No point in listing everything on this one. A 3CD compilation with two discs drawn from material on the band's previous HTD and Talking Elephant releases—*Illuminations, Bona Fide, Tracks, Tracks 2, Lost Pearls*—but adding a third disc featuring an audio interview with Andy and three exclusive live acoustic tracks from 2002: 'Strange Affair', 'The King Will Come', and 'Hard Times'.

Tracks 3 (Talking Elephant, 2007)
Surfing A Slow Wave / Ancient Remedy / The Ring / Healing Ground / Changing Tracks / Living Proof / Rock'n Roll Widow / Ballad Of

The Beacon / Lullaby / Candlelight / Wings Of Desire / Sorrell / Capture The Moment / Comfort Zone / Why Don't We / Baby What You Want Me To Do / Clousseau / The Raven / Valediction / Errors Of My Way / Wait Out The Storm / Dreams Outta Dust / Eyes Wide Open / Faith Hope And Love / Persephone / Cell Of Fame / Phoenix / Baby Don't Mind / Hard On You / Ship Of Dreams / Come In From The Rain / High Heeled Sneakers / Rock Me Baby / Jail Bait / Another Time / Motherless Child / Hard Times / Blind Eye / East Coast Boogie / Loose Change / Warrior (Orchestral Arrangement)
Personnel: Various
A 3CD third compilation of previously unreleased live tracks. Reissued as *Live History: Tracks Vol.3* by Happinet/Ward in Japan, 2009.

First Light (Talking Elephant, 2007)
Lady Whiskey / Roads Of Day To Day / Blind Eye / Joshua / Queen Of Torture / Alone / Handy / Errors Of My Way
Personnel: Wishbone Ash Mk I
Taken from the sole surviving acetate— bought at auction by Ash fan Dr John and generously made available for release—of a pre-first album studio session, this is the earliest known recording of Wishbone Ash. Reissued in 2014.

SELECTED DVD RELEASES

30th Anniversary Concert (Eagle, 2001)
Real Guitars Have Wings / The King Will Come / F.U.B.B. / Ballad Of The Beacon / Errors Of My Way / No Joke / Strange Affair / Living Proof / Blowin' Free / Phoenix / Come In From The Rain / Hard Times
Personnel: Wishbone Ash IX + guests

Recorded in London, 2000, with Laurie Wisefield and Claire Hamill guesting. Released in the US by Eagle as *30th Anniversary Concert—Live Dates 3*.

Phoenix Rising (Classic Rock Legends, 2004)
Vas Dis / The King Will Come / Blowin' Free / Phoenix / Warrior / Cosmic Jazz / Living Proof / Jail Bait / Wings Of Desire / Why Don't We / Ballad Of The Beacon / Real Guitars Have Wings / Blowin' Free / Bad Weather Blues / Where Were You Tomrorow?
Personnel: Wishbone Ash Mk I, Mk I (reunion) & Mk IX
Vintage performances from *The Old Grey Whistle Test* (BBC) 1971, ABC TV (Australia) 1972, Don Kirshner's *Rock Concert* (USA) 1973, Bristol 1989, and London 2003.

Live At The Spirit Of 66 (2006)
Outward Bound / Warrior / The King Will Come / Healing Ground / Underground / Why Don't We / Persephone / Leaf & Stream / Dreams Outta Dust / Tales Of The Wise / Changing Tracks / Almighty Blues / Living Proof / Phoenix / Surfin' A Slow Wave / Jail Bait
Personnel: Wishbone MK XI
Recorded in Belgium, 2006.

Live In Hamburg (BHM Productions, 2007)
Eyes Wide Open / Healing Ground / The King Will Come / The Warrior / Why Don't We / Dreams Outta Dust / The Raven / Sometime World / Valediction / Sorrell / Capture The Moment / Tales Of The Wise / Almighty Blues / Standing In The Rain / Phoenix / Blind Eye / Ballad Of The Beacon / Blowin' Free
Personnel: Wishbone Mk XI
Recorded in Hamburg, 2007.

40th Anniversary Concert: Live In London (C&B Productions, 2010)
Blind Eye / Runaway / Right Or Wrong / Growing Up / Sometime World / Rainstorm / The Way Of The World / Everybody Needs A Friend / The King Will Come / Throw Down The Sword / Cell Of Fame / Almighty Blues / Faith, Hope And Love / Engine Overheat / Phoenix / Jail Bait / Blowin' Free + Bonus: Road Movie
Personnel: Wishbone Ash MK XII
Recorded in London, 2010, with guests Mark Birch, Ben Granfelt, and Mervyn Spence.

This Is Wishbone Ash (A Rockumentary) (Wishbone Ash/Glasgow Production, 2010) Documentary including six full live performances.

WISHBONE ASH LIVE DATES 1969–2015

The 1969–2001 dates were very kindly provided by Simon Atkinson, with additional information from Big Harry, and are presented here with only a few editorial tweaks. Wishbone Ash performed many more dates in this period but these are all that can be currently retrieved, from numerous print sources. The 2002–15 dates were sourced from the official band website and represent virtually every show Wishbone Ash performed in this period.

All dates UK unless otherwise stated

1969
November
10 Civic Hall, Dunstable (with Aynsley Dunbar's Retaliation)
18 Tiffany's, Exeter
December
?   Klooks Kleek, London
20 Eel Pie Island, London (with Audience)

1970
January
14 Klooks Kleek, London (with Hard Meat)
February
3   Northern Poly, London (with Edgar Broughton Band, Steamhammer, Sam Apple Pie, and Forest)
6   Assembly Rooms, Wood Green
12 Polytechnic Kingston (with Caravan and Rare Bird)

19 The Temple, London (with Mighty Baby and The Grope)
20 Bedford College, London (with Heavy Jelly and May Blitz)
March
13 Connaught Hall, London
14 University College, London (with Rupert's People)
19 St Martin's School of Art, London (with Boris and Flesh)
21 The Swan, Yardley
23 Speakeasy, London
April
2–3 Le Bilbouquet, Paris, France
4–5 The Golf Druot, Paris, France
6–7 Le Rock 'n Roll Circus, Paris, France
12 Youth Club, Bletchley (supporting Van der Graaf Generator)
13 College of Agriculture, Leeds
16 Imperial College, London
17 Trent Park College, Barnet
18 The Cavern, Liverpool
29 Victoria Hall, Chelmsford
May
2   University College, London (with Heavy Jelly)
8   Marquee, London (with Slade)
9   Imperial College, London (with T.Rex, Taste, Smile, and Kevin Ayers)
14 Country Club, London (with Rupert's People)
15 College of Education, Coventry
16 Tofts, Folkestone
18 Civic Hall, Dunstable (with Deep Purple)

19 Speakeasy, London
23 Twerton Park, Bath City Pop Festival
June
? Guildford College
? Roundhouse, London
? Henry Blues House, Newcastle
4 Marquee, London (with Writing On
The Wall)
? Dorchester Hotel, London
? Country Club, London
15 Marquee, London
20 Hull University (with Taste)
July
? Old Granary, Bristol
? Farx Club, Southall
7 Ronnie Scott's, London
25 Civic Hall, Dunstable (with Aquila,
supporting The Who)
26 Brewery Tap, London
31 Town Hall, Torquay
August
1 Town Hall, Torquay (with Atomic
Rooster, Adolphus Rebirth)
6 BBC Paris Studios, London (*Sounds Of
The 70s*)
8 Starlight Rooms, Boston
9 National Jazz & Blues Festival,
Plumpton
14 Fishmonger's Arms, Wood Green
16 Roundhouse, London (with Writing
On The Wall, Heads Hands & Feet,
Trader Horne, Stoics, Supertramp)
21 Lyceum, London (with Hardin & York,
Keef Hartley Band)
22 Builders Exchange, Huddersfield
23 Edinburgh Festival
25 City Hall, St Albans
September
14 Cook's Ferry Inn, Edmonton
16 Marquee, London
24 Town Hall, Watford (with ELP)

25 City Hall, St Albans (with Farm, ELP)
26 Starlight Rooms, Boston (with Farm,
ELP)
27 De Montfort Hall, Leicester (with
Farm, ELP)
28 Guildhall, Portsmouth (with Farm,
ELP) *or* Nite Cat, Clacton
October
1 Town Hall, Leeds (with Farm, ELP)
or Hornsey Town Hall (with Juicy
Lucy)
4 City Hall, Newcastle (with Farm,
supporting ELP)
7 The Dome, Brighton (with Farm, ELP)
8 Lancaster University (with Free)
9 Dunhelm House, Durham (with Free)
10 Polytechnic, Kingston
16 Floral Hall, Hornsey (with Van der
Graaf Generator and Mandrake)
19 Ronnie Scotts, London
24 University College, London (with
Blodwyn Pig)
29 Acid Palace, Uxbridge (with Mogul
Thrash)
30 Rag Ball, University of Surrey (with
Keef Hartley Band, Yes, Jimmy James,
New Temperance Seven)
31 Starlight Ballroom, Boston (with Van
der Graaf Generator)
November
7 Imperial College, London (with
Brinsley Schwartz)
19 Paris Theatre, London (*John Peel
Sunday Concert*, with The Faces)
30 Winter Gardens, Cleethorpes (with
Stray and Mogul Thrash)
December
2 BBC TV Studios, London (*Disco 2*)
? 1932, Windsor
? Cooks Ferry Inn, Edmonton
? Railway Tavern, London

10 Locarno Mecca, Blackpool (with
Barclay James Harvest)

1971

January

1 BBC Maida Vale, London (*Sounds Of
The 70s*)
8 Sisters, Tottenham
9 Van Dyke Club, Plymouth
16 Dumfries University
17 Eel Pie Island, London
18 Civic Hall, Dunstable
22 Thames Polytechnic (with If)
27 Albert Hall, Nottingham (with
Mott The Hoople, Red Dirt,
Nothineverhappens)
28 City Hall, Newcastle (with Mott The
Hoople, Red Dirt, Nothineverhappens)
29 City Hall, Sheffield (with Mott The
Hoople, Red Dirt, Nothineverhappens)
30 City Hall, Hull (with Mott The
Hoople, Red Dirt, Nothineverhappens)
31 St George's Hall, Bradford (with
Mott The Hoople, Red Dirt,
Nothineverhappens)

February

2 Marquee, London (with Gordon
Giltrap)
5 Il Rondo Ballroom, Leicester
7 Youth Club, Bletchley
12 Co-op Hall, St Albans
19 Town Hall, West Bromwich (with Tea
& Symphony and Egg)
20 Shenstone College, Worcester
21 Roundhouse, London
25 Austin, USA (with The Guess Who)
26 Dallas, USA
27 Houston, USA

March

5–7 Whisky A Go Go, Los Angeles, USA
(with Ned)

9 San Diego, USA
11 Fillmore West, San Francisco, USA
(with Siegel-Schwall)
12–14 Fillmore West, San Francisco, USA
(with Poco and Siegel-Schwall)
19 Eastown Theatre, Detroit, USA (with
Eric Burdon, War, Badfinger)
20 Eastown Theatre, Detroit, USA (with
Mountain and McKendree Spring)

April

3 The Warehouse, New Orleans, USA
(with The James Gang; The Allman
Brothers?)
? Detroit, USA
? Chicago, USA
8–10 Fillmore West, San Francisco, USA
(with Seatrain and Elton John)
12 Virginia Theatre, Alexandria, USA
16 Cheltenham Town Hall
17 Country Club, Kirklevington
18 Boat Club, Nottingham
21 BBC Maida Vale, London (*Sounds Of
The 70s*)
23 Nag's Head, Wollaston
24 Dudley Technical College
25 Lyceum, London (with Wooden Horse
and Thin Lizzy)
27 Resurrection, Hitchin
28 Big Brother, Hertford
29 Westbridge College, Nottingham
30 Penthouse Club, Scarborough

May

1 Hull University
2 Bowes Lyon House, Stevenage
4 Marquee, London (with Stackridge)
5 Tooting Castle, London
6 Swansea University
7 Polytechnic, Lancaster
8 Van Dyke Club, Plymouth
14 Red Lion, Leytonstone
15 University College, London

21 Westfield College, London

June

5 The Phonograph, Finchley

All dates to June 22 with Stackridge and Renaissance unless otherwise noted.

7 Town Hall, Plymouth

9 Flamingo, Redruth

10 Colston Hall, Bristol

11 Guildhall, Southampton

12 Town Hall, Oxford

14 De Montfort, Leicester

15 St George's Hall, Bradford

16 Free Trade Hall, Manchester (with Stackridge and Mogul Thrash)

17 University, Warwick

18 Town Hall, Birmingham

19 City Hall, Newcastle

20 City Hall, Hull

22 City Hall, Sheffield (with Stackridge and Mogul Thrash)

23 Town Hall, Leeds

24 Albert Hall, Nottingham

25 Caird Hall, Dundee

26 Stirling University

27 Caley Cinema, Edinburgh

July

5 BBC Maida Vale, London (*Top Gear*)

17 Pioneer Club, St Albans

26 Reading Festival

August

All dates to August 16 with The Who

12 Public Hall, Cleveland, USA

13 Hara Arena, Dayton, USA

14 Cobo Arena, Detroit, USA

15 Sports Centre, Minneapolis, USA

16 Mississippi River Festival, Edwardsville, USA

September

3 Satsop River Festival, Seattle, USA (with Steve Miller, Flash Cadillac, Eric Burdon, War)

5 Austin, USA

? Alexandria, USA

? Performing Arts Centre, Saratoga Springs, USA (with Love and Humble Pie)

24 The Hove, Bournemouth

25 Slough College

26 Greyhound, Croydon

28 Osborne Hotel, Clacton

October

1 Polytechnic, Bristol

2 Roundhouse, Dagenham

3 Lyceum, London (with Renaissance, Burnt Oak, Armada)

5 Town Hall, Cheltenham (with Phillip Goodhand-Tait)

6 Patti Ballroom, Swansea

8 Mayfair, Newcastle

9 Sheffield University

10 Jazz Festival, Redcar

12 BBC TV Studios, London (*Old Grey Whistle Test*)

15 Chez, Leightonstone

16 Polytechnic, Isleworth (with Keith Christmas)

18 BBC Kensington House, London (*Sounds Of The 70s*)

24 Empire Theatre, Sunderland

28 Alsager College

29 Bath University *or* Technical College Ball at the Pavilion (with Stray and Edgar)

30 College of Technology, Watford (with Renaissance)

31 Starlight Ballroom, Boston (with Van der Graaf Generator)

November

12–13 Rainbow, London (with Gordon Haskell and Mountain)

18 Kinetic Circus, Birmingham

19 St Peters, York University

21 Caley Picture House, Edinburgh (with Glencoe—60p)
26 Stockport College (with In Crust)
27 Spa Hall, Bridlington
30 Southampton University
December
1 Lyceum, London (with Renaissance and Phillip Goodhand-Tait)
4 Technical College, Waltham Forest (with Camel)
31 Marquee, London

1972
January
14 Subscription Room, Stroud (with Renaissance)
15 University College, London (with Glencoe)
26 Civic Hall, Dunstable
27 De Montfort Hall, Leicester
28 Town Hall, Birmingham
29 Colston Hall, Bristol
31 Exeter University (with Glencoe)
February
5 Free Trade Hall, Manchester
6 Greyhound, Croydon (with Trapeze)
7 Oxford Polytechnic
8 Town Hall, Watford
9 Civic Hall, Guildford
10 City Hall, Sheffield
11 Town Hall, Leeds
12 City Hall, Newcastle
13 Caley Cinema, Edinburgh
14 City Hall, Glasgow
16 Guildhall, Southampton
17 Essex University
18 The Dome, Brighton
19 Guildhall, Portsmouth
20 Winter Gardens, Bournemouth
March
23 Schwabingerau, Munich, Germany

April
? Camden Festival
4 Kinetic, Kenilworth (with The Groundhogs)
13 Central Hall, Chatham (with Cat Iron)
14 Locarno, Sunderland
15 Sports Centre, Bracknell (with Glencoe)
16 King George's Hall, Blackburn (with Cat Iron)
17 Top Rank, Swansea
18 BBC Maida Vale, London (*Top Gear*)
19 City Hall, Salisbury (with Cat Iron)
20 Winter Gardens, Malvern
22 City Hall, St Albans (with Glencoe)
30 Camden Festival, Roundhouse, London (with Flash, Linda Lewis and Hookfoot)
May
5 Bickershaw Festival, Wigan
10 BBC Maida Vale, London (*Sounds Of The 70s*)
12 ? University
14 Locarno, Bristol
21 Germersheim Festival (with Humble Pie and Atomic Rooster)
25 Paris Theatre, London (*In Concert* taping)
27 Great Western Festival, Lincoln
31 BBC Aeolian Hall, London (*Sounds Of The 70s*)
June
10 Will Rogers Coliseum, Fort Worth, USA (with Jo Jo Gunne)
16 The Warehouse, New Orleans, USA (with ZZ Top and The Uncle Jam Band)
19 St Louis, USA
? Houston, USA (with Jo Jo Gunne)
? Memorial Stadium, Charlotte, USA (with Uriah Heep)

July

19 Hollywood Palladium, Los Angeles, USA (with Poco and The Kinks)

27 Civic Auditorium, San Francisco, USA (with ELP)

28 Long Beach Arena, USA (with ELP)

? Amphitheatre, Chicago, USA (with Alice Cooper)

30–31 Santa Monica, USA (with ELP)

August

1 Outdoor show, ? USA (with Black Sabbath; cancelled)

4 Idora Park, Youngstown, USA (with Quicksilver Messenger Service and Blue Oyster Cult)

7 Convention Centre, Louisville, USA (with Alice Cooper and Ursa Major)

? Armory, Minneapolis, USA (with Alice Cooper and Captain Beyond)

11 Mecca Arena, Milwaukee, USA (with ELP)

13 Arts Centre, Saratoga, USA (with ELP and Black Oak Arkansas)

16 The Warehouse, New Orleans, USA (with Nabasota)

17 Arie Crown Theatre, Chicago, USA (with ELP)

19–20 Convention Hall, Asbury Park, USA (with ELP)

21 WCNK Studios, Memphis, USA

23 Balboa Park Bowl, San Diego, USA (outdoors, with The New Riders Of The Purple Sage—$3)

24 Rainbow Ballroom, Fresno, USA (with Ballin' Jack)

September

10 Pavilion, Torquay

11 *West Country TV* taping

15 Locarno, Sunderland

16 Buxton Festival

29 Corn Exchange, Cambridge

30 The Oval, London (with ELP, Focus, Genesis)

October

10 Massey Hall, Toronto, Canada (with Gentle Giant)

11 Massey Hall, Toronto, Canada (with Phlorescent Leech and Eddie)

? Ontario, Canada (cancelled due to faulty sound system)

12 Niagara Falls, Canada (with Quicksilver Messenger Service)

13 Academy, New York, USA (with Boz Scaggs and Quicksilver Messenger Service—$5.50)

? Youngstown, USA (with Quicksilver Messenger Service)

24 Agora Ballroom, Cleveland, USA

27 Municipal Auditorium, San Antonio, USA

28 Ice Rink, Des Moines, USA (with Taj Mahal)

29 Aragon Ballroom, Chicago, USA (with Quicksilver Messenger Service and Elephant's Memory)

30 Electric Park, Waterloo, USA (with Blue Oyster Cult and REO Speedwagon—1000 capacity)

31 Cowtown Ballroom, Kansas City, USA (with Steve Miller Band)

November

1 Wharton Fieldhouse, Moline, USA

2 University of Kentucky, Lexington, USA

3 The Warehouse, New Orleans, USA (with Captain Beyond)

4 Music Hall, Dallas, USA (with Boz Scaggs)

5 Laurie Auditorium, San Antonio, USA (with Boz Scaggs)

8 Hollywood Palladium, Los Angeles, USA (with Hot Tuna and New Riders Of The Purple Sage)

? Western State College, Alamosa, USA

11 Arlene Schnitzer Hall, Portland, USA (with Boz Scaggs)

17 Rainbow, London

18 Rainbow, London (with Fumble)

All dates to December 2 with Curtiss-Maldoon

24 The Dome, Brighton

25 Winter Gardens, Bournemouth

26 Colston Hall, Bristol

27 Guildhall, Southampton

29 Town Hall, Birmingham

30 Stadium, Liverpool

December

1 City Hall, Sheffield

2 City Hall, Newcastle

4 Free Trade Hall, Manchester

6 Public Hall, Preston

7 Greens Playhouse, Glasgow

8 Empire, Edinburgh

9 Caird Hall, Dundee

12 Guildhall, Portsmouth

15 Town Hall, Leeds

17 Fairfield Halls, Croydon

19 Civic Hall, Dunstable

1973

January

10 Rainbow, London (with Stackridge and The Average White Band?)

March

17–18 Marquee, London

29 Massey Hall, Toronto, Canada (with Gentle Giant and Vinegar Joe)

30 Civic Centre, Ottawa, Canada (with Vinegar Joe)

31 Lutheran University Theatre, Waterloo, Canada (with Gentle Giant and Vinegar Joe)

April

1 State University, Pittsburgh, USA

3 Agora Theatre, Columbus, USA (with Vinegar Joe)

4 Palace Theatre, Dayton, USA (with Vinegar Joe)

5 Music Hall, Cincinnati, USA

6 Ford Auditorium, Detroit, USA (with Joe Walsh and Vinegar Joe)

7 Morris Civic Centre, South Bend, USA

8 Melody Skateland, Indianapolis, USA

10 Mary E Sawyer Auditorium, La Crosse, USA (with Joe Walsh and Vinegar Joe)

11 Minneapolis Civic Arena, Minneapolis, USA

12 Municipal Auditorium, Des Moines, USA

13 Cowtown Ballroom, Kansas City, USA (with Vinegar Joe and Finnegan & Wood)

14 Kinetic Playground, Chicago, USA

15 Kinetic Playground, Chicago, USA (with Joe Walsh)

16 Armory, Sheboygan, USA

17 PAC, Milwaukee, USA (with REO Speedwagon and Siegal Schwall)

18 Convention Centre, Louisville, USA (with Quicksilver Messenger Service)

19 Auditorium, Little Rock, USA

20 Municipal Auditorium, Shreveport, USA

21 Independence Hall, Baton Rouge, USA (with Vinegar Joe)

22 Warehouse, New Orleans, USA (with Vinegar Joe)

23 Louis Tech University, Ruston, USA

25 War Memorial, Nashville, USA (with Trapeze)

26 Municipal Auditorium, Atlanta, USA

27 Ellis Auditorium, Memphis, USA (with Vinegar Joe)

28 Municipal Auditorium, Mobile, USA

29 Municipal Auditorium, Birmingham, USA

May

10 Fairgrounds, Rochester, USA
11 Tower Theatre, Philadelphia, USA
12 Academy of Music, USA (with Elephant's Memory and Roy Buchanan)
13 Century Theatre, Buffalo, USA
15 Civic Centre, Hammond, USA (with The Strawbs and The Climax Blues Band)
16 Kiel Auditorium, St Louis, USA
18 Pirate's World, Miami, USA
19 Municipal Auditorium, Jacksonville, USA
20 Armory, Tampa, USA
21 Fort Collins, USA
22 Albuquerque, USA
23 Colorado Springs, USA
25 Seattle, USA
26 Paramount Theatre, Portland, USA
27 Hollywood Palladium, Los Angeles, USA (with Jo Jo Gunne)

June

3 San Diego Stadium, San Diego, USA (with ELO and Mason Proffit)
? Locarno, Bristol (with Fumble)
10 Theatre Royal, Norwich
11 Pink Pop Festival, Geleen (with Stealers Wheel, Jeff Beck—30,000 people)
13 Swansea
14 City Hall, Sheffield
16 Leeds University
17 Fairfield Halls, Croydon (with Upp?)
18 Free Trade Hall, Manchester (cancelled)
21 Guildhall, Portsmouth
22 Southampton University
23 Reading University
24 City Hall, Newcastle
25 City Hall, Hull
26 Stadium, Liverpool

July

14 Amsterdam, Netherlands

August

1 London Music Festival, Alexandra Palace, London (with SAHB)
8 Houston, Texas
9 Merriweather Post Pavilion, Columbia, USA (with Flash and Canned Heat)
10 Asbury Park, New Jersey, USA
11 Central Park, New York, USA (with Joe Walsh)
12 Jepperson Stadium, Houston, USA (with Savoy Brown, ZZ Top, The Doobie Brothers, Willie Nelson)
13 Auditorium Theatre, Chicago, USA (with Flash)
14 Pine Knob Theatre, Detroit, USA (with Flash)
15 Du Page County Fairgrounds, Wheaton, USA
16 Shubert Theatre, Philadelphia, USA (with Joe Walsh)
17 Hardrock Quarry, Akron, USA
? Field House, Wheeling, USA (with Vinegar Joe)
19 Municipal Auditorium, New Orleans, USA
? San Antonio, USA
21 Dallas, USA
22 Oklahoma City, USA
23 Wichita, USA

September

? Hardrock Quarry, Buffalo, USA
? Birmingham
9 Schessell Festival, Germany (with Lou Reed, Chuck Berry, Soft Machine, Chicago and Manfred Mann)

All dates to September 17 with Home

11 October Guildhall, Portsmouth
13 Kursaal, Southend
14 Colston Hall, Bristol

15 Stadium, Liverpool
16 City Hall, Sheffield
17 Apollo, Glasgow
23 Lincoln (with Fleetwood Mac)
24 Memorial Hall, Kansas City, USA
25 Oklahoma City, USA
26 Dallas, USA
27 San Antonio, USA
28 El Paso, USA
30 Coliseum, Denver, USA
31 Civic Auditorium, Colorado Springs, USA

November

2–3 Winterland, San Francisco, USA (with Robin Trower)
4 P&E Garden, Vancouver, Canada
5 Jubilee Theatre, Calgary, Canada
? Selland Arena, Fresno, USA
? San Diego, USA
7 Municipal Auditorium, San Bernadino, USA (with ZZ Top)
8 Hollywood Palladium, Los Angeles, USA (with ZZ Top and Robin Trower)
9 Spokane, USA
10 Salem Armory, USA (with ELO) OR Music Hall, Boston, USA
11 Arena, Seattle, USA (with ELO)
12 Ellensburg, USA (with ELO)
13 Orpheum Theatre, Boston, USA
14 Ohio Theatre, Columbus, USA
15 Music Hall, Cincinnati, USA
16 Tower Theatre, Philadelphia, USA
17 Academy of Music, New York City, USA
19 St Paul Civic, Minneapolis, USA
20 University of Winnipeg, Manitoba, Canada
21 Kiel Auditorium, St Louis, USA
22 Armory, Sheboygan, USA
23 High School, Wheeling, USA
24 Masonic Temple, Detroit, USA

25 Orchester Auditorium, Memphis, USA
26 Cleveland, USA
27 Municipal Auditorium, Shreveport, USA
29 Thibodaux, USA
30 Civic Centre or Municipal Auditorium, Mobile, USA (with ELO)

December

1 Jai Alai Fronton, Miami, USA
2 Curtis Nixon Hall, Tampa, USA
? Paris, France
22 Alexandra Palace, London (with Vinegar Joe, Al Stewart and Renaissance)

1974

January

18 Kleinhans Music Hall, Buffalo, USA (with the Climax Blues Band)
19 Capitol Theatre, Passaic, USA (with Climax Blues Band)
20 Aragon Ballroom, Chicago, USA
21 Coliseum, Des Moines, USA
22 Municipal Auditorium, Cedar Rapids, USA
23 Auditorium, Milwaukee, USA
24 Coliseum, Stevens Point, Wisconsin, USA
25 Rock Valley College, Rockford, USA
26 Civic Centre, Hammond, USA (with Heartsfield)
27 Dane County Coliseum, Madison, USA
30–31 Municipal Auditorium, Davenport, USA

February

1 Allen Theatre, Cleveland, USA (with Bruce Springsteen)
2 Palace Theatre, Dayton, USA (with Bill Wilson)
3 Agricultural Hall, Allentown, USA
4 University of Maryland, Baltimore, USA

14 BBC Paris Theatre, London (*In Concert*)

24 *King Biscuit Flower Hour* (with Seals & Crofts)

March

29 *Midnight Special* (US TV taping)

April

14 *King Biscuit Flower Hour*

May

12 *King Biscuit Flower Hour* (with Uriah Heep)

October

2 Guildhall, Portsmouth

3 Colston Hall, Bristol

All dates to October 19 with The Winkies

4 Town Hall, Leeds

5 City Hall, Sheffield

7 De Montfort Hall, Leicester

8 New Theatre, Oxford

10 Odeon, Newcastle

11 Apollo, Glasgow

12 Empire, Liverpool

13 Fairfield Halls, Croydon

14 The Dome, Brighton

15 Guildhall, Portsmouth

17 Rainbow, London

18 Free Trade Hall, Manchester

19 Odeon, Birmingham

22–23 Volkshaus, Zurich, Switzerland

24 Olympia, Paris, France

25 Marni, Brussels, Belgium

26 Turfschip, Breda, Netherlands

27 Evenementenhal, Groningen, Netherlands

29 Musichalle, Hamburg, Germany

30 Phillipshalle, Dusseldorf, Germany

31 Stadthalle, Offenbach, Germany

November

1 Friedrich Eberts Halle, Ludwigshafen, Germany

2 Killesberghalle, Stuttgart, Germany

3 Deutchemuseum (or Circus Krone), Munich, Germany (with American Gypsy, Steve Harley & Cockney Rebel)

5 Tivoli, Copenhagen, Demark

20 Tower Theatre, Upper Darby

? Academy, NYC, USA

? Academy, NYC, USA

26 Convention Centre, Indianapolis, USA (with Camel)

28 Keil Auditorium, St Louis, USA (with Camel)

29 Baseball Stadium, Miami, USA (with Camel)

December

2 Masonic Temple, Detroit, USA (with Camel)

3 State University, Bloomington, USA (with Reo Speedwagon)

4 Civic Centre, St Paul, USA

5 Dane County Coliseum, Madison, USA (with Camel and Foghat)

6 Auditorium, Milwaukee, USA (with Camel)

7 Forum, Chicago, USA (with Camel)

8 Western Illinois State University, Macomb, USA (with Camel)

9 Fort Wayne, USA

10 Brown City Arena, Green Bay, USA

11 Sports Arena, Toledo, USA (with Camel)

13 Public Arena, Cleveland, USA (with Camel)

15 Century Theatre, Buffalo, USA (with Camel)

16 State College, Grand Rapids, USA (with Camel)

18 Municipal Auditorium, Atlanta, USA

19 Mobile, USA

20 Jacksonville, USA

21 Lakeland, USA

22 West Palm Beach Auditorium, USA

23 Indiana, USA
? Palmer Auditorium, Davenport, USA
27 Vets Memorial Coliseum, Des Moines, USA (with Brownsville Station and Mountain)
28 Aragon Ballroom, Chicago, USA (with Eric Burdon, Camel, REO Speedwagon)
29 Roberts Municipal Stadium, Evansville, USA (with Eric Burdon, Camel, REO Speedwagon)
All dates to February 4 with Camel unless otherwise noted
30 Palmer College, Davenport, USA
31 Hara Arena, Dayton, USA

1975
January
2 Civic Hall, Baltimore, USA (with Ted Nugent and Camel)
3 International Building, Oklahoma City, USA
4 Music Hall, Houston, USA
5 Hoffehit Pavilion, Dallas, USA
6 Memorial Hall, Kansas City, USA
7 Ellis Auditorium, Memphis, USA
9 Hirsh Memorial Coliseum, Shreveport, USA
10 Independence Hall, Baton Rouge, USA
11 University, New Orleans, USA
15 Masonic Temple, Detroit, USA
17 Long Beach Arena, Los Angeles, USA (with KISS and Camel)
19 Golden Hall, San Diego, USA (with KISS?)
22 Regis College, Denver, USA
23 Terrace Ballroom, Salt Lake City, USA
25 Winterland, San Francisco, USA (with Johnny Winter and James Cotton)
26 Selland Arena, Fresno, USA (with KISS)

28 Kennedy Pavilion, Gonzaga University, Spokane, USA
29 County Fairgrounds, Eugene, USA
30 Paramount Theatre, Portland, USA
31 Center Arena, Seattle, USA
February
1 PNE Agrodome, Vancouver, Canada
2 Carver Gym WWSC, Bellingham, USA
3 Stampede Corral, Calgary, Canada (with Dr Hook)
4 Kinsmen Fieldhouse, Edmonton, Canada
7 Andrews Amphitheatre, Honolulu, Hawaii
15–17 Sun Plaza, Tokyo, Japan
19–20 Koseinenkin Hall, Osaka, Japan
21 Shi Kokaldo, Nagoya, Japan
27 Festival Hall, Brisbane, Australia
March
1 Festival Hall, Melbourne, Australia
2 Hordern Pavilion, Sydney, Australia
4 Festival Hall, Melbourne, Australia
6 Centennial Hall, Adelaide, Australia
13 Town Hall, Wellington, New Zealand
14 Christchurch, New Zealand
15 Western Springs Stadium, Auckland, New Zealand
April
3 Mets Sports Centre, Bloomington, USA (with Robin Trower)
12 Midnight Sun, Upper Darby, USA
22 Kolf Sports Centre, Oshkosh, USA (with Commander Cody)
May
All dates to June 6 with Aerosmith unless otherwise noted.
13 Lakeview Arena, Marquette, USA
27–28 Cobo Hall, Detroit, USA
30 Outdoor Arts Arena, Edwardsville, USA (with Headeast)
31 Convention Centre, Kentucky, USA

June
1   Roberts Stadium, Evansville, USA (with Aerosmith, Bob Seger and Silver Bullet Band)
2   Morris Civic Auditorium, South Bend, USA
3   Lakeview Arena, Marquette, USA
5   Brown County Arena, Green Bay, USA
6   Duluth Arena, USA

August
All August dates part of the Star Truckin' 75 tour with Caravan, Mahavishnu Orchestra, Soft Machine, Climax Blues Band, etc.
5   Falkener Theatre, Copenhagen, Denmark
7   Chateau Noir, Oslo, Norway
9   Runsala Folk Park, Turku, Finland
11 Tivoli, Stockholm, Sweden
14 Groendoorhallen, Lieden, Netherlands
15 Festival, Bilzen, Belgium
16 Stadion Gelende, Ludwigsberg, Germany
17 Amphitheatre, Orange, France
18 Plaza de Toros, Marbella, Spain
24 Reading Festival
27 Hallen Stadion, Zurich, Switzerland
28 Munich, Germany
29 Sporthalle, Vienna, Austria

September
6   Jaap Edenhal, Amsterdam (with Climax Blues Band and Soft Machine)

1976
March
4   Lubbock Arena, USA (with Black Oak Arkansas)
5   Municipal Auditorium, San Antonio, USA (with Black Oak Arkansas)
6   Kirsch Memorial Coliseum, Shreveport, USA
7   Summit, Houston, USA

8   Ector County Coliseum, Odessa, USA (with Black Oak Arkansas)
10 Oklahoma City, USA
13–14 Warehouse, New Orleans, USA (with Styx and Van Wilkes)
19 Arena, Milwaukee, USA
22 Philadelphia, USA
23 Spectrum, Philadelphia, USA (with ELO and Journey)
24 Madison Square Garden, New York, USA (with Robin Trower)
25 West Virginia University Coliseum, Morgantown, USA
26 Theatre for Performing Arts, Elizabeth, USA
28 Convention Centre, Indianapolis, USA
29 Largo Coliseum, Washington DC, USA (with ELO and Journey)

April
2   Winterland, San Francisco, USA (with Bachman Turner Overdrive and Styx)
3   Sports Arena, San Diego, USA (with Bachman Turner Overdrive and Status Quo)
5   Terrace Ballroom, Salt Lake City, USA (with Status Quo)
6   State Fairgrounds, Boise, USA
8   Selland Arena, Fresno, USA
9   Long Beach Arena, Los Angeles, USA (with Bachman Turner Overdrive)
10 Swing Auditorium, San Bernadino, USA (with Bachman Turner Overdrive)
12 Redding, USA
14 Medford, USA
16 Paramount Theatre, Portland, USA (with Status Quo)
17 Convention Centre, Spokane, USA (with Status Quo)
18 Arena, Seattle, USA
23 Hayes, USA (with Headeast and Henry Gross)

24 Uptown Theatre, Kansas City, USA
(with Henry Gross)
25 Moody Coliseum, Dallas, USA (with
Black Oak Arkansas)
27 University of Oklahoma, Tuscaloosa,
USA (with Elvin Bishop)
28 Pershing Auditorium, Lincoln, USA
30 City Auditorium, Hastings, USA (with
Status Quo)
May
1 Kiel Auditorium, St Louis, USA (with
Status Quo)
5 Bradley University, Peoria, USA (with
Foghat)
6 Davenport, USA
7 Dane County Memorial Coliseum,
Madison, USA
8 Mount Prospect, USA
June
6 Festival Frankfurt, Germany (with Bob
Marley)
7 Dusseldorf, Germany
8 Ernst Merke Halle, Hamburg,
Germany (with War and Van der Graaf
Generator)
October
3 Sun Plaza, Tokyo, Japan
5–6 Koseinenkin Hall, Osaka, Japan
7 Hiroshima, Japan
8 Kurashiki, Japan
10 Koseinenkin Hall, Osaka, Japan
11 Kokura, Japan
13 Shi Kokaido, Nagoya, Japan
14 Sun Plaza, Tokyo, Japan
All dates to November 20 with Supercharge
22 Victoria Hall, Hanley
23 City Hall, Sheffield
26 Festival Hall, Torbay
27 Exeter University
28 Capitol Theatre, Cardiff
29 Colston Hall, Bristol

30 Nottingham University
31 Fairfield Halls, Croydon
November
1 Pavilion, Hemel Hempstead
2 Guildhall, Portsmouth
4 Gaumont, Ipswich
5–6 Hammersmith Odeon, London
7 Odeon, Birmingham
8 De Montfort Hall, Leicester
12 The Dome, Brighton
13 Free Trade Hall, Manchester
14 City Hall, Newcastle
15 Empire, Liverpool
16 City Hall, Newcastle
18 Usher Hall, Edinburgh
19 Apollo, Glasgow (BBC *John Peel Show*
concert recording)
20 The Refectory, Leeds University
21 Lancaster University
*All dates to December 15 with Sutherland
Brothers and Quiver, Lake.*
25 Niedersachsenhalle, Hannover,
Germany
26 Eissporthalle, Berlin, Germany
27 Holstenhalle, Neumunster, Germany
28 Halle Munsterland, Munster, Germany
30 Stadthalle, Bremen, Germany

December
1 Sporthalle, Koln, Germany
2 Saarlandhalle, Saarbrucken, Germany
3 Walter Kobel Halle, Russelsheim,
Germany
4 Friedrich Eberts Halle, Ludwigshafen,
Germany
5 Messe Centrum Halle, Nuremberg,
Germany
6 Naue Sporthalle, Linz, Austria
9 Eishalle, Innsbruck, Austria
10 Pavilion des Sports, Geneva,
Switzerland (also with Gordon Giltrap)

11 Sporthalle St Jacob, Basel, Switzerland
12 Boblingen Sporthalle, Stuttgart, Germany
14 Stadthalle, Freiburg, Germany
15 Olympiahalle, Munich, Germany
17 Olympia, Paris, France
18 Ljsselhal, Zwolle, Netherlands

1977
September
10–15 Shepperton Studios (rehearsals)
All dates to October 7 with Steve Hillage and Country Joe
18 Osteseehalle, Kiel, Germany
20 Ernst Merke Halle, Hamburg, Germany
21 Bremen, Germany
22 Phillipshalle, Dusseldorf, Germany
23 Walter Kobel Halle, Russelsheim, Germany
24 Messehalle, Nuremberg, Germany
26 Stadhalle, Wolfsburg, Germany
27 Munsterlandhalle, Munster, Germany
29 Rhein Nicker Halle, Heidelberg, Germany
30 Edward Bauer Halle, Esslingen, Germany

October
1 Olympiahalle, Munich, Germany
2 Sporthalle, Winterthur, Germany
4 Toulouse, France
6 Lyons, France
7 Hippodrome, Paris, France
8 Tijenraan, Raalte, Netherlands
9 Beynishal, Haarlem, Netherlands
All dates to October 27 with The Motors
16 City Hall, Newcastle
17 Apollo, Glasgow (BBC *In Concert*)
18 City Hall, Sheffield
20 Odeon, Birmingham

21 Empire, Liverpool
22 King's Hall, Belle Vue, Manchester
24 De Montfort Hall, Leicester
25 Theatre, Coventry
26 Capitol Theatre, Cardiff
27 Gaumont, Southampton
29 Marquee, London
31 Wembley Empire Pool, London
November
5 Baden Baden (TV taping, Germany)
11 Aragon Ballroom, Chicago, USA (with Nils Lofgren and Brand X)
12 Rock Island, USA
14 *Mike Douglas Show* (TV taping with Georgia Brown, Marvin Hamlisch, Gary Crosby)
15 Masonic Temple, Detroit, USA
18 Fox Theatre, St Louis, USA (with Brand X and Dwight Twilly)
19 Kansas City, USA
All dates to December 11 with Robin Trower
21 Santa Barbara, USA
22 Civic Auditorium, Bakersfield, USA
23 Selland Arena, Fresno, USA
25 Long Beach Arena, Los Angeles, USA
26 Swing Auditorium, San Bernadino, USA (with Eddie Money)
27 Sports Arena, San Diego, USA
29 Arena, Seattle, USA (with Eddie Money)
30 Salem Armory, USA
December
2–3 Winterland, San Francisco, USA (with Eddie Money)
4 Aladdin Theatre, Las Vegas, USA (with Eddie & The Hot Rods)
7 Coliseum, Corpus Christi, USA
8 Tarrant County Coliseum, Fort Worth, USA (with Starcastle)
9 Joe Freemans Civic, San Antonio, USA
10 Sam Houston Coliseum, Houston, USA (with Starcastle)

11 Assembly Centre, Tulsa, USA
16 Philadelphia, USA (with Kansas)
17 Morristown, USA

1978
September
9 Open Air Festival, Stadion 1 F.C.P.,
    Pforzheim, Germany (with Status Quo,
    Uriah Heep, Climax Blues Band, David
    Coverdale)
October
1–5 Roxy Theatre, Willesden (rehearsals)
6 Gaumont, Ipswich
7 Odeon, Birmingham
8 The Great Hall, Lancaster University
9 Apollo, Glasgow
10 Odeon, Edinburgh
11 City Hall, Newcastle
12 Apollo Theatre, Manchester
13 Victoria Hall, Hanley
15 Gaumont, Southampton
16 The Dome, Brighton
17 Guildhall, Portsmouth
20 The Great Hall, Cardiff University
21 City Hall, Sheffield
22 Royal Spa Hall, Bridlington
24 Hammersmith Odeon, London
25 Hammersmith Odeon, London (BBC
    In Concert)
27 Colston Hall, Bristol
28 Leeds University
30 Winter Gardens, Bournemouth
31 De Montfort Hall, Leicester
November
2 Theatre, Coventry
3 Empire, Liverpool
10 Sun Plaza Hall, Tokyo, Japan
13 Festival Hall, Osaka, Japan
15 Japanese TV, Tokyo, Japan
15 Koseinenkin Hall, Tokyo, Japan

1979
November
22 Wembley Empire Pool, London (with
    David Essex, Cat Stevens, Sky, Gary
    Numan; BBC *Year Of The Child*)

1980
January
All dates to February 22 with The Dukes
18 Victoria Hall, Hanley
19–20 City Hall, Sheffield
21 City Hall, Newcastle
23 Odeon, Edinburgh
24 Caird Hall, Dundee
25 Capitol Theatre, Aberdeen
26 Apollo, Glasgow
27 Empire, Liverpool
29 De Montfort Hall, Leicester
30 Assembly Rooms, Derby
31 St George's Hall, Bradford
February
1 Hammersmith Odeon, London
2 Hammersmith Odeon, London (BBC
    In Concert)
3 Fairfield Halls, Croydon
4 Gaumont, Ipswich
5 Gaumont, Southampton
7 The Dome, Brighton
8 Apollo, Manchester
9 Odeon, Birmingham
10 New Theatre, Oxford
11 Pavilion, Hemel Hempstead
12 Civic Hall, Guildford
13 Winter Gardens, Bournemouth
15 Guildhall, Portsmouth
16 Colston Hall, Bristol
17 Festival Theatre, Paignton
19 Cardiff University
21 Stadium, Dublin
22 Whitla Hall, Belfast
29 Hall Roma, Antwerp, Belgium

March
All dates to April 3 with The Headboys
1 Palais des Sports, Cambrai, France
2 Maison des Sports, Reims, France
3 Hippodrome, Paris, France
4 La Rotonede, Le Mans, France
5 Maison des Sports, Clermont Ferrand, France
6 Palais des Sports De Gerland, Lyons, France
8 Parc des Expositions, Nancy, France
10 Deutches Museum, Munich, Germany
11 Stadthalle, Offenbach, Germany
12 Phillipshalle, Dusseldorf, Germany
14 Stadthalle, Kassel, Germany
15 Hemmerleinhalle, Nuremberg, Germany
16 Neue Welt, Berlin, Germany
17 Musichalle, Hamburg, Germany
18 Niedersachsenhalle, Hannover, Germany
19 Ausstellungshalle, Stuttgart, Germany
21 Freidrich Eberts Halle, Ludwigshafen, Germany
22 Eurogress, Aachen, Germany
23 Westfallenhalle, Dortmund, Germany
25 Volkshaus, Zurich, Switzerland
26 Sportshalle, Linz, Austria
27 Sofienshalle, Vienna, Austria
28 Udine, Italy
29 Turin, Italy
30 Milan, Italy
31 Udine, Italy
April
1 Ljubljana, Slovenia
2 Belgrade, Serbia
3 Zagreb, Croatia
May
5 Sheffield University
24 Sports Centre, Bracknell
25 Top Rank, Cardiff

27 Town Hall, Middlesbrough
28 Mecca Centre, Sunderland
29 King George's Hall, Blackburn
30 Sheffield University
31 Market Hall, Carlisle (with The Trend)
June
1 City Hall, Hull
2 Odeon, Ilford
3 Odeon, Chelmsford
4 Civic Hall, Wolverhampton
6 Pavilion, Bath
7 Odeon, Taunton
22 Loch Lomond Festival
August
20 Bullring, Santander, Spain
23 Lorelei Festival, Germany
24 Golden Summer Festival
September
20 Colmar Festival (with UFO)

1981
May
16 Manchester University
17 BBC Studios, London (*Simon Bates Show*)
18 Odeon, Taunton
19 Colston Hall, Bristol
21 Lancaster University
22 City Hall, Hull
23 Odeon, Birmingham
24 De Montfort Hall, Leicester
26 Empire, Liverpool
27 City Hall, Newcastle
28 Odeon, Edinburgh
29 Apollo, Glasgow
30 City Hall, Sheffield
June
1 Guildhall, Portsmouth
2 Hammersmith Odeon, London (BBC *In Concert*)
3 Rainbow, London

4   Civic Hall, Guildford
5   The Dome, Brighton
6   New Theatre, Oxford
9   La Rotonde, Le Mans, France
10 Palais des Congres, Nantes, France
    (with Live Wire)
11 Sal Omnisports de Rennes, Rennes,
    France
12 Palais des Sports, Dijon, France
13 Parc des Expo, Metz, France
15 Palais des Sports, Bordeaux, France
16 Palais des Sports, Paris, France
17 Palais d'Hiver, Lyons, France
18 Palais des Sports, Montpellier, France
19 Alpexpo, Grenoble, France
20 Halle Tivoli, Strasbourg, France
21 Hamar Festival, Norway (with Mike
    Oldfield, Roy Harper)
27 Macroom Festival, Ireland (with Elvis
    Costello, The Undertones)

July

14 Louis Rock City, Washington, USA
15 My Father's Place, New York, USA
16 The Ritz, New York, USA (with
    R.E.M.)
17 Tower Theatre, Audabon, USA
20 Agora, Atlanta, USA
21 Point After, Orlando, USA
22 Agora, Miami, USA
23 Brassy's, Cocoa, USA
25 Warehouse, New Orleans, USA
26 Cardis, Houston, USA
27 Randy's Rodeo, San Antonio, USA
28 Cardis, Dallas, USA
29 The Rox, Lubbock, USA
30 Cains Ballroom, Tulsa, USA
31 Uptown Theatre, Kansas City, USA

August

1   Casa Loma, St Louis, USA
3   Rockstage Festival, Chicago, USA (with
    Aretha Franklin, Albert King)

4   Studio 1, Champaign, USA
6   Point East, Lynwood, USA
7   Edgewater, Twin Lakes, USA
8   Harpo's, Detroit, USA
11 Paradise, Boston, USA
12 Concord, New Hampshire, USA
13 Sanctuary, Worcester, USA
14 Rusty Nail, Sunderland, USA
15 Poughkeepsie, USA
16 Bayou, Washington DC, USA
17 Margate Beach
30 Reading Festival

November

10 Casino Den Bosch, Netherlands
11 'T Heem, Hattem, Netherlands
19 Polytechnic, Plymouth (UK tour with
    Hanoi Rocks)
20 Brunel University
21 University of East Anglia, Norwich
24 Caird Hall, Dundee
25 Strathclyde University

December

1   Polytechnic, Hatfield
7   Bombay, India
8   Bombay, India
12 Madras University, India

1982

May

15 Great Hall, Huddersfield Polytechnic
All dates to May 17 with Mamas Boys
17 Queensway Hall, Dunstable
18 Rock City, Nottingham
19 Assembly Rooms, Derby
20 Pier Theatre, Colwyn Bay
21 Floral Hall, Southport
22 Pavilion, West Runton
23 Apollo, Oxford
24 Queen's Theatre, Barnstaple
26 Town Hall, Middleborough
27 Leisure Centre, Ashington

July

9   Lisdoonvarna Festival, Ireland
20 Iron Horse, Thibodaux, USA
21 Ricky's, Kenner, USA
22 Southpaws, Boiffer City, USA

September

21 Cliffs Pavilion, Southend
22 Civic Hall, Guildford
24 City Hall, Hull
25 Guildhall, Preston
26 Royal Court Theatre, Liverpool
27 Empire, Sunderland
28 Thameside Theatre, Ashton
29 Lyceum, Sheffield

October

1   City Hall, St Albans
2   Polytechnic, Plymouth
3   Winter Gardens, Margate
4   Guildhall, Southampton
6   Assembly Hall, Worthing
8   Dominion Theatre, London
9   Rock Theatre, Chippenham
10 Fairfield Halls, Croydon
11 Anglia TV, Norwich
11 Theatre Royal, Norwich
18 Hala Tivoli, Ljubljana, Slovenia
19 Dom Sportova, Zagreb, Croatia
20 Hala Pionir, Belgrade, Serbia
21 Skenderija, Sarajevo, Yugoslavia
22 Sportski Centar Gripe, Split, Croatia
24 Sportska Duorana, Pula, Croatia
26 Tivoli Hall, Strasbourg, France
27 Salle Lancey, Grenoble, France
28 Palais des Sports, Clermont Ferrand, France
29 Pavilion Baltard, Nogent sur Marne, France
30 Under Canvas, Lille, France
31 Under Canvas, Rouen, France

November

2   Salle du Baron, Orleans, France

3   Arenes-Rocade Est, Poltiers, France
4   Casino Municipal, Pau, France
5   Grand Parc, Bordeaux, France
7   Toursky, Marseilles, France
8   Salle des Fetes, Epinal, France
9   Palais d'Hiver, Lyons, France
10 TV Espanola Channel2, Barcelona, Spain
11 Palaus Blau Grana, Barcelona, Spain
12 Pavilion de Deportes, Madrid, Spain
13 Club Gares, Pamplona, Spain
14 Pabellon de los Deportes, San Sebastian, Spain
16 Salle des Fetes, Rouen, France
18 Stadthalle, Ludwigsburg, Germany
19 Donauhalle, Ulm, Germany
20 Jahnhalle, Pforzheim, Germany
22 Friedrich List Halle, Reutlingen, Germany
23 Volkhaus, Zurich, Switzerland
24 Kulturhaus, Mannheim, Germany
25 Zeche, Bochum, Germany
26 Nordseehalle, Emden, Germany
27 Markthalle, Hamburg, Germany
28 Aladin, Bremen, Germany
30 Rotation, Hannover, Germany

December

1   Metropol, Berlin, Germany
2   Redoutensaal, Erlangen, Germany
17 Wembley Arena, London (with Ian Gillan)
20 ?, Germany

1983

February

15 Bombay, India
16 Poona, India
18 Madras, India
19 Bangalore, India
22–23 Marquee, London
26 Queen's University, Belfast

March

4   Palasport, Gorizia, Italy
5   Teatro Tenda, Milan, Italy
6   Teatro Tenda, Brescia, Italy
7   Bologna, Italy
9   Club Manila, Florence, Italy
10 Teatro Tenda, Rome, Italy
11 Teatro Tenda, Naples, Italy
12 Teatro Comunale, Catanzaro, Italy
14 Palasport, Venezia, Italy
17 Alabama Halle, Munich, Germany
18 Stadthalle, Dornbirn, Austria
19 Waldseehalle, Forst, Germany
20 Elzberghalle, Dallau, Germany

April

13 Ons Huis, Venlo, Netherlands
14 Berg Stichting, Noordwijk,
    Netherlands
15 Alphen A/D, Riijn, Netherlands
17 Spuug, Vaals, Netherlands

June

5   Bayou, Washington, USA
8   Brandywine Club, Chadd's Ford, USA
9   Paradise, Boston, USA

July

1   Eucalypta, Winterswijk, Netherlands
2   Goero Europaweg, Schonebeek,
    Netherlands

November

30 Tampereen Yo-Talo, Tampere, Finland

December

1   Tawastia Klubi, Helsinki, Finland
2   Kisasuija, Saarijarvi, Finland
4   Kuopion Kaupunginhotelli Club,
    Kuopio, Finland
5   Tuiskula, Nivala, Finland
7   Glaedjehuset, Stockholm, Sweden
8   Club Trombone, Soedertailje, Sweden
9   Mudd Club, Gothenburg, Sweden

1984

June

19 Flensburg, Germany (with Joe Cocker)
24 Barcelona, Spain
26 Lycabetus Open Theatre, Athens, Greece

July

7   Parkzicht, Rotterdam, Netherlands
8   Paradiso, Amsterdam, Netherlands

August

25 Wakefield Music Festival

September

8   New Bingley Hall Showground Festival
    (with Man and Magnum)
21 Exo 7, Rouen, France
22 Grand Parc, Bordeaux, France
24 Gymnase des Rongieres, Toulon-
    Hyeres, France
25 Salle Victoire, Montpellier, France
26 Marseille, France
27 Theatre de Verdure, Nice, France
28 Apt, France
29 Palais d'Hiver, Lyons, France

October

1   Casino de Paris, Paris, France
3   Halle aux Grains, Toulouse, France
4   Altexpo, Grenoble, France
5   Chapiteau, Grenoble *or* Macon, France
6   Parx Expo, Nancy, France
28 Hala Torwar, Warsaw, Poland
30 Sporthall, Lodz, Poland
31 Sporthall Makaszowy, Zabrze, Poland

November

30 Basel, Switzerland

December

1   Igersheim Mehrzweckhalle, Bad
    Mergentheim, Germany
2   Hydepark, Osnabruck, Germany
    (cancelled)
3   WWF Convoy TV Show, Ahlen,
    Germany

4   Zeche, Bochum, Germany
5   Detmold, Germany
6   Wartesaal, Koln, Germany
7   Revolution, Simmern, Germany
8   Apolon, Neuenstadt, Germany
9   Sporthalle Flein,, Heilbronn, Germany
10 Donauhalle, Ulm, Germany
11 Stadthalle, Landau, Germany
12 Gewerkshafthaus, Rosenheim, Germany
13 Theaterfabrik, Munchen, Germany
14 Ruhresaal, Nuremberg, Germany
15 Tivoli Park, Pirmasens, Germany
16 Disco Schnaid, Bamberg, Germany
17 Maxim, Stuttgart, Germany
19 Paradiso, Amsterdam, Netherlands
20 Beethovenhalle, Bonn, Germany
21 Markthalle, Hamburg, Germany

1985
February
6–7 Club 7, Oslo, Norway
8   De Roede Sjoehus, Stavanger, Norway
9   Studentsenteret, Bergen, Norway
May
24 BBC Maida Vale, London (*Friday Rock Show*)
June
All dates to June 21 with IQ
1   Surrey University
2   Goldiggers, Chippenham
3   Cliffs Pavilion, Southend (cancelled)
4   Pink Toothbrush, Rayleigh
5   Odeon, Birmingham
6   Carnegie Theatre, Workington
7   Pavilion, Ayr
8   Playhouse, Edinburgh
9   Albert Hall, Stirling
10 Caird Hall, Dundee
11 Rock City, Nottingham
12 Manchester University
13 Assembly Hall, Worthing

14 Leas Cliff Hall, Folkestone
15 City Hall, St Albans
16 New Ocean Club, Cardiff
19 Theatre Royal, Lincoln
20 Apollo, Oxford
21 Hammersmith Odeon, London
28 TV Club, Dublin, Ireland
29 Larne Festival, Northern Ireland
July
25 Rock Festival, Vlissingen, Netherlands
26 Parkzicht, Rotterdam, Netherlands
27 Elkerlijk, Luttenberg, Netherlands
28 Paradiso, Amsterdam, Netherlands
September
14 Lorelei Festival (with Metallica)
18 Trondheim, Norway
20 Bergen, Norway
21 Odda, Norway
?   London Polytechnic
October
17 The Savoy, Limerick, Ireland
18 Stadium, Dublin, Ireland
19 Queen's University, Belfast
November
2   Blues and Booze Ringo Starr Charity Event, Waltham St Lawrence (with Andy Powell, Mick Ralphs, Jimmy Page, Simon Kirke, Pat Mraz)
December
2   Mutualite, Paris, France
4   Queen's Theatre, Barnstaple
5   Arts Centre, Poole
6   Bar Gates Centre, Burton
7   Spectrum, Willington
9   Hammersmith Odeon, London (with Alaska)
All dates to December 21 with Richie Havens.
14 Bombay, India
15 Goa, India
19 Madras, India
21 Calcutta, India

1986

January

7 Akzente, Tuttlingen, Germany
8 Maxim, Stuttgart, Germany
9 Drachtxhmidli Jugenhaus, Zurich, Switzerland
10 Kongress—Saal, Freiburg, Germany
11 Saalbau, Bamburg, Germany
12 Centre Culturelle, St Avold, Germany
14 Zeche, Bochum, Germany
15 Grosse Freiheit 36, Hamburg, Germany
16 Alte Piesel, Kunzell, Germany
17 Motown, Aarhus, Denmark
18 Musikcafer, Copenhagen, Denmark
20 Konserthuset, Gothenburg, Sweden
21 Broadway, Linkoping, Sweden
22 Folkets, Katrineholm, Sweden
23 Magasinet, Orebro, Sweden
24 Rackis, Uppsala, Sweden
25 Hard Rock, Stockholm, Sweden

March

14 Philadelphia, USA (cancelled)
16 Baltimore, USA (cancelled)
17 Trocadero, Philadelphia, USA (with The Kneetremblers)
19 Copa, Springfield, USA
20 The Ritz, New York, USA
21 Boat House, Norfolk, USA
22 Harpo's, Detroit, USA
25 Easy Streets, Des Moines, USA
26 Stages, East St Louis, USA
27 Uptown Theatre, Kansas City, USA
28 Metro, Chicago, USA
29 Zivko's, Hartford, USA

April

1 Rockers, Phoenix, USA
2 Grand Central Station, Albuquerque, USA
3 Roxy, Tucson, USA
4–5 Joshua's Parlor, Westminster, USA
7 Bacchanol, San Diego, USA

8 Oasis, Sacramento, USA
9–10 Keystone, San Francisco, USA
12 Starry Night, Portland, USA (with Foghat—$13.00)
13 Parkers, Seattle, USA
14 Commodore Ballroom, Vancouver, Canada
15–16 Parkers, Seattle, USA
17–18 Gatsby's, Spokane, USA
22 Club, Turlock, USA
23 The Hill, Oakland, USA
26 Rainbow Theatre, Denver, USA
28 Krackers, Las Vegas, USA

May

4 New West Club, San Antonio, USA
5 Cardis Houston, USA
7 Jimmy's, New Orleans, USA (with The Kneetremblers, formerly Foghat)
9 Boardwalk, Huntsville, USA
10 Kidnappers, Charlotte, USA
12 Lone Star Café, New York, USA

August

2 Folkestone Festival (with Bernie Torme and Black Roots)
8 Stadtbredimus, Luxembourg (with Jimmy Martin)

October

29 Lace, Horten, Denmark
30 Lace, Larvik, Norway
31 Laegreid Hotel, Sogndal, Norway

November

1 Rockefeller, Oslo, Norway
2 Manhattan, Sandnes, Norway
3–4 Rogers, Tromso, Norway
5 Sjohuset, Stord, Norway
6 Betzy, Haugesund, Norway
7 Hulen, Bergen, Norway
8–9 Ritz, Trondheim, Norway
29 Central Park, Burton

December

12–13 Messehalle, Leipzig, Germany

14 Theatre, Weimar, Germany
17 Marquee, London
18 Marquee, London

1987
January
2 Azotod, De Meern, Netherlands
3 Paradiso, Amsterdam, Netherlands
4 Noorderligt, Tilberg, Netherlands
6 Akzente, Tuttlingen, Germany
7 Rockfabrick, Bruchsal, Germany
8 Maxim, Stuttgart, Germany
9 Intertref, Heilbronn, Germany
10 Jurahalle, Neumarkt, Germany
11 Hotel de Ville, Saargemund, Germany
12 Theaterfabrick, Unterfohring, Germany
13 Steinbruchtheater, Darmstadt, Germany
14 Druckhaus, Hanau, Germany
15 Zeche, Bochum, Germany
16 Stollwerk, Koln, Germany
17 Freitzeitzentrum, Bremerhaven, Germany
18 Knopfs Music Halle, Hamburg, Germany
19 Sudhaus, Berlin, Germany
21 Jugend-Und Kulterzentrum, Bern, Switzerland
22 Rohrbach Bei Huttwill, Baeren, Switzerland
23 Gigelbergahalle, Biberach, Germany
24 Maintauberhalle, Wertheim, Germany
25 Rathaussaal, Schaan, Germany
26 Utopia, Innsbruck, Austria
27 Posthof, Linz, Austria
28 Metropol, Vienna, Austria
February
3 Belgrade, Serbia (with Alvin Lee)
15 Town and Country Club, London (Andy Powell with Albert Lee, Dave Gilmour, Andy Fairweather-Low)

March–May
? US tour
May
24–28 Sun City, South Africa (with Nazareth)
August
? Germany / Spain tour
December
7–15 Jubilejnuj, Leningrad, Soviet Union
18–20 Sporthall, Vilnius, Soviet Union

1988
February
All dates to March 9 with Pete Haycock
28 Leas Cliff Hall, Folkestone
28 Hummingbird, Birmingham (with Major Hero)
March
1 Gatehouse Theatre, Stafford
2 International 2, Manchester
3 Tivoli Ballroom, Buckley
4 Hammersmith Odeon, London (BBC *In Concert*)
5 Forum, Hatfield
6 Arts Centre, Poole
7 Assembly Hall, Worthing
8 Assembly Hall, Tunbridge Wells
9 Riviera Centre, Torquay
20 Roxy, Sheffield
25 Mayfair, Newcastle
28 Astoria, Nottingham
29 Roxy, Sheffield
April
6 Metropole, Aachen, Germany
7 Europasaal, Bayreuth, Germany
8 E Werk, Erlangen, Germany
9 Schutzenhalle, Buren Harth, Germany
10 Modernes, Bremen, Germany
11 Zeche, Bochum, Germany
12 Akzente, Tuttlingen, Germany
13 Capital, Hannover, Germany

14 Grosse Freiheit, Hamburg, Germany
15 Alte Piesel, Kunzell, Germany
16 Waldcafe, Dudweiler, Germany
17 Concertcentrum, Gieselwind, Germany
18 Garage, Rastatt, Germany
19 Theatrefabrik, Munich, Germany
22 Biberach, Germany
23 Herenthout, Germany
24 Hunky Dory Musichalle, Detmold, Germany
26 Darmstadt, Germany
28 Schlaghaus, Wels, Austria
30 Stadtest, Vienna, Austria

May

2 Burgerweeshuis, Deventer, Netherlands
3 Paradiso, Amsterdam, Netherlands
4 Festhalle, Frankfurt, Germany (with Rush)
5 Schleyerhalle, Stuttgart, Germany (with Rush)
6 Prasilia, Kiel, Germany

1989

July

14 Sao Paulo, Brazil (with Leslie West and Jan Akkerman)
16 Rio De Janeiro, Brazil (with Leslie West and Jan Akkerman)
21 Bachanaal, San Diego, USA
22 Theatre of the Living Arts, Pasadena, USA (with Spirit)
24 The Stone, San Francisco, USA
26 Coach House, San Juan, USA
27 Wadsworth Theatre, Redondo Beach, USA (with Spirit, Rob Krieger, Steve Hunter)
29 Coach House, San Capistrano, USA

August

2 Theatre of Living Arts, Philadelphia, USA ($16.50)
4 New Orleans, USA

September

8 Winter Gardens, Eastbourne
9 City Hall, St Albans
10 Odeon, Lewisham
11 Borderline, London
12 Assembly Hall, Tunbridge Wells
13 Beck Theatre, Hayes
14 Princess Hall, Aldershot
15 Assembly Hall, Worthing
16 Leas Cliff Hall, Folkestone
17 Stables, Milton Keynes
18 Riviera Centre, Torquay
20 Empire, Sunderland
21 Municipal Hall, Colne
22 Royal Spa Centre, Leamington Spa

All dates to September 28 with Spirit

23 Hammersmith Odeon, London
24 Festival Hall, Corby
25 Corn Exchange, Cambridge
26 Colston Hall, Bristol
27 Royal Court Theatre, Liverpool
28 Apollo, Manchester

October

1 Willem II, Den Bosch, Netherlands
2 Musichalle, Frankfurt, Germany
3 Akzente, Tuttlingen, Germany
4 Rockfabrik, Ludwigsberg, Germany
12 Capitol, Hannover, Germany
25 Music & Action, Bonlanden, Germany
26 Factory, Regensburg, Germany
28 Haus der Jugend, Ingolstadt, Germany
29 Meddox, Remscheid, Germany
30 Arche, Waldkirch, Germany
31 Kultursaal, Saarbrucken, Germany

November

1 Milieu, Hausach, Germany
3 Baumgarten, Bistensee, Germany
4 Miami Nice, Berlin, Germany
5 Top Act, Zapendorf, Germany
6 Hyde Park, Osnabruck, Germany
7 Garage, Luneberg, Germany

8   Felsenkeller, Hoxter, Germany
9   Zeche Karl, Essen, Germany
10 Audi Max, Giessen, Germany
11 Kulturfabrik, Krefeld, Germany
12 Gala, Bremen, Germany

1990
January
26 Winter Gardens, Margate
27 Civic Centre, Aylesbury
28 Civic Centre, Mansfield
30 Civic Centre, Camberley
February
1   The Dome, Brighton
2   Cliff's Pavilion, Southend
3   Hertsmere Centre, Borehamwood
4   Civic Centre, Farnham
7   Marquee, London
9   Hummingbird, Birmingham
10 Exeter University
March
2   East Meets West, Berlin, Germany
5   Town and Country Club, London
June
3   Villa Marina, Douglas, Isle Of Man
July
?   Zurich, Switzerland
7   Big Top Festival, Swansea
August
30 Congress Theatre, Eastbourne
31 Leisure Centre, Brentwood
September
1   Leas Cliff Pavilion, Folkestone
2   Towngate Theatre, Basildon
4   Guildhall, Portsmouth
6   Irish Centre, Birmingham
7   Civic Centre, Mansfield
9   Queen Elizabeth Hall, Oldham
10 Corn Exchange, Maidstone
12 Beck Theatre, Hayes
14 Assembly Hall, Worthing

15 Forum, Hatfield
16 Stables, Milton Keynes
19 Central Hall, Chatham
20 White Rock Theatre, Hastings (£8.50)
21 Theatre, Lewisham
22 Queen's Hall, Barnstaple
24 Civic Hall, Guildford
27 Ritz Theatre, Lincoln
28 Civic Hall, Wolverhampton
29 Royal Spa Centre, Leamington Spa
30 Leadmill, Sheffield
October
1   St George's Hall, Bradford
2   Cleethorpes
4   Arcadia Theatre, Llandudno

1991
April
12 Zurich, Switzerland
13 Rubigen, Switzerland
19 Madrid, Spain
20 Barcelona, Spain
May
3   Forum, Hatfield
4   Winter Gardens, Weston-super-Mare
5   Stables, Milton Keynes
6   Marquee, London
7   Marquee, London
8   Prince's Hall, Aldershot
9   Assembly Hall, Worthing
11 King George's Hall, Blackburn
12 Civic Hall, Mansfield
13 Thameside Theatre, Ashton
16 Assembly Hall, Walthamstow
20–21 Club Citta, Kawasaki, Japan
23 Bottom Line, Nagoya, Japan
24 Am Hall, Osaka, Japan
31 Festzelt, Babenhausen, Germany
June
2   Haus Neue Einheit, Chemnitz,
    Germany

3   Capital, Hannover, Germany
4   Music Hall, Koln, Germany
5   Longhorn, Heligenwiessen, Germany
    (with Golden Earring)
6   Theater Fabrick, Munich, Germany
7   Serenadenhof, Nuremburg, Germany
8   Stadthalle, Neuenstadt, Germany
9   Music Galerie, Uelzen, Germany
10 Fabrik, Hamburg, Germany

October
4–5 German Festival (with Ten Years
     After)
25   Springfield, USA
26   Biddy Mulligans, Chicago, USA
November
1   St Louis, USA
15   Rockhaus, Vienna, Austria (European
     tour with Man and Ten Years After)
16   Wiedhofen, Austria
17   Feldkirch, Austria
18   Longhorn, Stuttgart, Germany
19   St Josefhaus, Weiden, Germany
20   Resi, Nuremburg, Germany
21   Elzer Hof, Mainz, Germany
22   Schwabenhalle, Augsburg, Germany
23   Stadthalle, Saarburg, Germany
24   Westfelenhalle, Dortmund, Germany
25   Metropol, Berlin, Germany
26   Grosse Freiheit, Hamburg, Germany
27   Rockheaven, Herford, Germany
28   Stadthalle, Koln, Germany
29   Elysee Montmartre, Paris, France
30   Mulhouse, France
December
1   Rockfestival, Schinjndel, Netherlands
2   Aladdin, Bremen, Germany
3   Paradiso, Amsterdam, Netherlands
4   Schwabenhalle, Augsburg, Germany
5   Town and Country Club, London
6   Elysee Montmartre, Paris, France

7   Vooruit, Gaet, France
8   Town and Country Club, London

1992
January
24–25 Easy Street, Glenview, USA
April
10 Playhouse Theatre, Newcastle
11 Civic Hall, Wolverhampton
12 Bierkeller, Bristol
13 Marina, Swansea
15 Irish Centre, Leeds
17 Spring St Theatre, Hull
19 Leadmill, Sheffield
24 Cotton Bowl, Redcar
25 Olympia, Dublin
26 Carnegie Theatre, Workington
28 Civic Theatre, Mansfield
29 Old Frog Inn, Newcastle-u-Lyme
30 Rio Rokz, Bradford
May
1   Leisure Centre, Brentwood
2   Stables, Milton Keynes
3   University of East Anglia, Norwich
    (£7.50)
4   The Dome, Ipswich
5   Civic Hall, Camberley
8   Queen's Hall, Barnstaple
9   English Riviera Centre, Torquay
11 Marquee, London
13 Greater London Radio Studios
14 Playhouse Theatre, Newcastle
15 Legends, Dingwall
16 Pelican Club, Aberdeen
17 SECC, Glasgow
18 The Venue, Edinburgh
19 The Grand, Clapham
June
4   Villa Marina, Douglas, Isle Of Man
6   Antara Pub, Olastrom
20 Montgomery Hall, Wath

July
18 Biddy Mulligans, Chicago, USA
19 Big Kahuna, St Louis, USA
27 Cowboys, Shreveport, USA
29 Juanitas, Little Rock, USA
August
8 Olympia, Dublin, Ireland
10–11 Roadhouse, London
13 Harvey's, Stockton
15 Central Library Theatre, Birmingham
16 Civic Theatre, Barnsley (with the Frank White Band)
18 Wytchwood, Manchester
20 Bobby Browns, Nottingham
October
22 Robin Hoods, Dudley
24 Oval Rockhouse, Norwich
26 Arts Guild Theatre, Greenock
29 Kronprinzen, Malmo, Sweden
30 Bergan's, Gothenburg, Sweden
31 Antara, Olofstrom, Sweden
November
5 Wheatsheaf, Stoke
30 Gothenburg, Sweden

1993
All 1993 dates with Blue Oyster Cult, Nazareth, Uriah Heep, plus Girlschool from December 8
March
12 Flaherty's, Evergreen, USA
13 Club Metropolis, Glenview, USA
15 Juanita's, Little Rock, USA
16 Cowboys, Shreveport, USA
17 Sneakers, Austin, USA
18 Sneakers, San Antonio, USA
19 Sante Fe, Cantina, USA
20 Rockefeller's, Houston, USA
November
5–6 PNE Show Mart, Vancouver, Canada
7 Riverside Coliseum, Kamloops, Canada

9 Max Bell Centre, Calgary, Canada
10 Convention Centre, Edmonton, Canada
11 Titan Place, Saskatoon, Canada
12 Convention Centre, Winnipeg, Canada
13 Target Centre, Minneapolis, USA
14 Memorial Hall, Kansas City, USA
16 Convention Centre, Steven's Point, USA
17 Pierre's, Fort Wayne, USA
18 Seagate Centre, Toledo, USA
19 Rpm Warehouse, Toronto, Canada
20 Lulu's, Kitchener, Canada
21 Eastbrook Theatre, Grand Rapids, USA
22 Battelle Hall, Columbus, USA
24 Boomers, Martinsburg, USA
26 Music Fair, Westbury, USA
27 Valley Forge Music Fair, Devon, USA
29 Palmer Auditorium, Davenport, USA
30 Coronade Theatre, Rockford, USA
December
1 Club Eastbrook, Grand Rapids, USA
2 American Theatre, St Louis, USA
3 Rosemont Horizon, Rosemont, USA
4 The Palace, Auburn Hills, USA
8 Stadthalle, Offenbach, Germany
9 Stadthalle, Fürth, Germany
10 Heldenberghalle, Goeppingen, Germany
11 Eissporthalle, Halle, Germany
12 Phillipshalle, Dusseldorf, Germany
14 Wikinghalle, Flensburg, Germany
15 Musichall, Hannover, Germany
17 Hessenhalle, Alsfeld, Germany
18 Eberthalle, Ludwigshafen, Germany
19 Terminal 1, Munich, Germany
20 Kurhalle, Vienna, Austria

1995
March
30 Leisure Centre, Rotherham
31 Fibbers, York

April

1 Concert Hall, Blackheath
2 Robin Hood, Dudley
3 Tivoli Theatre, Wimborne
4 Wedgewood Rooms, Portsmouth
5 Lanterns, Ashburton
6 Arthur's Club, Geneva

May

13 Rock at the Quin's, Port Talbot
19 Soundgarden, Ingleheim, Germany
20 Park Kino, Pirmasens, Germany
21 Centre Culturel, Sandweiler, Germany

November

2 VH1 Studios, London
2 Bottom Line, London
4 Mean Fiddler, Dublin, Ireland
9 Never Never Land, Blackburn
11 Civic Theatre, Mansfield
12 Robin Hood, Dudley
14 Ladle Ballroom, Middlesbrough
15 Beachcomber, Cleethorpes
16 Irish Centre, Leeds
17 Civic Theatre, Barnsley
18 Wheatsheaf, Stoke
20 Wedgewood Rooms, Portsmouth
21 Lanterns, Ashburton
22 Tivoli Theatre, Wimborne
23 New Morning, Paris, France
24 First Rock Café, Geneva, Switzerland
25 Neuchatel, Switzerland

December

3 Leicester University
4 Filling Station, Newport
6 Brook, Southampton
7 Pavilion, Worthing
9 Cellar Club, South Shields
11 Fleece and Firkin, Bristol
13–15 Warsaw, Poland

1996

June

30 Festival, Budapest, Hungary

October

31 Irish Centre, Leeds

November

1 Municipal Hall, Colne
2 Civic Theatre, Barnsley
3 Wheatsheaf, Stoke
4 Fleece and Firkin, Bristol
6 Tivoli Theatre, Wimborne
8 Waterford
9 Mean Fiddler, Dublin
10 The Quays, Galway
14 Garage, Glasgow (£8.30)
15 Cellar Club, South Shields
16 Carnegie Theatre, Workington
17 Leisure Centre, Mansfield
18 Stables, Milton Keynes
19 Beachcomber, Cleethorpes
20 Victoria Theatre, Halifax
21 Ladle Ballroom, Middlesbrough
22 Cellar Club, South Shields
23 Wilbarston Hall
24 Robin Hood, Dudley
26 Power Station, Barry
27 New Pavilion, Rhyl
28 Fernham Hall, Fareham (with The Wild
    Turkeys)
30 Lanterns, Ashburton

December

1 Astoria 2, London
4 Esplanade, Southend
6 Grosse Freiheit, Hamburg, Germany
7 Rintelin, Germany
8 Leipzig, Germany
9 Berlin, Germany
10 Augsburg, Germany
11 Nuremburg, Germany
12 Midstedt, Germany
13 Warmelskirchen, Germany

15 Schloss, Wiessenfels, Germany
17 Brook, Southampton

1997
May
5–6 Atlantis, Basel, Switzerland
7 Scala, Zurich, Switzerland
8 Mehrzweckhalle, Ottenbach, Switzerland
9 Kammgarn, Schaffhausen, Switzerland
10 Rossli, Wattenwil, Switzerland
June
5–6 Summerland, Douglas, Isle Of Man
7 Stramrock, Hardenberg, Netherlands
8 Atlantis, Alkmaar, Netherlands
9 Spirit of 66, Verviers, Belgium
10 Stadsdanszaal, Middleburg, Netherlands
11 Zaal Schaaf, Leeuwarden, Netherlands
19 Tuxedo Junction, Danbury, USA
20 Jaxx Springfield, Virginia, USA
November
6 Stables, Milton Keynes
7 Wilbarston Hall
8 Leisure Centre, Mansfield
9 Robin Hood, Dudley
10 Brook, Southampton
11 Esplanade, Southend
12 Floral Pavilion Theatre, New Brighton
13 Rio Rock Club, Bradford
14–15 Cellar Club, South Shields
16 Boardwalk, Sheffield

1998
January
28 Old Oak, Cork, Ireland
29 Quays Bar, Galway, Ireland
30 Mean Fiddler, Dublin, Ireland
31 Empire Music Hall, Belfast
February
4 Lanterns, Ashburton

5 Tivoli Theatre, Wimborne
6 Recreation Centre, Bridgend
8 Standard, Walthamstow
9 Bier Keller, Bristol
10 12 Bar Club, London
11 Cellar Club, South Shields
12 Ladle Ballroom, Middlesbrough
13 Robin Hood, Dudley
14 Leisure Centre, Rotherham
15 Oval Rock House, Norwich
16 Wheatsheaf, Stoke
17 Concorde, Brighton
19 Horn, St Albans
20 Rotplombe, Erfurt, Germany
21 Grosse Freiheit, Hamburg, Germany
22 Flensburg, Germany
23 Bad Hannover, Germany
24 B9, Aachen, Germany
25 Hirsch, Nuremburg, Germany
26 Alte Malzerei, Regensburg, Germany
27 Anker Club, Leipzig, Germany
28 Hafenbahn, Offenbach, Germany
March
1 Rock Haus, Salzburg, Germany
2 Jazz Galerie, Bonn, Germany
3 Schlutzenhaus, Stuttgart, Germany
4 Colos Saal, Aschaffenburg, Germany
5 Substage, Karlsruhe, Germany
6 Star Club, Oberhausen, Germany
7 Spektrum, Solingen, Germany
8 Kufa, Krefeld, Germany
9 Rock House, Cologne, Germany
10 Aladdin Club, Bremen, Germany
11 Jovel Music Hall, Munster, Germany
12 Alts Zollhaus, Leer, Germany
13 Ostend, Belgium
14 Spirit of 66, Verviers, Belgium
15 Arnhem, Netherlands
July
17 Summer Night Festival, Weil Der Stadt, Germany

18 Burg Herzberg Festival, Alsfeld,
Germany
19 Spirithaus, Frankfurt, Germany
August
6 Camden Palace, London
October
31 Wilbarston Hall
November
1 Robin Hood, Dudley
2 Riddles Music Bar, Stoke
3 Beachcomber, Cleethorpes
4 Fleece and Firkin, Bristol
5 Swan, Swindon
6 Rio Rock Club, Bradford
7 Leisure Centre, Mansfield
9 Boardwalk, Sheffield
10 Brook, Southampton
11 Blues W14, London
12 Lanterns, Ashburton
13 Standard, Walthamstow
14 Stables, Milton Keynes
16 Lucky Break, Bury St Edmunds
19 Carnegie Theatre, Workington
21 Ladle Ballroom, Middlesbrough
22 Wytchwood, Ashton
23 Gwyn Hall, Neath
24 Ludwigs, Swansea
26 Quays Bar, Galway, Ireland
27 Whelans, Dublin, Ireland
28 Village Hall, Narbeth
30 Blue Note, Gottingen, Germany
December
1 Bruckentorsaal, Rinteln, Germany
3 Alter Schlachthof, Soest, Germany
4 Kulterhaus Markers, Dorndorf,
Germany
6 Substage, Karlsruhe, Germany
7 Jazz Galerie, Bonn, Germany
8 Hirsh, Nuremburg, Germany
9 Alte Malzerei, Regensberg, Germany
11 S'fon, Renningen, Germany

12 Star Club, Oberhausen, Germany
13 Tivoli Club, Freiburg, Germany
15 Colos Saal, Aschaffenburg, Germany
16 Borderline, Diest, Germany
17 Schwimmbad Club, Heidelberg,
Germany
18 Stadthalle, Rheinberg, Germany
19 Grosse Freiheit, Hamburg Hal,
Germany

1999
January
20 Whisky A Go Go, Los Angeles,
USA
March
11 Horn Reborn, St Albans
12 Recreational Centre, Bridgend
14 Ronnie Scott's, Birmingham
18 Leisure Centre, Market Harborough
19 Park Hotel, Tynemouth
20 Oakwood Centre, Rotherham
21 Robin Hood, Dudley
23 The Brook, Southampton
24 The Standard, Walthamstow
25 Blues W14, London
26 Krone, Worms, Germany
27 Ebertbad, Oberhausen, Germany
30 Jazz Haus, Frieberg, Germany
31 Longhorn, Stuttgart, Germany
April
1 Spectrum, Augsberg, Germany
2 Apeldoorn, Netherlands
3 The Roots, Meyel, Netherlands
4 Spirit Of '66, Verviers, Belgium
? Florence, Italy
30 House Of Blues, Chicago, USA
May
1 The Beaumont, Chicago, USA
? St Louis, USA
? Cleveland, USA
? Saloon, Georgetown, USA

June

3   Villa Marina, Douglas, Isle Of Man
6   Town Hall, Cheltenham
?   Peavey Electronics, Meridian, USA
26 University, Duisburg, Germany
?   Trimedia, Switzerland

July

4   Festival, Burg Herzburg, Germany
13 Festival, Pont Auclemer, France
23 Open Air Freilichtbuhne, Eichtal, Germany
24 Open Air Festival, Buga, Germany
30 Burgergfestival, Hamburg, Germany
31 Open Air Festival, Hameln, Germany

August

7   Nunningen Festival, Basel, Switzerland
14 Festival, Clermont Ferrand, France

September

10 Le Gourde d'Or Bike Festival, France
28 Basel, Switzerland
29 Zurich, Switzerland
30 ?, Switzerland

October

1   Gonfreville L'Orcher, Le Havre, France
2   Salle Oceanis, Ploemeurs, France
5   Cabaret Sam, Boulognes Sur Mer, France
6   ?, France
7   Le Splendide, Lille, France
8   La Luciole, Alencon, France
9   Run Ar Pens, Chateaulin, France
10 Le Bacandi, Callac, France
13 L'Orange Blue, Vitry Le Francois, France
14 La Forge, St Etienne, France
15 L'Usine, Arles, France
16 Café Rex, Toulouse, France
17 Valence, France
20 New Morning, Paris, France
21 EuroDisney, Paris, France
22 Le Plan, Ris Orangis, France

23 Festival, La Rochelle, France

November

2   Telford Warehouse, Chester
3   Blues West 14, London
4   The Stables, Milton Keynes
5   The Corn Hall, Cirencester
6   Mansfield (*AshCon*)
7   Robin Hood, Dudley
8   Wellington Club, Hull
9   The Brook, Southampton
10 The Royal Standard, London
11 Wakefield
12 The Dome, Whitley Bay
13 Rio Rock Club, Bradford
14 The King's Head, Dursley
17 The Horn, St Albans
18 Unna Lindenbrauerei, Germany
19 Locomotive, Bad Nenndorf, Germany
24 Haus Der Jugend, Wuppertal, Germany
25 Fabrik, Hamburg, Germany
26 Riders Café, Lubeck, Germany
27 Gasthof zur Linda, Afalter, Germany
28 Prague, Czech Republic
30 Budapest, Hungary

December

3   Schutzenhaus, Stuttgart, Germany
4   Colosaal, Aschaffenburg, Germany
5   Die Weberei, Gutersloh, Germany
6   Jazz Galerie, Bonn, Germany
7   Cobra, Solingen, Germany
8   Alte Matzerei, Regnsburg, Germany
9   Hirsch, Nurnberg, Germany
10 Juz Komplex, Schuttorf, Germany
11 Helendoorn, Lantarn, Netherlands
12 Helmond, Netherlands

2000

February

25 Chiddingfold Club, Guildford

March

25 Eurodisney, Paris, France

28 Cri Art, Auch, France
30 Le Thelonius, Bordeaux, France
31 Le Psyche Café Gap, France
April
1   Le Variete, Sommieres, France
4   013, Tilburg, Netherlands
5   Blues Café, Appeldoorn, Netherlands
6   Le Terminal Export, Nancy, France
7   Reims, France
8   Le Splendide, Lille, France
9   Spirit of '66, Verviers, Belgium
15 Victoria Inn, Pontypridd
16 Nighthawks, Swindon
17 Guildhall, Gloucester
19 The Cavern, Liverpool
22 Shepherds Bush, London
23 Robin 2, Bilston
24 Wedgewood Rooms, Portsmouth
27 Waterfront, Norwich
28 Fibbers, York
29 Century Theatre, Coalville
August
4   Guitar Festival, Bath
5   Pigs Nose, East Prawl
7   Riverside Festival, Gravesend
12 Eject Garden Part, Dreisen, Germany
19 Festival, Kortenarken, Belgium
September
29 Recreation Centre, Bridgend
October
1   Robin 1, Birmingham
2   Stables, Milton Keynes
3   The Army & Navy, Chelmsford
4   Medina Theatre, Newport
5   The Standard, Walthamstow
6   Classic Rock Society, Rotherham
7   Wilbarston Hall, Wilbarston
8   The Cavern, Liverpool
9   Limelight Club, Crewe
11 Balne Lane WMC, Wakefield
12 Opera House, Newcastle

13 Lochgelly Centre, Lochgelly
14 Glasgow
15 Aberdeen
19 The Brook, Southampton
20 Zodiac Club, Oxford
21 Ashcon, Mansfield
23 Phoenix Theatre, Exeter

2001
January
10 Bluescafe, Appeldoorn, Netherlands
11 Kulturfabrik, Krefeld, Germany
12 Ducsaal, Freudenburg, Germany
13 Villa Berg, Stuttgart, Germany
14 Hirsch, Nurnberg, Germany
16 Quasimodo, Berlin, Germany
17 Spectrum, Augsburg, Germany
18 Jazzhaus, Freiburg, Germany
19 Kammgarn, Kaiserslautern, Germany
20 Colos Saal, Aschaffenburg, Germany
21 Zur Linde, Affalter, Germany
23 Iduna, Drachten, Netherlands
24 Elfenbein, Bielefeld, Germany
25 Fabrik, Hamburg, Germany
26 Blues Garage, Hannover, Germany
27 Gasthof Schluter, Olsberg, Germany
28 Jazz Galerie, Bonn, Germany
30 Kulturetage, Oldenburg, Germany
31 Spirit of '66, Verviers, Belgium
February
1   Pumpehuset, Kopenhagen, Denmark
2   Rytmeposten, Odense, Denmark
3   Train, Aarhus, Denmark
5   Rockefeller, Oslo, Norway
7   Travestia Club, Helsinki, Finland
9   Music Hall, Worpswede, Germany
10 Logo, Ahaus, Germany
11 Tavenu, Waalwijk, Denmark
May
11 Chiddingfold Club, Guildford
12 Cheese & Grain, Frome

13 Patti Pavillion, Swansea
14 Concorde, Brighton
16 The Standard, Walthamstow
17 The Springhead, Willerby
19 The Soundhaus, Northampton
20 Robin 2, Bilston
21 The Army & Navy, Chelmsford
22 The Waterfront, Norwich
23 The Flowerpot, Derby
24 The Brook, Southampton
25 Tivoli Theatre, Wimborne
26 Opera House, Newcastle

September

1   Ashcon-at-Sea, Conzumel, Mexico
21 Chiddingfold Club, Guildford
22 Bass Museum, Burton-on-Trent
27 The Buckley, Anglesey
28 Recreation Centre, Bridgend
29 Wilbarston Hall, Wilbarston
30 Robin 1, Birmingham

October

1   Stables, Milton Keynes
2   Astor Theatre, Deal
3   The Standard, Walthamstow
4   The Flowerpot, Derby
5   The Springhead, Willerby
6   Oakwood Centre, Rotherham
7   The Cavern, Liverpool
8   Limelight Club, Crewe
9   The Irish Centre, Leeds
10 Opera House, Newcastle
12 Lochgelly Centre, Lochgelly
17 Medina Theatre, Newport
18 The Brook, Southampton
19 Phoenix Theatre, Exeter
20 Pigs Nose, East Prawl
21 Princes Hall, Aldershot
31 The Witchwood, Ashton-under-Lyne

November

1   The Springhead, Willerby
2   Astoria, London

2002

January

10 Quasimodo, Berlin, Germany
11 Gewerkschaftshaus, Erfurt, Germany
12 Weisbierstadl, Abensberg, Germany
13 Pratteln, Switzerland
16 Colos Saal, Aschaffenburg, Germany
17 Elfenbein, Bielefeld, Germany
18 Gasthof Schluter, Olsberg, Germany
20 Zur Linde, Affalter, Germany
22 Jazz Galerie, Bonn, Germany
23 Roxy Music Hall, Ulm, Germany
24 Sudhaus, Tubingen, Germany
25 Schulturnhalle, Winterbach, Germany
26 Kammgarn, Kaiserslautern, Germany
27 Ducsaal, Freudenburg, Germany
28 Matrix, Bochum, Germany
29 Hirsch, Nurnberg, Germany
30 Logo, Ahaus, Germany
31 Fabrik, Hamburg, Germany

February

1   Blues Garage, Hannover-Isernhagen, Germany
2   Twist, Twist, Germany
3   Live Club Barmen, Wuppertal, Germany
5   Werkhof, Lübeck, Germany
6   Pumpehuset, Kopenhagen, Denmark
7   Rytmeposten, Odense, Denmark
9   Stadthalle, Betzdorf, Germany
10 Kulturetage, Oldenburg, Germany

April

11 The Brook, Southampton
12 The Point, Cardiff
13 Amulet, Shepton Mallet
14 The Robin R'n'B Club, Wolverhampton
15 The Flowerpot, Derby
16 The Limelight Club, Crewe
17 Bury Met, Bury
18 Band On The Wall, Manchester

19 Pacific Road Arts Centre, Birkenhead
20 Pierpoint, Hastings
21 Y Theatre, Leicester
23 Fibbers, York
24 The Springhead, Hull
26 Astoria 2, London
May
11 Centre Culturel de Sarlat, Sarlat, France
June
3 LeTransbordeur, Lyon, France
13 Toscanini Theatre Chiari, Chiari, Italy
15 Villanova di San Daniele, Udine, Italy
July
18 La Cooperative de Mai, Cleremont Ferrand, France
19 Les Voix de Gaeu, Six-Fours-Les-Plages, France (with Johnny Winter)
22 Theatre de Le Mer, Sate, France (with Johnny Winter)
September
7 Georgetown Saloon, Georgetown, USA
10 Magic Bag, Ferndale, USA
12 Shank Hall, Milwaukee, USA
13 Thirsty Ear, Columbus, USA
15 Generations, St Louis, USA
16 Generations, St Louis, USA
19 Variety Playhouse, Atlanta, USA
20 Jannus Landing, St Petersburg, USA
22 Miami, USA (*AshCon at Sea*)
17 12th and Porter, Nashville, USA
30 Stables, Milton Keynes
October
2 The Standard, London
3 The Flowerpot, Derby
4 Tivoli Theatre, Wimborne
5 Oakwood Centre, Rotherham
6 The Buckeley, Beaumaris
7 The Limelight Club, Crewe
8 Irish Centre, Leeds
9 Opera House, Newcastle-upon-Tyne
10 The Cathouse, Glasgow

11 Lochgelly Centre, Lochgelly
12 The Citadel, St Helens
14 Telford's Warehouse, Chester
13 Robin 1, Brierley Hill
16 Assembly Hall, Tunbridge Wells
17 Queen's Theatre, Barnstaple
18 Exeter Phoenix Theatre, Exeter
19 Pigs Nose Inn, Devon
20 The Point, Cardiff
21 Patti Pavilion, Swansea
23 The Springhead, Hull
24 The Brook, Southampton
25 Chiddingfold Club, Chiddingfold
26 Chesterfield (*AshCon*)
27 Cheese & Grain, Frome
December
5 Psyche Live Café, Gap, France
6 Le Pleiade, Tours, France
7 Le Saxaphone, Montpelier, France
11 Spirit of 66, Verviers, Belgium
12 C.C. Sandweiler, Sandweiler, Luxembourg
13 Manifesto, Hoorn, Netherlands
14 Plato, Helmond, Netherlands
15 De Sprong, Winterswijk, Netherlands
16 De Boerderij, Zoetermeer, Netherlands
17 De Kroeg, Oldenzaal, Netherlands
18 BluesCafe, Apeldoorn, Netherlands

2003
January
11 Frankfurter Hof, Mainz, Germany
12 Ducsaal, Freudenburg, Germany
13 Georg-Elser-Halle, Munich, Germany
14 Hirsch, Nurnberg, Germany
16 Sudhaus, Tubingen, Germany
17 Colos Saal, Aschaffenburg, Germany
18 Zur Linde, Affalter, Germany
20 Stadthalle, Betzdorf, Germany
22 Musiktheater Rex, Lorsch, Germany
23 Substage, Karlsruhe, Germany

24 Live Club Barmen, Wuppertal, Germany
25 Baumgarten, Bistensee, Germany
26 Elfenbein, Bielefeld, Germany
28 Matrix, Bochum, Germany
29 Quasimodo, Berlin, Germany
30 Fabrik, Hamburg, Germany
31 Music Hall, Worpswede, Germany

February
1 Blues Garage, Hannover-Isernhagen, Germany
2 Heimathaus, Twist, Germany
15 Coach House, San Juan Capistrano, USA
19 Sweetwater, Mill Valley, USA
20 Foxfire, Springfield, USA
21 Aladdin Theater, Portland, USA
23 The Yale, Vancouver, BC, Canada
25 The Mint, Sun Valley, USA
26 Zephyr, Salt Lake City, USA

March
1 Tres Hombres, Woodland Park, USA
2 The Grand Emporium, Kansas City, USA
3 Generations, St Louis, USA
4 Shank Hall, Milwaukee, USA
5 Synergy II, W. Chicago, USA
6 The Tralf Music Hall, Buffalo, USA
7 Jaxx, Springfield, USA
8 Towne Crier, Beacon, USA
9 The Social, Orlando, USA
12 Havana Café, Toulouse, France

April
7 Patti Pavilion, Swansea
8 Tivoli Theatre, Wimborne, Dorset
9 The Brook, Southampton
10 The Wharf, Tavistock, Devon
11 Gloucester Guildhall, Gloucester
12 Cheese & Grain, Frome
13 The Mount Stuart, Cardiff
14 Central Station, Wrexham

16 The Springhead, Hull
17 Pacific Rd Arts Centre, Birkenhead
18 The General Wolfe, Coventry
19 Wilbarston Hall, Wilbarston
20 Robin 1, Brierley Hill
21 The Limelight Club, Crewe
23 The Boardwalk, Sheffield
24 The Waterfront, Norwich
25 Astoria 2, London
26 Bisley Pavilion, Bisley
27 The Lowry, Manchester
28 The Flowerpot, Derby
29 The Cauliflower, Ilford

June
8 Sweden Rock, Solvesborg, Sweden
21 Rock & Bike Festival, Weeze, Germany
23 Matrix, Bochum, Germany
24 Phoenix Club, Liege, Belgium
25 Patronaat, Haarlem, DN, Netherlands
26 013, Tilburg, Netherlands
27 Arrow Classic Rock Fest, Lichtenvoorde, Netherlands
29 Troubadour, Hardenberg, Netherlands

July
2 Milwaukee Fest, Milwaukee, USA
5 Rib Fest, Naperville, USA
19 Burg Herzberg Festival, Fulda, Germany

August
23 Coach House, San Juan Capistrano, USA
24 Rhythm Room, Phoenix, USA
25 Nimbus Brewery, Tucson, USA
28 Cactus Cafe, Austin, USA
30 Cardi's, Houston, USA
31 Prog Day, Chapel Hill, USA

September
1 LA House of Blues, New Orleans, USA
3 The Social, Orlando, USA
4 The State Theater, St Petersburg, USA
5 Variety Playhouse, Atlanta, USA

8 Georgetown Saloon, Georgetown, USA
9 The North Star, Philadelphia, USA
11 The House Of Blues, Boston, USA
12 Bull Run, Shirley, USA
13 The Bottom Line, New York, USA
14 Ramshead Tavern, Annapolis, USA

October

3 Tivoli Theatre, Wimborne
4 Y Theatre, Leicester
5 Robin 2, Wolverhampton
6 The Flowerpot, Derby
7 Irish Centre, Leeds
8 Park Hotel, Tynemouth
9 The Ferry, Glasgow
10–11 Lochgelly Centre, Lochgelly
13 The Limelight Club, Crewe
14 Neptune Theatre, Liverpool
15 The Platform, Morecambe
16 Life Café, Manchester
17 Carnegie Theatre, Workington
18 Oakwood Centre, Rotherham
19 The Springhead, Hull
21 The Stables, Milton Keynes
22 The Standard, London
23 T.J.'s, Newport
24 Queen's Hall, Narbeth
25 Muni Arts Centre, Pontypridd
26 The General Wolfe, Coventry
28 Medina Theatre, Newport
29 The Brook, Southampton
30 Exeter Phoenix Theatre, Exeter
31 Pavilions, Plymouth

November

1 The Landmark, Ilfracombe
2 Cheese & Grain, Frome
4 Trades Council Club, Barnsley
6 Guildford Civic Hall, Guildford
7 Astor Theatre, Deal
8 Hurst School, Tadley (charity event)
16 Opinião Cidade Baixa, Porto Alegre, Brazil

18 Teatro Municipal de Macao, Macao, Brazil
20 Caneceo, Rio de Janeiro, Brazil
21 Directv Music Hall, Sao Paulo, Brazil
23 Palacio das Artes, Belo Horizonte, Brazil

December

1 Le Rouge Gorge, Avignon, France
2 Le Poste a Galene, Marseille, France
3 Havana Café, Toulouse, France
4 Le Reservoir, Perigueux, France
5 New Morning, Paris, France
6 Plato, Helmond, Netherlands
7 Club de Noot, Hoogland, Netherlands
8 Le Bayou, Rouen, France

2004

January

10 Tivoli Theatre, Wimborne
14 Spectrum, Augsburg, Germany
15 Ducsaal, Freudenburg, Germany
16 Blues Garage, Hannover-Isernhagen, Germany
17 Raeucherei, Kiel, Germany
18 Kulturetage, Oldenburg, Germany
19 Fabrik, Hamburg, Germany
21 Quasimodo, Berlin, Germany
22 Centrum, Erfurt, Germany
23 Zur Linde, Affalter, Germany
24 H2O, Reichenbach, Germany
27 Hirsch, Nurnberg, Germany
28 Colos Saal, Aschaffenburg, Germany
29 Musiktheater Rex, Lorsch, Germany
30 Substage, Karlsruhe, Germany
31 Lagerhalle, Osnabruck, Germany

February

2 Harmonie, Bonn, Germany
3 Elfenbein, Bielefeld, Germany
4 Live Club Barmen, Wuppertal, Germany
5 Zur Linde, Affalter, Germany

6   Music Hall, Worpswede, Germany
7   Antonianum Geseke, Geseke, Germany
28 Towne Crier, Beacon, USA
29 Sellersville Theater, Sellersville, USA

March

1   Georgetown Saloon, Georgetown, USA
2   Tribeca Rock Club, New York, USA
3   The Van Dyck Club, Schenectady, USA
4   Rockits, Toronto, ONT, Canada
5   The Tralf Music Hall, Buffalo, USA
6   The Stephen Talkhouse, Amagansett, USA
7   New Jersey Proghouse, Metuchen, USA
9   Checkered Flag, Appleton, USA
10 Luther s Blues, Madison, USA
12 Magic Bag, Ferndale, USA
13 Chicago City Limits, Schaumburg, USA
14 Shank Hall, Milwaukee, USA
15 Generations, St Louis, USA

April

2   The Venue, Chichester
3   Bridgend Recreation Centre, South Wales
5   The Waterfront, Norwich
8   The Wharf, Tavistock, Devon
9   Pigs Nose Inn, Devon
10 Cheese & Grain, Frome
11 Honiton Motel, Honiton
13 The Limelight Club, Crewe
14 The Rescue Rooms, Nottingham
15 The Springhead, Hull
16 The Corporation, Sheffield
17 Pacific Road Arts Centre, Birkenhead
18 The Buckeley, Beaumaris
19 Telford's Warehouse, Chester
20 The Lowry, Manchester
22 The Brook, Southampton
23 Astoria 2, London
24 Bisley Pavilion, Bisley
25 Rock Cafe 2000, Stourbridge

26 Cox's Yard, Stratford Upon Avon

June

11 Redwood Run, Piercy, USA
12 Breeze Nightclub, Tahoe, USA

July

8   BluesCafe, Apeldoorn, Netherlands
9   Bospop, Weert, Netherlands
10 Caracol, Madrid, Spain
11 Luz de Gas, Barcelona, Spain
19 Winchester Music Hall, Lakewood, USA
20 Magic Bag, Ferndale, USA
22 Estes Amphitheater, Des Moines, USA
23 Porter's Oyster Bar, Crystal Lake, USA
24 Checkered Flag, Appleton, USA
25 Taste of Lincoln, Chicago, USA
27 Generations, St Louis, USA
29 Shank Hall, Milwaukee, USA
30 Thirsty Ear, Columbus, USA
31 Recher Theatre, Towson, USA

August

10 Fete du Vin Festival, Colmar, France
22 Rockinbeerfest, Huntingdon

October

1   Tivoli Theatre, Wimborne
2   Muni Arts Centre, Pontypridd
3   Honiton Motel, Honiton
5   Princess Pavilion, Falmouth
6   Fiddlers, Bristol
7   Gloucester Guildhall, Gloucester
8   Minsterley Parish Hall, Shrewsbury
9   Wilbarston Hall, Wilbarston
10 Robin 2, Wolverhampton
12 The Flowerpot, Derby
13 The Springhead, Hull
14 Festival Hall, Bolton
15 The Citadel, St Helens
16 The Platform, Morecambe
18 The Limelight Club, Crewe
19 Irish Centre, Leeds
20 Park Hotel, Tynemouth

21 The Ferry, Glasgow
22 Lochgelly Centre, Lochgelly
23 Lochgelly Centre, Lochgelly
24 O'Donoghue's, Aberdeen
25 Magnum Theatre, Irvine
26 The Stables, Milton Keynes
27 The Standard, London
28 The Brook, Southampton
29 Chiddingfold Club, Chiddingfold
30 Mansfield (*AshCon*)
November
17 The Tralf Music Hall, Buffalo, USA
18 Northern Lights, Clifton Park, USA
20 Bull Run, Shirley, USA
21 Sellersville Theater, Sellersville, USA
22 XM Radio Live Broadcast, Washington DC, USA
23 Ramshead Tavern, Annapolis, USA
27 Neil's, Memphis, USA
28 Granada Theater, Dallas, USA
30 Community Center, Los Alamos, USA
December
1 Rhythm Room, Phoenix, USA
2 Boulder Station Casino, Las Vegas, USA
3 Coach House, San Juan Capistrano, USA
4 Humphrey's by the Bay, San Diego, USA
6 The Jungle, Eugene, USA
7 Aladdin Theater, Portland, USA
9 The Yale, Vancouver, BC, Canada

2005
January
14 Yeni Melek Gosteri Merkezi, Istanbul, Turkey
15 Saklikent, Ankara, Turkey
19 Colos Saal, Aschaffenburg, Germany
20 Die Halle, Reichenbach, Germany
21 Ducsaal, Freudenburg, Germany

22 Blues Garage, Hannover-Isernhagen, Germany
23 Fabrik, Hamburg, Germany
25 Heimathaus, Twist, Germany
26 Harmonie, Bonn, Germany
27 Elfenbein, Bielefeld, Germany
28 Music Hall, Worpswede, Germany
29 Live Club Barmen, Wuppertal, Germany
30 Lagerhalle, Osnabruck, Germany
February
1 Musiktheater Rex, Lorsch, Germany
2 Substage, Karlsruhe, Germany
3 Hirsch, Nurnberg, Germany
4 Quasimodo, Berlin, Germany
5 Zur Linde, Affalter, Germany
6 Alte Molzerei, Regensburg, Germany
9 Spirit of 66, Verviers, Belgium
10 De Boerderij, Zoetermeer, Netherlands
11 Iduna, Drachten, Netherlands
12 Plato, Helmond, Netherlands
13 Doornroosje, Nijmegen, Netherlands
14 Off Broadway, St Louis, USA
March
4 Recher Theatre,Towson, USA
5 JAXX, Springfield, USA
6 Gatsby's, Johnson City, USA
9 Waverly Beach, Menasha, USA
10 Shank Hall, Milwaukee, USA
11 Chicago City Limits, Schaumburg, USA
12 House of Tunes, Poplar Grove, USA
14 Off Broadway, St Louis, USA
15 Thirsty Ear, Columbus, USA
16 Winchester Music Hall, Lakewood, USA
18 Moondog's, Blawnox, USA
April
1 The Lowry, Manchester
2 Pacific Road Arts Centre, Birkenhead
3 Hare and Hounds, Keresley

4   The Junction, Cambridge
5   Park Hotel, Tynemouth
7   Loreburn Hall, Dumfries
9   Villa Marina Royal Hall, Douglas
10 The Boardwalk, Sheffield
11 The Limelight Club, Crewe
12 The Rescue Rooms, Nottingham
13 The Springhead, Hull
14 The Flowerpot, Derby
15 The Venue, Chichester
16 Birthday Bash, Godmanchester
17 Robin 2, Wolverhampton
21 Community Theatre, Abertillery
22 Pigs Nose Inn, Devon
23 Cheese & Grain, Frome
24 NCLA, Newport
26 The Waterfront, Norwich
27 The Stables, Milton Keynes
28 The Brook, Southampton
29 Astoria 2, London
30 Bisley Pavilion, Bisley
June
3–4   Moonshine Theater, Scranton, USA
11 Cancer Benefit, Vlissingen, Netherlands
16 Le Plan, Ris Orangis, France
17 Le Rouge Gorge, Avignon, France
18 Noumatrouff, Mulhouse, France
20 Festival du Parc, Compiegne, France
21 Fete de La Musique, Marcq En Bareuil, France
23 Club Atlantis, Alkmaar, Netherlands
24 Club Zwaanje, Deesd, Netherlands
25 Congresova Place, Warsaw, Poland
July
3   Rib Fest, Naperville, USA
15 Moondance Jam, Walker, USA
16 Rock Fest 2005, Cadott, USA
18–31   Recording, Boston, USA
September
24 Ayr Town Hall, Ayr

25 Melton Mowbray Theatre, Melton Mowbray
26 Green Room, Welwyn Garden City
27 Hare and Hounds, Keresley
28 The Springhead, Hull
30 Corn Hall, Cirencester
October
1   Wilbarston Hall, Wilbarston
2   Robin 2, Wolverhampton
3   The Stables, Milton Keynes
4   Huntingdon Hall, Worcester
5   Assembly Rooms, Derby
6   The Maltings, Farnham
7   Tivoli Theatre, Wimborne
8   Queen's Hall, Narbeth
9   Swindon Art Centre, Swindon
11 Miners Institute, Blackwood
12 The Standard, London
13 The Brook, Southampton
14 Princess Pavilion, Falmouth
15 Cheese & Grain, Frome
16 Axminster Guild Hall, Axminster
18 Irish Centre, Leeds
19 The Cluny, Newcastle upon Tyne
20 The Ferry, Glasgow
21 Lochgelly Centre, Lochgelly
22 Station Hotel, Perth
23 O'Donoghue's, Aberdeen
25 The Limelight Club, Crewe
26 Theatr Gwynedd, Bangor
27 The Platform, Morecambe
28 Academy 3, Manchester
29 Mansfield (*AshCon*)
November
11 Sellersville Theater, Sellersville, USA
12 Bull Run, Shirley, USA
13 The Old Franklin Schoolhouse, Metuchen, USA
16 Intersection, Grand Rapids, USA
17 Durty Nellies, Palatine, USA
19 Star Central, Minneapolis, USA

20 Surf Ballroom, Clear Lake, USA
21 Grand Emporium, Kansas City, USA
22 Granada Theater, Dallas, USA
23 307 Jazz and Blues, LaFayette, USA
25 Neil's, Memphis, USA
26 House of Rock, St Louis, USA
28–29 Gatsby's, Johnson City, USA
30 Handlebar, Greenville, USA

2006

January
19 Kulturetage, Oldenburg, Germany
20 Quasimodo, Berlin, Germany
21 Zur Linde, Affalter, Germany
22 Alter Schlacthof, Dresden, Germany
24 Hirsch, Nurnberg, Germany
25 Muffathalle, Munich, Germany
26 Spectrum, Augsburg, Germany
27 Sudhaus, Tubingen, Germany
28 Schulturnhalle, Winterbach, Germany
29 Musiktheater Rex, Lorsch, Germany
31 Die Kantine, Koln, Germany

February
1   Matrix, Bochum, Germany
2   Rosenhof, Osnabrueck, Germany
3   Music Hall, Worpswede, Germany
4   Halle 400, Kiel, Germany
5   Amager Bio, Kobenhavn S, Denmark
6   Fabrik, Hamburg, Germany
8   Blues Garage, Hannover-Isernhagen, Germany
9   Colos Saal, Aschaffenburg, Germany
10 Z7, Pratteln, Switzerland
12 Theatercafe Schuttershof, Middelburg, Netherlands
13 De Kade, Zaandam, Netherlands
14 Spirit of 66, Verviers, Belgium
15 De Boerderij, Zoetermeer, Netherlands
16 Metropool, Hengelo, Netherlands
17 Hedon, Zwolle, Netherlands
18 Plato, Helmond, Netherlands

March
9   The Ferry, Glasgow
10 Pacific Road Arts Centre, Birkenhead
11 O2 Academy, Newcastle-upon-Tyne
12 The Boardwalk, Sheffield
13 The Limelight Club, Crewe
14 The Springhead, Hull
16 The Rescue Rooms, Nottingham
17 Invicta Hall, Maidstone
18 Y Theatre, Leicester
19 Robin 2, Wolverhampton
20 Honiton Motel, Honiton
21 Cox's Yard, Stratford Upon Avon
22 Burnley Mechanics, Burnley
24 Whelan's, Dublin, Ireland
26 The Lowry, Manchester
27 The Stables, Milton Keynes
28 Swindon Art Centre, Swindon
29 The Brook, Southampton
31 Pigs Nose Inn

April
1   Cheese & Grain, Frome, Somerset
2   Muni Arts Centre, Pontypridd, Wales
4   The Waterfront, Norwich
5   Martlet's Hall, West Sussex
6   Gloucester Guildhall, Gloucester
7   Astoria 2, London
8   The Maltings, Farnham
9   The Junction, Cambridge
20 Hungry Tiger, Manchester, USA
21 InterMedia Arts Center, Huntington, USA
22 Recher Theatre, Towson, USA
24 Winchester Music Hall, Lakewood, USA
25 Intersection, Grand Rapids, USA
26 Chicago City Limits, Schaumburg, USA
27 Shank Hall, Milwaukee, USA
28 Clark Place, Stevens Point, USA
29 The Chesterfield, Sioux City, USA

May

1 Little Bear Saloon, Evergreen, USA
3 The Santa Fe, Las Vegas, USA
4 Boulder Station Casino, Las Vegas, USA
5 Coach House, San Juan Capistrano, USA
6 Humphrey's by the Bay, San Diego, USA
9 The Last Day Saloon, Santa Rosa, USA
12 Aladdin Theater, Portland, USA
13 JazzBones, Tacoma, USA
14 The Yale, Vancouver, BC, Canada

June

2 Festival de Guitare, Morzine, France
3 Le Cargo, Arles, France
5 Le New Morning, Paris, France
6 De Nieuwe Wijngaard, Oeffelt, Netherlands
7 Club de Bosuil, Weert, Netherlands
8 Arrow Classic Rock Fest, Lichtenvoorde, Netherlands

July

5 Festival Bulgaria, Bulgaria
7 Legends of Rock Festival, Wiesen, Austria
8 Burg Clam Festival, Clam, Austria
22 Burg Herzberg Festival, Fulda, Germany
28 Rock of Ages Festival, Stuttgart, Germany
30 Museumsmeile, Bonn, Germany

October

4 Huntingdon Hall, Worcester
5 Mr Kyps, Poole
7–8 Redstack Playhouse, Bexhill on Sea
9 Theatr Brycheiniog, Brecon
10 The Stables, Milton Keynes
11 The Standard, London
12 The Brook, Southampton
13 Pontardawe Arts Centre, Pontardawe

14 The Wharf, Tavistock
15 The Fleece, Bristol
16 Glee Club, Cardiff
18 Chiddingfold Club, Chiddingfold
19 Brindley Arts Centre, Runcorn
20 Picturedrome, Holmfirth
21 Wilbarston Hall, Wilbarston
22 Robin 2, Wolverhampton
24 Irish Centre, Leeds
25 O2 Academy, Newcastle-upon-Tyne
26 Perth Concert Hall, Perth
27 Lochgelly Centre, Lochgelly
28 Lemon Tree, Aberdeen
30 Cox's Yard, Stratford Upon Avon
31 The Limelight Club, Crewe

November

1 Festival Hall, Bolton
2 The Ferry, Glasgow
3 The Platform, Morecambe
4 Chesterfield (*AshCon*)
15 Sellersville Theater, Sellersville, USA
16 Bank Street, New London, USA
17 Bull Run, Shirley, USA
18 The Van Dyck Club, Schenectady, USA
19 Infinity, Buffalo, USA
20 Moondog's, Blawnox, USA
21 Thirsty Ear, Columbus, USA
24 House of Rock, Eau Claire, USA

December

9 G Lawrence Sportshall, Hartenhoom, Germany

2007

January

5 Plato, Helmond, Netherlands
6 Club Lantaarn, Hellendoor, Netherlands
7 Spirit of 66, Verviers, Belgium
8 Cape Holland Studio 62, Den Helder, Netherlands
10 Musiktheater Rex, Lorsch, Germany

11 Gewerkschaftshaus, Erfurt, Germany
12 Substage, Karlsruhe, Germany
13 Die Halle, Reichenbach, Germany
14 Ducsaal, Freudenburg, Germany
15 Z7, Pratteln, Switzerland
16 Spectrum, Augsburg, Germany
17 Alte Molzerei, Regensburg, Germany
19 Colos Saal, Aschaffenburg, Germany
20 Live Club Barmen, Wuppertal,
   Germany
21 Die Kantin, Koln, Germany
22 Rosenhof, Osnabrueck, Germany
23 Fabrik, Hamburg, Germany
24 Quasimodo, Berlin, Germany
26 Zur Linde, Affalter, Germany
27 Music Hall, Worpswede, Germany
28 Meier Music Hall, Braunschweig,
   Germany
29 Blues Garage, Hannover-Isernhagen,
   Germany

March
16 Apelsin Club, Moscow, Russia

April
6 The Boardwalk, Sheffield
12 The Platform, Morecambe
13 Robin 2, Wolverhampton
14 Corn Exchange Theatre, Stamford
15 The Boardwalk, Sheffield
16 The Limelight Club, Crewe
17 Kite Club, Blackpool
18 The Springhead, Hull
19 The Rescue Rooms, Nottingham
20 Pacific Road Arts Centre, Birkenhead
21 Cheese & Grain, Frome
22 Gloucester Guildhall, Gloucester
24 Aberystwyth Arts Centre, Abersystwyth
25 Queen's Hall, Narbeth
26 Phoenix Theatre, Exeter
27 Pigs Nose Inn,Devon
28 The Acorn, Penzance
30 Beaufort Theatre, Ebbw Vale

May
1 The Maltings, Farnham
2 Cox's Yard, Stratford Upon Avon
4 Redstack Playhouse, Bexhill on Sea
5 Y Theatre, Leicester
6 Robin 2, Wolverhampton
8 The Stables, Milton Keynes
9 The Waterfront, Norwich
10 The Junction, Cambridge
11 Astoria 2, London
12 The Lowry, Manchester
13 The Ferry, Glasgow
14 O2 Academy, Newcastle-upon-Tyne
15 PJ Molloy's, Dunfermline
26 Kammena Vourla, Athens, Greece

August
4 Guitar Festival, Zajecar, Serbia
9 Cropredy Festival, Cropredy
10 Waerdse Tempel, Heerhugowaard,
   Netherlands
11 Pink Pop Festival, Netherlands
18 The Woolpack, Doncaster
19 Rockinbeerfest, Huntingdon
25 Logopak, Hartenholm, Germany

October
4 Harlequin Theatre, Redhill
5 Mick Jagger Centre, Dartford
6 Wilbarston Hall, Wilbarston
7 Robin 2, Wolverhampton
8 The Stables, Milton Keynes
10 Mr Kyps, Poole
11 The Wharf, Tavistock
12 Princess Pavilion, Falmouth
13 The Landmark, Ilfracombe
14 The Fleece, Bristol
16 Cox's Yard, Stratford Upon Avon
17 Glee Club, Cardiff
18 Arts Centre, Pontardawe
19 Carling Academy 2, Liverpool
20 Brewery Arts Centre, Kendal
22 The Limelight Club, Crewe

23 Irish Centre, Leeds
24 Picturedrome, Holmfirth
25 The Ice Factory, Perth
26 Lemon Tree, Aberdeen
27 Ironworks, Inverness
28 The Ferry, Glasgow
29 O2 Academy, Newcastle-upon-Tyne
31 Huntingdon Hall, Worcester
November
1 The Citadel, St Helens
2 Academy 3, Manchester
3 Chesterfield (*AshCon*)
8 The Nerve Centre, Derry
9 Spring & Airbrake, Belfast
10 The Village, Dublin, Ireland
24 Ramshead Tavern, Annapolis, USA
25 Towne Crier, Beacon, USA
26 The Tralf Music Hall, Buffalo, USA
27 Thirsty Ear, Columbus, USA
29 Voodoo Café, Maryland Heights, USA
December
1 Chicago City Limits, Schaumburg, USA
2 The Narrows, Orono, USA
4 Shank Hall, Milwaukee, USA
5 Winchester Music Hall, Lakewood, USA
6 Moondog's, Blawnox, USA
8 Bull Run, Shirley, USA
10 Iron Horse Music Hall, Northhampton, USA
11 The State Theatre, Falls Church, USA
13 Sellersville Theater, Sellersville, USA

2008
January
16 Outbaix, Ubach-Palenberg, Germany
17 Die Kantine, Koln, Germany
18 Rosenhof, Osnabrueck, Germany
19 Zur Linde, Affalter, Germany
20 Gewerkschaftshaus, Erfurt, Germany
22 Quasimodo, Berlin, Germany

23 Meier Music Hall, Braunschweig, Germany
24 Fabrik, Hamburg, Germany
25 Amager Bio, Kobenhavn, Denmark
26 Blues Garage, Hannover-Isernhagen, Germany
27 Zeche, Bochum, Germany
February
6 Le Ziquodrome, Compiegne, France
7 Le Plan, Ris Orangis, France
8 De Kade, Zaandam, Netherlands
9 Plato, Helmond, Netherlands
10 Metropool, Hengelo, Netherlands
12 Hirsch, Nurnberg, Germany
13 Colos Saal, Aschaffenburg, Germany
13 Jazzhaus, Freiburg im Breisgau, Germany
16 Substage, Karlsruhe, Germany
17 Z7, Pratteln, Switzerland
18 Roxy Music Hall, Ulm, Germany
19 Georg-Elser-Halle, Munich, Germany
21 Musiktheater Rex, Lorsch, Germany
22 Ducsaal, Freudenburg, Germany
23 Lehenbachhalle, Winterbach, Germany
24 Spirit of 66, Verviers, Belgium
28 Chollerhalle, Zug, Switzerland
29 Bahnhof Fischbach, Friedrichshafen, Germany
March
1 Sounddock 14, Zurich, Switzerland
April
4 Pacific Road Arts Centre, Birkenhead
5 The Lowry, Manchester
6 The Boardwalk, Sheffield
7 The Limelight Club, Crewe
9 Carnegie Theatre, Workington
10 The Ferry, Glasgow
11 Liquid Room, Edinburgh
12 The Platform, Morecambe
13 Robin 2, Wolverhampton
15 Martlets Hall, West Sussex

17 The Brook, Southampton
18 Cheese & Grain, Frome
19 Pigs Nose Inn, Devon
21 Daddy Cool's, Knaresborough
22 Cox's Yard, Stratford Upon Avon
23 Intake, Mansfield
24 Savoy, Monmouth
25 Bridgend Recreation Centre
26 The Wyeside, Builth Wells
27 Harpenden Public Halls, Hertfordshire
29 The Stables, Milton Keynes
30 The Waterfront, Norwich

May

1 The Junction, Cambridge
2 Astoria 2, London
3 Corn Exchange, Bourne
4 Rites of Spring Festival, Glenside, USA
5 Ramshead Tavern, Annapolis, USA
6 XM Radio Live Broadcast, Washington DC, USA
8 Boulder Station Casino, Las Vegas, USA
9 Coach House, San Juan Capistrano, USA
10 Humphrey's by the Bay, San Diego, USA
12 Little Fox Theatre, Redwood City, USA
15 Macos Place, Silverton, USA
16 Aladdin Theater, Portland, USA
17 JazzBones, Tacoma, USA
18 The Yale, Vancouver, BC, Canada
29 Het Spoor, Harelbeke, Belgium
30 Alem Pop, Alem, Netherlands
31 Fenix, Sittard, Netherlands

June

1 Iduna, Drachten, Netherlands
28 Blues En Bourgogne, Le Creusot, France

August

17 Lovely Days Festival, A-Wiesen, Austria
23 Rock Op n Dorp, Hartenholm, Germany

September

4–7 AshFest: Club Med Sandpiper, St Lucie, USA
9 B.B. King's, New York, USA
10 Sellersville Theater, Sellersville, USA
11 Chan's, Woonsockett, USA
12 Ridgefield Playhouse, Ridgefield, USA
13 Boulton Theater, Bay Shore, USA
14 Bull Run, Shirley, USA
27 Chesterfield (*AshCon*)

October

2 Muni Arts Centre, Pontypridd
3 Harlequin Theatre, Redhill
4 Tivoli Theatre, Wimborne, Dorset
7 The Stables, Milton Keynes
8 The Standard, London
9 Wedgewood Rooms, Portsmouth
10 Phoenix Theatre, Exeter
11 Hall for Cornwall, Truro
12 The Maltings, Farnham
13 12 Bar, Swindon
15 Thekla, Bristol
16 Huntingdon Hall, Worcester
17 Picturedrome, Holmfirth
18 Academy 2, Manchester
19 Blackpool Tower, Blackpool
22 Rio's, Leeds
23 The Ferry, Glasgow
24 Lochgelly Centre, Lochgelly
25 The Caves, Edinburgh
26 Ironworks, Inverness
29 Pocklington Arts Centre, Pocklington
30 O2 Academy, Newcastle-upon-Tyne
31 Corn Exchange Theatre, Stamford

November

1 Wilbarston Hall, Wilbarston

December

2 Le New Morning, Paris, France
4 LA Forge 92, Le Chambon-Feugerolles, France
5–6 Le Moods, Monaco

2009

January

7 Spirit of 66, Verviers, Belgium
8 Mezz, Breda, Netherlands
9 De Pul, Uden, Netherlands
10 P3, Purmerend, Netherlands
11 Schuttershof, Middelburg, Netherlands
13 Kulturfabrik, Krefeld, Germany
15 Ducsaal, Freudenburg, Germany
16 Outbaix, Ubach-Palenberg, Germany
17 Centre Culturel, L-Dudelange, Luxembourg
18 Jazzhaus, Freiburg im Breisgau, Germany
19 Z7, Pratteln, Switzerland
21 Sudhaus, Tubingen, Germany
22 Musiktheater Rex, Lorsch, Germany
23 Die Scheuer, Idstein, Wörsdorf, Germany
24 Blues Garage, Hannover-Isernhagen, Germany
25 Quasimodo, Berlin, Germany
27 Hirsch, Nurnberg, Germany
28 Colos Saal, Aschaffenburg, Germany
29 Die Kantine, Koln, Germany
30 Capitol, Paderborn, Germany
31 Music Hall, Worpswede, Germany

February

10 Szene, Vienna, Austria
11 Spectrum, Augsburg, Germany
12 Alte Mulzerei, Regensburg, Germany
13 Zur Linde, Affalter, Germany
14 Gewerkschaftshaus, Erfurt, Germany
15 Alte Stadthalle, Melle, Germany
16 Fabrik, Hamburg, Germany
17 Pumpe, Kiel, Germany
19 Trudgorn, Goteborg, Sweden
21 Byscenen, Haugesund, Norway
22 Rick's Theatre, Bergen, Norway

April

10 Blues Rock Legends Night, La Poudriere, France
23 The Brook, Southampton
24 The Globe, Cardiff
25 Cheese & Grain, Frome
26 Honiton Motel, Honiton
28 Kiddlington FC, Kidlington
30 Theatre Royal, Wakefield

May

1 The Boardwalk, Sheffield
2 Pacific Road Arts Centre, Birkenhead
3 The Lowry, Manchester
6 The Volunteer Hall, Galashiels
7 The Ferry, Glasgow
8 The Crypt, Middlesbrough
9 M Club, Crewe
10 Robin 2, Wolverhampton
12 The Stables, Milton Keynes
13 The Waterfront, Norwich
14 The Junction, Cambridge
15 Peterborough Park, Peterborough
16 Shepherd's Bush Empire, London

June

6 Working Class Hero Festival, Drammen, Norway
13 La Loco, Mézidon-Canon, France

August

15 Jagdschlopark, Arnsberg-Herdringen, Germany
27 Bibelot, Dordrecht, Netherlands
28 Open Keuken, Doetinchem, Netherlands
29 Fiesta City, Verviers, Belgium
30 The Rock Temple, Kerkrade, Netherlands

September

17 Olsztyn Bohema Club, Olsztyn, Poland
18 Od zmierzchu do switu, Wroclaw, Poland
19 Rzeszow Imperium Hotel, Rzeszow, Poland

20 Lizard King Club, Torun, Poland
October
2   The Globe, Cardiff
3   The Regal, Oxford
4   Sin City, Swansea
5   Gibson-Planet Rock, London
6   Hawth Theatre, Crawley
7   Komedia, Bath
8   Queen's Theatre, Barnstaple, Devon
9   Princess Pavilion, Falmouth
10 City Hall, Salisbury
11 Rock'n'Blues Festival, Cromer
12 Cox's Yard, Stratford Upon Avon
13 The Rescue Rooms, Nottingham
15 The Festival Hall, Bolton
16 Picturedrome, Holmfirth
17 Forum 28, Barrow-in-Furness
18 Grand Opera House, York
22 The Ferry, Glasgow
23 Lochgelly Centre, Lochgelly
24 Queen's Hall, Edinburgh
25 Lemon Tree, Aberdeen
27 O2 Academy, Newcastle-upon-Tyne
29 Theatre Royal, St Helen's
30 Town Hall, Birmingham
31 Wilbarston Hall, Wilbarston
November
1   Mick Jagger Centre, Dartford
2   The Stables, Milton Keynes
4   Stadtkeller, Luzern, Switzerland
5   Bahnhof Fischtold, Friedrichshafen,
    Germany

2010
January
14 Mezz, Breda, Netherlands
15 De Kelder, Amersfoort, Netherlands
16 De Pul, Uden, Netherlands
17 Paradiso, Amsterdam, Netherlands
19 Harmonie, Bonn, Germany
20 Borse, Wuppertal, Germany

21 Ducsaal, Freudenburg, Germany
22 Alte Piesel, Fulda, Germany
23 Lokschuppen im Brenzpark,
    Heidenheim, Germany
24 Substage, Karlsruhe, Germany
25 Z7, Pratteln, Switzerland
27 Colos Saal, Aschaffenburg, Germany
28 Musiktheater Rex, Lorsch, Germany
29 Gewerkschaftshaus, Erfurt, Germany
30 Blues Garage, Hannover-Isernhagen,
    Germany
31 Pulp, Duisburg, Germany
February
6   Le Bois Aux Dames, Samoëns, France
10 Seifenfabrik, Graz, Austria
11 Rockhouse, Salzburg, Austria
12 Die Halle, Reichenbach, Germany
13 Zur Linde, Affalter, Germany
14 Retro Music Hall, Prague, Czech
    Republic
16 Proxima, Warsaw, Poland
17 Eskulap, Poznan, Poland
18 Quasimodo, Berlin, Germany
19 Zum Rautenkranz, Barby, Germany
20 Music Hall, Worpswede, Germany
21 Rosenhof, Osnabrueck, Germany
23 Fabrik, Hamburg, Germany
24 Roxy, Flensburg, Germany
25 Amager Bio, Kobenhavn, Denmark
26 Herr Nilsen, Oslo, Norway
27 Tribute, Sandnes, Norway
March
1   Bingo, Lillehammer, Norway
4   On The Rocks, Helsinki, Finland
13 Abbeville Theatre, Abbeville, France
    (Andy with Pat McManus)
17 Le Trabendo, Paris, France (Andy with
    Pat McManus)
19 La Luciole, Alençon, France (Andy
    with Pat McManus)
24 Ramshead Tavern, Annapolis, USA

25 Sellersville Theater, Sellersville, USA

26 Bull Run, Shirley, USA

27 Boulton Theater, Bay Shore, USA (with Roger Filgate)

28 Moondog's, Blawnox, USA

29 Winchester Music Hall, Lakewood, USA

30 Callahan's, Auburn Hills, USA

April

1 Voodoo Café, Maryland Heights, USA

2 Fitzgerald's, Berwyn, USA

3 Shank Hall, Milwaukee, USA

7 Kammgarn, Schaffhausen, Switzerland

8 Moonwalker, Aarburg, Switzerland

9 Naima Club, Forli, Italy

10 Cinema Teatro Parrocchiale, Cologne, Italy

11 Crossroads Live Club, Rome, Italy

23 Phoenix Theatre, Exeter

24 Cheese & Grain, Frome, Somerset

25 Mr Kyps, Poole

26 Pontardawe Arts Centre, Pontardawe

28 The Caves, Edinburgh

29 The Ferry, Glasgow

30 Academy 2, Manchester

May

1 The Brickyard, Carlisle

2 The Sugarmill, Hanley

4 Irish Centre, Leeds

5 Birdwell Venue, Barnsley

6 The Platform, Morecambe

7 Brindley Arts Centre, Runcorn

8 Pacific Road Arts Centre, Birkenhead

9 Robin 2, Wolverhampton

10 The Stables, Milton Keynes

13 The Junction, Cambridge

14 The Maltings, Farnham

15 Shepherd's Bush Empire, London (with Mostly Autumn / Panic Room)

16 Gloucester Guildhall, Gloucester

28 The Coca-Cola Dome, Johannesburg, South Africa (with Uriah Heep / Deep Purple)

30 ICC Durban Arena, Durban, South Africa (with Uriah Heep / Deep Purple)

June

1 Grand Arena, Cape Town, South Africa (with Uriah Heep / Deep Purple)

July

10 Classic Rock Night, Nuremburg, Germany

17 Kloster Open Air Festival, Benediktbeuern, Germany (with Toto)

27 Humphrey's by the Bay, San Diego, USA

28 Arcadia Blues Club, Arcadia, USA

29 Coach House, San Juan Capistrano, USA

30 Aladdin Theater, Portland, USA

31 Satsop River Rock Festival, Hoquiam, USA

August

14 Club Citta, Kawasaki, Tokyo, Japan

15 Club Citta, Kawasaki, Tokyo, Japan

21 Rock Knights Festival, La Couvertoirade, France

September

11 Burgkultur Open Air, Herzogburg, Klagenfurt, Austria

17 Festival Place, Sherwood Park, Alberta, Canada

24 Edmond Town Hall, Newtown, USA (with Roger Filgate)

October

8 City Hall, Salisbury

9 Wilbarston Hall, Wilbarston

10 The River Rooms, Stourbridge

11 The Rescue Rooms, Nottingham

13 The Grand, Clitheroe (live CD recording)

15 Fat Sams, Dundee

16 The Ferry, Glasgow
17 The Caves, Edinburgh
20 Fibbers, York
22 O2 Academy, Newcastle-upon-Tyne
23 Picturedrome, Holmfirth
24 Bridgend Recreation Centre
25 Telford's Warehouse, Chester
26 The Horn, St Albans
27 The Standard, London
28 White Rock Theatre, Hastings, East
Sussex
30 Harlequin Theatre, Redhill
November
1 Sub 89, Reading
2 The Stables, Milton Keynes
6 The Winding Wheel, Chesterfield
(*AshCon*)
December
2 La Boite à Musique, Wattrelos, France
3 Paulette, Pagney derrière Barine, France
4 La Loco, Mézidon-Canon, France
5 Le Plan, Ris Orangis, France

2011
January
8 Zaal Art-Cube, Gent, Belgium
9 De Kelder, Amersfoort, Netherlands
10 Spirit of 66, Verviers, Belgium
11 De Kade, Zaandam, Netherlands
12 De Boerderij, Zoetermeer, Netherlands
13 Hedon, Zwolle, Netherlands
13 De Pul, Uden, Netherlands
15 Open Keuken, Doetinchem,
Netherlands
16 Schuttershof, Middelburg, Netherlands
18 Harmonie, Bonn, Germany
19 Kulturfabrik, Krefeld, Germany
20 Kulturetage, Oldenburg, Germany
21 Rosenhof, Osnabrueck, Germany
22 Blues Garage, Hannover-Isernhagen,
Germany

23 Vest Arena, Recklinghausen, Germany
25 Colos Saal, Aschaffenburg, Germany
26 Musiktheater Rex, Lorsch, Germany
27 Centre Culturel, L-Dudelange,
Luxembourg
28 Cafe Hahn, Koblenz, Germany
29 Die Scheuer, Idstein, Wörsdorf,
Germany
30 Jazzhaus, Freiburg im Breisgau,
Germany
February
5 Le Bois Aux Dames, Samoëns, France
9 Reigen, Wien, Austria
10 Spectrum, Augsburg, Germany
11 Muehle Hunziken, Rubigen,
Switzerland
12 Schüür, Luzern, Switzerland
13 Z7, Pratteln, Switzerland
15 Sudhaus, Tubingen, Germany
16 Hirsch, Nurnberg, Germany
17 Malzhaus, Plauen, Germany
18 Zur Linde, Affalter, Germany
19 Quasimodo, Berlin, Germany
20 Der Speicher, Schwerin, Germany
21 Fabrik, Hamburg, Germany
22 Pumpe, Kiel, Germany
24 Club Eter, Wroclaw, Poland
25 Kwadrat, Kraków, Poland
26 Proxima, Warsaw, Poland
27 Klub Parlament, Gdańsk, Poland
28 Od Nowa, Torun, Poland
March
1 Kawon, Zielona Góra, Poland
4 Music Majestic Club, Bratislava,
Slovakia
5 Sportovni Hala, Zlínský kraj, Kunovice,
Czech Republic
6 Retro Music Hall, Prague, Czech
Republic
26 Cheese & Grain, Frome
29 Muni Arts Centre, Pontypridd

30 The Brook, Southampton
31 Islington Academy, London
April
1 Corn Exchange, Bourne
2 The Arkenstall Centre, Haddenham
3 Kiddlington FC, Kidlington
6 The Flowerpot, Derby
7 Brewery Arts Centre, Kendal
8 Pacific Road Arts Centre. Birkenhead
9 The Ferry, Glasgow
11 The Stables, Milton Keynes
14 Spring & Airbrake, Belfast (Pat
   McManus Band + Andy Powell)
15 TLT Theatre, Drogheda, Ireland (Pat
   McManus Band + Andy Powell)
16 Slaughtered Lamb, Swords, Ireland (Pat
   McManus Band + Andy Powell)
25 Tupelo Music Hall, Londonderry, USA
26 Tupelo Music Hall, White River
   Junction, USA
27 Sellersville Theater, Sellersville, USA
28 Ramshead Tavern, Annapolis, USA
29 B.B. King's, New York, USA
30 The Van Dyck Club, Schenectady,
   USA
May
2 Winchester Music Hall, Lakewood,
   USA
3 Callahan's, Auburn Hills, USA
4 4D's, Fort Wayne, USA
5 Midway Tavern, Mishawaka/South
   Bend, USA
6 Fitzgerald's, Berwyn, USA
7 Shank Hall, Milwaukee, USA
11 Sioux City Community Theater, Sioux
   City, USA
12 Whiskey Roadhouse, Council Bluffs,
   USA
13 Knuckleheads, Kansas City, USA
14 Wildey Theatre, Edwardsville, USA
15 Cosmic Charlie's, Lexington, USA

16 Moondog's, Blawnox, USA
17 Bridge Street Live, Collinsville, USA
July
23 Silverstone Classic Festival, Towcester
August
27 Club Citta, Kawasaki, Tokyo, Japan
28 Hibiya Park Music Hall, Tokyo, Japan
   (with Kansas and PFM)
October
5 New Morning, Paris, France
7 Tivoli Theatre, Wimborne
8 Miners' Institute, Blackwood
9 Robin 2, Wolverhampton
12 The Waterfront, Norwich
13 The Standard, London
14 Martlets Hall, West Sussex
15 The Grand, Clitheroe
17 Buxton Opera House, Buxton
19 Doncaster Civic Theatre, Waterdale
22 O2 Academy, Newcastle-upon-Tyne
23 The Stables, Milton Keynes
29 The Ferry, Glasgow
30 Lemon Tree, Aberdeen

2012
January
11 Spirit of 66, Verviers, Belgium
12 Dru Frabriek, Ulft, Netherlands
13 De Boerderij, Zoetermeer, Netherlands
14 De Pul, Uden, Netherlands
15 Gebouw T, Bergen op Zoom,
   Netherlands
17 Die Kantine, Koln, Germany
18 Outbaix, Ubach-Palenberg, Germany
19 Live Club Barmen, Wuppertal,
   Germany
20 Rosenhof, Osnabrueck, Germany
21 Blues Garage, Hannover-Isernhagen,
   Germany
22 Pulp, Duisburg, Germany
24 Hirsch, Nurnberg, Germany

25 Quasimodo, Berlin, Germany
26 Musiktheater Piano, Dortmund, Germany
27 Ducsaal, Freudenburg, Germany
28 Cafe Hahn, Koblenz, Germany
29 Scala, Ludwigsburg, Germany
31 Freiheiz, Munich, Germany

February

1 Sounddock 14, Dietikon, Zurich, Switzerland
2 Alte Molzerei, Regensburg, Germany
3 Alte Piesel, Fulda, Germany
4 Komma, Wurgl, Austria
5 Reigen, Wien, Austria
7 Kulturladen, Konstanz, Germany
9 Musiktheater Rex, Lorsch, Switzerland
10 Zur Linde, Affalter, Germany
11 HsD, Erfurt, Germany
12 Spectrum, Augsburg, Germany
13 Colos Saal, Aschaffenburg, Germany
15 Fabrik, Hamburg, Germany
16 Music Hall, Worpswede, Germany
17 Amager Bio, Kobenhavn, Denmark
18 KB, Malmo, Sweden
19 Sticky Fingers, Gothenburg, Sweden

March

2 Theatre de Sochaux, Sochaux Cedex, France

April

6 La Poudriere, Leffrinckoucke, France
7 Le Forum, Vaureal, France
24 Bridge Street Live, Collinsville, USA
25 Ramshead Tavern, Annapolis, USA
26 Sellersville Theater, Sellersville, USA
27 Tupelo Music Hall, Londonderry, USA
28 Mauch Chunk Opera House, Jim Thorpe, USA
29 American Ukranian Cultural Center, Whippany, USA
30 B.B. King's, New York, USA

May

1 Winchester Music Hall, Lakewood, USA
2 Callahan's, Auburn Hills, USA
3 Midway Tavern, Mishawaka/South Bend, USA
4 Fitzgerald's, Berwyn, USA
6 Shank Hall, Milwaukee, USA
7 Wildey Theatre, Edwardsville, USA
8 Knuckleheads, Kansas City, USA

June

2 Highlands Festival, Amersfoort, Netherlands

July

21 Burg Herzberg Festival, Fulda, Germany

August

6 La Foire Aux Vins, Colmar, France (with Thin Lizzy and Toto)

September

20 Theatre Krizanke, Ljubljana, Slovenia
22 Fest Les Grosses Guitares, Messimy, France

October

4 The Guildhall, St Ives
5 Tivoli Theatre, Wimborne
6 Cheese & Grain, Frome
7 Corn Exchange, Exeter
8 Swindon Art Centre, Swindon
9 The Maltings, Farnham
11 Huntingdon Hall, Worcester
12 Pontardawe Arts Centre, Pontardawe
13 Robin 2, Wolverhampton
16 The Flowerpot, Derby
17 O2 Academy, Newcastle-upon-Tyne
18 The Ferry, Glasgow
19 The Jam House, Edinburgh
20 Lochgelly Centre, Lochgelly
21 Lemon Tree, Aberdeen
23 Bootleggers Music Bar, Kendal
26 Mick Jagger Centre, Dartford
27 Floral Pavilion Theatre, New Brighton

28 The Lowry, Manchester
30 The Stables, Milton Keynes
31 King Edward VII Hall, Newmarket
November
2 Picturedrome, Holmfirth
3 The Winding Wheel, Chesterfield
   (*AshCon*)
December
8 Espace Athena, Saint-Saulve, France
9 Le Bota, Brussels, Belgium
10 New Morning, Paris, France
11 Le Cafe-Musiques Portail, Salon de
   Provence, France
12 Luz de Gas, Barcelona, Spain
13 Sala Cats, Madrid, Spain

2013
January
15 Spirit of 66, Verviers, Belgium
16 De Boerderij, Zoetermeer, Netherlands
17 Mezz, Breda, Netherlands
18 Pop Podium Romein, Leeuwarden,
   Netherlands
19 De Pul, Uden, Netherlands
20 ECI Cultuurfabriek, Roermond,
   Netherlands
22 Twist, Germany
23 Harmonie, Bonn, Germany
24 Kulturzentrum Dieselstrasse, Esslingen,
   Germany
25 Substage, Karlsruhe, Germany
26 Ballhaus, Rosenheim, Germany
27 Alte Seilerei, Mannheim, Germany
29 Ampere, Munchen, Germany
30 Hirsch, Nurnberg, Germany
31 Jazzhaus, Freiburg im Breisgau,
   Germany
February
1 Chollerhalle, Zug, Switzerland
2 Muehle Hunziken, Rubigen,
   Switzerland

3 Gewelbe Haiming, Haiming, Germany
5 Colos Saal, Aschaffenburg, Germany
6 Sudhaus, Tubingen, Germany
15 Rosenhof, Osnabrueck, Germany
16 Zur Linde, Affalter, Germany
17 Meier Music Hall, Braunschweig,
   Germany
19 Zentrum Altenberg, Oberhausen,
   Germany
20 Fabrik, Hamburg, Germany
21 Moritzbastei, Leipzig, Germany
22 Blues Garage, Hannover-Isernhagen,
   Germany
23 Quasimodo, Berlin, Germany
24 Musiktheater Piano, Dortmund,
   Germany
28 Tupelo Music Hall, Londonderry, USA
March
1 Towne Crier, Beacon, USA
2 Record Collector, Bordentown, USA
3 American Ukranian Cultural Center,
   Whippany, USA
5 Bridge Street Live, Collinsville, USA
6 Bull Run, Shirley, USA
7 Sellersville Theater, Sellersville, USA
8 Iridium, New York, USA
9 Mauch Chunk Opera House, Jim
   Thorpe, USA
10 Wellsboro House, Wellsboro, USA
11 Winchester Music Hall, Lakewood,
   USA
12 Callahan's, Auburn Hills, USA
13 Fitzgerald's, Berwyn, USA
14 Pabst Theater, Milwaukee, USA
16 Festival Place, Alberta, Canada
19 The Venue, Vancouver, BC, Canada
20 JazzBones, Tacoma, USA
21 Aladdin Theater, Portland, USA
April
10 Le Ziquodrome, Compiegne, France
11 Le Plan, Ris Orangis, France

12 Toulon Omega Live, Toulon, France
29 Stary Dom Club, Domecko, Poland
30 Bielskie Centrum Kultury, Bielsko
Biala, Poland

May

1 Sala Urzedu Gminy, Kolbudy, Poland
2 Klub Wytwornia, Lodz, Poland
3 Centrum Kultury Grodzisk, Mazowiecki, Poland
4 Rock Festival, Krosno, Poland
5 Burnley Rock & Blues Festival
9 Jolly Joker, Istanbul, Turkey
10 Jolly Joker, Ankara, Turkey

July

20 Montraker Live Festival, Vrsar, Croatia

August

24 Fiesta City Festival, Verviers, Belgium

October

4 Tivoli Theatre, Wimborne
5 Cheese & Grain, Frome
6 Robin 2, Wolverhampton
7 Swindon Art Centre, Swindon
8 Islington Academy, London
10 The Globe, Cardiff
12 Wilbarston Hall, Wilbarston
13 The Wharf, Tavistock
15 The Stables, Milton Keynes
16 King Edward VII Memorial Hall, Newmarket
17 Dorking Halls, Dorking
18 Picturedrome, Holmfirth
19 Floral Pavilion Theatre, New Brighton
20 The Box, Crewe
22 The Flowerpot, Derby
23 The Cluny, Newcastle upon Tyne
24 Bootleggers Music Bar, Kendal
25 The Jam House, Edinburgh
26 Ironworks, Inverness
27 The Ferry, Glasgow
30 The Artrix, Bromsgrove
31 The Brook, Southampton

November

2 The Winding Wheel, Chesterfield (*AshCon*)
16 Bluesonalia Festival, Konin, Poland

2014

January

15 Rockfabrik, Uebach, Germany
16 Patronaat, Haarlem, Netherlands
17 De Boerderij, Zoetermeer, Netherlands
18 De Pul, Uden, Netherlands
19 Burgerweeshuis, Deventer, Netherlands
20 Spirit of 66, Verviers, Belgium
22 Twist, Germany
23 Die Kantine, Koln, Germany
24 Die Scheuer, Idstein, Wörsdorf, Germany
25 Cafe Hahn, Koblenz, Germany
26 Zeche, Bochum, Germany
28 Reigen, Wien, Austria
29 Ampere, Munchen, Germany
30 Hirsch, Nurnberg, Germany
31 Zum Rautenkranz, Barby, Germany

February

1 Zur Linde, Affalter, Germany
2 Alte Piesel, Fulda, Germany
4 Rosenhof, Osnabrueck, Germany
5 Fabrik, Hamburg, Germany
6 Quasimodo, Berlin, Germany
7 Blues Garage, Hannover-Isernhagen, Germany
8 Music Hall, Worpswede, Germany
9 Zentrum Altenberg, Oberhausen, Germany
11 Colos Saal, Aschaffenburg, Germany
12 Kulturladen, Konstanz, Germany
13 Spectrum, Augsburg, Germany
14 Ducsaal, Freudenburg, Germany
15 Die Halle, Reichenbach, Germany
18 Alte Seilerei, Mannheim, Germany
19 Burghof, Lurrach, Germany

20 Casino Theater, Burgdorf, Switzerland
21 Chollerhalle, Zug, Switzerland
22 Muehle Hunziken, Rubigen, Switzerland
25 Eskulap, Poznan, Poland
26 Oerodek Kultury Andaluzja, Piekary Slaskie, Poland
27 Dom Kultury, Kety, Poland
28 Muzyczna Owczarnia, Szczawnica, Poland

April
5 Arc En Ciel, Lievin, France
9 3 Frontieres, Bartenheim, France
10 Divan du Monde, Paris, France
11 Salle Des Fetes, Savigny Sur Orge, France
12 Atelier Des Moles, Montbeliard, France
15 Lou's Blues, Indialantic, USA
16 The Plaza Live, Orlando, USA
17 Bamboo Room, Lake Worth, USA
18 Ringside Café, St Petersburg, USA
19 Variety Playhouse, Atlanta, USA
21 Rhythm & Brews, Chatanooga, USA
22 Neil's, Memphis, USA
23 Duling Hall, Jackson, USA
24 The Warehouse Live, Houston, USA
26 Poor David's Pub, Dallas, USA
27 The Roost, Austin, USA
29 The Dirty Bourbon, Albuquerque, USA

May
1 Hard Rock Cafe Las Vegas, Las Vegas, USA
2 The Rhythm Room, Phoenix, USA
3 Ramona Mainstage, Ramona, USA
4 Coach House, San Juan Capistrano, USA
5 Throckmorton Theatre, Mill Valley, USA
6 Auburn Event Center, Auburn, USA
8 Aladdin Theater, Portland, USA
9 JazzBones, Tacoma, USA

11 Triple Door, Seattle, USA

July
25 Rock of Ages Festival, Stuttgart, Germany
26 Chateau De Beaufort, Luxembourg

August
10 Cambridge Rock Festival

September
5 Stargazer Theater, Colorado Springs, USA
6 Soiled Dove, Denver, USA
8 Knuckleheads, Kansas City, USA
10 Famous Dave's, Minneapolis, USA
11 Turner Hall, Milwaukee, USA
12 Fitzgerald's, Berwyn, USA
13 Alton Amphitheater, Alton, USA
14 Midway Tavern, South Bend, USA
15 Callahan's, Auburn Hills, USA
17 Music Box, Cleveland, USA
18 Record Collector, Bordentown, USA
19 Mauch Chunk Opera House, Jim Thorpe, USA
20 Center for the Performing Arts, Natick, USA
21 Ramshead Tavern, Annapolis, USA
23 Sellersville Theater, Sellersville, USA
24 B.B. King's, New York, USA
25 Boulton Theater, Bay Shore, USA
26 Narrows Center for the Arts, Fall River, USA
27 Towne Crier, Beacon, USA
28 Infinity Hall, Norfolk, USA
29 Sportsmen's Tavern, Buffalo, USA
30 Hugh's Room, Toronto, ON, Canada

October
24 Tivoli Theatre, Wimborne
25 The Wharf, Tavistock
26 The Scene, Swansea
27 Llandudno Junction Labour Club, Llandudno
29 Quarterhouse, Folkestone

30 Harpenden Public Halls, Hertfordshire
31 Picturedrome, Holmfirth
November
1   Chesterfield (*AshCon*)
2   Yardbirds, Grimsby
4   The Stables, Milton Keynes
5   The Waterfront, Norwich
6   The Brook, Southampton
7   Martlets Hall, West Sussex
8   Islington Assembly Hall, London
9   King Edward VII Memorial Hall,
    Newmarket
11 The Flowerpot, Derby
12 The Cluny, Newcastle upon Tyne
13 The Ferry, Glasgow
14 The Jam House, Edinburgh
16 Lemon Tree, Aberdeen
18 Bootleggers Music Bar, Kendal
19 The Grand, Clitheroe
20 Leamington Assembly, Leamington Spa
21 Corn Exchange, Bourne
22 O2/2, Leicester

2015
January
9   Spirit of 66, Verviers, Belgium
10 Sudhaus, Tubingen, Germany
11 Spectrum, Augsburg, Germany
13 Hirsch, Nurnberg, Germany
14 Colos Saal, Aschaffenburg, Germany
15 Substage, Karlsruhe, Germany
16 Musiktheater Piano, Dortmund,
    Germany
17 Cafe Hahn, Koblenz, Germany
18 Kulturfabrik, Krefeld, Germany
20 Z7, Pratteln, Switzerland
21 Muehle Hunziken, Rubigen,
    Switzerland
22 Ampere, Munchen, Germany
23 Jazzhaus, Freiburg im Breisgau,
    Germany

24 Zur Linde, Affalter, Germany
25 Quasimodo, Berlin, Germany
27 Fabrik, Hamburg, Germany
28 Pumpwerk, Wilhelmshaven, Germany
29 Amager Bio, Kobenhavn, Denmark
30 Blues Garage, Hannover-Isernhagen,
    Germany
31 Music Hall, Worpswede, Germany
February
1   Forum Berufskolleg Schloss Neuhaus,
    Paderborn, Germany
3   Harmonie, Bonn, Germany
6   Podium Victorie, Alkmaar, Netherlands
7   De Pul, Uden, Netherlands
8   Club Gigant, Apeldoorn, Netherlands
9   Parktheater, Alphen aan den Rijn,
    Netherlands
March
28 Le Forum, Chauny, France
April
8   Rickshaw Theatre, Vancouver, Canada
9   One-Eyed Jack's Roadhouse,
    Lynnwood, USA
11 Aladdin Theater, Portland, USA
12 Triple Door, Seattle, USA
14 The Catalyst, Santa Cruz, USA
15 Yoshi's, Oakland, USA
17 Hopmonk Tavern, Sebastopol, USA
18 Bar and Grill, Corona, USA
23 Coach House, San Juan Capistrano,
    USA
25 Ramona Main Stage, Ramona, USA
26 The Rhythm Room, Phoenix, USA
29 The Roost, Austin, USA
30 Poor David's Pub, Dallas, USA
May
1   Aztec Theatre, San Antonio, USA
2   Dosey Doe, Conroe, USA
4   Duling Hall, Jackson, USA
5   WorkPlay, Birmingham, USA
6   Variety Playhouse, Atlanta, USA

16 Metropolis Studios, London (vinyl recording)

21–23 Le Triton, Les Lilas, France (live DVD recording)

25 Le Portail Coucou, Salon De Provence, France

26 Cafe del Teatre, Lleida, Spain

27 Sala Caracol, Madrid, Spain

28 Sala Razzmatazz, Barcelona, Spain

29 Private Show, London

July

5 Wutzdog Open Air, Dornstadt, Germany

11 Barnyard Cresta, Johannesburg, South Africa

12 Barnyard Parkview, Pretoria, South Africa

15 Rivonia, Johannesburg, South Africa

18 Barnyard, Willowbridge, Cape Town, South Africa

24 Keitelejazz, Äänekoski, Finland

October

2 The Haymarket, Basingstoke

3 Islington Assembly Hall, London

5 Dorking Halls, Dorking

6 The Stables, Milton Keynes

7 The Assembly, Leamington Spa

8 The Lowry, Salford

10 Chesterfield (*AshCon*)

11 The Engine Shed, Lincoln

13 Fibbers, York

15 Floral Pavilion Theatre, Merseyside

16 The Picturedrome, Holmfirth

18 King Edward VII Memorial Hall, Newmarket

20 Theatre Severn, Shrewsbury

22 Swindon Arts Centre, Swindon

23 Huntingdon Hall, Worcester

25 Ropetackle Arts Centre, Shoreham-By-Sea

27 The Flower Pot, Derby

28 Bootleggers, Kendal

29 The Ferry, Glasgow

30 The Jam House, Edinburgh

31 Lochgelly Centre, Lochgelly

November

1 Riverside Lodge, Morpeth

3 The Grand, Clitheroe

5 The Brook, Southampton

6 Tivoli Theatre, Wimborne Minster

7 Cheese & Grain, Frome

8 Phoenix Theatre, Exeter

ACKNOWLEDGEMENTS

Our thanks to Nigel Osborne and Tom Seabrook at Jawbone Press for taking on the book, and to Tom for all his hard work on proofing, typesetting, and indexing. Huge thanks to the following, who all contributed to the end result: Hannah Lawrence for undertaking the research at BBC Written Archives Centre in Caversham (a location not wholly convenient to either Belfast or Connecticut); Olwyn Dawson (always awesome) for help with interview transcribing; Rainer Frilund for generously checking the Select Discography and suggesting additions and corrections; Simon Atkinson for generously providing the 1969–99 concert listings; Mark Case for the cover design; Bob Lefsetz for allowing us to reproduce his Letter about 'Blowin' Free'; and the eagle-eyed Tony Bacon.

Andy thanks
All our fans who have supported us through the years and those who have urged me to pen this book. Pauline, and our sons Richard, Aynsley, and Lawrence, for their love, patience, and understanding on this journey. The current members and former members of Wishbone Ash, who have kept it real through the years. Leon Tsilis, Dr. John Brady, Guy and Sue Roberts, Andy Yates. Mike, Pauline and Guy Holt, Dave and Daniel Moore for their unswerving support, help and continued inspiration. Kate Goldsmith and Billy James for their work in publicising what we do.

Simon Atkinson, Rainer Frilund, Detlef Assenmacher for their help and studious cataloguing of the band archives. Patrick Fuchs for his insightful interviews. Pat Hyre for her exquisite Wishbone Ash jewelry. Kevin and Lyn Chilcott and family for their inspiration and incredible guitars. Jon Case for his amazing hand-crafted guitars and graphic design work. Andreas Kloppmann for the pickups. Our crew members through the years: Kevin Harrington, Chris Runciman, Terry Finn, Mark Emery, Mel Baister, Mal Ross, Richard Ames, Howard Barrett, Dudley, Mal Craggs, Granny Grange, Tom Hagan, Nick Sholem, Tony Self, Penny Gibbons, Sandro, Russell Sidelsky, Daniel Vetter, Holger Brandes, and Chris Boast. Our merchandisers: Carol Farnworth, Jan Krinsky, Susanne Panhans, Gema Dilf. There will be some crew folks that I've missed but I thank you all for helping us on our way. Thanks also to Christian Guyonnet, Mikaël Samson, and Martin Müller for the visual cataloging of our recent shows, and Tom Greenwood and Stephan Ernst for our recorded sound production. Barry Riddington and Malcolm Holmes plus Ralf Blasberg at our record labels. Special thanks to our agents: Patrik Mertens at A.S.S. Concerts and Promotion GmbH (Germany), Andy and Sarah Nye at Andy Nye Music (UK), Döm Bérard at 106 db (France), Rudolph Heiniss at NeBeLux (Netherlands), David Salter and Norman Dugdale (South Africa), and Steve Ozark at Oz Talent (USA). Our excellent legal team at Walker Morris: Patrick, Sam, Phil, Helen, Rose, et al.

To you Colin, my co-writer, for your boundless enthusiasm and passion for all things cultural from the latter part of the twentieth century, and for the taciturn wit and responses from the inimitable Heather.

Colin thanks

Heather, for putting up with all the Rock, be it Classic, Progressive, or Pantomime. Thanks to all the chaps in Wishbone Ash (band, crew, and Pauline) for being so welcoming—even Muddy. Thanks to

Bewley's Airport Hotel, Dublin, for several splendid bar/restaurant experiences along the way and to the discreetly unnamed hotel near Milton Keynes for providing so much fun with the rhubarb crumbles. And thank you Andy for making the process of working on this book such an enjoyable experience.

Photo credits

Front cover image by Juergen Spachmann/ bigface.de. Title page image by Michael Putland/Getty Images. All other interior photography from the author's collection. If you feel there has been a mistaken attribution, please contact the publishers.

CO-AUTHOR'S NOTE

Wishbone Ash today, as Andy once said to me, is about total transparency: interacting with fans in person and online, listening to their suggestions and observations, making time for them—because it's only through respect for the people who come to the shows that the good ship Wishbone continues. With that in mind, perhaps it would be of interest to explain the process of creating this book.

During 2012, in the early stages of working on a John McLaughlin book (*Bathed In Lightning*, published by Jawbone in 2014), Andy was kind enough to give me a phone interview toward it. I had the impression, from shooting the breeze after the interview, that Andy had thoughts around writing a book himself. When the McLaughlin project was completed I got

in touch again and offered my services if Andy felt he could use some help with it. We convened at Bewley's Airport Hotel, Dublin, in early April 2014—one hundred miles down the road from me, midway (ish) from Connecticut to Europe for Andy—to at least discuss how such a collaboration might work. We would stay over and Andy would fly on to his commitments in Europe early the next morning.

Andy has often said that, while taking his music and the business around keeping the show on the road very seriously, part of the package these days, for him, has to be fun. The ideal is a mix of creative energy, viable logistics, comfortable hotels, and a happy atmosphere. Count me in for all of the above. We got on very well at that first meeting on the book trail and certainly had a few laughs. After two or three hours of intensive discussion around the still-speculative project, we recorded an interview for another couple of hours—mostly around growing up in the 1950s. I went off and transcribed the interview, turned it into prose, with a small amount of ghostwriting around it (mostly contextual information on the period), and also entirely ghosted a few hundred words of Introduction to the book, capturing Andy's vision for it based on the intensive discussion we had had.

The ghosted Intro and draft opening chapter was enough to give Andy a feel for what the book might be, to fire him up with the knowledge that (a) he really did have a story to tell, and (b) we could productively work together on it. Andy is a musician first and foremost: he has long experience of giving interviews, presenting his thoughts with clear diction and clear sentence structure, and also writing short-form essays for online blogs. Writing a book is a different challenge. What I brought to the table was experience and instinct in creating long-form narratives. I'm also a fan of Wishbone Ash but helpfully (we both thought), not a diehard fan. I knew the Wishbone story in broad form but not the details; I knew the bigger picture of rock history very well. I could, in effect, be the 'everyman' in terms of conducting the interviews with Andy—asking questions a casual reader might want to ask about this or that situation without assuming knowledge. My feeling was that this should be a book which anyone interested in music history, not only confirmed Wishbone Ash fans, could read with pleasure. Andy agreed.

The process continued with further periodic meetings in Dublin thereafter.

Quality fare would be consumed, decent wine quaffed, and then intensive interviews conducted. These would then be written up as prose, with on average 80 percent in Andy's words, 20 percent in mine, ghostwriting around Andy. There was also an interview session get-together for a couple of days around Wishbone Ash's annual show at the Stables, Milton Keynes, in November 2014, which was a terrific insight into how the band operate on the road. Additional interviews were also conducted by phone in late 2014. In general we would focus each interview around a particular projected chapter. The main chapters would be essentially chronological, though both of us were keen to avoid a straight album/tour/album narrative within that. It was Andy's memoir so that, in a way, meant that he had the freedom to major on the things he most *remembered*—the things which were most important to him at the time or subsequently. There was no obligation to write a thousand words on every album or even mention every tour. I had also given Andy a few themes to explore in 'Interlude' chapters—fun chapters which could range across the decades on subjects such as hotels, fans, guitars, Pauline, and so on.

December 2014, with Andy off the road for a few weeks, saw intensive work on the book on both sides of the Atlantic, and much communication across it. Throughout the previous few months, with time being snatched literally in the back of vans and in hotel rooms around Europe, Andy had been revising the various chapters I had been sending him. Using each chapter as a draft, having something solid to work with and to spark further memories, Andy would add information and observations, tweak the way he had expressed some things in the interviews and generally finesse each chapter until it 'felt right', in tone and content, as a representation of that time and place, from his experience. It was, as intended, a personal history in tandem with it being, inevitably, a band history. He had also by now written a new Introduction—my ghostwritten one, rightly, acting only as a template.

By this stage, we had secured the involvement of Jawbone Press. For the first few months we had been happy to work on the book speculatively. In tandem with Andy's book, I was also working on a history of uilleann piping while Andy, of course, continued to put in serious work on the road. The process, for both of us, became challenging in the first quarter of 2015. Andy had a particularly arduous tour of Germany to contend with, with much driving and adverse weather, and then a similarly gruelling tour across the Southern States of the US, while I was trying to complete a quarter of a million heavily footnoted words on 300 years of Irish piping by an immutable deadline. Coincidentally, the deadline for both books, for different reasons, was more or less the same: April/May 2015. Yikes.

Nevertheless, necessity is the mother of invention. I finished the piping book by the end of April and Andy continued to somehow find time to complete the Interlude chapters (all of which were originated by him, edited only very slightly by me) and to further enhance the already revised main chapters. Some chapters would go through four significant revisions, with much material from a personal and family perspective from Andy being woven into the tale, with the effect that any ghostwriting I might have done to fill the odd narrative gap or suchlike from the original interview material has been very largely replaced with the real thing. A final intensive period of writing and revising took place during the first three weeks of June 2015, with Andy having at last a productive period of connected time off the road.

The result is a book which readers can be confident represents Andy Powell 100 percent. My input was necessary to get the project off the starting blocks—to an extent, giving Andy confidence as a writer and storyteller in this format—and to give it shape throughout. But no one should be in any doubt that the finished product has the authorship of Andy Powell. To give a Powell-esque analogy, I 'produced' Andy Powell: it was akin to taking his song and arranging it in the studio, mixing the performance, and mastering it for the maestro's approval. Andy liked the result but knew it could be better, so he remixed it a few times; I agreed with every remix (only suggesting we notch the bass down a little or brighten up the mid-range here or there), and then we remastered it together. We're both delighted with the end result. We hope you are too.

INDEX